Piety and Power

DAVID LANDAU

Piety and Power

THE WORLD OF JEWISH FUNDAMENTALISM

HILL AND WANG
A division of Farrar, Straus and Giroux
New York

Printed in the United States of America
Published simultaneously in Canada by HarperCollins*CanadaLtd*
Published in England in 1993 by Martin Secker & Warburg Ltd, London
First American edition, 1993

LIBRARY OF CONGRESS CATALOGING-IN-PUBLICATION DATA
Landau, David.
Piety and power : the world of Jewish fundamentalism / David
Landau. — 1st American ed.
p. cm.
Includes index.
1. Hasidim—History—20th century. 2. Judaism—20th century.
3. Hasidim—England—London. 4. Hasidim—New York (N.Y.)
5. Hasidim—Jerusalem. I. Title. II. Title: Jewish
fundamentalism.
BM198.L26 1993 296.8′332′09045—dc20 92-37540 CIP

To N.L., who found favour

Contents

Part IV LIVE AND LEARN

Part V BY BREAD ALONE

Part VI SPECTRE OF SCHISM

List of Illustrations

Credits: photographs nos. 1, 3, 8, 9, 14, 20: Flash 90; no. 2: J.B./Select; nos. 4, 6, 10, 11, 15, 16, 18: Joel S. Fishman; no. 5: Yaron Kaminsky; no. 7: Leonard Freed/Magnum; nos. 12, 13: Mike Abrahams/Network; no. 17: Bruce Davidson/Magnum; no. 19 Patrick Zachmann/Magnum

Tables

Acknowledgements

This book had four editors. The brilliant and incisive Sara Bershtel of Hill & Wang in New York whipped the original manuscript into shape. Later, Steve Cox, on behalf of Secker & Warburg, combed through it again with all the trenchant sensitivity and perceptiveness that make him one of the most sought-after editors in England. I was aided in meeting their stringent requirements – and not losing heart – by a journalistic colleague, Lisa Clayton, herself a gifted editor. And finally – but also firstly, and indeed throughout the entire endeavour – my wife, Jacqueline, was my most stringent and most sensitive editor of all.

The book came into being because my agent, Toby Eady, believed in it and believed, rightly, that Dan Franklin, the publisher of Secker, would see its value too. Dan remained an unfailing source of reassurance and encouragement throughout the long process of researching, writing and editing. In the United States, Steve Wasserman, then publisher of Hill & Wang, responded with enthusiasm to the initial proposal, and that enthusiasm was sustained by his successor, Arthur Rosenthal, and by the head of Farrar, Straus & Giroux, Roger Straus.

This is the place to acknowledge my gratitude to my late mother; I wish she had lived to see this book in print. Chaim Lewis of London, poet and teacher, was an inspiration. Councilman Noach Dear of New York opened doors for me – including his own door, behind which he and his wife Rickli offered relaxed hospitality on my many visits to their city. David Kornbluth, my learned friend, provided constant support and sympathy, and came up with the pithy title that I had sought in vain. Malcolm Walker was always a ready source of information and advice. To Jonathan Landau I offer my thanks for his help throughout the project, and for his painstaking reading of the manuscript. A *haredi* himself, who is wise as well as knowledgeable, he confined his criticism to points of fact.

Interviews

A great many people kindly agreed to be interviewed 'on the record' for this book. I list them here in alphabetical order, and with the titles they held when interviewed, and gratefully acknowledge their help.

Many other men and women also gave me of their time and patience, but preferred no explicit, individual acknowledgement. To them therefore – discreet collective gratitude.

Rabbi Baruch Abuhatseira, Sephardic Rebbe, Netivot, Israel; Dr Yaacov Ariel, Department of Comparative Religion, Hebrew University, Jerusalem; Rabbi Zvi Bakst, Mashgiach, Yeshiva Ketana, Gateshead, England; Rabbi Mordechai Becher, Lecturer, Ohr Somayach Yeshiva, Jerusalem; Dr Yossi Beilin, Member of Knesset, Jerusalem; Mr Yosef Ben-Aharon, Director-General, Prime Minister's Office, Jerusalem; Dr Yehuda Ben-Meir, Department of Psychology, Bar-Ilan University, Ramat Gan, Israel; Rabbi Yitzhak Berger, Dayan of the Ecclesiastical Court, London, England; Prof. Eugene Borowitz, Hebrew Union College-Jewish Institute of Religion, New York, USA; Rabbi David Bowden, Principal, High School for Girls, Gateshead, England; Mr Marshall J. Breger, Chairman, Administrative Conference of the United States, Washington DC, USA; Rabbi Menahem Nahum Breier, Hasidic Rebbe of Boyan, Jerusalem; Rabbi Sidney Brichto, Executive Vice-President, Union of Liberal and Progressive Synagogues, London, England; Rabbi Avraham Brun, Director, Hesder Yeshiva Programme, Jerusalem; Rabbi Yosef Buxbaum, Director, Machon Yerushalayim Publishing House, Jerusalem; Rabbi Menahem Carmel, Secretary-General, Degel Hatorah Party, Tel Aviv; Mr Pinhas Castnett, Director, Jewish Learning Exchange, New York, USA; Mr Binyamin Chen, Director, Baba Sali Yeshiva, Netivot, Israel; Mr Haim Yitzhak Cohen, Executive Director, Sadagora Hasidic Centre, Jerusalem; Mrs Paula Cohen, Newcastle, England; Mr Yossi Cohen, Newcastle, England; Rabbi Menahem Deutsh, Principal, Habad School, Aubervilliers, France; Mr Tom Dine, Executive Director, AIPAC, Washington DC, USA; Mr Yisrael Eichler, Editor, *Hamahane Haharedi*, Jerusalem; Mr Nahum Elbaum, Director, Ideal Tours, Jerusalem; Rabbi Avraham Farbstein, Dean, Hevron Yeshiva, Jerusalem; Mr Abraham Foxman, Vice-President, Anti-Defamation League of Bnai Brith,

New York, USA; Yechiel Michel Goodfarb, Jerusalem; Rabbi Shlomo Goren, Chief Rabbi (ret.), Tel Aviv; Rabbi Joseph Grunfeld, Director, 'Project Seed', Gateshead, England; Rabbi Naftali Halberstam, Bobov Hasidic Center, Brooklyn, New York, USA; Mr Yisrael Harel, Editor, *Nekuda*, Ofra, Israel; Prof. Samuel C. Heilman, Department of Sociology, City University of New York, USA; Rabbi Moshe Hirsch, Netorei Karta, Jerusalem; Rabbi Robert Hirt, Vice-President, Yeshiva University, New York, USA; Mr Malcolm Hoenline, Executive Director, Conference of Presidents of Major American Jewish Organizations, New York, USA; Rabbi Victor Hoffman, Director (ret.), Masorti Movement, Jerusalem; Rabbi Levi Yitzhak Horowitz, Rebbe, New England Hasidic Center, Brookline, Mass., USA; Mr Moshe Ishon, Editor, *Hatzofe*, Tel Aviv; Rabbi Louis Jacobs, New London Synagogue, England; Lord Jakobovits, Chief Rabbi (ret.) of Great Britain and the Commonwealth, London, England; Greville Janner MP, London, England; Mr Jerome Kadden, Associate Director, Ner Israel Yeshiva, Baltimore Md, USA; Mrs Batya Kalmanson, Habad emissary, Aubervilliers, France; Rabbi Sholem Mendel Kalmanson, Habad emissary, Aubervilliers, France; Prof. Jacob Katz, Emeritus Professor, Hebrew University, Jerusalem; the late Rabbi Wolfe Kelman, Executive Director, Rabbinical Assembly, New York, USA; Advct. Theo Klein, President (ret.) CRIF (Representative Council of Jewish Organizations), Paris, France; Mr Teddy Kollek, Mayor, Jerusalem; Dr Lionel Kopelowitz, President, Board of Deputies of British Jews, London, England; Dr Barry Kosmin, City University of New York, USA; Dr Yerahmiel Kugielsky, Chairman, Agudat Yisrael, Buenos Aires, Argentina; Rabbi Dr Norman Lamm, President, Yeshiva University, New York, USA; Mr Naftali Lavie, Director, United Jewish Appeal, Israel Office, Jerusalem; Sen. Joseph I. Lieberman, US Senate, Washington DC, USA; Prof. Charles Liebman, Department of Political Science, Bar-Ilan University, Ramat Gan, Israel; Prof. Avishai Margalit, Department of Philosophy, Hebrew University, Jerusalem; Dr Peter Medding, Department of Contemporary Jewry, Hebrew University, Jerusalem; Rabbi Yissachar Meir, Dean, Yeshivat Hanagev, Netivot, Israel; Prof. Ezra Mendelsohn, Department of Contemporary Jewry, Hebrew University, Jerusalem; Mr Dan Meridor, Minister of Justice, Jerusalem; Mr Baruch Merzel, Jerusalem; Mr Elimelech Neiman, Council of Jewish Organizations of Boro Park, New York, USA; Rabbi Herman N. Neuberger, Vice-

President, Ner Israel Yeshiva, Baltimore Md, USA; Mr Moshe Nissim, Minister of Commerce, Jerusalem; Mr Ehud Olmert, Minister of Health, Jerusalem; Geoffrey Paul, Editor (ret.), *Jewish Chronicle*, London, England; Mr Shimon Peres, former Prime Minister, Tel Aviv; Mr Menahem Porush, Deputy Minister of Labour, Jerusalem; Rabbi Bezalel Rakov, Gateshead, England; Rabbi Bezalel Rapoport, Editor, *English Yated Ne'eman*, Jerusalem; Rabbi David Refson, Dean, Neve Yerushalayim Women's College, Jerusalem; Mr Elazar Rokach, Director, Rokachman Industries, Ramle, Israel; Mr Gary Rosenblatt, Editor, *Baltimore Jewish Times*, Baltimore Md, USA; Mr Elyakim Rubinstein, Cabinet Secretary, Jerusalem; Rabbi Jonathan Sacks, Chief Rabbi of Great Britain and the Commonwealth, London, England; Mr Uri Savir, Consul-General of Israel, New York, USA; Rabbi Hanina Schiff, Gabbai, Gerer Hasidic Centre, Jerusalem; Rabbi Nota Schiller, Dean, Ohr Somayach Yeshiva, Jerusalem; Rabbi Alexander Schindler, President, Union of American Hebrew Congregations, New York, USA; Dr Avner Shaky, Minister of Religions, Jerusalem; former Prime Minister Yitzhak Shamir, Jerusalem; Rabbi Moshe Sherer, President, Agudath Israel of America, New York, USA; Rabbi Nosson Sherman, General Editor, ArtScroll/Mesorah, New York, USA; Rabbi Israel Singer, Executive Vice-President, World Jewish Congress, New York, USA; Rabbi René Samuel Sirat, Chief Rabbi (ret.), Paris, France; Prof. Hayim Soloveitchik, Yeshiva University, New York, USA; Rabbi Pinhas Stolper, Executive Director, Union of Orthodox Jewish Congregations, New York, USA; Mr Avraham Tanenbaum, City Clerk, Bnei Brak, Israel; Mr Wayne Tanenbaum, President, Runnymede Development Corpn, Scarborough, Ontario, Canada; Prof. Yisrael Ta-Shma, Department of Talmud, Hebrew University, Jerusalem; Rabbi Yaacov Toledano, Dean, Merkaz Hatorah, Le Raincy, France; Dr Zorach Warhaftig, National Religious Party, Jerusalem; Rabbi Mendel Weinbach, Dean, Ohr Somayach Yeshiva, Jerusalem; Mr Dov Ber Wolf, Director of Public Affairs, Habad Movement, Kfar Habad, Israel; Rabbi Ovadia Yosef, Chief Rabbi (ret.), Jerusalem; Dov Zackheim, Defence Consultant, Washington DC, USA; Mr Dedi Zucker, Member of Knesset, Jerusalem.

'They that wait upon the Lord shall renew their strength.'
Isaiah 40:31

'There is a holy mistaken zeal in politics as well as in religion. By persuading others, we convince ourselves.'
'Junius', Letter 35, 19 Dec. 1769

Introduction

King of Israel

Millions of Israelis sat riveted to their television screens. In the stadium the crowd erupted into song and rhythmic clapping. Never, even at the most fateful moments of the most critical games, had such electric excitement gripped the national basketball centre in south Tel Aviv, radiating across the country. But then, never had such fanatical fans packed the stands, such passionate devotees of the stars on the parquet. Tier upon tier of bearded, black-hatted men and youths sang in lusty unison: 'Add days to the days of the king, O Lord, make his years as many generations.'

The parquet had in fact been covered with protective boards in preparation for this first national convention of Degel Hatorah, the newest of Israel's *haredi* parties, which represent the ultra-Orthodox Jews in the Jewish State. (*Haredi* is Hebrew for 'fearing' or 'trembling'; the *haredim* are those who fear God.) At one end of the court, instead of the basket, a broad dais had been set up with rows of chairs on it for the party's rabbis and elders. The other end was reserved for the press. Hundreds of cameramen and reporters from Israel and abroad jostled to get a first look at 'the king'.

He made his way slowly from a side-entrance, a bent diminutive figure, surrounded by uniformed security men and by his own dark-suited attendants. The television arc-lights scanned back and forth anxiously, seeking him out. Eventually he reached the centre of the dais, and sank into a chair. An aide quickly placed a book on the table before him and he pored over it, as though oblivious to the deafening chorus resounding from thousands of throats. The emcee exhorted the audience to sing louder, conducting vigorously with both arms. Over and over, the same verse from Psalms. Give him days, give him years, many more years.

Some of the audience had paid ten times the ten shekels ($5) marked on their tickets for the chance to experience this event.

Veteran sports reporters said there had never been such sharp scalping outside this stadium. Hundreds of *yeshiva* students had queued the whole previous night for the chance of a ticket. Those who failed to obtain one, but came nevertheless, were accommodated in an outdoor amphitheatre nearby, where a huge screen conveyed the proceedings by closed-circuit television. For women – barred from the convention itself – Degel Hatorah hired the largest concert hall in Jerusalem for a live hook-up. Fleets of buses ferried the women from the haredi town of Bnei Brak and other haredi centres around the country.

Unlike most Israelis, Degel Hatorah followers could not have stayed at home to watch their leader. For *haredim*, television sets are strictly forbidden. They pervert the young, instil alien values, and poison the purity of a traditional Jewish family. The rest of the country, unfettered by this restriction, watched and waited. At stake was, almost literally, the fate of the nation. The government of Prime Minister Yitzhak Shamir, leader of the right-wing Likud Party, had fallen eleven days earlier, on 15 March 1990, over the fundamental policy issue of negotiations with the Palestinians. Now the Labour Party, under Shimon Peres, was trying to put together a 'government of peace'. The 120 members of the Knesset, fragmented into fifteen parties, were evenly divided between hawks and doves. Degel Hatorah's two members could clinch the majority for Peres.

Rabbi Eliezer Menahem Shach, ninety-two-year-old spiritual leader of Degel Hatorah, the 'king' whose days and years were the subject of the singing, slowly rose to speak. The explosion of sound ceased instantly. Silence. Everyone straining to hear every syllable.

In the past, he had frequently spoken in favour of political moderation. The avoidance of war and the preservation of human life were the noblest goals, he taught. Haredism, in fact, had always been hostile, or at best ambivalent, towards Zionism and the Jewish State. It certainly did not support the policy of territorial aggrandizement advocated by the hardline Likud. Yet in this present political crisis Rabbi Shach had been acting unpredictably.

'Let me tell you the truth,' he began, in a quaint, uncolloquial Hebrew. 'I did not intend to address this vast gathering here today . . . But I am so happy when I see this great thirst for *Torah* . . . so many people, thank God, coming together to hear words of spiritual strength, true and sincere words, without any politics, without any ulterior motives, just the pure, honest truth . . .'

In ten minutes it was all over. The politicians and pundits were explaining why Rabbi Shach had dashed Labour's hopes, why he had thrown in his lot with the Likud – despite the apparent chasm between his political views and those of Yitzhak Shamir. Labour's Peres fought back as best he could, trying to cobble together a moderate government despite Degel's desertion. In the event, it was another venerable haredi rabbi who dealt the *coup de grâce* to Labour's chances. Just hours before the Knesset was due to convene on 11 April to endorse a Labour-led government, the octogenarian Rabbi Menahem Schneerson of Brooklyn, New York, *Rebbe* or spiritual leader of the hasidic sect of Lubavitch, sent instructions to two members of another haredi party, Agudat Yisrael, to switch sides and support Shamir. As his loyal followers, the two men obeyed.

At least Rabbi Schneerson, the Lubavitcher* Rebbe, was consistent. He had always espoused the 'Greater Israel' position, ever since Israel took the occupied territories in the 1967 Six Day War. Questioned by an Israeli reporter soon after the government fell in March, he said he was confident the Messiah would be coming very shortly, 'and for the few minutes until then, we need the "not-one-inch [of withdrawal] policy" of Mr Shamir, which will bring peace to the Land and to the region. Once they start making concessions, there will be no end to it.'

Between them, Rabbi Shach and Rabbi Schneerson had decided the course of Israeli history by determining policy on the most central issue facing the Jewish State. They had done so by wielding

* Lubavitch was the small town in White Russia where this sect originated. The various sects and groups within haredism usually identify themselves by their town or village of origin in pre-Holocaust Europe – hence Gerer, Belzer, Satmarer, Boyaner, adding the Yiddish suffix '-er' to the name of the place. A contemporary hasidic rebbe from New England, whom we shall encounter later, styles himself the Bostoner. Where a hasidic house or sect has split into more than one group, a double-barrelled designation is sometimes used to denote each separate branch: hence 'Vishnitz-Monsey' (Vishnitz was the village of origin in Eastern Europe, Monsey is in upstate New York) and Vishnitz-Haifa (after the port-town in Israel).

the political power that the vigorous resurgence of haredi Orthodoxy, in Israel and in the Diaspora, had placed in their hands.

Ironically, the two old men, thrown together in political alliance, loathed each other with a vengeance. Shach had accused Schneerson of heresy and had seriously questioned whether Lubavitch hasidism under Schneerson could be considered authentic Judaism at all. Some saw their feud as a renewal of the historic enmity between hasidism (lit. piety), the revivalist movement that swept through Eastern European Jewry from the late eighteenth century, and its dour detractors, the *mitnagdim* (opponents), who considered themselves the true guardians of the Talmudic law and traditions.

Ironically too, it had been a third haredi rabbi, unloved by either of the other two, who had actually triggered the downfall of the Shamir-led government. Rabbi Ovadia Yosef, a Sephardic (Oriental) sage some twenty years younger than Shach and Schneerson but by no means their inferior in Talmudic scholarship, had gone on television to announce that he could no longer face God and his conscience if he continued to support an 'extremist, warmongering government'. He instructed the Knesset members of Shas, the haredi-Sephardic party, to vote for a motion of no-confidence tabled by Labour.

Now, chastened and humiliated by Shach, and bowing to the Ashkenazic (Occidental) sage's seniority, Yosef ordered Shas to join with the parties of the Right in the new coalition under Shamir.

The world looked on incredulously. *Time* magazine wrote of the 'outright disgust' that American Jews felt at the 'vulnerability of Israel's political system to the demands of fanatical ultra-Orthodox sects'. That system is based not on districts or constituencies, but on nationwide proportional representation. Thus, it encourages small parties to compete. Any party that can pick up 1.5 per cent of the national vote can get a member into the Knesset. With the Right and Left often evenly balanced, the haredi parties have proven adept at exploiting their tie-breaking power. Time after time, they wring concessions out of Likud or Labour – funding for their yeshivas and building projects, for instance, or legislation tightening public sabbath observance or limiting abortions – in return for their support.

This time, the drama of the intervention by Rabbis Shach and Schneerson transformed a widespread but dim awareness – sometimes benign, sometimes uncomfortable – of the haredim's resurgence, into shock and fear.

The writing had appeared on the Knesset wall two years earlier, when the haredi parties won 11 per cent of the vote in an election, more than doubling their representation. They immediately brought Israel and the bulk of the Jewish Diaspora into bitter conflict by demanding, as their coalition price, a change in the Israeli Law of Return that defines who is a Jew (see chapter 33). Millions of non-Orthodox Jews in the Diaspora – that is, Jews who belong to the Reform or Conservative movements or are unaffiliated – were appalled and alienated by what they saw as a haredi attempt to hijack the Jewish State. Haredism seemed on the march, trampling the more moderate forms of Orthodoxy, spoiling for a fight with the rest of Jewry.

In 1992, the haredim of Israel proved that the previous election result was no flash in the pan and that their growing power is no transient phenomenon. Despite the immigration since 1989 of nearly 400,000 Jews from the Soviet Union – hardly any of whom are Orthodox, let alone haredi – the haredi parties still won close to 10 per cent of the vote. This time Rabbi Yosef had his way, leading his party, Shas, into a coalition alliance with Labour, under its new leader Yitzhak Rabin.

The haredim's electoral showing provides a fair picture of their present numbers, though some non-haredim too – among them thousands of Arab citizens – vote for haredi parties. Informed estimates put the Israeli haredim at around 350,000, out of a Jewish population of some 4 million (see tables on p. xxii), and the haredim in the Diaspora at 300–325,000.

Despite the shock-waves generated by the haredi rabbis' political diktats, haredism's assertion of power is not a sudden development, either in Israel or in the Diaspora. The haredim themselves have long felt that the tide of Jewish history is turning their way, that after two centuries of retreat and shrinkage in the face of advancing Modernity, old-style Orthodoxy is on the ascendant

Table 1: *Estimated Jewish Population, by Continents and Major Geographical Regions, 1939–92*

	1939	1947	1969	1989
United States & Canada	4,965,620	5,176,500	6,186,000	5,825,000
South and Central America	524,000	578,000	782,250	436,700
Europe[1]	9,739,000	3,920,000[2]	4,030,950	2,558,400
Asia (including Israel)	771,500	917,000	2,605,500	3,750,700
Australasia	33,000	35,000	77,000	89,600
Africa	609,000	639,500	193,950	149,900
	16,643,120	11,266,000	13,875,650	12,810,300

[1] Includes former USSR.
[2] Based on reports received by the Joint Distribution Committee from their European Sources.

Table 2: *Estimated Jewish Population Distribution in Israel, USSR, France & United Kingdom, 1989*

Israel	3,717,100
USSR[1]	1,370,000
France	530,000
UK	320,000

[1] Including Asian regions

Table 3: *Estimated Immigration to Israel, 1989–92*

	1989	1990	1991	1992 until 30/6
Total	24,050	199,516	170,500	33,309
USSR	12,924	185,227	144,800	27,330
Ethiopia	1,289	4,137	14,194	—

Sources: American Jewish Year Book, 1947–48, 1970, 1991 (New York & Philadelphia: American Jewish Committee & Jewish Publication Society, 1948, 1970, 1991).
Ministry of Absorption, Israel.
Jewish Agency for Israel.
Israel Central Bureau of Statistics.

again, capturing new ground. What has been sudden is the impact of this haredi triumphalism on the consciousness of the rest of Jewry and of the watching Gentile world. The isolated pockets of haredism – in New York's Brooklyn and the Diamond District, Jerusalem's Mea Shearim, London and Antwerp – can no longer be dismissed as fading, irrelevant remnants of the pre-Holocaust world. They are bursting at the seams, swelling in numbers, growing in self-confidence and in their determination to influence the world around them.

The *shtetl* has entered the City. Canadian realtor Paul Reichmann's large black *yarmulka* and rabbinical beard were prominently noted as he hosted presidents and prime ministers to kosher canapés at the vast construction projects that he and his brothers, all of them haredi, erected in major cities before their over-extended Olympia & York property empire fell victim in 1992 to the economic recession. The modest, synagogue-centred lifestyle of these multi-billionaire brothers itself became a subject of public interest. People are intrigued, too, to learn of the dimensions of haredi philanthropy. Haredi businessmen pour funds into schools and yeshivas around the world, where the traditional Torah scholarship is recycled to power the haredi renaissance.

In the United States, haredi dynamism is challenging the established order of Jewish life. Formerly a minority even within the Orthodox minority of American Jewry, the haredim now set the tone in Orthodoxy with their increasingly stringent religious standards and their uncompromising rejection of the non-Orthodox majority. Key Orthodox figures in the US now bluntly predict an outright schism in the Jewish community within one generation. The non-Orthodox, as they see it, will cease to be Jews. The Orthodox, led by the haredim, will cease to recognize them as Jews. Given the haredim's growth-rate and their single-minded militancy, such warnings seem not nearly so eccentric or bombastic as they would have sounded just a few short years ago. Haredi leaders speak out and lobby Congress with self-assurance on national and political issues – abortion, gay rights, affirmative action, government funding for parochial schools. They make common cause with Christian fundamentalist groups and take positions far removed from the liberalism espoused by most Jewish organizations. Significantly, their positions are closely in step with the conservative spirit that propelled Ronald Reagan and George Bush to power. Unlike the majority of Jews, they overwhelmingly voted for these Republican presidents.

In 1988, for the first time, an Orthodox Jew was elected to the US Senate. Joseph Lieberman (Democrat, Connecticut) is

'Modern-Orthodox' rather than haredi, but all Orthodox Jews in America, and especially the haredim, see in him a symbol of their own evolution from the fringes to the mainstream of society. And he readily acknowledges that perceived role.

In Mrs Thatcher's Britain too, the former Chief Rabbi, Lord Jakobovits, was widely seen as the cleric closest to the Prime Minister in his political outlook. As head of the United Synagogue, he was spiritual leader of the large majority of Anglo-Jewry, but his own place on the religious spectrum was close to haredism, and under his long stewardship (1964–91) the British Jewish community, and especially its rabbinate, shifted markedly to the religious right. Before he took office, it was rare to find a British rabbi with a full beard, which is *de rigueur* for haredi rabbis – and indeed for laymen too in some haredi sects. A few wore small goatees. Now it is hard to find a shaven chin in a mainstream Jewish pulpit throughout the British Isles.

Haredism today, throughout the Jewish world, is self-confident and aggressive. It believes in its divine right to win souls and influence the Jewish People and the Jewish State. Its leaders imbue their followers with the conviction that the 'competing' ideologies – Zionism, Modern-Orthodoxy, Reform and Conservative Judaism, secular modernity in general – are becoming steadily weaker and less attractive. They point up the crises and malaises that afflict other societies. Communism, once the godless ideal of a generation of young Jews, has receded around the world, haredi leaders point out, partly in the face of resurgent religion. Zionism, the other 'ism' that offered idealistic young Jews a spiritual and national alternative to religious tradition, is undergoing a wrenching crisis of purpose and identity, say the haredim – witness the deep divisions in Israeli society.

The terms fundamentalism and khomeinism are frequently invoked as people search for analogies to explain the haredi resurgence. (Ironically, the same terms are sometimes applied to the ultra-nationalist settlers in the occupied territories, who believe they are paving the way for the coming of the Messiah. Haredism, by contrast, believes in an apocalyptic coming.) But embarrassment, prejudice, and above all ignorance, hamper efforts to understand this important and powerful Jewish movement.

This book is an attempt to dispel at least the ignorance. It tries to describe the haredi world, and, more importantly, the haredi mind, to Gentiles and Jews from the world outside. It does not argue for or against the haredim, but seeks to examine haredism against the backdrop of Jewry as a whole. It delves into the complexities of Israeli politics and society to show how the haredim, despite their theological reservations over the very existence of a non-messianic Jewish State, nevertheless adroitly work the system to their own advantage.

More controversially, perhaps, it points to the timebomb ticking beneath the surface of worldwide Jewish unity and threatening in particular the integrity of American Jewry. The question 'Who is a Jew?' has triggered a series of shock waves in the past. Now, with hardline haredi rabbis dictating religious dogma throughout the Orthodox camp, and with a simultaneous polarization 'leftwards' on the non-Orthodox side, there is real danger of an irreversible explosion that will split the Jewish People in two. The haredim, in their buoyant confidence, do not flinch from that prospect. Many of the others do not understand its imminence.

Before confronting this startling scenario, the book takes the reader inside haredi society, into the yeshivas which are the intellectual core of the community, into the colourful 'courts' of the hasidic rebbes, into the haredi home with its warm family life and stern sexual codes, and into the international structure of philanthropy and mutual aid that help sustain a rapidly growing 'society of learners' in which young men may aim to spend decades of their lives as full-time students of the Talmud. In Israel, they are able to gain immunity from national service by doing so – a radical divide, in a country so dominated by the burden of military service. Above all, this book seeks to explain the mindset of the haredim. Their lives are ruled by 'the Torah', which for them is a concept that embraces God Himself, all His prophets and scribes, a vast body of legal and ethical literature, and a chain of spiritual leaders down to the rabbis of today, charismatic men like Rabbis Shach and Schneerson and Ovadia Yosef who wield temporal power as well as spiritual authority.

For the haredim themselves, their present prospering, like their previous long decline, is God's work. If explanations are to be sought, they say, they lie in the stubborn faith of tiny groups of haredi Holocaust survivors who were determined to live and flourish in the modern world – but on their terms.

PART I

CONTEXTS

1

Fear and Trembling

'Five hundred Tsarist soldiers killed, please God . . . And another five hundred Tsarist soldiers killed . . .' With each morbid imprecation, the hasidic Rebbe of Rymanov, Rabbi Menahem Mendel, tossed a round, flat matza dough into the oven.

It was late winter of 1813. The decimated remnant of Napoleon's Grand Army had staggered back from Moscow, battling and bloodied every step of the way. In Rymanov, a nondescript village in Galicia, the argument raged as it did in Jewish shtetls and ghettos throughout Eastern Europe: good for the Jews, or bad? The age-old question of an impotent people.

The Rebbe's outstanding disciple, Naftali of Ropczyce, grew increasingly agitated as he watched the matza-baking. Finally, he leapt up and seized Menahem Mendel's long-handled shovel. 'Rebbe, stop! Napoleon is unclean!' A moment of frozen silence as the two men stared at each other. Then, the hasidic story continues, Naftali turned and fled. He took refuge with the venerable *Maggid* (preacher) of Kozienice, sheltering there from the Rymanover's wrath.

Hasidic leaders of the time were profoundly exercised by the meta-historical significance of contemporary events. They saw Napoleon's invasion of Russia as the 'War of Gog and Magog', the massive military upheaval prophesied by Ezekiel (Ezek. 38–9) which was to precede Israel's miraculous restoration to its Land. Russian Jewry lived for the most part in conditions of penury and discrimination. The accounts, therefore, of Napoleon's Emancipation of their co-religionists seemed to some Russian Jewish leaders truly to portend the Biblical apocalypse. Throughout Western Europe, Jewish disabilities were being swept away. During his Palestine campaign in 1799, Napoleon had even issued a vague call to the Jews of Asia and Africa to join him, and receive in return the Holy Land. But among the hasidic rebbes there were those who regarded Napoleon's invasion of Russia as an insidious threat. They knew that Jewish life in the West had been infiltrated during the previous half-century by new and alien ideas, spread by scholars who had 'grazed in foreign pastures'. These men had studied Gentile philosophy, science and literature. They proposed novel interpretations of the Bible, and openly challenged rabbinic authority.

Jewish demands for equality and civil rights – which Napoleon liberally granted – were a direct outgrowth of these changes. But so was a novel and alarming levity, and even brazen disregard, towards the hallowed laws and customs of the faith. Progressive Jewish circles in Berlin, Paris and Vienna, basking in the Age of Enlightenment and in their newly won political freedoms, were casting off not only the traditional Jewish garb and the Yiddish of the ghetto, but also the traditional education, the age-old rituals, and – this had already happened in disturbing numbers among the more radical – the bonds of the religion itself. There had been group conversions to Christianity, freely undertaken as a means of assimilating more quickly into Christian society.

Emancipation, Enlightenment, the French Revolution – perhaps the rebbes in benighted Russia could not fully understand the import of these cataclysmic developments. But they understood enough to know they did not like them, and did not want them for their own flocks. 'If Bonaparte wins,' wrote Rabbi Shneur Zalman, founder of Lubavitch hasidism, 'the nation of Israel will enjoy much wealth and prestige. But it will come undone, and the hearts of the people will grow distant from their Father in Heaven. Whereas if our Master Alexander wins, there will be much poverty and suffering, but the hearts of the People will draw close to their Father in Heaven.' He had been 'shown this in a vision,' he wrote, during *Rosh Hashana*, the Jewish New Year.

Shneur Zalman was under no illusions about 'our Master Alexander'. He had twice seen the inside of the Tsar's prisons at St Petersburg, the victim of framed accusations levelled by his *mitnaged* opponents. Nevertheless, he prayed for a Tsarist victory over Napoleon, fleeing with his family before the advancing French forces. His son and successor Rabbi Dov Ber later recalled a turning-point in the war: 'Father called us together and spoke words of comfort and joy. "Today," he said, "I saw in my prayers that a change for the better has occurred; even though the enemy may take Moscow he will not recover from it, and we shall be saved."'

In modern-day New York, where Shneur Zalman's seventh successor issues political instructions rather than merely praying to influence current events, most of the city's two million-odd Jews live lives far removed from the devout Orthodoxy of the early nineteenth-century shtetls of Eastern Europe. Yet they are all, as are Jews worldwide, descendants of Orthodox forebears – inasmuch as all Jews were 'Orthodox' before the Enlightenment and the Emancipation began to make inroads in the unitary character of Judaism. The very word 'Orthodoxy' only came into being, and took on meaning, when Jews began moving away from the traditional, 'Orthodox' faith of their fathers. With the advent of other, 'non-Orthodox', trends in Judaism during the nineteenth century – principally the Reform and Conservative movements – 'Orthodoxy' became defined as such by contrast.

But Orthodoxy itself underwent splits, as some rabbis sought to fuse the tradition with modern culture and civilization, into which the Jews were belatedly, grudgingly, gaining admittance. Haredim today are sometimes referred to as 'ultra-Orthodox' or 'strictly Orthodox', to distinguish them from other more 'Modern' forms of Orthodoxy. They invariably bridle at such adjectival appendages. As they see it, theirs is the sole authentic form of Jewish Orthodoxy. Therefore, they should be referred to as 'Orthodox', while the other – in their eyes lesser – forms should be duly qualified: 'Modern-Orthodox', 'centrist-Orthodox' or 'Zionist-Orthodox'. This etymological sensitivity has encouraged the use of the Israeli Hebrew term 'haredi', which is now slowly making its way into English. Originally the biblical word meant 'fear' or 'trembling', but it already appears in Isaiah in the metaphorical sense of 'God-fearing'.

Pre-Enlightenment Judaism, though 'Orthodox', was by no means one-dimensional. There were theological disputations through the ages, in which one side might hurl the charge of heresy at the other. But the other would usually hurl it right back, and both insisted they remained firmly within the fold of traditional dogma. There was always backsliding too, of course, in the *practice* of the religion. Moses himself had no sooner received the Ten Commandments than he had to chastise the people for worshipping the Golden Calf; and successive generations of admonishing prophets and preachers had their work cut out ever after.

But the Age of Enlightenment ushered in challenges of an entirely new kind, by questioning the authority of religion itself. The Emancipation of the Jews meant that Judaism, like Christianity, was exposed to the cold blasts of Modernity. 'The new reality,' writes one Orthodox Jewish historian, 'was completely contrary to the Word of God. In the view of the Word of God, the individual personality is not a gift, but a duty; humanism is merely a prior condition for the loftier goal of serving God . . . Science is an instrument for Man to conquer Nature, but certainly not the source of Truth.'*

The Reform Movement in Judaism, which began in Germany in the early 1800s and later spread to America, was a direct outgrowth of the Emancipation. It was an attempt to remould the faith in the spirit of the age. Led by men who were steeped in secular as well as Jewish learning, the movement sought to apply a modern, critical approach to the ancient Jewish texts. Reform's first divergences from Orthodox norms were in the realm of ritual: services were conducted in German rather than Hebrew; expressions of longing for Zion or for the Temple sacrifices were omitted; women were allowed to sing in formerly all-male choirs. More flagrant violations of the *halacha* (the corpus of laws) quickly followed, such as the use of an organ during the *shabbat* (sabbath) service, and soon Reform rabbis were openly breaking with traditional teachings and dismissing the halacha as largely an anachronism.

The transfer of Saturday worship to Sundays was an extreme

* Dr Isaac Breuer, Introduction to vol. 2 of *The Cycles of the Year* by Rabbi Samson R. Hirsch (Bnei Brak: Netzah 1966) (Hebrew).

expression of Reformist zeal. It was not widely adopted (and was subsequently reversed in most American congregations that did adopt it). But as far as the Orthodox rabbis were concerned, and especially the haredi rabbis of Eastern Europe, the entire Reform movement was a vindication of their principled objection to the lures of the Emancipation, and of their opposition to anything smacking of modernity. Reform's iconoclastic vigour was too drastic for some non-Orthodox moderates, too, who wanted change but not indiscriminate upheaval. This, in very basic terms, accounts for the creation of the Conservative Movement in the United States at the turn of the twentieth century. (Some of the early impetus for this movement originated in Germany too.)

Beyond the different 'streams' that developed within Judaism during the nineteenth and early twentieth centuries, many young Jews in Eastern Europe and in the West were discarding the trappings of the faith altogether, in favour of socialism, Zionism, or other modern ideologies. They were not especially interested in any revamped version of the religion.

Among the Sephardim, the Oriental Jews of North Africa and the Middle East, the divisions between Orthodoxy and non-Orthodoxy were never so pronounced, nor the disputes so bitter. Enlightenment brought major changes to the Sephardic communities too, but Reform never presented a serious challenge to the established Orthodox rabbinate, and the vast majority of lay people, even those who grew lax in their halachic observance, remained attached to the traditional rituals in the synagogue and the home.

By the end of the First World War, when the mass migration from Eastern Europe was halted by strict new immigration laws, the trend in North America was unmistakable: those Jewish immigrants who had not abandoned their faith tended to move towards a watered-down style of Orthodoxy, and then on to Conservatism, and their children or grandchildren to Reform. By the 1950s, barely 10 per cent of America's Jews described themselves as Orthodox. Social scientists saw this trend as the inexorable course of Jewish history, at least in America. They pointed to material and sociological phenomena that accompanied and seemed to explain the movement away from traditional religion: increasing affluence, acculturation, suburbanization.

In Britain, though these phenomena were also present, the national Jewish leadership always remained formally Orthodox; the non-Orthodox movements, while strong, have never achieved the pre-eminent role, numerically and communally, that they have in America. In Israel, where the State-run Rabbinate is Orthodox – and half of the Jewish population are Sephardim – efforts by local branches of the American Reform and Conservative movements to build a grass-roots following have achieved negligible success. Despite the widespread unpopularity of the Orthodox rabbinical establishment, Israelis do not seem drawn to non-Orthodox religious alternatives.

It is only in recent years that scholars and students of Jewry have begun to take note of the Orthodox revival, reflected both among the Modern-Orthodox and especially among the haredim. While this does not negate the other, still-ongoing trend away from Orthodoxy, it plainly does represent a novel, indeed revolutionary counter-trend.

Among Sephardic Jews too, the economic and cultural dislocations brought on by mass emigrations in the 1950s and 1960s seemed to quicken a drift away from tradition. But recent years have seen a significant 'return to roots' movement among young Jews, both in Israel and in the Diaspora, with substantial numbers of Sephardim in particular drawn into it.

If the pursuit of affluence was long regarded as a catalyst of Orthodoxy's decline, the achievement of affluence is now understood as a cause of its renaissance. Historians of Jewry argue, metaphorically, over whether the masses of East European Jewish immigrants to the United States at the turn of the century threw their *tefillin* (phylacteries, worn for prayer) into the ocean the day *before* they docked at Ellis Island, or the day after, when they realized they would have to give up Orthodoxy and work on shabbat, in order to make a living in the New World. A century later, all that has changed. The sweat-shops have gone, at least for the Jews. Today it is no longer startling, nor even noteworthy, to see Orthodox Jewish residents of the most affluent suburbs of New York or Los Angeles, decked out in their shabbat finery, walking to their synagogues through snow or stifling heat. Walking – because driving is halachically forbidden on the day of rest.

2

Keeping Kosher

Shabbat, the sabbath, is one of the three cardinal societal precepts of Judaism which are invariably invoked by Orthodox thinkers to define Judaism and distinguish it from other monotheistic faiths. The two others are *kashrut* (the dietary laws) and *taharat hamishpacha* (lit. 'the purity of the family' – the sexual laws). Asked to define the 'essence of Judaism', an Orthodox rabbi or Orthodoxly observant layman will automatically cite three broad areas of his life which are minutely regulated by his religion.

For the majority of Jews, however, who are not Orthodox, these three *mitzvot* (commandments) describe the way of life of Jewish Orthodoxy; they do not define Judaism. A non-Orthodox rabbi, asked for *his* definition of Judaism, might prefer to cite the Talmudic sage Hillel, who, challenged by a Gentile to 'teach me the Torah while I stand on one leg', replied: 'That which is hateful to you – do not do unto others. The rest is commentary.' Another sage, Rabbi Akiva, declared that the biblical verse 'Love your neighbour as yourself' (Lev. 19:18) is 'the greatest principle of the Torah'. Indeed it is that verse that is emblazoned in stone over the portals of the Union of American Hebrew Congregations, the movement for Reform Judaism, on New York's Fifth Avenue.

Without getting entangled in this theological thicket, the different ways that different Jews observe – or ignore – shabbat, kashrut, and taharat hamishpacha *are* a useful tool in describing (though not defining) the wide spectrum of modern-day Jewry and placing the haredim within that spectrum.

Shabbat

All Jews are vaguely aware and proud of the fact that Judaism gave the world the idea of a seventh day of rest. Beyond that unanimity, there is vast variety in the ways Jews choose to mark the sabbath.

For the Orthodox, 'resting' on the sabbath translates into a huge codex of do's and don't's. It is no use arguing that to flick on an electric light switch does not entail 'work', and does not impinge on the day of rest, as 'kindling a fire' did when the biblical injunction forbidding it on the sabbath was originally enacted. The halacha, the code of Jewish law, is immutable. A fire is a fire, and kindling it is forbidden, no matter how effortless modern technology has now rendered that action. Driving, which entails igniting an internal combustion engine, is therefore equally an offence. Similarly, it is pointless to contend that riding a bus or a train is not the same as riding a horse, which was prohibited by the Talmud 'in case he pulls a twig off a tree'. (The biblical injunction forbids 'reaping'.) Riding remains riding.

On the Jewish spectrum from 'left' to 'right', there are firstly many Jews the world over who do nothing whatever to celebrate or mark the Jewish day of rest. Millions more, who are not religious in the synagogue-going sense, will nevertheless light the traditional two candles on Friday evening and have a family dinner – both now social activities of obvious (and freely acknowledged) religious origin. Committed Conservative and Reform Jews, while they will drive and switch on electric lights – because they believe the halacha must move with the times – will recite the *kiddush* (sanctification) prayer over wine at Friday-night dinner, which is another halachic requirement on the sabbath.

In general, then, non-Orthodox Jews intent on marking shabbat in a religious way accentuate the do's of the traditional halacha and dismiss the host of technical don't's.

Orthodoxy, next along the spectrum, is doctrinally committed to the immutability of the halacha. Nevertheless, it seeks a modicum of modern convenience within that immutability. Thus, for instance, the Orthodox will have time-clocks in their homes and synagogues which, set before the sabbath, will switch their various electrical appliances on and off as desired. Or they will use 'shabbat elevators' which are pre-set to stop on every floor or every second floor, obviating the need to press the buttons, which is forbidden ('kindling' again).

The permissibility of these devices proves, in their view, that the halacha does move with the times, and is not ossified or archaic as the non-Orthodox movements contend. Indeed, the Talmud itself provided such devices. For instance: it is forbidden to carry anything, even a prayer-book or a handkerchief, in the public domain on the sabbath; but the Talmud explains how by means of poles and pieces of string one can symbolically close off a public domain and nominally render it a private domain, where carrying is permitted. The arrangement, called *eruv*, is in effect in most Israeli cities and in several cities in the US and Europe. With the cooperation of the local authorities, the rabbis incorporate seashores, rivers, highways and existing telephone cables or power lines into their symbolic perimeter fence, adding their own poles and string when no demarcation of any form exists.

The haredim, on the extreme right of the spectrum, cannot condemn convenience-devices on shabbat, which after all are well founded in halacha and precedent. But some nevertheless forbid 'shabbat elevators' and some prefer not to rely on an eruv in case a part of it falls down during the shabbat. They refrain from carrying anything out of their homes – though even they have to resort to halachic 'devices', fashioning their front-door keys into belt-buckles or tie-clips so as to be considered as 'wearing' and not carrying them.

In Israel, some haredim refuse to use electric power on shabbat, since it is generated by Jews who are thereby breaking the halacha. Instead they use gas- or battery-operated appliances. Haredi yeshivas have their own petrol-run electricity generators. Some haredim do not even use running water on shabbat, because it is pumped by electric power. They prepare buckets of water before the sabbath. The Modern-Orthodox, however, and some of the haredim, do use electricity, on the grounds that it has to be generated anyway for hospitals, where it is needed to save lives. Saving life, under the halacha, takes precedence over observing the sabbath.

Haredi shabbat observance is not focused solely on complying with all the halachic minutiae (that is taken for granted), but also on preserving the traditional pattern of the holy day as transmitted over the centuries. Haredim cook the same shabbat foods their great-grandmothers cooked – especially *cholent*, a stew left simmering all night and eaten for shabbat lunch. They wear the same shabbat clothes their great-grandfathers wore: the black satin caftan and, among the hasidim, the fur *shtreimel* hat. They sing the same mealtime hymns, to the same tunes, around the shabbat table, and faithfully recreate precisely the same ritual in their synagogue or rebbe's court that was in vogue in their particular community '*in der Heim*' – back home in Eastern Europe.

Although reading a newspaper or kicking a ball around the backyard are not halachically forbidden on shabbat, the more high-minded haredim will discourage such mundane pursuits on the holy day. Shabbat is meant for prayer, study, and seemly relaxation. While an afternoon stroll is quite proper, serious haredim will be at pains to keep their shabbat conversation, even while at leisure, appropriately sober and religious.

As the haredi communities have grown in numbers and in self-confidence, they have become more rigorous in observing these various extra-halachic practices and restrictions, investing them with neo-halachic status. Thus, despite the doctrine of halachic immutability, the halacha is changing for the haredim too. But it is changing by adopting new requirements, and requiring greater stringency in the fulfilment of the old ones.

In part, the reasons for the increasing stringency and intolerance among the haredim are to be found in the growing tolerance of the world around them. For example, there are haredim still alive today, especially women, who remember having to go to (Gentile) school on Saturday mornings, while their fathers went to synagogue. In some European countries, school on Saturday was mandatory. They would walk to the school-house, sit in on the classes, but refrain from writing, which is a halachic offence. Today such conduct would be entirely unthinkable in any haredi family anywhere in the world. Virtually all haredi children attend haredi, or at least Jewish, schools. Even the few who do not would immediately be removed from their Gentile school by their parents if they were required to attend on Saturday. Alternatives are readily available. Haredi parents today who nevertheless sent their child to school on Saturday, even though no technical halachic offence was committed, would be instantly ostracized by the community.

Kashrut

A similar improvement in objective conditions of affluence and availability, especially in Western countries, has enabled the haredim to develop increasingly stringent standards in the way they apply the laws of kashrut, the second of the major societal mitzvot. New restrictions are briskly evolving into accepted norms within their community, and serving as additional demarcations between them and other Jews.

The Bible itself specifies which animals may be eaten and which are unkosher. And it implies the second basic requirement of kashrut – that the animal must be slaughtered in a certain way. But there is less clarity on that, while on the third basic rule, the separation of milk and meat, the Bible commands only that 'You shall not seethe a kid in its mother's milk' (Exod. 23:19). Here too, as with the laws of shabbat, it was left to the Oral Law to elaborate on the halachic method of slaughter – slitting the windpipe and oesophagus – on drawing off the blood by a process of salting and washing, and on keeping meat and dairy products rigorously apart.

As with shabbat, classical Reform threw over the entire edifice as a vestige of primitive rules of health and hygiene, while irreligious Jews simply discarded the dietary restrictions as a cumbersome, meaningless burden. Nevertheless, two centuries later, some of the old beliefs, primitive or not, still linger on with remarkable resilience even among the most thoroughly non-Orthodox sections of the Jewish spectrum. Millions of Jews who do not otherwise 'keep kosher' will refrain from eating pork and/or seafood. Many cannot rationally explain their conduct, even to themselves.

Moving 'rightwards' on the spectrum, there are many Jews who 'keep a kosher home', at least to the extent of buying only kosher meat for their domestic needs. When they eat out, however, they are not particular, and will eat non-kosher meat. This latter group is represented both within the Reform and the Conservative communities in the Diaspora, and among non-Orthodox Israelis.

Farther along, there are those who eat only kosher meat – that is, meat from a kosher animal slaughtered in the halachic way by a qualified slaughterer. This entails a certain financial as well as gastronomic sacrifice, as kosher meat is usually more expensive, due to the added cost of religious supervision. People in this group do not insist, however, that every food product they eat must be certified kosher by a rabbi. If the ingredients are kosher – that is, if they contain no animal substance – these Jews will eat the product. A small number of Reform Jews, a larger number of Conservatives, and many Modern-Orthodox observe that standard of kashrut, especially those living in countries other than the US, where rabbinically certified products are not as plentiful nor as generally available as in America.

Until barely a generation ago, many haredim were content to live at this standard too. But today the line dividing the haredim from the merely Orthodox runs along this matter of *hechsherim*, rabbinical kashrut certifications. Haredim will not eat any processed or manufactured foodstuff that does not carry a *hechsher*. The reasoning is that even if the ingredients are kosher, small quantities of unkosher substances might have infiltrated during the production process. The hechsher attests that a rabbinical inspector has checked to ensure that does not happen.

But the matter does not end there. In America and Israel, thousands of products carry hechsherim. A kashrut-observant Jew can walk into a supermarket virtually anywhere in the US, and emerge with armfuls of popular brand-makes all displaying a tiny 'OU' (Orthodox Union) sign or a 'K' on their packaging. (The average consumer does not even notice these signs, or is unaware of their significance.) But for many haredim this is not good enough. They will insist on the particular hechsherim of particular rabbis, rejecting those of other rabbis as not reliable. For example, a young British haredi woman flying from Israel on British Airways rejected the special kosher breakfast provided for her on the grounds, as she explained to the English stewardess, that it only carried the hechsher of the Israeli Chief Rabbinate, not of the haredi community of Jerusalem.

The Jerusalem community is one of several haredi sects that run their own kashrut certification systems, supervised by their own *batei din* (rabbinical courts). (Eventually the hunger pangs of her small daughter persuaded the woman to relent and allow the child to eat.) The hechsherim business, which is a major money-maker, is consequently awash with internal haredi rivalries. It is also fraught, as is so much else in haredi life, with ideology and politics. The haredi community of Jerusalem and its rabbis are anti-Zionist. By rejecting the State Rabbinate's hechsher, the woman on the BA flight was making a political statement as well as a religious one.

The Zionist issue becomes especially relevant each seventh year, when the Jewish calendar marks *shemitta*, the year when fields in the Holy Land must be left fallow (Lev. 25). Early in this century, when the first Zionist farmers began to settle in Palestine, sympathetic rabbis ruled that this law, which would have been crippling for the fledgeling homesteads and kibbutzim, could be circumvented by 'selling' the land to a Gentile. This subsequently became the halachic policy of the Israeli Chief Rabbinate. But it was consistently rejected by the largely anti-Zionist haredi rabbinical leadership. Thus haredim in Israel today make a point of eating only genuinely Gentile produce, grown by Arab farmers, during the shemitta year; and Diaspora haredim shun any Israeli exports that are not certified by haredi rabbis as 'shemitta' free.

Kashrut is also complicated by differences in halachic tradition between the Ashkenazic majority and the Sephardic minority in Jewry. An Ashkenazic haredi will not eat meat slaughtered under the hechsher of a Sephardic rabbi, and vice-versa. The differences are particularly pronounced on Passover, when Sephardim will eat rice, beans and other legumes which are all forbidden to Ashkenazim. The Shulhan Aruch code of laws expressly permits these foods, but the Shulhan Aruch, written by the Sephardic sage Rabbi Yosef Karo in Palestine in the sixteenth century, was overruled in many halachic details, as far as Ashkenazim are concerned, by the commentary of Rabbi Moshe Isserles published in Poland in the seventeenth century. What this means in practice is that an Ashkenazi may not eat in a Sephardi's home in Passover, because the dishes and silverware are regarded as contaminated.

Taharat hamishpacha

Of the three major societal mitzvot, it is taharat hamishpacha, the code of sexual 'purity', that provides the most clear-cut distinction between the Orthodox minority and non-Orthodox majority of Jews.

The non-Orthodox, barring a handful of Conservative rabbis' wives and a minuscule number of their congregants, simply reject or ignore the basic halacha in this code, which requires a woman to dip in a special ritual bath after her period. No Conservative or Reform congregation has a *mikve* (ritual bath) for this purpose, while most Orthodox congregations do have one or share in a district mikve, even though far from all their women members actually use it. Among non-affiliated Jews in the Diaspora, these laws are even more remote, or entirely unheard of. All Israelis, though, do face one brief, unavoidable encounter with the halacha of sex. Marriage between Jews is within the exclusive legal jurisdiction of the (Orthodox) State Rabbinate, and the Rabbinate requires every bride to dip in the mikve before her wedding night.

Once again, the original Pentateuchal prohibition is tersely stated: 'You shall not approach a woman to uncover her nakedness while she is in her menstrual uncleanness' (Lev. 18:19). The Pentateuch itself frequently refers to ritual immersion as a means to attain or restore purity. The halacha accordingly ordained that a menstruant woman must undergo this procedure before she is 'permitted to her husband', that is, allowed to have intercourse again. There are vast and complex canons about the timing of the immersion (at least seven days after the end of menstruation, leaving barely a fortnight of permitted sex each cycle), the method, the size of the bath, the type of water and so forth. But the fundamental provision is that a woman remains menstruant in the eyes of the halacha, unless and until she duly immerses herself. Passage of time does not change that forbidden status, neither does pregnancy or even the menopause.

The complex canons proscribe not only the act of intercourse itself, but a whole gamut of actions and situations between husband and menstruant (i.e. unimmersed) wife which might lead them to desire intercourse. Some are obvious enough, like kissing or sleeping in the same bed. But some seem far-fetched in modern society – like drinking consecutively from the same glass, or sitting on the same couch. Such restrictions, moreover, apply with even greater stringency – and seem to the modern mind even more far-fetched – between men and women who are not husband and wife. Two unrelated persons of opposite sex are not even allowed to be alone together in the same room. Haredi society starts enforcing a rigid separation of the sexes from nursery-school age.

On paper, the Modern-Orthodox subscribe to the letter of the halacha as faithfuly as the haredim, and ought therefore to feel bound by these restrictions. In practice, though, they have made substantial compromises with modernity in this area. On the 'left' of Modern Orthodoxy, children attend co-educational schools and youth movements, and mix freely in social settings. Modern-Orthodox youngsters will not openly admit to premarital sex, but clearly it is widespread among circles whose observance of the other two key societal mitzvot, shabbat and kashrut, is stricter than their compliance with the sexual constraints of the halacha. Similarly, many Modern-Orthodox married couples who observe the basic rule of immersion are lax about the layers of desire-curbing prohibitions.

'Right-of-centre' Modern Orthodoxy, however, influenced by the puritanical haredim, is currently embracing more restrictive sexual norms. Co-education is now frowned on by Modern-Orthodox parents, both in America and Israel, who themselves were sent to co-educational schools. Mixed swimming is forbidden where once it was enjoyed as a matter of course. And many Modern-Orthodox married women now cover their hair with a hat, scarf or wig, because the halacha determines that 'a woman's hair is lust-provoking'. One consequence of these changing values is a rise in social pressures on young Modern-Orthodox people to marry early, as the haredim do.

Still, the gulf between haredism and Modern Orthodoxy in this area of sexual and social mores is profound. Here, too, sexual rules bring the differences between the different groups into sharp focus. But here, on the extreme right of the Jewish spectrum, the nomenclature changes – from taharat hamishpacha, in the sense of post-menstrual immersion, which is taken for granted and is not a subject of polite conversation among haredim, to *tsniut* or modesty, a term incorporating a broad range of halachic and quasi-halachic law and custom.

It incorporates, too, a broad range of subtle differences between the different haredi sects. While some haredi women make do with a hat, scarf or wig, others, such as the Belzer hasidim, wear two forms of headgear together: a wig with a little hat on top. The Sephardic sage Ovadia Yosef, however, forbids wigs altogether, because they can look too natural. And while most haredi women trim their own hair short, some, such as the women of Jerusalem's Mea Shearim quarter, shave their heads quite bald when they marry, and keep them that way, under their black scarves, for the rest of their lives.

Stockings, another essential of female tsniut, also account for wide variety within haredism. Some hasidic women wear only thick black ones. In other, slightly more modern haredi circles black or any coloured tights are thought to be too suggestive, and only flesh-coloured hose is allowed. Each group has its own by-laws about how many denier thick the stockings must be.

But tsniut is concerned with more than clothes. It is a code of conduct and attitude of mind that affects every aspect of life, from the most public to the most intimate. In some haredi groups, a man will not refer to his wife in public (and certainly not to anybody else's wife) by her first name. Gerer hasidim, who are especially strict regarding tsniut, take this practice even further; the men will not refer to their wife as 'wife' even in casual conversation with other men, but will use an elliptical euphemism.

The Gerers are considered extremist even among haredim. One English-speaking haredi recalled teasing a Gerer friend, also English-speaking, who kept asking him in Yiddish: '*Bei dir in der Heim arbeit-men?*' (lit. 'At your home, does one work?'). 'Well, we had the decorators in . . .' the non-hasid replied disingenuously. '*Nein, nein – bei dir in Shtub . . . ?*' (No, no – in your house . . . ?) But the other kept up his façade of incomprehension until the exasperated hasid blurted out, in English: 'I mean, does your wife work?'

Obviously, tsniut entails a flat ban on any physical or vocal expression of affection between husband and wife in public. Holding hands, or even a gentle steering of the arm, is forbidden in front of strangers, lest it arouse lascivious thoughts (which in turn could result in a wanton emission of semen, which is a halachic offence and a spiritual/metaphysical calamity) according to the

Kabbala. The Gerers, again, go to extremes: Gerer husbands and wives are expected not to walk together in the street, at least until they reach middle age. Getting from point A to point B for a Gerer family, therefore, requires careful planning and logistics. This too gives rise to jokes within the broader haredi community. (Non-hasid: 'Who was that woman I saw you with last night?' Gerer hasid: 'Not my wife! Not my wife!').

But Gerer prudery extends to the connubial bedroom too, and it has become a subject of fierce if muted controversy within the haredi world. The Gerers, especially under a previous rebbe, Rabbi Yisrael Alter (1895–1977), campaigned against 'too much sex' within marriage. But how much is too much? Gerer hasidim took to calling each other up in the small hours with exhortations to get up and 'go to the synagogue instead of lolling alongside' their wives. Community elders, however, guided by the Rebbe, would instruct newly wed young men that sex once a week is sufficient, and that they have no duty to make the sex act prolonged or pleasurable for their wives. The women had been educated as to what to expect, and not to expect. Apparently they too accepted this approach to marriage as a religious ideal.

The Gerers, whose headquarters are in Israel with branches in America and Europe, are a large and influential grouping within haredism, and their ideas have taken hold in recent years in other sects too, to the chagrin of leading non-hasidic figures. These latter argue – the arguments, by their nature, are conducted discreetly – that haredi Judaism, for all its social restrictions and hedges of modesty, is basically positive towards human sexuality and encourages frequent and enjoyable sex within marriage. Myriad biblical and Talmudic statements are cited to bear this out. There is no monasticism in Judaism; to the contrary, the High Priest himself, in Temple times, was required to be married.

At any event, neither the regular haredi rules of tsniut nor the Gerers' excesses have any negative effect on fecundity. Haredi couples in all sections of the community are prolific by any standards. This is accountable only in part to a religious disapproval of contraception and abortion. In fact, while the condom is almost always forbidden (wanton emission), many haredi rabbis do permit women to use the IUD or the Pill if there are medical or psychological grounds to avoid pregnancy. These grounds need be less convincing, moreover, once the couple has fulfilled the *mitzva* 'Be fruitful and multiply' (Gen. 1:28), which according to halachic interpretation means having at least one boy and one girl.

But such small families are very much the exception, and will give rise to rumours that 'something is wrong.' As a rule, haredi families are large families; seven or eight children is normal; eleven or twelve is unexceptional. Haredim regard with scarcely veiled pity the average 'modern' family of two or three children. For them, a home teeming with little children is the epitome of joyful living. Among the Modern-Orthodox too, in America and in Israel, the birth-rate tends to be higher than the Jewish average.

3

'I've Never Been to Brooklyn!'

Orthodox leaders, especially in the United States, are convinced that the surging demographics – and economics – of their community are not fully taken into account, whether by design or by negligent omission, in the surveys that national Jewish organizations commission from time to time. 'They're all liars!' says Rabbi Israel Singer, the Orthodox director of the World Jewish Congress, referring to statisticians who estimate Orthodoxy still today at only 10 per cent of American Jewry. 'The federations commission their studies . . . [implying that the powerful Jewish philanthropic federations in the major cities are inherently anti-Orthodox]. The reason they can get away with it is the baby-boom. They ignore the Orthodox baby-boom and just count sample households and extrapolate. Look at me; I have five kids, my sister has six, none of our cousins have any less.'

Malcolm Hoenlein, executive director of the Conference of Presidents of Major American Jewish Organizations, and also Orthodox, is usually less vehement than Singer, but he too waxes resentful on this issue. 'Bullshit is what I think of the so-called findings of the statisticians. If you look at the next generation of committed Jews – you come up with a very different figure from ten per cent Orthodox . . .'* Hoenlein cites philanthropy, especially educational charity, as a significant indicator. In one month, he says, he was invited 'to twenty-six major dinners – that is four hundred guests or more – all held by Orthodox sponsors in

* In *Highlights of the Council of Jewish Federations 1990 National Jewish Population Survey* (New York: CJF 1991), the authors note that: 'The current levels of Orthodoxy may have been somewhat under-reported as terms unfamiliar to some interviewers such as the names of Hasidic sects may have been recorded as miscellaneous, traditional or just Jewish.'

aid of Orthodox schools. And people are paying $200 to $500 a plate.'

Rabbi Pinhas Stolper, long-time director of the Union of Orthodox Jewish Congregations of America (the organization responsible for the 'OU' kosher food supervision), also asserts that: 'The statistics lie. The surveys are taken by secular Jews in secular neighbourhoods and extrapolated. Ninety per cent of them don't factor in the Orthodox areas. I know what's happening. Just look at the housing situation in Flatbush, or in Borough Park [largely Orthodox sections of Brooklyn, the latter predominantly haredi]. In Flatbush today, seven yeshivas are putting up new buildings, each costing between two million and seven million dollars. That is a community that's bursting at the seams. And the attrition rate is extremely low. It's tiny; maybe one per cent.'

But Rabbi Alexander Schindler, head of the Union of American Hebrew Congregations (Reform), is prepared to grant, at most, that the Orthodox 'are holding on . . . They seem to be stable at around twelve per cent.

'And that's wonderful,' he adds. 'I have no problem with Orthodoxy. My *ahavat Yisrael* [love of Israel] embraces my traducers! Though I must say the Orthodoxy that I respected had humility in it. I do have problems with politicized Orthodoxy, with triumphalized Orthodoxy, with rabbis who preach that a Jew should sooner take refuge in a church than in a Reform synagogue.' He would 'like to see the Orthodox grow,' Schindler says generously. But they aren't. 'I know what the sociologists tell us, that there has been a steady crumbling of Orthodoxy, that the fourth and fifth generations of American Jews choose Reform. And the figures have been substantiated by community studies. We have 850 congregations, and our rolls have increased by twenty-five per cent in a decade. There is nowhere near that growth in Orthodoxy. Maybe there's a growth in urban centres. But let's talk about Middle America. Let's talk about Worcester, Massachusetts. Orthodoxy has virtually disappeared.'

Gary Rosenblatt, editor of the *Baltimore Jewish Times*, one of the leading American Jewish weekly newspapers, says of this remarkable difference in perception: 'The Reform feel that yes, the Orthodox are having a resurgence – but how long can it last in

America in the twentieth and twenty-first centuries? Federation-type people don't have any real sense of what's going on inside Orthodoxy, of what's being taught in the schools. Take Lubavitch for instance. Most of the people who give it most of its money don't know much about it. The Orthodox for their part simply feel that the others are dying, that eventually they will fade away.'

Another shrewd observer of American Jewish life, the late Rabbi Wolfe Kelman, who headed the Rabbinical Assembly (Conservative) for many years, said Orthodox resurgence 'is not quite what the Orthodox make it out to be, but it's there all right. Forty years ago, when I began at the Rabbinical Assembly, Orthodoxy was weak and dependent. It didn't have rich *baalei batim* [householders – figuratively, philanthropic supporters]. Now, the Orthodox are probably the richest per capita community in Jewish America.'

Kelman's father was a hasidic rabbi in Toronto. 'I remember how people would come round every Saturday night, wringing their hands about their children who were turning away from Orthodoxy. But not any more; the attrition has ended; they're holding on to their young. Any attrition is in the opposite direction; the Modern-Orthodox are losing ground to the haredim.'

The fundamental difference of perception regarding the viability of Orthodoxy, and especially of haredism, between the Orthodox and non-Orthodox, is both a cause and a consequence of deepening alienation between the haredim and the non-Orthodox majority of Jewry. Tom Dine, executive head of the pro-Israel lobby in Washington, the America-Israel Public Affairs Committee (AIPAC), and another key player in the national Jewish 'establishment', confides that 'In nine years at this job I've never been to Brooklyn! . . . The congressmen from there are so pro-Israel anyway, there's no need to work on them.' But then he adds: 'I don't think mainstream Jews feel very comfortable with the ultra-Orthodox. It's a class thing, I suppose. Their image is – smelly. That's what I'd say now you've got me thinking about it. Hasids and New York diamond dealers. United Jewish Appeal (UJA) people have told me several times they don't want to fly El Al because of "those people". Actually, I prefer Swissair or Lufthansa myself. But I fly El Al to Israel because it's direct. Yes, TWA flies direct too. But it's low-class, like the Orthodox. Yes, that's still the image. Still the poor immigrant image. That's the perception of a lot of people I mix with.'

On the haredi side one can hear similar expressions of alienation. Haredim commonly refer to non-Orthodox Jews in disparaging Yiddish terms that the Jews of the Russian shtetl used to describe the unloved local peasantry. Children are raised to shy away from the non-Orthodox and at the same time to look down on them with a mixture of pity and antipathy.

On the political and organizational level, haredi leaders in the United States are building independent structures outside those of the general Jewish community. They have their own photo-opportunities in the Oval Office, their own representatives in Washington lobbying for their own social services, and their own Federally funded employment offices and vocational training programmes. Their campaign in favour of Federal and state support for parochial schools – fought alongside Christian groups and traditionally opposed by mainstream liberal Jewish organizations – steadily gained ground during the Reagan-Bush years. Transportation, meals and grants are available today to yeshiva students as a result of this sustained campaign, and the haredi lobbyists are hopeful of eventually winning tax credits for tuition fees.

'We've built a new type of Orthodox Jew. We've given him self-esteem,' says Rabbi Moshe Sherer, head of Agudath Israel in America, which is the foremost haredi public organization. In the old days, he recalls, a haredi young man who spoke up for the community in accent-free English was something of a hero in the ghetto. '*Er ken redn tzu a policeman*' (he can talk to a policeman), he remembers people whispering admiringly behind his back.

Sherer believes that social and halachic alienation between Orthodox and non-Orthodox will ultimately lead to a complete rupture in Jewry. The alternative community agencies that he is building up, though not originally intended for this purpose, will serve as a ready-made organizational infrastructure for the Orthodox in the event of outright schism. By the same token, though, the vigour and success of the haredim's separatist efforts catalyse the process of schism. 'Would you rather we died?' is Sherer's reply. 'We see what's coming. Our job is to shore up our side, to save our souls.'

4

Comfort and Joy

Newspaper headlines often use the word 'hasidic' as a generic term to describe all haredim – both the hasidim and their opponents, the mitnagdim. For most Jews today, descended from one side or the other of this hoary dispute, the distinction is quaintly esoteric and entirely irrelevant to their own lives. For the haredim, however, committed to making the past live on, the hasidic-mitnagdic divide is still a matter of meaning and practical significance.

The origins of hasidism are shrouded in legend and mystery. Basic facts and key events are unclear, even though they took place in relatively recent times. The movement's founder, Rabbi Yisrael Baal Shem Tov, 'Master of the Good Name' (1698–1760), and his successor Rabbi Dov Ber, the Maggid of Mezritch (d. 1772), preached a new joy and spontaneity in Judaism. They reached out to the masses, teaching that simple devotion, if performed with sincerity and zeal, can bring a believer to spiritual elevation. They stressed the importance of prayer and song, of comradeship and the intimate, heady study of the kabbala. They seemed to play down the traditional value-system, based on Talmudic learning and halachic casuistry.

But their life-stories are full of lacunae, and despite the efforts of historians we have no clear picture of their personalities nor a full understanding of their activities and the meteoric success of their religious revolution. The early movement, in what is now the Ukraine, was untouched by the Jewish Emancipation in the West. Hence there was no scholarly and dispassionate recording of contemporaneous events from within. Such contemporary chronicling as there was flowed from the pens of virulent mitnagdic enemies of the Baal Shem Tov and the Maggid of Mezritch, or from occasional brief visits by *maskilim* (Enlightened literati), who had their own axes to grind.

The hasidim themselves wrote biographical accounts that tended to be long on miracle-making, prophecy and telepathy, but woefully short on the more mundane aspects of the subject's personal development and public career. That is still a favoured literary genre in the haredi world, and is now equally popular among hasidim and mitnagdim. In haredi biographies, the rabbi or rebbe hero invariably exhibited academic genius by the age of three, was endowed solely with good and kindly character-traits, and usually had supernatural or at least extra-sensory powers.

Scholars have sought the sociological roots of hasidism in the collapse of the messianic pretensions of Shabtai Zvi in the previous century and of Jacob Frank in the mid-eighteenth century. Both men, particularly Shabtai Zvi, attracted large followings throughout the Jewish Diaspora and aroused great hopes which, when dashed (Zvi eventually converted to Islam), brought on a period of despondency.

Certainly the contemporary enemies of early hasidism, led by the most eminent Talmudist of the age, Rabbi Elijah, the Gaon of Vilna, made the connection between the Baal Shem Tov and the earlier messianic pretenders. Only thus can the vehemence and fanaticism of their opposition – replete with book-burning and false accusations to the Tsarist authorities – be understood at all. They thought they were dealing with dangerous heretics who, left uncurbed, would wreak yet another historic disaster of betrayal and apostasy upon the Jewish people. The mitnaged informers who engineered the imprisonment of Rabbi Shneur Zalman of Lubavitch in St Petersburg must have presumed that he would not return alive. The accusation of false messianism pretty much died out thereafter – until its recent revival by Rabbi Shach against the present Lubavitcher Rebbe (see chapter 11).

Historians also see in the Baal Shem Tov and his movement a rebellion against the stuffiness of rabbinic scholarship at that time, which tended to haughty exclusivism, with little room for the non-intellectual to develop his spiritual potential. At the rebbe's 'court', on the other hand, caught up in the fervour and magic of a collective spiritual experience, the hasid could forget the daily grind of eking out a living. He could forget, too, his nagging sense of inadequacy in the face of the abstruse and convoluted Talmudic texts. His spirit could soar with the lofty, mystical *torot* (homilies) of his rebbe. This at any rate is the romantic – and often somewhat disdainful – image conjured up by writers on the period. It served to support the mitnagdic accusation that the early hasidic leaders, and indeed later rebbes too, were ignorant men who disparaged learning.

The ignorance canard became the strongest motif in the hasid–mitnaged rivalry. It has proved remarkably resilient, given that some of the most distinguished Talmudists of the past 200 years have been hasidim, and in some cases hasidic rebbes. The Baal Shem himself attracted several leading rabbis to his original following, and several of the adherents of the Maggid were noted halachic authors, including Shneur Zalman of Lubavitch. Nevertheless, the oft-repeated generalization that hasidim are *amei-haaretz* (unlearned) continues to this day to imbue many a student and alumnus of a mitnagdic yeshiva with a smug sense of superiority, and to fuel a feeling of defensiveness and resentment among the hasidim.

Hasidim say the misunderstanding began with the Baal Shem himself, who 'concealed' his great gifts, living for years as a simple forester and later as a *heder* (elementary school) teacher before finally 'revealing himself' to his family and close disciples. His purpose, they explain, was to struggle against the pernicious pride that comes with public recognition of scholarly accomplishments or piety. Better – for the spirit, that is – to be thought of as a simpleton and ignoramus. The story may be apocryphal, or a post-factum rationalization of that strand of anti-intellectualism that certainly exists in hasidism. But it does encapsulate early hasidism's constant striving to flout social norms and pressures that inhibit the free flight of the spirit.

Plainly there were excesses and provocations on both sides. One disciple of the Maggid, Rabbi Haim Haike of Amdur, set up a community of like-minded men who (if the outraged fulminations of the local mitnagdim are to be believed) were wont to jump and skip and stand on their heads during prayer. They would invariably pray later than the halachically permitted time. And they would deliberately dress bizarrely, wearing their boots on the wrong feet and their hats inside out – all in their efforts to smash the natural human desire for honour and respect from society. In this they duly succeeded: they were excommunicated by the mitnagdic rabbis, and driven out of town.

The mitnagdic pamphleteering that accompanied these early battles made out that the 'new sect' did little else but stand on their heads. But the same Haim Haike was the author of a hardly-known book, published long after his death, which shows him to have been a homileticist of delicate sensitivity and insight.

Under the Maggid, hasidism spread throughout the Ukraine and into Poland, Galicia and White Russia. Many of his disciples became rebbes in their own right after his death, setting up courts and founding dynasties. Some retained the simplicity and spirituality of the early movement; others developed a taste for high living, waxing fat on the cash contributions of their followers. This in turn gave rise to charges of venality, levelled both by the embattled mitnagdim, who remained strong, particularly in Lithuania and parts of White Russia, and by the scoffing scholars of the *haskala* (Enlightened intellectualism) in the West, who regarded hasidism as a throwback to primitivism. 'After the death of the founder,' wrote the nineteenth-century German-Jewish historian Heinrich Graetz, 'barbarism and degeneracy increased . . .'

Hasidism's critics directed their scorn at the dynastic excesses of what they contemptuously called 'zaddikism'. Not only was the crown in most hasidic courts passed down from father to son, sometimes with scant regard for the son's suitability, but in many cases every son, and even every son-in-law, of a deceased rebbe or *tzaddik* (saintly man) set up a court of his own. And the hasidim were expected and required to keep all these princes-turned-kings in the state to which their predecessor had become accustomed.

The animosity between the two brands of haredism was mitigated to some extent by their common fight against the haskala in its various manifestations. This was the rationale behind the creation in 1912 of Agudat Yisrael, a joint hasidic–mitnagdic political organization designed to fight against Zionism and against the growing non-Orthodox movements in Jewry, which were all regarded by the haredim as outgrowths of the haskala.

It was hasidism, though, with its religious fervour and populist appeal, that proved the more resilient arm of haredism in the battles against the various incursions of modernity. Among the Jews who remained in Eastern Europe and did not emigrate to the West, hasidic families were somewhat less prone than mitnagdim to secularist erosions. The few who survived the Holocaust with their haredi faith intact have been the nucleus of the revival of haredism in recent decades.

This indeed was the conclusion of one of the most eminent mitnagdic rabbis of this century, Yehezkel Abramsky (1886–1976). He saw Lubavitch hasidism at work in conditions of deprivation and danger in post-revolutionary Russia, before himself escaping to England, where he became head of the London Beit Din (rabbinical court). In his later years as the dean of Slabodka, a leading mitnagdic yeshiva in Israel, he would encourage the hasidic students to spend shabbat with their rebbes, explaining that the hoary rivalry was no longer valid, and that haredi history had vindicated the hasidim.

5

Shades of Black

Hasidism's enemies of yesteryear have in fact absorbed many of the traits that they previously spurned. One obvious case is the important matter of dress. Today's haredi male – hasidic or mitnagdic (Sephardic haredim generally follow the mitnagdic lead) – deliberately sets out to *look* different from other people. This was not always the case. In the past, the hasidim made a point of looking different from the world around them, while the mitnagdim tried to look the same.

The great mitnagdic *yeshivot* of Lithuania encouraged their students early in this century to dress in the fashion of the time: sober-coloured suits, white shirts with starched collars, ties and modish hats, smoothly shaven cheeks (achieved with an evil-smelling powder, not with a razor, which is halachically forbidden). This 'modern' and elegant appearance accorded with their philosophical teaching of '*gadlut ha'adam*', the greatness of man: the Torah scholar was taught to feel that he could hold his head up high in any society. The hasidim meanwhile, true to their own teachings, defiantly retained their unkempt beards and curly sidelocks, their long coats deliberately buttoned the wrong way just to be different, their shabbat shtreimel, knickerbocker trousers and unfashionable boots. There was no attempt to change with the times; quite the opposite.

A century later, both camps remain essentially unchanged in their external appearance. But for the mitnagdim what this means is a radical revision of their previous approach, and an acceptance, in effect, of the hasidim's belief that haredim must look different from the rest of society, and that one obvious way to achieve this is to wear outdated or incongruous clothes.

There is no mistaking a haredi-mitnagdic man today. Who else wears a dark suit, black hat, white shirt and tie in the middle of a sweltering New York or Tel Aviv heat-wave? Yet the 'Lithuanian' yeshivot insist that their students retain this long-unfashionable wardrobe. The yeshiva deans themselves, and some haredi pulpit rabbis, wear Edwardian frock-coats. This sartorial profile that was *de rigueur* in polite society decades ago has been endowed with almost religious significance.

Some of the mitnagdim now also sport long *peyot* (sidelocks) like the hasidim, and many have taken to wearing long coats instead of standard-length suit jackets, particularly on shabbat. A close inspection can still tell them apart from the hasidim though: their peyot are not usually as long as the hasidim's, and they tend to wear them tucked behind their ears rather than curled and hanging down to their shoulders like some hasidim, or gathered up under their hats like some others, or wound round and round their ears in a third common hasidic variation. (This latter practice produces entire hasidic communities in which the males have small, shell-shaped ears). Their black hats, moreover, are usually in the fedora or homburg style, whereas hasidim spurn any indentation of the crown.

The long coats of the mitnagdim are also distinguishable from those of the hasidim to the tutored eye, at least on shabbat. They are made of the same suiting material as their trousers, not of the shiny black gabardine or patterned silk (or synthetic silk-substitute) that is a hasid's sabbath and festival pride.

And the mitnagdim, whatever the length of their coats, eschew the black rope-like belt or *gartel* without which no hasid will pray, approach his rebbe, or perform any ritual or ceremonial act. The halacha requires a 'separation between the heart and the sexual organs'. Mitnagdim say this is achieved by the modern-day trouser waistband. But hasidim cite other halachic and kabbalistic reasons to back their position. The division of opinion over this relatively minor accoutrement runs deep. The gartel, more than anything else, is the hallmark of the hasid.

Among the hasidic sects themselves there are subtle differences in dress. Some wear breeches tied below the knee, so that their black- or white-stockinged calves (depending on the sect) are visible below their long coats. Others have knickerbockers that are more like plus-fours, gathered above the ankle. Some sects have adopted regular trousers; some wear regular trousers midweek, and the traditional shorter ones on shabbat. The hasidim's trousers, of whatever length, are usually of dark material; but in certain sects the rebbe wears breeches in a dog-toothed check.

The Gerers and other Polish hasidic sects do not wear shtreimels, which are flat and round and made of thirteen pelts – in some sects twenty-six; both numbers have kabbalistic significance – but *spodiks*, which are taller and narrower, rather like Cossack caps. A good quality sable-skin spodik can set a new bridegroom (or his father-in-law) back by several hundred dollars; but a fine shtreimel can cost thousands. The Lubavitchers, alone among the hasidim, do not wear fur hats at all, but regular black trilbies both midweek and shabbat.

If you see a haredi today in the cool, colourful, comfortable clothes favoured by most of mankind, it is fair to assume that he is sliding from haredism to mere Orthodoxy, or perhaps even beyond. But the pervasive influence of hasidism upon the generality of haredism today goes beyond clothes. There is an ongoing absorption and internalization by the mitnagdim of key hasidic values – spiritual spontaneity, song and dance, unabashed emotionalism in prayer. Mitnagdism, almost despite itself, is not nearly so dour as it was in the heyday of its battles against hasidism.

A wedding among haredi mitnagdim today is as loud and lively as among the hasidim. The young men and women swirl round in sweating circles, dancing the same flashing steps to the same tunes – hasidic tunes, usually belted out by five- or seven-piece bands equipped with the latest in high-decibel amplification.

The circles of dancers are entirely separate, of course: haredi men and women do not sit together at weddings or other public events, much less dance with each other, which is halachically forbidden. At most weddings, the separation is achieved by means of a room-divider – curtains, potted ferns or movable screens – strategically placed down the centre of the hall. Sometimes this physical separation stops short of the bride and groom themselves; they are allowed to sit side-by-side at the head table. But that is not usually the case, and among most mitnagdim, and all hasidim, bride and groom (who have spent hardly any time together before their nuptials) must bid farewell after the religious ceremony, the *huppa* (lit. canopy, under which the ceremony is held), and spend the rest of their wedding apart, the bride dining and dancing with the women and the groom with the men.

Some hasidic wedding feasts actually take place in two separate halls – one for each sex. The halacha requires that the bride must hear the blessings recited after the meal, and taste the wine, and for these, therefore, she is grudgingly permitted to enter and sit at the edge of the 'men's hall'. Hasidim, however, conclude their weddings with the ancient and beautiful custom of the *mitzva-tensl*, when the bride dances briefly in turn with her various male relatives and with rabbis and other honoured guests who are invited to stay for this intimate and very moving moment.

The dance is performed with a handkerchief or napkin (sometimes a gartel is used), since any direct physical contact between a man and a woman is strictly prohibited by the halacha. As the *klezmer* (traditional music) band plays a slow and gentle melody, the bride and her partner circle gravely, while the other men dance around them and the women watch from a distance. After a few revolutions, the man drops his end of the connecting cloth and rejoins the other dancers. The high point is the bride's dance with the groom. Here the cloth is dispensed with, and the young couple hold hands and shuffle demurely to the music.

There is something quintessentially hasidic about this scene; a blend of the earthy and the sublime that runs through much of the movement's religious thought. (The early hasidic masters were much taken with the kabbala with its explicit sexual imagery, invoked in poetry and esoteric texts, to represent the mystical union of God and Israel.)

A mitzva-tensl at a wedding of hasidic 'royalty' in Bnei Brak some years ago created a colourful tableau. The groom was the son of a local hasidic rebbe of Romanian origin, the Nadvorner. The rebbe-grandfather, venerable patriarch of the clan, had come from New York for the occasion, and he, resplendent in a shimmering blue *bekeshe* (silk coat), regaled the company with his violin. One by one, the groom's uncles and brother, all of them rebbes in Israel or America, each wearing a different-coloured brocaded bekeshe, took their turn to dance with the bride.

*

Mitnagdim would argue that there has been a much more significant transfer of influence than their absorption of the hasidic clothes-culture, namely the adoption by the hasidic side of the fundamental mitnagdic value of systematic Talmud study. The first all-hasidic yeshiva in Poland run on Lithuanian yeshiva lines, Hachmei (Wise Men of) Lublin, was founded less than a decade before the Holocaust, and was considered a great innovation. Before that, Talmudic education in the hasidic communities was very much an informal, unstructured process (though the hasidim would counter that it produced many fine scholars, and an educated laity).

Today, every self-respecting hasidic court must have a yeshiva, and the larger ones have developed entire educational networks, with institutions for boys and girls at the rebbe's headquarters and in the main centres of the sect elsewhere. They provide instruction from infancy to marriage, and for the men there are *kollelim* too – advanced yeshivas where they can 'stay in learning' beyond marriage. Indeed, the adoption and adaptation of the 'Litvisher' (Yiddish: Lithuanian) yeshiva structure has proved, perhaps paradoxically, modern-day hasidism's shrewdest success. The hasidic yeshivot produce not merely Torah-trained graduates, but hasidim.

'The secret of our phenomenal growth, thank God, is one word,' says Rabbi Naftali ('Reb Naftolche') Halberstam, son and heir-presumptive of the Bobover Rebbe of Brooklyn, New York: 'Yeshiva'. He described how his father, scion of a major hasidic house in Galicia largely obliterated by the Nazis, had arrived in America in 1946, lonely and indigent. He set up a *shul* (synagogue) on Manhattan's upper west side, unknown and unnoticed. 'We hardly had a *minyan* [prayer quorum of ten men] on *shabbos*,' the son recalled wryly. Eventually he moved to more hospitable surroundings in Brooklyn, first to the Crown Heights section, then to Borough Park.

But there were many such refugee rebbes in New York at that time, some of them irreparably broken men, others, like Rabbi Shlomo of Bobov, determined to recreate the life that had been destroyed. The Bobover was aided by a warm, outgoing personality, a welcoming smile, a rare gift for story-telling and an inexhaustible fund of hasidic tales that attracted people to his *tishen* (plural of *tish*, table), or festive meals (see chapter 9). But the key to his success was the yeshiva that he quickly founded alongside his then modest court. He hired the best teachers, irrespective of their hasidic or mitnagdic affiliations. And he accepted any Orthodox youngster looking to learn.

Students entered without sectarian loyalty and emerged as Bobover hasidim. Today, in the huge, marbled yet tastefully understated Bobover synagogue in Borough Park – completed in 1988 but already too small for the burgeoning community – there are precious few worshippers who can claim to be of Bobover stock '*fun der Heim*', that is from back in pre-war Poland. But they are all Bobover now, body and soul, part of a fast-growing sect with thousands of adherents. The branch-communities in Israel and England also maintain thriving yeshivas.

The hasidic yeshiva, in other words, unlike a regular university, does not aim to turn out graduates who keep up only occasional contact with the alma mater and may be approached in later life for philanthropic support. The hasidic alumni never really leave. Rather, if the study-course has succeeded, they have been turned into life-long 'fellows'. Their fellowship, moreover, transcends borders. For haredim, and especially for hasidim, geography is remarkably irrelevant. In the words of an Israeli political scientist: 'Whether in Jerusalem or Bnei Brak, in Brooklyn or Antwerp, they share a common universe of discourse: synagogue and rabbinical authority, halacha and observance, Torah and study . . . [They] maintain tight networks of family and "sectarian" loyalties to rabbis and schools, cutting across boundaries and seas.'*

The rebbe's court is the centre of the hasid's life, his home-from-home. Its specific location – in Israel, America or Europe – is unimportant, an accident of history, which in many cases, after the traumas and disruptions of the Holocaust, it was. The well-to-do think nothing of crossing the Atlantic, or the Mediterranean, four or five times a year to spend a shabbat or festival with their rebbe. But even down-at-heel Breslever hasidim in Jerusalem manage to

* Avraham Avi-Hai, 'The Three Jewish Peoples', *Jerusalem Post*, 5 Feb. 1989.

come up with several hundred dollars for a four-day Rosh Hashana round-trip to the Ukraine and back – where their rebbe, Rabbi Nachman of Breslev, has lain buried in the town of Uman for 180 years. The Breslevers, who are called 'the dead hasidim', believe themselves still bound to the soul of their one and only rebbe. After decades during which Uman was classified a closed Soviet military area, this focus of their thoughts and mystical longings has become accessible once again.

The Baal Shem Tov himself, founder of hasidism (and great-grandfather of Rabbi Nachman), taught his disciples: 'Where a man's mind is, that's where the whole man is.' Today, when Lubavitcher hasidim speak of 'Lubavitch', they are usually referring to their Rebbe's headquarters in the Crown Heights section of Brooklyn, New York, not to the village in White Russia where the famous dynasty originated. The row of brownstones on Eastern Parkway has *become* Lubavitch. Rabbi Schneerson, the Rebbe, maintains his own peculiar ambivalence towards the confines of geography. On the one hand, he refuses to leave New York and has not been out of the city for close to forty years; on the other, he has had a precise replica of his New York headquarters built in Kfar Habad, the main Lubavitcher village in Israel. The house stands there in all its architectural incongruity, waiting for its owner who has never visited.

When hasidim meet and mingle at their rebbe's court, the atmosphere is truly international – even though they all look the same to an outsider, dressed in the special garb of their particular sect. Business deals are concluded, and marriages arranged – all serving to draw the community still closer across the continents. Where will the young couple live? In the groom's country, or the bride's, or perhaps in a new community that the sect is building in a provincial town in Israel or in upstate New York? This decision is left to the rebbe, who weighs the interests of the sect as well as those of the individual families.

Philanthropy, like business, spans continents. A wealthy haredi in New York is expected to support his sect's yeshivas in Israel and Europe as well as its institutions in his own city and elsewhere in North America. But this global haredi economics has its flip-side: when business is bad in New York, yeshivas in Israel and Europe suffer. By the same token, when the financial empire of a millionaire haredi businessman collapsed in London in 1991, haredim in New York, Antwerp and Bnei Brak were among those ruined. As a son of the hasidic Rebbe of Sassov, they had trusted him with their money.

When the hasidic rebbe of Belz, Rabbi Yissachar Dov Rokeach, celebrated the bar-mitzva of his only son, Aharon, in Jerusalem in March 1989, he rented the city's main convention hall for a festive gathering of his followers. Reading in Yiddish from a prepared speech, he described the central role of 'that little village, Belz' in the lives of tens of thousands of Jews in pre-Holocaust Europe. Rabbi Rokeach, born in Israel in 1948, had never actually visited Belz. The Belzer community was almost totally wiped out by the Nazis. The former Rebbe and his brother, Yissachar Dov's father, escaped through Hungary to Palestine. When Yissachar Dov became Rebbe, in 1968, his following was still small and weak, a sad remnant of the pre-war community. Now he read out a long list of Belz's yeshivas, schools and synagogues, from Montreal to Melbourne.

Ger, the largest hasidic sect in pre-war Poland, was all but annihilated, like the others. The Rebbe, Rabbi Avraham Mordechai Alter, escaped to Palestine with some of his family. His sons, Yisrael, a charismatic figure who was Rebbe from 1949 to 1979, and then Simcha Bunim, presided over the process of regeneration. Today there are eleven Gerer yeshivas spread throughout Israel. In Borough Park, Brooklyn, there are eight Gerer *shtieblach* (hasidic synagogues; sing., *shtiebel* – lit. small room).

The largest hasidic sect is the Satmarer, whose centre before the Holocaust was in Hungary, where the Nazi death machine moved in only in 1944. Relatively more Hungarian Jews therefore survived the war than Polish Jews. The main Satmarer communities are in the Williamsburg section of Brooklyn, and in Monroe, a small town north of New York City. They too have branches in Israel, Britain, Belgium and other countries.

The Satmarers' dramatic post-war growth is accountable to their magnetic leader, Rabbi Yoel Teitelbaum (1887–1977). His fiery extremism – he was a bitter foe of Zionism and Israel – was matched by great personal warmth. Many Hungarian haredi refugees who reached the US in the Forties, and in a second wave after the brief Hungarian uprising of 1956, were drawn to him and became Satmarers.

When a Satmarer or Gerer hasid takes to the road, he can find his own kind in a dozen cities around the world. A Lubavitcher will encounter his colleagues in literally hundreds of locations, including such tiny, far-flung Jewish communities as Hong Kong and Bangkok, and in college campuses all across the United States. Lubavitch's speciality is spiritual outreach, and the Rebbe runs a Peace Corps-like programme of 'emissaries' (see Chapter 10). But any hasidic Jew walking into any shtiebel anywhere can be confident of a warm welcome and generous hospitality.

One historian of modern Jewry, Professor Ezra Mendelsohn, considers this 'internationalism' the most salient feature of haredism's current resurgence. 'They're like the Jewish socialists of the pre-war world. If you were a Jewish socialist, then wherever you were, you could find like-minded people with whom you had a common language. Today it's the haredim who enjoy this advantage.'

PART II

LINES OF AUTHORITY

6

Keeping His Word

The San Francisco earthquake in October 1989 came during the opening ceremonies of the third game of the baseball World Series and rendered the stadiums of both teams – Oakland and San Francisco – unusable for more than a week.

A few days after the earthquake, the Israeli haredi newspaper *Yated Ne'eman*, in its English-language edition which is sold mainly in America, published the following item prominently on its front page: 'The Jerusalem Talmud on Earthquakes (Tractate Berachos 64a)' (this was the headline). '*HaKadosh Boruch Hu* [The Holy One, Blessed Be He] sees their theaters and amphitheaters in tranquility while the *Bais Hamikdosh* [Holy Temple] lies in ruins, and He wants to destroy the world, as it is written, "He shall roar mightily because of His dwelling place." '

The baseball spectators, in fact, were unhurt. Most of the earthquake's victims were drivers on the Oakland Bridge. But *Yated*'s point was that the timing of the quake was no random coincidence. God was signalling to Man. Baseball, a twentieth-century 'amphitheatre' activity, displeases Him, especially because His dwelling place lies in ruins – that is, the ancient Jewish Temple in Jerusalem, destroyed nearly 2,000 years ago, is now the site of a Muslim mosque.

A similar lesson in the workings of Divine retribution had been delivered to the Israeli public two years earlier by the haredi interior minister, Rabbi Yitzhak Peretz, after a bus carrying children on a school outing stalled on a level-crossing and a train ploughed into it. Peretz, in a public statement, pointed out that the dead children were from the town of Petah Tikva, where a cinema had opened on Friday nights, thereby transgressing the sabbath. Local haredim had demonstrated each week outside the cinema, and clashed with the police. But the shows went on. God, said Rabbi Peretz, had now visited a terrible punishment on the sabbath-desecrating town. His remarks caused an outcry.

According to the haredim – and this is a fundamental tenet of their belief – the 'Holy One Blessed Be He' actively runs the world. He did not merely create it and then leave it to run itself by rules of Nature which He had previously ordained. Nor does He let it run itself while intervening supernaturally from time to time. He is constantly and directly involved – both in the affairs of Man and in the operation of Nature.

There have been broad variations of this doctrine in Orthodox Jewish thinking through the ages. Rabbis and scholars have grappled with the mysteries of immanence and transcendence; some Jewish mystics have come close to a pantheistic approach, so imbued were they with an overwhelming sense of Godliness all around them. The common denominator of all strands of Orthodox faith is that God *can* intervene. In the words of a contemporary Jewish theologian: 'On waking each morning, a Jew at prayer acknowledges the Creation renewed, for not only he but the world might have passed out of existence overnight.'

For haredim today, He not only can, but does. God is a constant presence in their lives, and they for their part must try to live in a constant state of awareness of Him. They invoke Him frequently in mundane conversation. 'With God's help' the train will leave on time; 'Thank God' the train left on time. It is a *façon de parler*; but they mean it too. The standard haredi response to the question 'How are you?' is '*Boruch Hashem*,' Blessed be the Name (of God). The haredi will reply in this way even if all is not well, thus observing the Talmudic ruling: 'Just as one must bless God for the good things, one must bless him for the bad things too.' In the same vein, the Talmud and subsequent halacha lay down a special blessing on hearing of a death or other bad news: 'Blessed be the True Judge.'

But haredim are not passively fatalistic (at least not in their private lives: haredi anti-Zionism can be seen as a form of fatalism on the national, historical level). Some fundamentalists, in other religions, prefer to rely on Divine intervention in sickness rather than submit to medical treatment. Some forbid surgery; others balk even at blood-transfusions. Haredim reject such conduct as perverse and presumptuous. 'One may not rely on miracles,' the Talmud teaches. It expressly enjoins the sick man to seek medical advice. Many haredi rabbis, in fact, maintain their own worldwide network of contacts with the top men in every branch of medicine, and are able to refer their followers to the best hospitals and the most advanced treatments.

In some cases a rabbi or hasidic rebbe will recommend one doctor or proposed treatment as against another. Rarely, he might counsel against undergoing a particular treatment or operation even though it is unanimously prescribed. The haredi patient in effect shifts the decision-making, and the responsibility, onto the holy man's shoulders. This is called the acceptance of *daat Torah* (lit., the knowledge of the Torah: Torah means literally the Pentateuch or Five Books of Moses; but by extension it has come to mean the entire corpus of religous law) or *emunat hachamim* (faith in wise men). The haredi accepts that his rabbi, in his superior wisdom, knows best.

One memorable example of emunat hachamim occurred in January 1991, as the United Nations deadline to Iraq approached and war clouds gathered over the Middle East. The Lubavitcher Rebbe declared that Israel was 'the safest place on earth'. Accordingly, his hasidim in Israel put aside any thought of leaving – though thousands of foreign passport-holders, including haredim, were fleeing the country. Lubavitcher hasidim in the Diaspora planning to visit Israel went ahead without hesitation. 'The Rebbe said everything will be all right,' one hasid explained, landing at the semi-deserted Tel Aviv airport. 'The Rebbe said that the Torah says that God looks after the Holy Land . . .'

The haredim's blind obeisance to rabbis is one of the most alienating characteristics of haredism in the eyes of the outside world, both Jewish and Gentile. For the haredim themselves, however, the profundity of this disapproval is hard to understand, because for them religious reverence is a seamless web. God Himself, the Bible, the Talmud, the rabbinical writings, the rabbis themselves – all are intertwined in an unbroken thread that extends from Abraham and Moses to the *gedolim* (great rabbis) of the present day, and on into the future. Strict fidelity to Holy Writ, which is a characteristic of every form of religious fundamentalism, is a key component of haredism too. But for haredim, scriptural reverence is not confined to the Bible. In fact, in a paradoxical way, it does not actually apply to the Bible: Talmudic tradition forbids a literal reading of Scripture. The Bible must be read and understood only through the eyes of later exegesis.

Haredism is therefore sometimes described as 'Talmudic fundamentalism', meaning that the haredim relate to the Talmud, the vast body of law and legend compiled between the first and fifth centuries CE,* with the same religious reverence as Christian fundamentalists relate to the Bible. But the 'Talmudic fundamentalism' of the haredim does not stop with the Talmud. It extends to all the subsequent centuries of post-Talmudic literature – thousands of commentaries, codes, responsa, mystical tracts, homiletics – down to the present day. Thus the writings of the twelfth-century sage and philosopher Maimonides, or of the sixteenth-century mystic Isaac Luria, are regarded with reverence too; not with quite the same degree of reverence as the earlier works, but with profound, uncritical reverence nonetheless.

And it extends beyond the texts themselves, to their authors. Thus the rabbis who wrote the Talmud and all the subsequent literature were holy, wise and righteous, and must be uncritically revered. From there it is just a short hop to applying the same fundamentalistic reverence to holy, wise and righteous rabbis, dead or alive, who may not have actually written a particular text in question, but are regarded as human embodiments of the sacred literature. Their every utterance is imbued with the knowledge – daat Torah – or at least the spirit, that is contained in the totality of the texts, which collectively are the Word of God.

It is this veneration, says a Jerusalem physician, this acceptance of daat Torah as an all-embracing way of life, that sets apart the haredim from the rest of the Orthodox. An Orthodox Jew, he says – he is himself devoutly (Modern-)Orthodox – lives his religious life by the Shulhan Aruch, the authoritative codification of the

* Common Era, used by Jews in preference to AD, Anno Domini; hence BCE, Before Common Era.

halacha. He will consult a rabbi if he has a question regarding a point of halacha, and will be bound by the rabbi's ruling. He might consult with a rabbi on a problem unrelated to halacha, but that would be by way of seeking advice; there would be no binding authority in the rabbi's response. A haredi, on the other hand, will consult his rabbi or hasidic rebbe on every aspect of his life, and will obey the advice he receives as though it were an halachic ruling.

For the physician, a gynaecologist serving a mixed haredi/Modern-Orthodox area, this is no mere semantic or even theological distinction; it bears direct and often far-reaching practical consequences for his everyday work. Thus, he will always try to ascertain the precise affiliation of a haredi patient – to which hasidic sect she or her husband adheres, or which mitnagdic rabbi they follow – and record it in the patient's file. He knows that his diagnoses and treatments will be 'monitored' by the rebbe or rabbi.

In the course of a pregnancy, and sometimes in the delivery room itself, there will be a constant flow of medical information from the doctor through the patient to the rebbe/rabbi. A problem or complication will result in a stream of queries, and often detailed advice, in the other direction. Often, to save time and energy, the doctor and the rebbe/rabbi will set up their own direct channel of communication to discuss cases. Some rebbes have a particular aide (with no formal medical training) who handles contacts with doctors and hospitals. In some cases, a rebbe – or *rebbitzin*, for several pious women are active in the medical, and especially gynaecological, sphere – will actually write out a prescription, and there are pharmacies in Jerusalem that will dispense the drugs.

This doctor, and others like him in Jerusalem and other cities around the world with significant haredi communities, protests of course at such interference. But not too loudly; the haredim represent an important clientele. They zealously take care of their health as a matter of religious duty as well as of sensible self-interest. They prefer to pay for private treatment rather than rely on public medicine. For doctors whom their rabbis favour and recommend, and especially for gynaecologists, they are a prolific source of work and income.

*

The physician was exaggerating when he equated Orthodoxy with total observance of the Shulhan Aruch, the book of rules written at the end of the sixteenth century, which regulates the most minute aspects of life. Many Jews who define themselves as Orthodox, and indeed who strive to *be* Orthodox, will admit, if they are prepared to be honest, that they cannot or do not keep every detailed ordinance of the rule-book. They do not necessarily get dressed while under the bedclothes out of modesty (Shulhan Aruch 2:1), or tie their left shoe-lace before their right one (2:4), or deliberately wear different clothes from the Gentiles (Kitzur Shulhan Aruch 3:2), or refrain from walking between two women, two dogs or two pigs (3:8).

This is a deliberately tendentious selection, but it serves to illustrate how Modern-Orthodox Jews, Jews who observe shabbat, kashrut and taharat hamishpacha, do in fact make their quiet compromises with the Shulhan Aruch in matters that they consider anachronistic and/or marginal. These Jews, though, would feel offended to be excluded from the doctor's definition of Orthodoxy.

Modern Orthodoxy attempts to steer its own course not only in religious practice, but in doctrine too. It rejects the haredim's extension of their fundamentalistic faith from the ancient texts and sainted figures of the past to the rabbis of the present. For the Modern-Orthodox, this is an abdication of Man's duty to think for himself, to reflect on his world and make decisions about his life. Yet Modern Orthodoxy is fundamentalist too, up to a point. 'If Judaism commands us to be fundamentalists, let us be so, proudly and undefensively,' says the new British Chief Rabbi, Jonathan Sacks, a leading spokesman for Modern Orthodoxy. 'But let us be so, also, precisely and accurately. Orthodoxy involves belief in a proposition denied by most non-Orthodox Jews, namely that the Five Books of Moses are the unmediated word of God.'

That does not mean, Sacks explains, that the Bible is literal truth. Rather, it is 'instruction, legal and ethical', as expounded by the Jewish sages in their interpretation of the Bible. 'It does not set out to answer the question, "What happened?" but the question, "How then shall I live?" . . . There is no reading of Torah which is not accompanied by faith. If this is fundamentalism, so be it. On it, I stake my faith as a Jew.'

Sacks's Bible reading, then, is steeped in the Oral Law. His answer to the question, 'How then shall I live?', is delivered by the sages. But that in turn begs the question: Which sages? The haredim have their comfortably comprehensive answer, extending sage status down through time all the way to their here-and-now leaders, and across the entire spectrum of life's decisions. That, for the Modern-Orthodox like Sacks, is *too* fundamentalist. But Modern-Orthodox doctrine, as Sacks acknowledges, is too fundamentalist for most Jews. A brilliant British rabbi and scholar, Dr Louis Jacobs, was barred from becoming Chief Rabbi in the early 1960s, in a celebrated row that still echoes in Anglo-Jewry, precisely because he would not accept the Torah as 'the unmediated word of God', but taught that while it was inspired by God, it was the product of human creativity too.

Walking the narrow middle ground in both religious practice and doctrine, the Modern-Orthodox have to defend a line that is inherently subtle and vulnerable. It is easy for the haredim to attack them as compromisers, and today's stridently self-confident haredim are attacking hard and scoring points. 'The emphasis [in Modern Orthodoxy],' one observer has remarked, 'is shifting from Modern to Orthodox.' A controversial New York Modern-Orthodox rabbi, Irving Greenberg, accuses some of his colleagues of 'shifting positions. Others have become silent . . . A struggle for the soul of Modern Orthodoxy is now raging.'

A key figure in this struggle, Rabbi Dr Norman Lamm, president of New York's Yeshiva University, also rails against 'ideological wimpishness' in the Modern-Orthodox camp. 'The way of moderation is open to attack by extremists,' he warns. 'We must not be intimidated.' But within his own institution, which is the academic and rabbinical bastion of Modern Orthodoxy, there are strong trends towards haredism. Lamm himself fell victim to these trends, as we shall see (chapter 37), when he sought to negotiate with Reform and Conservative rabbis over the crucial question 'Who is a Jew.'

The retired British Chief Rabbi, Lord Jakobovits, is resigned to the shift of power within the Orthodox camp. 'Personally,' he says, 'by upbringing and conviction, I am deeply committed to the philosophy of "Torah im Derech Eretz" ["religion-with-life": this was the original doctrine of Modern Orthodoxy, developed by the nineteenth-century German rabbi Samson Raphael Hirsch]. It is my way of life, my ideology. But I am realistic enough to appreciate that such a religious–secular fusion, as a movement, is not likely to prevail in our generation . . . We must recognize the growing ascendancy of the yeshiva/hasidic world and come to terms with it.'

In that world, as we have seen, the rabbi is much more than a jurist, merely dispensing the halacha. He wields temporal as well as judicial and spiritual authority. The Pentateuch itself (Deut. 17:9, 11), is deemed to have spelled out this all-inclusive role: '. . . You shall come to the priests, the Levites, and to the judge that shall be in your day, and they shall show you the judgement . . . And you shall not deviate, neither to the right nor to the left.' The Talmud remarks on this that the rabbis of the contemporary generation must be obeyed 'even if they say that right is left and left is right.' That interpretation was cited in haredi circles in 1990 when Rabbi Shach, in his speech in the stadium, unexpectedly switched his political allegiance from Left to Right.

Israeli politics is one obvious example of a non-halachic area of life where the haredi will seek out the daat Torah from the particular rabbi to whom he adheres or whom he especially respects. Each haredi party in Israel has its own council of sages, and every haredi politician pledges not only allegiance, but disciplined subservience, to his party's sages. Similarly the extremist groups that reject any participation in the politics of the Zionist State have their own rabbis and batei din who issue periodic fulminations against the other haredim.

In America, too, haredim have their political choices made for them by their rabbis. Every candidate for elected office in the state of New York – and many a presidential candidate too – recognizes this fact, and makes sure to pay well publicized court to the leading hasidic rebbes and yeshiva deans in Brooklyn. The haredim are considered one of the last deliverable blocs of disciplined, ethnic voters in American politics. By the same token, elected officials who represent the heavily haredi areas on the city or state levels are careful to consult with local rabbis. This is the surest way for them to take the political pulse of that section of their constituency.

Noach Dear, a New York City councilman who is himself Orthodox and represents a largely haredi district of Brooklyn, says he is guided by a leading haredi rabbi on all controversial council votes.

There need be no disingenuousness here. The rabbis and their disciples sincerely believe that the process of leadership and consultation, guidance and acceptance, is a joint, genuine seeking after God's will and God's blessing.

The rabbi's authority was not always so pervasive or intense in the individual haredi's life. In the shtetl, people lived their lives, of necessity, largely cut off from the outside world – which included the next shtetl, and certainly the big city several days' travel away. Even hasidim would visit their rebbe only once or twice a year. For the rest of the time, they were on their own, dealing with everyday problems as best they could. Mitnagdim lacked even that minimal regular contact with a figure of authority.

Today, the rebbe's court, or venerated rabbi's yeshiva, is only a phone-call or a flight away. Indeed, haredism has embraced state-of-the-art communications with the same energy that it eschews most other aspects of modernity. The haredi world is a global shtetl. Lubavitcher hasidim hook into their New York headquarters by satellite link. Rabbi Shach's latest instructions are faxed to his followers in real time. Haredi weekly newspapers carry the doings and sayings of their readers' various spiritual leaders fresh every Friday, complete with radio-photos of the holy men in action. There is little to distinguish nowadays, moreover, between the hasid-rebbe relationship and the reliance of the mitnaged disciple upon his rabbi, in matters both temporal and spiritual. Rabbi Shach himself, the arch-mitnaged, is, paradoxically, the best illustration of this blurring of the former distinction.

Different haredim venerate different rabbis, which is what makes for much of the contentiousness, but also the vigour and intensity, of haredi life. It is virtually impossible for a haredi to be merely a haredi, of no particular stripe. Everyone is a follower of someone.

7

'A Saint Decrees'

Yosef Levy (not his real name) began to fear something was amiss about two years after his marriage. His wife Adina was still not pregnant. An alumnus of the famous Ponevezh yeshiva in Bnei Brak, of which Rabbi Shach is the dean, Yosef was now studying in a *kollel*, an advanced yeshiva for married students.

Rabbi Shach had always been particularly kind to Yosef during his years at Ponevezh. He knew the family slightly, having taught Yosef's father a generation earlier, at another yeshiva. When Yosef first began to catch the eye of the *shadchanim* (marriage-brokers), both professional and amateur, he sought Rabbi Shach's advice. 'Ignore them,' was the Rabbi's response. 'Carry on learning quietly for another half a year at least – unless, that is, you're offered something really special.'

Some months later, Yosef, then twenty-two years old, returned to his rabbi with 'something really special'. She must have had a special personality, Yosef explains, 'because she went to a Modern-Orthodox high-school until the age of fifteen, and was then accepted by a prestigious haredi seminary.

'The *rosh yeshiva* [head or dean of the yeshiva; Rabbi Shach is known in the haredi world as "*the* rosh yeshiva"] never says no straight out. You have to listen closely, and catch the hints. He told me to "make more inquiries". I understood it wasn't for me.'

Yosef bided his time, confident in the rosh yeshiva's guidance. When he married Adina, the following year, Rabbi Shach delivered a homily at the engagement party. A rare honour.

Confronted two years later with his young pupil's fear of barrenness, Shach sent the couple to a succession of doctors. Their verdict: an irreversible case of female infertility. In his desperation, Yosef learned of a Yemenite *mekubbal* (mystic, master of the kabbala) living in a small village, who dealt in natural medicine and ancient charms, and had something of a reputation in such matters.

'Rabbi Shach agreed that we go to him. For nearly three years we went. He gave us *kameyot* [kabbalistic formulae written on parchment] which we were to wear. But mainly he dispensed herbal cures, laced with honey. He also rubbed my wife's body with liniment – always in my presence; there was nothing immodest.

'What was he like? Like any ordinary Yemenite. With a beard. He didn't behave especially mystically. Anyway, at one point he informed us that my wife was cured. Her Fallopian tubes were now open. I reported back to Rabbi Shach, and he said we should check it out with a doctor.

'Sure enough, the X-rays showed no change. The tubes were still blocked. Rabbi Shach said I was to tell the Yemenite. I was reluctant to tell him, because his attitude all along had been, if you don't want to rely on my treatment, don't bother to come any more. But Rabbi Shach insisted. I told the Yemenite the whole situation, in the name of Rabbi Shach. He took it very calmly, and said he would try something else.

'I reported back to Rabbi Shach who said: That's enough with the Yemenite. If he can try something else, so can I. Go abroad! He didn't say where to, he just said go abroad.'

Shach set in motion a series of inquiries, among haredi figures involved in medical matters in Israel and overseas. It turned out that there were two leading micro-surgeons in the field, one in Canada and the other in London. Rabbi Shach said: 'Why go as far away as Canada?'

Rabbi Shach also discreetly directed Yosef to a free-loan fund to help finance the trip and the treatment. But Adina was still uncertain. 'Rabbi Shach told me to bring her to him. He sat her down opposite him as we are sitting now. "Don't worry," he encouraged her. "It isn't such a serious operation. God will help . . ." Whenever he met me at a *brit* [circumcision] or any *simcha* [celebration] he would say: "Mazeltov – Please God you too will be helped."

'When our first daughter was born, I phoned Rabbi Shach from the hospital. I can't describe his joy, the way he wished me happiness.'

But there was more worry and grief before that happy moment. The surgery in London was successful, but hormonal problems triggered a series of miscarriages. Yosef went to several hasidic rebbes to receive their blessings, and also to the late Steipler Rav, Rabbi Yaacov Yisrael Kanievsky of Bnei Brak. He too, like Rabbi Shach, was a mitnaged. But his celebrated scholarship and unassuming piety gave him wide recognition as a *tzaddik* (righteous or saintly man), and his blessings were sought by haredim of all denominations.

He would receive *kvitlach*, written requests for succour bearing the full Hebrew name of the person in distress and his or her mother, in the manner of hasidic rebbes. 'But that was because he was deaf,' Yosef explains. 'At any rate, I sent him such a note each mikve night. I would write our names, and add "Please pray" with four dots. He would understand.

'Once I told him Adina was in danger of miscarrying. He said he would pray, and we would have a healthy child. But we lost it.

'That doesn't mean the prayer was lost, though. If it didn't work for that, it helped for something else . . .'

Yosef explains the efficacy of a sage's blessing by citing the Talmudic adage: 'A saint decrees, and the Lord obeys.' He gives a more recent example from his own life. Adina, now the radiant mother of four delightful daughters, is a school teacher (Yosef is still studying in a kollel, with no 'career' plans other than 'to learn more and more'). She had been teaching an hour's bus-ride from Bnei Brak, but now, with her growing domestic duties, she applied for a transfer to a school nearer home. The decision was in the hands of an anonymous Education Department bureaucrat.

'I went to Rabbi Shach and asked "That the Rosh Yeshiva should give a blessing that she should get the transfer."' Needless to say, she got it.

8

Root of the Soul

'There was a concept among *tzaddikim* [righteous men; used here to mean rebbes] that the first answer that comes into one's mind is the right answer. Sometimes, I feel it too. A piece of advice comes to me that I wouldn't have thought of myself.'

The hasidic Rebbe of Boyan, Rabbi Menahem Nahum Breier, was trying to explain the essence of a rebbe's role, and the religious and psychological profundities of the rebbe–hasid relationship.

'I find this ability developing with time. But it's not in my *zechus* [merit]. I don't attribute it to myself. It's the collective zechus of our community. In the zechus of the faith that a person has in the rebbe, he is helped in this way, with this piece of advice.

'Sometimes – this was observed by many tzaddikim in the past – the rebbe feels at first that he is simply unable to help, that he has no advice to give. But the hasid, through his faith, can generate the help he needs, can elicit the right advice. In hasidic thought, faith is not only belief; it is a force through which a person can bring about the thing he needs. If a person believes that God can help him, if he believes in the zechus of the tzaddik, then it happens. Even if the tzaddik feels that it is not through his zechus.'

Aged thirty-two, the Boyaner Rebbe has seven years of experience as Rebbe behind him, and regards himself as still learning and growing in the job. Soft-spoken, bespectacled and ascetic-looking, he spends his days studying and praying in a small office-synagogue complex near his home in the Geula quarter of Jerusalem.

He wears a broad felt hat and a black silk bekeshe, which ordinary hasidim wear only on shabbat or festive occasions, but which rebbes wear all the time. Unlike the more conservative hasidic sects, the Boyaners, including their Rebbe, wear regular trousers, reaching to their shoes. Of particular note: the Boyaner Rebbe wears a neck-tie. This is the tradition among rebbes of his

House, although ties are disparaged and eschewed by most hasidim as a symbol of modern, decadent fashion, which, to boot, serve no useful purpose.

Menahem Nahum Breier was born and brought up in New York, the son of a professor of psychology at the Modern-Orthodox Yeshiva University. But his grandfather, his mother's father, was a hasidic rebbe of illustrious ancestry, much loved by New York haredim, Rabbi Mordechai Shlomo Friedman of Boyan. The fourth son of the original Boyaner Rebbe, Mordechai Shlomo left Europe for America after the First World War. Boyan, in Galicia, had been ravaged in the fighting. His father, the Rebbe, had fled to Vienna where he died in 1917. The eldest of his brothers moved to Czernowitz, in Romania, after the war. Another brother set up a Boyaner court in Lemberg (Lvov), Poland; the third moved to Leipzig, Germany. Rabbi Mordechai Shlomo chose the Lower East Side of Manhattan.

The original Boyaner was a son of Rabbi Yisrael of Sadagor, a grandson of the renowned Ruzhiner Rebbe (1796–1850), who was a great-grandson of Rabbi Ber, the Maggid himself, disciple and successor of the Baal Shem Tov. The Ruzhiner drove in a gilded coach drawn by fine white horses. The Sadagorer lived in a palatial residence. Theodor Herzl (1860–1904), founder of the Zionist Movement, proposed him as the 'archbishop' of the new Jewish State that he hoped to create. Rabbi Yisrael was one of the very few haredi leaders at the turn of the century who was prepared to give the Zionist statesman and visionary a sympathetic hearing.

When Rabbi Mordechai Shlomo died in 1973, the hasidim in Israel and America – a pale remnant of the thousands who flocked to the Boyaner tzaddikim before the Holocaust – cast their hopes on young Menahem Nahum to rebuild the dynasty's former glory. He was sent to learn in the Ruzhin-Boyan yeshiva in Jerusalem, where he was tutored and groomed by the elders of the community.

'When someone asks me for advice, I think: how would I advise myself in the same situation? If it's a business problem, I'll discuss all the aspects with him, then perhaps refer him to a specific person, within our community, who has expertise in that field, or to a lawyer or another professional.

'Similarly in a medical matter, I'll refer a person to someone who has ties to doctors and hospitals. In our family, the rebbes didn't usually give straight yes or no advice on whether to undergo an operation. Rarely, my grandfather would give an explicit opinion. But usually not, though he might suggest that the doctors try some particular treatment or procedure. I'm not on that *madreiga* [level] yet, not on the spiritual plane to answer yes or no on an operation. Slowly I'm getting more involved, hearing more information, getting more experience.

'Is it madreiga that counts, or experience and expertise? Expertise can help. But it also has to do with the madreiga of a tzaddik. The greater a person is in *zidkus* [righteousness], the more *siyata dishmaya* [help from Heaven] he has to give the right answer.'

Since Rabbi Breier's 'coronation' in 1985, the Boyaner community has grown steadily. At present, there are some 400 families in Israel (mainly in Jerusalem and Bnei Brak), and another 150 'close hasidim', as the Rebbe calls them, in the United States. 'There are lots more who are not so close, but who consider themselves Boyaner hasidim and are gradually coming closer. Many people come to me because their father or grandfather was a hasid of our family, or had some connection with my grandfather. Slowly they're coming back . . .'

The yeshiva, now in a splendid new building with a domed roof, reminiscent of Ruzhin-Sadagora-Boyan's grander days, is growing too. The Rebbe supervises the curriculum and tests the students.

'It's the old hasidic story of the dream,' says Rabbi Levi-Yitzhak Horowitz, the Bostoner Rebbe, when asked to explain how one becomes a rebbe and makes a success of it. 'A hasid comes to the rebbe and says: "Rebbe, I dreamed that I became a rebbe." To which the rebbe replies: "Yes, but did any hasidim dream it too . . . ?"'

Rabbi Horowitz, spiritual leader of the 'New England Hasidic Center' in Boston since the early 1940s, says he never wanted to be a rebbe, even though his father, whom he revered, functioned as one – in Boston of all places – ever since he arrived in America from Palestine after the First World War. 'I tried to find other work. I went into business; I learned diamond cutting. But I was a *shlimazzel* [hopelessly and chronically unlucky] in both . . .

'Now, looking back, thinking of the thousands of lives that I touched over the years, I feel it would have been a cop-out. Not just a cop-out – a criminal cop-out!'

Rabbi Horowitz, whose Boston accent and colloquial English at first seem incongruous with his rebbe's garb, is hugely proud of his outreach work among Jewish students and faculty at Boston's many universities. 'We were the first in the *baalei teshuva* [penitents; born-again Orthodox Jews] field,' he says. Of his thousands of followers and admirers, a high percentage came from the campuses, with little prior knowledge of Judaism or commitment to Orthodoxy, and certainly no previous familiarity with hasidism. But though many of his hasidim are 'modern', and not all would classify themselves as haredi, his role as Rebbe, he says, is no different from the traditional one. He cites a tale of Rabbi Moshe Lev of Sassov, an early nineteenth-century hasidic master who, searching for 'lost Jewish souls' in a Russian ale-house, overheard a conversation between two drunken peasants. 'I love you.' 'No you don't.' 'Yes, I really love you.' 'If you really loved me, you would know what pains me.'

'A rebbe has to know what pains the other person,' he says. 'If someone comes to you with a messy divorce, or with problems with children, you have to think: How would *you* handle it if this were you, if these were your children?'

He offers another story by way of illustration. A mitnaged watched as the 'Seer of Lublin' (1750–1815) received kvitlach, the small notes on which hasidim write their name and their mother's name and outline their problem. The rebbe is expected to pray on behalf of the hasid – a practice the mitnagdim have always found religiously reprehensible because, as they see it, it leaves the hasid feeling he has no need nor duty to pray for himself.

The Seer spent no more time at his prayers than the rest of the congregation. 'How do you pray for all those people so fast?' the mitnaged challenged him. 'I ask, Please God, help Yaacov Yitzhak son of Maatel [his own name]. Their problems are my problem . . .'

'That is not an exaggeration,' says Rabbi Horowitz. 'It's part of what one experiences when one gets close to other people's problems.

'Sometimes, the hasid or *hasideste* [Yiddish feminine form] just wants to let me know of their desperate situation. The dialogue itself is the solution. You want to draw strength from stating your difficulty. If there is a *shoresh neshama* [root of the soul] connection between the hasid and the rebbe, then for sure the feeling of being linked-in spiritually helps the hasid to be able to make it.

'Of course, desperate situations are relative. It can be a little kid has fallen on the floor, and the husband's not home, and she can't reach the doctor. So she puts a call through just to say, this is what's happened. At times you'll call your mother; at times your best friend. And at times you'll feel comfortable to call your rebbe and just to know there's someone holding your hand, from a distance . . .

'Hasidism opened up the inner sanctum – the rabbi's study – to women. Until then, the woman was effectively shut out. The rabbi's role was to answer halachic questions, to teach and study and preach in the synagogue. The hasidic rebbe,' says the Bostoner, 'does all that and much more. He's there twenty-four hours a day.' His wife, listening in on the conversation, remarks that 'Most of the calls seem to come after midnight.'

On the desk in front of Rabbi Horowitz is a brass box, with its lid discreetly ajar. This is where the hasid deposits his *pidyon* [literally ransom], the cash gift – great or small, depending on the giver – that accompanies the *kvitl*.

Most rebbes take *pidyonot*. Among those who do not are the Gerer, whose family is independently wealthy, and the Lubavitcher, who, before an illness in February 1992 drove him into seclusion, would hand out a crisp dollar bill to everyone who visited him. But the pidyon is semi-symbolic. Hasidim are expected to contribute frequently and generously to the upkeep of the rebbe's court, and of the yeshivas, seminaries, synogogues and other institutions maintained by the House.

Rabbi Horowitz's Jerusalem apartment (he divides his time between Jerusalem and Boston) in the suburb of Har Nof is small and modest. He helped found this all-Orthodox neighbourhood in the early 1980s and his synagogue/kollel, standing imposingly on a nearby hill, is the hub of the community's life.

*

Just as the hasid's psychological needs and expectations from the rebbe have remained essentially unchanged since the beginnings of the movement – 'Hasidism antedated Freudian psychology; actually you can find it all in the Talmud,' Rabbi Horowitz says – so too the supernatural still plays an important part in the hasid's perception of the rebbe, and indeed in the rebbe's perception of himself. But the outgoing Bostoner, like the more diffident Boyaner, is cautious when addressing this subject. 'Polish hasidism, of which we were a part, generally frowned on any expectation of supernatural events from a rebbe, though the fact is that a rebbe can accomplish things through his prayer. My father used to say about the stories of the Baal Shem Tov and other tzaddikim that we don't have to believe that they're all true – but we have to believe that they all *could* have been true. We saw certain things at home. But if we tried to discuss them my father would just shut us up.

'I understand people who put their lives and futures in a rebbe's hands, who ask his advice on the big decisions in their lives, expecting him to be special. But there's a difference between appreciating the greatness of a person, and saying to him, You've *got* to provide me with what I need.

'When someone asks me for a blessing, I'm not just going to give him my blessing without trying to find out a little more about him, finding something on which to build the confidence that person should have in what may happen, and on which my blessing should be able to take effect.

'What's the uniqueness of being tuned in to a rebbe? The question that comes up all the time is why should the rebbe's prayers be more acceptable, more effective, than anyone else's? After all, God listens to all our prayers . . .

'The rebbe and the hasid are two people who can find each other spiritually. There is a connection between their heartbeats. And the rebbe, being the holy person he's supposed to be, serving God the way he's supposed to, is serving on behalf of the hasid too. As we've seen, the hasid's problem becomes the rebbe's problem. And now, in Heaven, the question is whether this person should continue suffering. In the bed of this sick person – who is lying sick maybe because of some things he's done wrong, or whatever – there are suddenly two people instead of one. The rebbe is lying there next to him.

'Now the rebbe's not supposed to suffer. Why should he suffer? But the rebbe says, This guy's suffering, and I'm suffering along with him.'

The rebbe's *zechusim* are thus entered onto the divine balance-sheet, and accrue to the credit of the hasid. In his own case, says Rabbi Horowitz, he has helped thousands of young people rediscover their Jewishness and, in many cases, live Orthodox lives. They, and by now their children too, 'are doing mitzvas all the time', and thereby building up the Rebbe's credit. Every time he prays for someone, that too redounds to his credit, and so he stays 'in the black'.

The Boyaner Rebbe makes essentially the same points, in his more introspective style. 'I have the peoples' names on the kvitlach, and I try to pray for them. Praying doesn't just mean three times a day, the set prayers. One can ask of God all the time that someone should be helped. Throughout the day I have in mind specific cases who need help, that the zechus of my learning or of other mitzvas should help this person.

'In years past, there certainly was an expectation of supernatural intervention by rebbes – and many times it was realized. Nowadays there is too. Maybe it's not so open and exposed as it was years ago. But it is there today as well.

'What does that mean for me? It makes a person expect more of himself. Every person has to be careful about what he says. A rebbe, who realizes that everything he says will be seen by the hasidim in different aspects, will be analysed in all different ways, has to be very careful.

'When a hasid come to consult his rebbe, that is a special occasion. The hasid prepares himself. The rebbe has prepared himself too. I don't feel that I talk any differently. I try to think and act the same way with people as when I'm by myself. I don't see any difference in myself. But I know there is. I know there is siyata dishmaya. The people who are being helped are being helped through siyata dishmaya.'

9

High Table

For the Boyaner Rebbe, acting naturally and consistently in all situations is an important personal and spiritual aspiration. 'A rebbe,' he says, 'is someone whose behaviour is the same at his *tish*, as in his private quarters, in his bedroom. He won't change if there are a lot of people at his tish, or a few. I try to work on myself that there shouldn't be a difference. One of our family's rebbes, the Husyatiner, had thousands of hasidim in Europe before the war. In Tel Aviv years later, he barely had a minyan. Yet people said they saw no difference at all in his behaviour. It was exactly the same.'

The tish, the ceremonial shabbat or festival meal of hasidic rebbes, is surely the most strenuous test of this quality. In Boyan, the tish takes place in the big synagogue/study-hall of the yeshiva building. The Rebbe sits at one end of a long, white-covered table. At either side down the length of the table sit the elder hasidim. Banked up behind them are sturdy metal-and-wood stepped terraces which are wheeled and levered into place before the tish begins, and on these the younger hasidim and the yeshiva students stand and watch.

They watch the Rebbe. He eats and drinks, and hands out fruit and little plastic cups of wine. He says '*lechaim*', the traditional Jewish toast, to everyone in turn. He can't reach all their hands of course, and so he makes eye contact, and a slight shaking movement with his hand, which is returned enthusiastically by each hasid in turn. As his gaze passes down the rows of hasidim, the hands go up in a wave of salutation. When he speaks, they all crane forward to hear his torah, spoken softly and full of allusions to midrashic and hasidic books. He weaves in ideas of his own. When he starts a song, they all join in with gusto, swaying together and singing as he keeps time and exhorts them on with delicate arm movements. At a sign from him, they stop at once. All the time – and a tish can last for hours – all eyes are glued on the Rebbe.

From the gallery upstairs, the women and girls peep through an almost opaque lattice screen. But they are passive participants; the Rebbe does not relate to them.

In hasidic thought, every human activity is a means of divine service, and that includes eating. According to the kabbala, the act of ingesting food, if performed with the proper purpose, releases 'holy sparks' which are 'trapped' in that food, as in all matter, and 'yearn to return' to their heavenly origin. On a more prosaic level, the rebbe's tish is the focus of the week at the hasidic court, the main social event, imbued with religious content by the shabbat songs and by the rebbe's homilies, which are memorized by select students (writing and recording are forbidden on the sabbath). These are often edited later, and published, by these students or by the rebbe himself. Most hasidic books, in fact, comprise discourses originally delivered at the tish.

There is not much food at the Boyaner tish. The Rebbe eats his shabbat or festival meal at home with his family. He feels that he is spiritually 'not yet ready' to hand out *shirayim* (leftovers) – another key element of tishen.

At Vishnitz in Bnei Brak, as in most other hasidic communities, the Rebbe, Rabbi Moshe Yehoshua Hager, eats his hearty shabbat or festival meals at the tish, and everyone present partakes of the shirayim. Vishnitz, a large community with wealthy supporters in Europe and America, has a separate, custom-built building especially for the tishen, next to the elegant synagogue. The layout is basically the same as in Boyan, but on a much larger scale. The stands rise five or six rows into the air. The section closest to the Rebbe is reserved for the official choir, with their conductor and composer, who give harmonized renditions of Vishnitzer songs and hymns.

A Friday-night tish begins with the Rebbe's kiddush prayer, recited over a silver or golden goblet of wine. Halachically, this is the high point of the shabbat (or festival) meal, and most rebbes will put much energy and emotion into their kiddush while the audience listens and watches in rapt attention. Hasidic stories tell of rebbes who became so ecstatic during their kiddush that most of the wine would spill out of the goblet. The Rebbe of Boyan-Czernowitz, Menahem Nahum Friedman (1869–1936), is reported to have dropped the goblet itself, but carried on, entranced, his hand outstretched as though still holding it.

The Bialer Rebbe, Rabbi Yehiel Yehoshua Rabinowitz, who died in 1984, would take half an hour over his kiddush (a regular recitation of the text need take about a minute), jumping and stamping, and shouting out the words in torrents of emotion. In Jerusalem people used to gather beneath the windows of his small synagogue to listen as the sounds of his worship eddied out into the night.

Kiddush completed, the Vishnitzer Rebbe ceremonially washes his hands and begins to cut huge loaves of *halla* bread arrayed before him. His aides complete the task, handing out pieces of bread to the hundreds – sometimes thousands – of onlookers.

From the kitchens behind the Rebbe's seat, a generous platter of fish appears: a large whole fish in the middle, surrounded by slices of gefilte (chopped and stuffed) fish that is the pride of traditional European Jewish cuisine. The Rebbe attacks first the big fish, then the surrounding pieces, dipping his halla into the sauce, eating slowly, as though oblivious to the eyes fixed on his every move, and the many watering mouths. He hands out small plates of fish to his close relatives and several of the leading hasidim seated at the table, and then the aides take over again, carving up the remaining fish and handing the pieces down the table and up into the banks of seats. From hand to hand they go, with the Rebbe sometimes indicating a particular morsel for a particular hasid. Soon everyone has had a taste, and now the wine-drinking and 'lechaim' ceremony starts, much as in Boyan but again on a far larger scale.

The modern age of disposable plastic crockery and cutlery has helped hasidism overcome some of the more problematic logistics and aesthetics (and hygienics) of the tish. In the days of the previous Vishnitzer Rebbe, Rabbi Haim Meir (1888–1972), for instance, an aide would walk down the table in his white-stockinged feet literally spooning the soup from the Rebbe's capacious tureen into the appreciative mouths of the hasidim.

Old customs die hard, however, especially when they are invested with an intrinsic significance. In Ger, the obvious convenience of stepped stands is spurned, in favour of a veritable scrum of squashed and sweating hasidim, all crowding together on the flat floor and trying to gain a glimpse of the Rebbe. This is considered socially cohesive, character-building, and religiously meritorious. The hasidim recall proudly that in pre-war Ger, near Warsaw, the eminent Rabbi Menahem Zemba (1884–1943) consistently refused a rightful place of honour seated at the tish, preferring to do battle in the *shura* (line), the serried, seething ranks of standing participants.

The Gerer hasidim keep special bekeshes for use at the tish – torn to shreds and saturated with perspiration. But there are rules, which everyone understands; steady pressure from the shoulder is allowed, but a jab from the elbow is foul play. The few lucky young hasidim are the ones who draw lots to sit *under* the table, from where they can hear the Rebbe, if not see him.

This, at any rate, is the Gerer tradition; it remains to be seen if the new Rebbe, Rabbi Pinhas Menahem Alter (b. 1926), will preserve it when the sect's new $13 million synagogue-headquarters in Jerusalem is completed. He succeeded his brother, Rabbi Simcha Bunim Alter, who died in 1992.

At every rebbe's tish, whether the tradition encourages pushing or not, all present will bestir themselves, and at least go through the motions of pushing and crowding up, when the rebbe begins to speak. Some rebbes speak several times during each tish. But, especially in the long, late evening of summer Fridays, it can be an uphill struggle to gain and keep the congregation's attention. The Bobover Rebbe in New York, who is a sprightly eighty-five, takes much care over his homilies, preparing them, according to his son Reb Naftoli, while the hasidim are at home eating their dinners. By the time they all regroup for the tish, however, it can be close to midnight, and heads loll one by one as the Rebbe tries manfully to hold his week-worn flock with moralistic interpretations of the next day's Torah reading. He keeps his popular story-telling for Saturday night tishen. By then the hasidim have slept their shabbat fill, and are wide-eyed and attentive.

At most tishen, the hasidim will have usually eaten their own meals at home, and the yeshiva students at their refectory. They do not therefore expect full portions of the rebbe's various shirayim from his main dishes – just a symbolic morsel. The *kugel*, however (some hasidim pronounce it *kigel*, depending on their particular Yiddish dialect), is a different matter. The advent of this quintessentially Eastern European Jewish culinary delight, made of noodles or potatoes, represents the gastronomic climax of the evening. The cooks will make not just one kugel, but five or six of the huge, steaming puddings, so that everyone can have a sizeable slice.

Between courses the choir leads the entire congregation in rendering the traditional mealtime hymns. These are variously squeezed or drawn out to fit into the *niggun* (tune; piece of music) selected by the choirmaster. Every hasidic house has its own musical tradition, and all share some of the most poignant, ancient melodies that hasidic lore dates back to the Baal Shem Tov and his original disciples.

In Modzhitz, whose headquarters is a modest synagogue on Tel Aviv's bustling Dizengoff Street, the Rebbe himself leads the singing and many of the main prayers. He is expected to know by heart the hundreds of Modzhitzer *niggunim* composed by his predecessors. Some are relatively simple tunes, in march or waltz tempi. But others are long and intricate works, full of longing and sadness, though usually building up to a triumphant affirmation of faith in a rousing 'last movement'.

The present Rebbe, Rabbi Dan Taub, knows all the music and has even begun composing his own works. Unfortunately, though, he is not endowed with an especially mellifluous voice. The Kalever Rebbe on the other hand, Rabbi Menahem Mendel Taub (no relation), of Bnei Brak, has a sweet and moving voice, and he sings solo at his tishen to the delight of his hasidim.

What, then, is a rebbe supposed to think about while 'starring', week after week – and some rebbes hold two or even three tishen each shabbat – in this one-man show?

True to his striving for consistency, the Boyaner Rebbe observes that 'there are things that a person has to think about not only at his tish, but always. I don't think specifically in terms of having an effect on the onlookers. I have to do what I have to do, and *Hakadosh Boruch Hu* [the Holy One Blessed Be He] should help these people to feel what they have to feel.

'A rebbe's handing out food or fruit is a symbolic act of kindness, of doing goodness to the other people. If the hasid thinks of it in magical or mystical terms – that's his side of the story.'

Some hasidim plainly do think in those terms. Many will pocket a sliver of shirayim to share at home later with their wife and children. In Lubavitch hasidism, there is no tradition of tishen as such, but the Rebbe, before his illness, would hand out wine or vodka, sometimes standing on his feet for hours as an endless line of hasidim and visitors filed past him to receive a lechaim drink and a blessing, while the Rebbe's gaze rested momentarily on the face of each man or boy. The vodka was treasured, and carefully decanted into other bottles of vodka, and those into others, so that no Lubavitch house was ever without its precious stock of 'the Rebbe's vodka'.

10

Batya the Bus-Driver

Lubavitch or Habad* hasidism is a case apart, and always has been. This was due in part to the movement's main geographic location until the 1920s – in Lithuania and White Russia, where hasidism never managed to defeat the established rabbinical order. Mitnagdim and hasidim lived side by side in, at best, suspicious coexistence. Habad, moreover, was always considered more cerebral than other hasidic groups. The mitnagdim say this was a consequence of the geography: the Lubavitchers were 'Litvaks' – Lithuanians, hailing from the heartland of mitnagdism – and thus they naturally cultivated a more learned and academic approach, even in their hasidism.

Hasidim look at it differently. They say that every major hasidic house 'specialized' in a particular aspect of religious life or thought. Thus Breslev put the stress on service-through-joy; the school of Kotzk emphasized truth and sincerity; Vishnitz focused on ahavat Yisrael, love of fellow Jews. Habad's speciality, according to this reading, was theological meditation.

Certainly the 'Tanya', written by the founder of Habad, Rabbi Shneur Zalman, has remained the classic of hasidic theology. Shneur Zalman also wrote his own Shulhan Aruch, or code of laws, reportedly at the behest of the Maggid Reb Ber, who wanted to show that the hasidim had among them a top-notch halachist – and also that they were not deviating from the halacha in any important detail. Rabbi Shneur Zalman tried to get an audience with the Gaon of Vilna, leader of the mitnagdim, in the hope of persuading him that he was being misled about hasidism. But he was repeatedly rebuffed.

* The name Habad is an acrostic of the three Hebrew words *hochma*, *binah*, *daat*, meaning wisdom, understanding and knowledge.

One peculiar manifestation of Habad's 'cerebralism' is the movement's driving urge to print books. The average Lubavitcher hasid has in his home whole bookcases full of the teachings, sayings, speeches, letters and all other writings of the movement's seven rebbes, and dozens of histories, biographies, story-books and associated literature. While some of the works are edifying and profound, others seem boringly mundane, chronicling the workaday doings of the rebbes and their aides. All are beautifully produced and bound by Habad's publishing company in New York.

The present Rebbe, Menahem Mendel Schneerson (b. 1902), introduced a particular quirk of his own: he wanted the 'Tanya' printed in every place on earth where Jews live. (By Habad tradition, the 'Tanya', like the Talmud itself, is invariably printed with the same pagination, so all that really changes in the different editions is the title-page.) Since 1973, when the Rebbe's order was issued, 'Tanyas' have been produced in such unlikely places as Grenada and New Caledonia. Habad hasidim trundled a press across the Suez Canal after the 1973 Middle East war to print their venerated text in the enclave of Egyptian territory captured during the fighting (and returned soon after). That particular edition was invested by the Israeli right wing with political significance, for the Rebbe was already firmly opposed to returning any land taken from the Arabs.

For outsiders and non-haredim, Habad is different and special not because of its geographical origins, its intellectual bent (or its bibliomania), but because it, much more than any other haredi community, has sought to bridge the gulf of ignorance, and often hostility, between haredim and other Jews. 'Habadskers' can be found haranguing students on a campus in middle America, operating a hasidic shtiebel in a hotel in Hong Kong, or running a Passover Seder for tourists in Kathmandu. They hold high-profile public happenings designed to promote Judaism – their opponents say Habadism – in the general media: lighting a huge Hannuka menora in downtown Milan or Melbourne, making a presentation to the President at the White House on the Rebbe's birthday, explaining the 'seven Noahide Laws' to the King of Swaziland.

(According to the halacha, Gentiles, or 'descendants of Noah', are required to observe seven commandments – compared to the Jews' 613. They are injunctions against idolatry, blasphemy, murder, robbery, incest, and tearing flesh from a living animal; and the duty to set up courts of law. Rabbi Schneerson has instructed his emissaries around the world to bring this concept to the attention of statesmen and political leaders 'as a cardinal foundation for ethical behaviour'.)

Wherever there are Jews, no matter how few, or how distant they are from Orthodoxy, the Rebbe sends his *shlichim*, emissaries. They come uninvited, nail up a notice, 'Habad House' – and launch their indefatigable search for Jewish souls. They set up schools and summer camps, visit the sick, run shabbat services on college campuses, invite the students to their homes. They try to blend into the established community, but in some communities they are resented as sectarian missionaries and marginalized by the local leadership. Some Jews respond hostilely to the Habadskers' persistent pestering. Often – and this was especially the case in Russia before glasnost – they operate in places where there is no other organized Judaism.

Habad says it has 3,000 shlichim. The number includes the shlichim's wives, who are regarded as full partners in the *shlichuss* (mission) and have to work as hard as their husbands. They are deployed in thirty-three countries around the world, and forty states of the US. It is a network that makes Habad far and away the largest organization in haredism.

Sustained by a constant flow of spiritual encouragement from the Brooklyn headquarters, the shlichim set up synagogues, yeshivas, schools, nurseries, adult education programmes, student hostels, coffee-shops – even drug-abuse centres. Wherever possible, they are expected to raise their own funds from within the community. They preach, speak and lecture whenever they can get onto a pulpit or platform, apparently impervious to attacks, unspoiled by success, undaunted by failure. Habad's man in Madrid, US-born Yosef Goldstein, has been there for a dozen years, but is still regarded as an outsider by the tight-knit, traditionalist but largely non-Orthodox Sephardic community in the Spanish capital. He sends his children to Habad schools in

France or the UK from the age of nine. Yet he has no thought of moving. The duration of a *shaliach*'s (emissary's) service in any particular place is determined only by the Rebbe's command.

Batya Kalmanson, for example, has begun her working day at 6 a.m. each morning for the past eighteen years, cooking lunch at the Lubavitch school in the Paris suburb of Aubervilliers. Recently, she says, she has been arriving a little later – not because a 6 a.m. start is hard for a woman in her late sixties, but 'because our school has grown so large, thank God, that we now have additional kitchen staff.' She still gets up at dawn on Fridays, when she drives in her minibus to a wholesale fruit and vegetable market to buy provisions for the coming week. 'I like to come early,' she explains, 'to have the best choice.' She takes her husband Sholem Mendel with her, but it is Batya who drives the van. 'I'm a bit nervous when someone else drives.'

Batya, her hair covered by a wig in the haredi fashion, and most comfortable in Yiddish despite her forty-five years in France, is an accomplished bus-driver. In the 1960s, when the school was just beginning, she would pick up the children in Aubervilliers and the surrounding suburbs, and bring them home again in the afternoon. During the day she would run the office. She still fills in at the wheel if a driver doesn't turn up.

'I would quite like to stop working,' she says. 'I've often thought about it. I'd have plenty to do. I like reading, for instance. And I could spend more time with my grandchildren. But they'd have to get three people to replace me. And the Rebbe, may he be healthy, he keeps demanding and demanding. He's so demanding! And he himself works so incredibly hard . . .'

Batya Kalmanson and her husband Sholem Mendel are not typical Habad shlichim. They were not sent to Paris from the headquarters in Brooklyn, but arrived there long before the shlichim system formally came into being. But in a deeper sense, Batya is the prototype Lubavitch hasid and *shlicha* who lives her whole life in the service of the Rebbe and the movement. Batya and Sholem Mendel instilled their values into their family: eight of the Kalmansons' nine children are Habad shlichim or teachers in Paris or Jewish communities around the world.

Batya was born into the Chen family, prominent Lubavitcher hasidim in Russia. Her childhood memories, of a small village and later of Moscow, are full of tension and danger as her father and his friends tried to keep up the old traditions in defiance of the new regime and its Jewish catspaw, the Yevsektsia, the Jewish Department of the Communist Party. In 1941, the family fled eastwards, ending up in Samarkand with other groups of Jewish refugees from Russia and Poland. Physically, life was hard there, but the harassment of religion was less intense, and soon the Lubavitchers had a 300-student yeshiva going in a cellar, for the local Jews who were mostly Sephardic. When the war ended Polish nationals were repatriated, and Batya's family managed to pass itself off as Polish too. After seven months in a Displaced Persons camp near Vienna, they found themselves in a run-down château outside Paris, which the Joint Distribution Committee, an American Jewish charity, put at the Habad group's disposal. They set up a girls' school on the ground floor, while several of the families lived above. (Today the Beis Rivka girls' high school and teacher-training seminary occupy separate campuses nearby, while the château serves as French Lubavitch's yeshiva.)

After two years in Ireland, where Sholem Mendel slaughtered beef for export – 'There weren't any Lubavitchers there, but we were used to being with other sorts of Jews,' says Batya – 'We thought of going to America. My father, may he be healthy, had gone on to America, with my brother and two sisters. We asked [the Rebbe] and the reply was: "Ask your friends in Paris" which we understood meant that we were to stay here.'

They stayed. Sholem Mendel worked as a *shochet* (ritual slaughterer) and *mohel* (circumciser). Life was quiet, and apparently not very enjoyable. 'One old man went to the Rebbe to complain,' Batya recalls. 'He said there wasn't even a minyan in Aubervilliers. "Really!" the Rebbe replied. "But there are 200 Jewish families there. Why don't you make contact with them? Maybe you could start a school . . ."

'The old man said that he had never seen a single Jew other than our few families. But Sholem Mendel took the phone-book, and started looking for Jewish names. He sent out invitations to come to a *melave malka* [lit. 'seeing off the queen', which refers to dinner on a Saturday night because in the imagery of the kabbala, the sabbath is the queen or bride]. You should have seen what a celebration that turned out to be. They had all come fairly recently from North Africa. Some met people they hadn't seen in years, and didn't know were living in the neighbourhood. When we totted up the names, we found there were exactly 200 families!

'So we started the school. My husband put in days and nights. He paid the bills out of his shochet's wages. He criss-crossed Paris raising money, but he was never any good at it. Our daughters were the first teachers. Gradually, girls graduating from the Beis Rivka school took over as teachers. The Rebbe, may he be healthy, said, "Make a day-camp in the summer." We said we can hardly make ends meet in term-time. But he said the camp would bring in money, and it did.

'At first the school was for boys only. But the parents pressed us to take in girls. So we set up a separate girls' school. Slowly, we grew. My husband would go round the houses, knocking on doors and asking people to send their kids to the school. My parents in New York were worried about me working so hard. But the Rebbe, may he be healthy, said: "God rejoices in your work. Work harder! Send your parents in to see me and I'll deal with them."

'From that day on, families began applying to send their kids to the school, and soon we were bursting. This was obviously the result of the Rebbe's blessing. You can't understand it any other way. After all, in such an out-of-the-way place . . . such a hole. But we have a wonderful family feeling in the school. All the parents say so too. And the education is really good.

'Twelve years ago, my husband wrote to New York that the school and its finances were getting too big for him to handle, and they should send someone over. The answer was, "You have someone right there" . . . our son-in-law Menahem Deutsh. They were just married, and were about to go back to Israel.'

The school today has 550 pupils, up to the age of fourteen. Rabbi Deutsh, now thirty-five, is the principal. His wife's sister, Haya Nisselevitch, is the headmistress. Another sister, Sarah, runs the kindergarten, and the youngest brother, Yosef-Yitzhak, is a teacher. Fees are $2,200 a year, but not everyone pays. Deutsh says he must raise $500,000 each year from private sources. There is some support available from the government and (communist) local authority for such *écoles privés*; Deutsh notes proudly that the school's curriculum is 'fully recognized' and its examination results are consistently good. The children study Jewish subjects in the morning and general subjects in the afternoon. Most of them go on to Jewish high schools.

The school is squeezed into a series of old buildings and prefabricated huts. But the children seem cheerful enough, and, if a chance meeting with two sets of parents in a kosher pizza parlour off Place Pigalle at 2 a.m. on a Saturday night is any indication, the parents do indeed feel a warmth and respect for the Kalmansons and their extended family of educators.

The Place Pigalle restaurant, its Shield of David neon sign shining out among the other advertised temptations of the district, is an indication of the surging popularity of eating kosher in Paris these days. There are more than sixty kosher restaurants under rabbinical supervision in the French capital, from milk bars and felafel counters to elegant, haute cuisine establishments. A decade ago there were barely ten. Does the restaurant boom reflect a rise in religious Orthodoxy among France's 700,000-odd Jews, the largest community in Europe? Plainly it reflects the growing prosperity of the hundreds of thousands of Sephardim who immigrated from Morocco, Algeria and Tunisia in the 1950s and 1960s, and who now outnumber by far the original Ashkenazic Jews.

'They just like to be together; they feel good,' says a prominent communal leader of the ancien régime, Theo Klein, referring to 'this gastronomic Orthodoxy. They like to feel as though they're in Israel.' But for Algerian-born former Chief Rabbi René Samuel Sirat, there is no doubt. 'There is a return to religion,' he says. 'You see it in the number of restaurants, of Jewish butchers, of new synagogues and Jewish centres even in the most remote places, and above all in the number of schools. In 1988, there were seventy-seven Jewish schools and 111 kindergartens, and there are more opening all the time.'

Lubavitch is not the only, nor the largest, Orthodox education network in the French Jewish community. 'Otzar Hatorah', an international Sephardic movement, runs schools in Paris and several provincial towns, and there are other organizations active in Orthodox 'outreach'. But Lubavitch takes the credit (for the Rebbe, of course) for being in there right at the start of the Orthodox revival. 'I was still an unmarried yeshiva student,' Rabbi Shmuel Azimov recalls. 'The Rebbe summoned me at 5.30 one morning and told me to go to France. He wished me success. "Do you know what that means?" the Rebbe said. "It means success so great that you can't imagine it." '

Today Azimov directs 'Jeunesse Loubavitch' in Paris, which offers eighty *shiurim* (classes) a week for adults around the city. On Sundays its main centre bustles with activity. 'There are literally thousands of Orthodox Jews in this city whom I personally first drew in. There was nowhere else for them at that time. Nothing at all. You see that man,' says Azimov, pointing out a Lubavitcher hasid with a long beard. 'He is a senior aeronautical engineer at Dassault. The Rebbe insists that high-school and university students continue their studies . . .'

There are hundreds of such baalei teshuva newcomers in the Habab community in Paris. They throng the Lubavitcher shtieblach. Many of them wear the Habad shabbat 'uniform': black trilby hat, long black coat belted by a thick gartel with its two tassels reaching to the knees.

The 'uniform' makes them indistinguishable from the (relatively few) born-Orthodox, or indeed from the born-Jewish. One bearded and be-garteled lecturer at a Habad gathering in Paris, who clearly seemed to have lost most of his audience – including a couple of rabbis – in a complicated kabbalistic discourse, turned out to be a convert to Judaism. He had begun to be interested when his Jewish wife encountered Habad many years before.

But though the hasidic apparel and bushy beard may signal much sincerity and enthusiasm, they may also conceal much ignorance. Baalei teshuva sometimes make the metamorphosis from non-Orthodoxy to a Habad hasidic appearance in a matter of months. They *look* like hasidim, but they don't talk like hasidim. This incongruity exposes the movement to much criticism and ridicule from other haredi groups. It causes criticism even from their own. Says one Paris bookseller, a scholarly graduate of a

Habad yeshiva in Morocco, 'Too many of the Habad baalei teshuva are ignorant. They shout and shake, but they don't study.'

Batya and Sholem Mendel Kalmanson fly to New York each Passover to spend the festival near the Rebbe. She goes again alone in the summer, to be with her father. Her modest apartment, in a barracks-like block largely inhabited by Aubervilliers Lubavitchers (one apartment serves as their shtiebel), is adorned with small photographs of her family, and large photographs and paintings of the Rebbe and of his predecessors. In some of these portraits Rabbi Schneerson is shown with a halo-like lustre around his head.

Batya confides that her two sons, born after seven daughters, came 'in response to my request from the Rebbe, may he be healthy'. She is a little vague about when she first raised this matter with the Rebbe. Was it only after the seventh daughter? Or was it before, and some more daughters arrived before his blessing was fulfilled? She can't recall. But she distinctly remembers how she had to pluck up courage to ask for a second son after she had already been delivered of one.

Now the first son is a Habad shaliach with his wife in Australia, where one Kalmanson daughter is also serving with her husband as shlichim. Another daughter is 'on schlichuss' with her husband in Italy; another daughter and son-in-law are shlichim in New Haven, Connecticut; another is married to a teacher in a Habad yeshiva in Morristown, NY. Just one daughter and her husband, living in New York, are not employed by Habad – though they, too, Batya hastens to assure, are staunch hasidim of the Rebbe.

The Rebbe and his late wife Chaya Moussia Schneerson, who was the previous Rebbe's daughter, spent most of the pre-war decade in Paris, where he studied at the Sorbonne. This is obviously an unusual episode in a hasidic rebbe's biography, yet Sholem Mendel, himself a Parisian for forty-five years, shows no interest in knowing more about it. 'We know the place at the back of a shul in the Pletzel [the former Jewish quarter] where the Rebbe stood and davened [prayed],' he says with reverence, as though referring to some ancient archaeological find. Where did he live? What did he do? Who were his friends? Sholem Mendel can't help with any of that.

Nor indeed would he be able to find out much from reading the various official biographies; the Paris period is only sketchily outlined. 'What did he do? He learned Torah of course!' Sholem Mendel says dismissively.

Who was his *chavrusa*, his learning-partner? Sholem Mendel seems astounded by the question. 'The Rebbe couldn't have had a chavrusa. Who could learn with the Rebbe . . . ?'

11

'We Want Messiah NOW!'

Every Sunday, until he suffered his stroke early in 1992, the Lubavitcher Rebbe would stand for hours as the crowds filed past: a random mix of his own hasidim and Jews of all denominations, from the world over. He handed each person a crisp dollar bill (for charity) from a large brown paper bag, listened, advised, comforted, smiled, blessed. The scene was constantly recorded on a VCR camera; each visitor could buy his or her video clip.

His sermons and homilies, always unscripted, often lasted for hours too, with intermissions for drinking 'lechaim', and fervent singing. They were broadcast live to Habad centres across the country and overseas. Most of the songs were devotional, the melodies sometimes dating back to the beginnings of the movement. But some were crude jingles in praise of the Rebbe, which Rabbi Schneerson appeared to enjoy without embarrassment.

In autumn 1992 the Rebbe, partially paralysed, appeared in public for the first time since his stroke. His hasidim hoped and believed that despite his great age he could recover to resume his active leadership of the sect. His aides insisted that despite his illness he remained in touch both with world events and with the running of Habad. Letters and faxes continued to stream in from shlichim and hasidim around the world with questions and requests, and the aides wrote replies in the Rebbe's name.

The personality cult surrounding Rabbi Schneerson is the major cause of Habad's controversiality, especially among other haredim. His sworn enemy, Rabbi Shach, accuses him of harbouring messianic pretensions: the paramount leader of the mitnaged haredim brands the most prominent hasidic rebbe a heretic.

The charge of messianism – that is, false messianism – is probably the most damning that can be hurled in a rabbinical dispute. Any reference in haredi speech or writing to the seventeenth-century false messiah, Shabtai Zvi, is invariably followed by the Hebrew words '*yimah shmo*' ('may his name be blotted out'). The sensitivity surrounding that tragic episode in Jewish history seems hardly to have waned over the intervening centuries, especially among rabbis, perhaps because many of the leading rabbis of that time were taken in by Zvi.

At the same time, messianic faith is still one of the most potent and soul-stirring motifs in Jewish Orthodoxy. For many Modern-Orthodox the State of Israel is a tangible harbinger of the fulfilment of the prophecies of redemption. Haredim, who reject any such interpretation of the prophecies, cherish a fervent faith in an ultimate, apocalyptic Coming. Every sermon or homiletic discourse in haredi circles ends with a formulaic: 'And may the Almighty send our Righteous Messiah speedily in our days,' or: 'And may the Holy One Blessed Be He help so that the True Redemption come speedily, as the Bible says: "And the Redeemer shall come to Zion [Isaiah 59:20]." ' The audience responds with a ritual 'Amen'.

The thirteenth and last of the Principles of Faith listed by the medieval sage Maimonides, which many haredim recite each morning after their prayers, is a declaration of the classical messianic credo: 'I believe with a perfect faith in the Coming of the Messiah, and even though he may tarry, nevertheless I will await him every day.' Many a believing Jew has gone to the stake, or to the gas-chamber, with that declaration on his lips.

Supporters of Rabbi Shach say his attacks on the Rebbe are intended to point up a potential tragedy and thereby try to head it off. Schneerson's focus on the Messiah in his sermons and writings, and his repeated assurances that the messianic Redemption is at hand, have fostered an atmosphere of acute, hope-filled tension throughout the movement. Children go to sleep with their best clothes laid out at the end of their beds, ready to greet the Messiah. Shach fears a dangerous wave of disillusionment among thousands of naïve and misguided Lubavitcher hasidim, when the Rebbe eventually dies without fulfilling the heady messianic promise.

The Habad counter-argument is not publicly articulated, because no scenario predicated on the Rebbe's demise is discussed openly by his hasidim. It contends that if the Messiah does not reveal himself in this generation, that will be because the generation is 'unworthy' – and Rabbi Shach will have a lot to answer for. For the present, though, and for the record, official Habad spokesmen carefully stop short of claiming outright that the Rebbe is, or will reveal himself to be, the Messiah. Their invariable line, when questioned by outsiders, is that all Jews are required to believe in the coming of the Messiah, that the Talmudic sources say the Messiah will arise from amongst the people, and: 'Do you know of anyone alive today who fits the bill better than the Rebbe?'

But the other side refuses to be fobbed off with this sort of discreet double-talk. In 1989, still smarting from Habad's successful intervention in Israeli electoral politics (Habad backed Agudhat Yisrael against Shach's Degel Hatorah, promising the Rebbe's personal blessing to everyone voting Agudah), Shach's party newspaper *Yated Ne'eman* compiled a dossier of Habad writings and statements over recent years. Among the counts on the charge-sheet were these:

> 'Contrary to the traditional formulation of Jewish yearning for the *coming* of the Messiah, today's Lubavitch speaks of the *revelation* of the Messiah, for obvious reasons . . .'
>
> 'In a seemingly innocuous advertisement in a Habad publication in 1984, placed by a Habad-owned dairy, the following greeting appeared: "May the New Year be a year of the propagation of the teachings of hasidism, until the coming of the kingdom of the House of David, when [the Rebbe] reveals himself, may it be soon in our days – Now."' (The text of the advertisement was in Hebrew, but the word 'Now' appeared in English, a reference to a popular Habad bumper sticker in America and Israel: 'We Want Moshiach NOW!')*
>
> 'A 1983 Israeli Habad publication described the scene in New York at the inauguration of the Lubavitch youth movement, Tsivot Hashem ["The Armies of the Lord"]: "Tsivot Hashem is the army of redemption, the army of the king-messiah. At its

* In 1991, the neo-Christian proselytizing group 'Jews for Jesus' chose as its slogan: 'We've GOT Moshiach Now – His name is Yeshua [Jesus].' The legend appeared on posters and T-shirts throughout Manhattan. Habad publicists said this only proved the effectiveness of their own slogan.

inauguration we all witnessed a heavenly sight when . . . the pure-souled Jewish children encircled the tzaddik of our generation . . . and this holy flock, crouching at the feet of the shepherd and leader of Israel, all pointed at him with their fingers and, in voices both beseeching and demanding, called out, We want Moshiach Now. We are not prepared to wait any longer." '

'In a discourse one shabbat in 1984, the Rebbe stressed that every single Jew has the power and duty to help bring about the coming of the Messiah, "and not just tomorrow or some time in the future, but right here and now . . . as though you could open your eyes and see that the Messiah is here with us in this synagogue, flesh and blood, body and spirit . . ." '

Yated added: 'Anyone determined to be disingenuous can claim that the Rebbe was merely seeking to strengthen their faith in the principle that the Messiah can appear imminently. But anyone familiar with the special messianic fervour and tension of Lubavitch must understand that the words "here with us in this synagogue, flesh and blood . . ." had a very particular significance.'

Maimonides, describing the attributes of the Messiah, writes that he will 'fight the battles of the Lord'. *Yated* cited Habad writings – including a reported discourse by the Rebbe in 1975 – to the effect that the Messiah's battles will be for 'the integrity of the Land' and 'the integrity of the Nation' – the names of Lubavitch's political campaigns for 'Greater Israel' and for halachic 'Who is a Jew' legislation. The fact that the Rebbe has never visited the Jewish State, despite his intense involvement with its life and politics, is also adduced by his foes as an implicit proof of his messianic aspirations – as though his advent to the Holy Land can only take place in an apocalyptic context.

It is an impressive indictment, though not quite as damning as the opposition makes out. Despite the deliberate and obvious hints that suffuse its rhetoric, Habad deliberately stops just short of crossing the boundary of ambiguity. It does not say outright that the Rebbe is or will become the Messiah. On the other hand, it certainly does lead its people to believe or expect that.

In the spring of 1991 the Messianic tension within Habadd

reached an explosive point when the Rebbe suddenly announced to his hasidim that he had failed in his efforts to hasten the Coming and that it was 'up to you now'. After an anguished outcry from followers around the world, he explained that he meant it would need a joint effort by all of them, and they must try even harder to persuade Heaven that the time was ripe. His illness the following year threw the faithful into renewed consternation. Some of the most diehard believers suggested that his suffering was itself added evidence of his Messianic potential and of the imminence of the historic moment.

Rabbi Shach for his part insists that the bitter feud, unprecedented in Orthodoxy since the rivalry between the Gaon of Vilna and the founders of hasidism, is not a new outbreak of the original hasidic-mitnagdic rift. Then too, as we have seen, associations of false messianism fuelled the controversy. Shach claims his argument is with today's Lubavitcher Rebbe, not with hasidism in general, nor even with Lubavitch hasidism in the past. His rhetoric, however, is distinctly reminiscent, in its style and vocabulary, of the diatribes against the hasidim in the late eighteenth century. He has even gibed, according to his followers, that 'Habad is the nearest thing to Judaism . . .'

There is no ambiguity or reticence on Habad's part in attributing to the Rebbe supernatural powers. An Israeli Habad booklet described the Rebbe's regular visits to the tomb of his father-in-law, the previous rebbe:

> He fasts during that day, and stands there without shoes, even in the cold and snow, for hours on end . . . What he does there no man knows . . . He stands alone. It has often happened that the Rebbe returns from the tomb and calls an 'instant' gathering, where he issues new instructions or launches a new 'campaign.' Sometimes he speaks of the tomb in terms of 'I was told . . .' 'I was pressured . . .'

The tomb is in the New York City borough of Queens. Apart from his drives there, which increased in frequency during 1990–1, until the stroke felled him while standing at the graveside, the Rebbe never left Brooklyn for four decades, conduct which heightened the supernatural speculation surrounding him, which in turn fed the personality cult. 'He has been described as the most phenomenal Jewish personality of our time,' proclaimed a recent Habad brochure, as glossily produced as any Madison Avenue prospectus. 'To his hundreds of thousands of followers and millions of sympathizers and admirers around the world, he is "the Rebbe," today's most dominant figure in Judaism and, undoubtedly, the one individual more than any other singularly responsible for stirring the conscience and spiritual awakening of world Jewry.'

Apart from the messianism controversy, many non-partisan Orthodox Jews, and many non-Orthodox, are troubled by Habad hasidim's almost total abdication of personal responsibility for their own lives. Intelligent and accomplished individuals will apply to the court in Brooklyn for guidance on the most mundane personal decisions, which they then accept as binding. There is also in Habad's outreach work, according to the movement's critics, a deliberate blurring between Habad and Judaism itself, so that some newcomers to the movement come to regard the two as synonymous.

This is not quite fair, because Habad, far more than any other brand of haredism, claims to accept the equality of all Jews, observant and non-observant alike. The glossy booklet explains:

> When the question is raised, 'Why do you put on tefillin in the street, or hand out shabbat candles, to men and women whom you have never met before?' the hasid of Lubavitch responds: Because of what they already *are*, not because of what they may become; not so that he or she may one day become 'Orthodox', but because right now they are already Jewish, and tefillin and shabbat candles *belong* to them. It is their right and their obligation to perform the mitzva, and it is our privilege, honor and obligation to respectfully help them to do so . . .

The critics would dismiss that as soft-sell proselytizing, ultimately aimed at recruiting non-Orthodox 'converts' to Habad hasidism. Sympathizers might find it moving and sincere. Which only serves to point up the depth of the controversy surrounding this movement.

One fact is beyond controversy: Rabbi Schneerson is a magnetic personality. The brief Sunday-morning encounters with him generally left visitors impressed. When he spoke to anyone – rabbi, tycoon, or little girl – he seemed to have neither eyes nor mind for anything else. The publicity hype, moreover, contains an unassailable truth: the Lubavitcher Rebbe has indeed been the dominant haredi personality of the post-war era. Alone among the haredi rabbis, he has sought direct contact with, and impact on, the largest possible numbers of Jews.

The vast majority of these Jews have not become Lubavitcher hasidim. Indeed, for all its much-criticized missionary work, Habad's actual ranks of card-carrying members have stayed relatively small; there are more Satmarer hasidim in New York than there are Lubavitchers. A certain number of non-Orthodox Jews who were influenced by Habad have gone on to become Orthodox, even haredi, without joining Habad. A much larger number though, whose lives were touched only fleetingly by Habad, have experienced a warmth for their religion that they would not otherwise have felt – and certainly not from contact with other haredim. In times of personal crisis – hospitalization or bereavement, for instance – people often find the solicitous presence of a Habad hasid consoling. In Israel's wars, the Lubavitchers manage to reach the furthest outposts, cheering the troops with a shot of vodka and a lively hasidic dance.

Granted, Habad's militancy over the question of 'Who is a Jew' (see chapter 33) has recently tarnished its 'tolerant' image in the eyes of non-Orthodox Jews. Granted too, some Jews, including Orthodox Jews, squirm self-consciously at Habad's Jewish exhibitionism, and many resent the Lubavitchers' insistent and unsolicited religious ministrations. But many others feel religiously enriched. And many more, who remain spiritually unmoved, nevertheless feel a certain pride or satisfaction at the sight of the Lubavitchers unabashedly, indefatigably, doing their thing.

12

Simple Sage

'We are fortunate,' the bearded, fruity-voiced emcee croons into the microphone, as an expectant hush stills the audience. 'Fortunate indeed.' His voice rises. 'Fortunate to be alive in this generation.' It reaches a crescendo. 'This generation, whose pride, whose glory, whose magnifience is here to speak to you tonight . . .'

The audience leap to their feet, cheering and clapping, as Rabbi Ovadia Yosef, resplendent among the other black-coated rabbis in his gold-embroidered robe and matching purple turban-like hat, makes his way to the podium. They break into song. 'Add days to the days of the king; make his years as many generations. . .'

It is the same song as that which greets Rabbi Shach. The words, though, are pronounced in the Sephardic way, which is also the way of modern, Israeli Hebrew, instead of in the old Ashkenazic, European way. *Shanim* (years) instead of *shonim, tosif* (add) instead of *toisif*. But the rhythm is the same, and the tune, repeated over and over. It is a distinctly Western rhythm; it has none of the delicate modes of Sephardic music.

The scene was repeated at dozens of Shas Party election rallies around the country in the early summer of 1992, when Rabbi Yosef attracted larger crowds than either of the two contenders for the prime ministership: Yitzhak Rabin of Labour and Yitzhak Shamir of the Likud. Unlike the politicians, who campaigned conventionally by car or minibus, he travelled by helicopter from one meeting to the next. This was no novelty for him: Shas's educational arm, El Hamaayan ('To the Source'), hires a helicopter each year for the revered spiritual leader's nationwide campaign of 'repentance and awakening' during the month of Elul, before the High Holydays. Some nights, he flies to three or four different locations. Twice a year at least, he travels abroad to visit Sephardic communities.

The audiences vary, but the warm-up routine is always the same. It is the substance of this routine, this particular patter of superlatives, that expresses the uniqueness of current Sephardic haredism, unique in its unanimous reverence of this one man. No Ashkenazic speaker, however adulatory he might wax, would ever think of extolling a living rabbi over those of the past, or the present generation over the previous ones. 'If the earlier [rabbis] were like angels then we are like men,' says the Talmud. 'If they were like men then we are like donkeys.' The unwavering rule, that informs every aspect of haredi life among Ashkenazim, is that 'the generations are declining.' And therefore, in learning and leadership, saintliness and personal example, haredim look backwards, always backwards.

Rabbi Shach, for instance, by virtue of his great age and eminence, is referred to as 'a remnant of a wise generation', or 'a vestige of the Greats'. The most generous homage that can be paid to a venerable scholar is to link him to the bygone age. Rabbi Yosef, on the other hand, sits impassively wearing dark glasses (he suffers from an eye condition) while the emcee proclaims that no one like him has arisen 'in decades, in a century, in long generations'.

He does not demur because, quite simply, the statement is accurate. Sephardic Jewry has not produced a sage of his stature in a hundred years. Not in North Africa, nor in Iraq, Syria and the Yemen, which were the principal Sephardic communities until they all began moving to Israel or to the West after 1948.

He knows, moreover, that his own outstanding scholarship (see chapter 25), and the reverence and admiration that this induces, are themselves key elements in the current religious revival among Sephardim. Wherever he goes, in Israel or abroad, people flock to kiss his hand or the hem of his robe. Many are yeshiva students or yeshiva alumni, a new phenomenon in Sephardic society. Many are baalei teshuva, recent adherents to Orthodoxy. For them he is a hero, the ultimate role-model. But he is also honoured and feted by Sephardim who are not strictly Orthodox. The personal honour accorded to him extends to the yeshivas, the rabbis, and the baalei teshuva – and translates into philanthropic support. Haredism among Sephardim is suddenly popular, even fashionable.

In Buenos Aires, to cite a distant example, while the Ashkenazic community is rapidly assimilating and dwindling demographically, the much smaller Sephardic community is holding its own numerically, and is increasingly shifting 'to the right' religiously, under the influence of a new cadre of haredi rabbis. All of them regard themselves, directly or indirectly, as disciples of Yosef.

For Sephardim the world over, Rabbi Yosef is a focus of their Sephardic pride. He took on and beat the Ashkenazim at their own game, Talmud study; yet he jealously guards the Sephardic tradition, vigorously asserts the superior authenticity of Sephardic rules and rituals, and, if just mildly provoked, reveals a remarkably vehement streak of anti-Ashenazic sentiment.

Asked why Sephardic Jewry did not produce a halachist of his stature for so long, Yosef explained: 'The reason is very simple. There weren't any yeshivas. Whoever learned, learned alone. But it's hard to learn alone. The Talmud itself says that he who learns alone is liable to stray off the proper path of understanding.

'The first yeshiva we had was Porat Yosef [in Jerusalem], and that was tiny. Very few familes wanted to send their sons to a yeshiva. Until twenty or thirty years ago, it was the only [Sephardic] yeshiva in the world. But now, thank God, everyone wants to learn. There are lots and lots of yeshivas. Parents beg yeshivas to admit their sons, and there isn't enough room. This is due, too, to the Great Sages of the Generation, who "went down" to the people, and explained to them what yeshiva means, what learning means, why it's important for their sons to be *talmidei hachamim* [scholars]. Before, there was no such value in our society.'

Yosef's modestly vague reference to the 'Great Sages of the Generation' is his way of pointing to his own cardinal role in the growth of Sephardic yeshivas. 'Now we have a growing generation of fine young men, steeped in learning. And they will increase and multiply, with God's help.

'Of course,' he adds drily, 'there are Ashkenazic yeshivas too which take in Sephardic pupils, up to a certain proportion at any rate.' The comment is a side-swipe at the ambivalence of the 'Lithuanian' yeshivas towards Sephardic students. But it also reflects Yosef's own ambivalence towards the 'Lithuanians'. 'They think their rabbis are the best,' he says. 'They think they know it all.'

After the 1992 election, in which Shas held its own while Agudah and Degel, running as one bloc, lost ground, Yosef finally broke free of Shach's paternalistic and sometimes downright contemptuous tutelage. In an ill-advised comment shortly before the election, Rabbi Shach had told a meeting of rabbis in Bnei Brak that the Sephardim were 'not sufficiently mature to lead, either in Torah or in national affairs'. Once the election was over – and his nightly campaigning efforts vindicated – Yosef promptly instructed the Shas MKs to negotiate a coalition agreement with Labour. He ordered them to abide by it, moreover, even when Prime Minister Rabin, in a tactically ill-conceived move, handed the education ministry to Mrs Shulamit Aloni, the leader of the strongly secularist Meretz Party. Rabin and Aloni pledged effective autonomy for haredi education, under a Shas deputy minister. Rabin also promised Yosef, in a personal letter, that the 'Jewish heritage' curriculum taught in all the country's schools would not be cut.

Nevertheless, Rabbi Shach led a strident outcry against 'the abandonment of one million children [meaning the country's non-haredi children] to apostasy', and he and other mitnagdic rabbis issued an 'halachic edict' forbidding the haredim to join the government. Yosef, his own man at last, ignored the edict.

Despite his vast scholarship, or perhaps because of it, Rabbi Yosef exemplifies a tradition of populism that distinguished the Sephardic rabbinate from its Ashkenazic counterpart. The imagery he uses is always simple and graphic. For every public appearance he has a story or parable. He tells them in straightforward, colloquial Hebrew (he knows no other language), and unerringly strikes a responsive chord with the most disparate audiences. His Ashkenazic detractors privately call him primitive and unsophisticated. They poke fun at his wife Margalit, a down-to-earth woman who speaks her mind too freely, and bustles around him like a bodyguard.

He, too, on occasion, gets swept away by his own crude banter. Prime Minister Shamir is 'a rodent-eater', he told a group of Shas rabbis at one frustrating stage of his political manoeuvring in 1990 (a reference to Shamir's penchant for frog's legs and other French gourmet delights, which are unkosher). Mrs Shulamit Shamir 'is the one who won't eat in a Jewish restaurant if she can eat in a Gentile one'; Ariel Sharon 'doesn't eat rodents, but he loves pig'; the State Comptroller (a powerful and prestigious super-ombudsman, investigating the charges of Shas misappropriations) is 'a real enemy of Judaism'; and as for the Attorney-General, 'May his house be destroyed' (a common Arabic curse).

Of course, this is hardly the manner in which a sage and spiritual leader is expected to express himself. But those who know Yosef well know that his common way of talking is a form of inverse snobbery. He feels that his credentials are so unassailable that he can afford to play to the gallery, to pander to his Sephardic constituency's ethnic resentments, never far beneath the surface, while his more strait-laced rivals gnash their teeth at his popularity with the masses.

Although he was required by law to retire as Sephardic Chief Rabbi of Israel in 1983, at the end of his ten-year term, he still wears the robes of that office, and insists on keeping the title 'Rishon LeZion' ('First in Zion'), to the chagrin of his successor. For virtually his entire term as Chief Rabbi, Yosef feuded and bickered with his Ashkenazic counterpart, the brilliant and tempestuous Shlomo Goren. Stuck once in an elevator between floors in a Manhattan hotel, Margalit suggested, in all seriousness, that Rabbi Goren's agents had somehow tampered with the electricity. But never, even in their most unbridled moments, did either man impugn the other's scholarship. Today, mellowed and generous, Goren says of Yosef: 'He knows ten times as much as Shach.'

But if that is even approximately the case, why did Yosef defer to the Ashkenazic sage for so long? In trying to understand him, political pundits would generally point to the make-up of the Shas constituency. Shas voters were 'hawks', they said. Some were extremists, outright Arab-haters. In late 1988, when Yosef first proposed an alliance with Labour, Margalit received threatening phone-calls from Shas supporters. They harassed her when she went out shopping. It was this reaction, as he himself admitted in a private conversation at that time, that stopped him from acting on his own doveish political convictions.

By 1990 he had overcome that inhibition. He intended to educate and moderate his constituency. And he believed that a period in government alongside Labour, with concomitant pecuniary benefits for Shas's educational movement, El Hamaayan, would win more and more adherents to the party. He was no longer afraid to confront angry voters. But he was still afraid to face down Rabbi Shach.

The roots of that fear are to be found deep in the lingering mutually ambivalent attitudes of Sephardim and Ashkenazim in the haredi world. Yosef himself is clad in gold and purple; but the other rabbis on the dais at his public appearances, dressed in dour black frock-coats, are indistinguishable from Shach's 'Lithuanians'. Even Yosef himself, when in 'mufti', dresses in the 'Lithuanian' style. In fact, it took desperate cajoling from Margalit and his aides, in an emptying plane at Kennedy Airport, to persuade him – this was back in 1984, shortly after his election as Chief Rabbi – to put on the Sephardic robes of office for the first time.

Many of the Shas rabbis studied at Ponevezh and other Ashkenazic yeshivas. Some excelled there. But none made it to the top: none were encouraged to marry into faculty families, as the best Ashkenazic students vie to do. They were torn between the unrequited urge to be accepted by the Ashkenazim, and the desire to preserve their ethnic separatism.

They gravitated to Shas not only because they themselves felt a need for an independent Sephardic haredi voice, but because Rabbi Shach determined that there was such a need. (Objectively, there certainly was: Agudah – including Shach – had regularly double-crossed its own Sephardic voters, promising them effective representation in the Knesset and in the party's policy-making forums, and always reneging once the elections were over.) Yosef was the father of Shas and its main electoral asset; but Shach was its godfather. He nurtured it in order to hit back at the hasidic rebbes and politicians who would not give him his own way in Agudah Yisrael. He packed the new party's Knesset list with his Sephardi disciples, outmanoeuvring the naïve and inexperienced Yosef. When the crunch came, in March 1990, they dared not defy him.

Nor, in the final analysis, did Yosef, although he insisted, looking back later, that he 'was not cowed'. There was simply no point in fighting Rabbi Shach, he explained, since the venerable Ashkenazic rabbi's writ ran throughout the haredi world. 'The Talmud teaches: Just as it is a mitzva to say something which will be listened to, so too is it a mitzva not to say something that will not be listened to.

'Let me tell his honour [Yosef always uses the formal third-person] a story, about the third Lubavitcher Rebbe, Rabbi Menahem Mendel, the "Tsemach Tsedek".* One day he said to his servant: "Let's go." He didn't say where, and the servant, of course, didn't ask.

'They reached the home of a certain bank manager, a non-Orthodox man. But he was respectful. He welcomed the Rabbi, offered him refreshments. The Rabbi just sat, and said nothing. The host felt it impolite to ask the Rabbi what had brought him, so he asked the servant. "I don't know either," he said. So they all sat in silence.

'After some time, the Rabbi rose, said to the servant: "Let's go," and headed for the door. The bank manager could no longer restrain himself and asked, very politely, to what had he owed the honour. So the Tsemach Tsedek said: "Our Talmud tells us, Just as it is a mitzva to say something that will be listened to, so too is it a mitzva not to say something that will not be listened to. If I stay at home, I can't fulfil that mitzva. So I come here, I sit with you, and I don't say something that will not be listened to. Having done that, I'm now leaving."

'The manager, of course, demanded to know what it was he wouldn't listen to. After much pressure, the Rabbi told him: a poor widow could not afford the repayments on her mortgage. "And your bank has sent her an eviction notice. Where is your mercy? The Torah commands us to protect the widow. . ."

* Lit. 'Flowering of Righteousness'. This is the name of Rabbi Menahem Mendel's book, published in 6 volumes in Vilna (1871–84).

'The manager remonstrated that it was not his bank, and he had to follow procedures.

' "There you are! I knew you wouldn't listen. But now you've foiled my intention of fulfilling the mitzva!" '

In the end, Yosef concluded the story, the manager paid the debt from his own pocket, and the Rabbi blessed him with lifelong prosperity.

Yosef's point was well taken. But by 1992 he himself had apparently had enough of biding his time and believed that if he spoke out he would be listened to, at least by his own followers, despite Rabbi Schach's opposition.

13

Murky Waters

'The water is a family tradition going back hundreds of years,' says Baruch Abuhatseira, smoothing his long brown gown over his knees. Baruch, a large man in his early fifties, with dark, limpid eyes, sensuous lips and a greying beard, is known as Baba Baruch, son and heir of the famous tzaddik of Netivot, Baba (lit. father) Sali. 'I recite a secret blessing over it, which was handed down in our family from father to son. Then I give it to the person. Of course, if he doesn't believe in it – it won't help him.'

His aide prepares several bottles of water on a low table in front of his armchair. In a few minutes, audience time will begin. A handful of people are already queuing outside. Some clutch plastic bottles which they have filled with water from a row of taps in the front yard of the building. Most are women; they seem to be traditional rather than haredi.

Baba Sali, whose full name was Rabbi Yisrael Abuhatseira, came from Morocco in the early 1960s and settled soon after in Netivot. He died in 1984. He lived in this imposing white building, which also houses a synagogue, for the last year of his life. Before that his home was a small apartment in a run-down block in this sleepy Negev township.

People flocked to him from all over the country and from overseas. Ashkenazim as well as Sephardim. Non-Orthodox, traditional and haredim. There was a tap in the yard of the apartment block, and the believers brought him water to bless. Others just poured out their troubles, and listened as the wizened old man, half-hidden in a white cowl, whispered his advice and blessing. Some gave him money, which he disbursed among the poor. The haredim would write their name and their mother's name on a small piece of paper, a kvitl, as they would to a hasidic rebbe.

Rabbi Yissachar Meir, German-born, a graduate of the first class of Ponevezh, who founded and heads the large 'Lithuanian'-style Yeshivat Hanegev in Netivot, speaks with reverence of the late Baba Sali. Once, he recounts, Baba Sali was visiting the yeshiva when a lame man accosted him. The tzaddik asked him if he observed the principal mitzvot: shabbat, kashrut, mikve. The man admitted that he did not. 'Then you deserve to be lame!' The man burst into tears. He begged for a blessing. 'Go away,' Sali said. 'I can't.' 'You can! Get up and walk.'

The man walked. The yeshiva students crowded around him. They danced with him.

'Next day,' Rabbi Meir ends his story, 'Baba Sali sent me a message: "Please have the students at the yeshiva say Psalms for me. I invoked a miracle for someone who did not merit it. He benefited from my merit; now I need your prayers." '

Rabbi Ovadia Yosef, too, says that Baba Sali was 'a saintly man, a man engrossed in Torah and prayer all the days of his life. Many of his blessings were fulfilled.' When he visited him, Yosef says, Baba Sali would stand up and kiss his hand, 'though he was a good thirty years older than I. He encouraged me to become Chief Rabbi. I consulted with him, and took his advice.'

Yosef's and Meir's respect for the memory of the father exacerbates their contempt for the son, whose colourful career includes a jail term for bribery and a much-publicized extramarital affair. And yet Baruch can rightly claim – and indeed does claim – a pivotal role in the religious revival among Sephardic Jews.

On the anniversary of the death of his father, more than 200,000 people, mostly Moroccan Israelis, stream into Netivot to attend the *hilula*, the gathering to mark the anniversary of a death. (Ashkenazic haredim, too, mark the hilula – or *yahrzeit* in Yiddish – of their parents or rabbis, the mitnagdim by learning Mishna, the hasidim by learning Mishna and drinking schnapps. Non-Orthodox as well as Orthodox Jews go to synagogue on the hilula/yahrzeit of a parent to recite a special prayer, the *kaddish*.) Hundreds of policemen direct the traffic to vast temporary car-parks in the desert. Courtesy buses shuttle the throngs to the glistening, white-domed tomb.

Their prayers said, they move on to large picnic areas, where they build charcoal fires and roast meat. Some pitch tents for an extended stay of two or three days. Some bring sheep or goats to slaughter and eat at the tomb site. Hawkers sell pictures of Baba Sali and Baba Baruch, video-cassettes, records, charms and baubles. People play musical instruments, or raucous tape-recorders; women dance and ululate. Ministers and Knesset members come to see and be seen; they can hardly ignore a popular gathering of this size. Rabbis come too, led by the Sephardic Chief Rabbi, Mordechai Eliahu. They pray at the grave, but pay their respects, too, to Baba Baruch in his exquisite Moorish-style courtyard built alongside the synagogue-residence.

The fact that Baruch spent four years in prison, from 1980 to 1984, convicted of fraud, forgery and taking bribes while serving as a local politician in the town of Ashkelon, seems to recede with each passing anniversary. A messy legal scrap between Baruch and his long-time mistress, which reached the courts and made the headlines two years *after* he took over as the Baba, has also rapidly faded into insignificance in the face of his huge and undeniable success.

In addition to the annual hilula jamboree, the grave-site and Baruch himself are year-round attractions. A daily stream of pilgrim/visitors, and frequent weddings and bar-mitzvas at the tombside restaurant, ensure constant activity and steady income. Baruch's aides defend the instant transformation, from rascal to rabbi, explaining that he is a new man, a baal teshuva. The Talmud declares that 'Where a baal teshuva stands, even the perfectly righteous cannot stand.'

One public figure who still shuns Baruch is Moshe Nissim, a Likud Party leader who was Minister of Justice when Baruch's jail term was commuted by the President of the State. Nissim, an Orthodox man himself, whose Iraqi-born father was the Sephardic Chief Rabbi before Yosef, regrets his role in advising the President to commute the sentence. 'The pressures on me were enormous,' he recalls. 'Shamir, David Levy, Shimon Peres, the trade union bosses, Chief Rabbi Eliahu. It was disgusting.'

Baruch's more temperate critics focus on what they say is his ignorance of religious and Talmudic matters. Rabbi Yosef, who condemned him publicly when he donned his father's mantle almost as soon as he left the prison, says he urged him more recently to sit and learn. Baruch had by this time opened a kollel in Netivot, which, despite his own dubious reputation, has established itself as a serious institute for advanced Talmud students. He himself notes pointedly and proudly that his graduates excel in the nationwide examinations for rabbis and *dayanim* (rabbinical court judges). A visit to the kollel, which is housed in a wing of the Moorish-style courtyard, finds more than thirty young men studying hard, and paying no heed to the activities surrounding Baruch in the adjacent building. They are drawn to this kollel in part, no doubt, by the fact that it pays a higher monthly salary than almost any other kollel in the country.

Rabbi Yosef says he congratulated Baruch for all that, when they met by chance in Bnei Brak. But he cited to him the verse in the Song of Songs (1:6): 'They made me the keeper of the vineyards, but my own vineyard I have not kept.' 'I told him to take a young scholar who would learn with him several hours a day. He said he's got no time. So too bad, I don't really care.'

Rabbi Yissachar Meir, who taught in a yeshiva in Morocco before opening his own yeshiva in Netivot, has known Baruch since his youth. 'Bright, but bone-idle,' he says. 'Doesn't know much and never wanted to learn. Gave his father no end of grief. I offered to learn with him myself. I gave him one of our best scholars to coach him. But all to no avail.'

Meir, though strait-laced in the German-Jewish way, is worldly-wise, and quickly recognized the significance of Baruch's succession to his father's title, and above all of his commandeering of the grave-site. On the first anniversary of Baba Sali's death, a fight erupted at the site between Baruch's men and followers of his own nephew, Baba Elazar Abuhatseira of Beersheba (of whom more below). The interlopers were driven off and Baruch remained sole master of the hilula. Meir decided to live in pragmatic amity with the new Baba.

Subsequently, though, relations between Meir and Baruch deteriorated, and they have become outright enemies since the 1988 Knesset elections, when Baruch backed Agudat Yisrael and Meir, as a 'Lithuanian' yeshiva dean, supported Rabbi Shach's Degel Hatorah Party. The feud has spilled over into municipal

Netivot politics and into bitter struggles over land and building rights. Yet even Meir praises Baruch's charitable activities. Hundreds of needy families in Netivot and throughout the region receive generous support at holiday times. And the recipients do not have to come and queue shamefacedly: Baruch's aides tour the countryside in vans, depositing large hampers of festival fare on the doorsteps of the families being helped in this way.

Baruch himself says he has raised and spent 'between $10 and $13 million' during his brief stewardship, much of it on charity. 'Meir's lot would have to work for decades to spend that much,' he says contemptuously. He has wealthy supporters abroad, in North America and France. 'I take from one and give to another, that is the tradition of our family.'

He wanted, he says, to be friends with Meir and the yeshiva community, which numbers close to 200 families in addition to some 350 students in the yeshiva and in a seminary for girls. 'I even gave him a letter of recommendation to people I know in France, for his fund-raising. There was a period of mutual respect. But the hostility began when I founded my educational institutions. He couldn't bear it. He had to have the monopoly in Netivot. But who would ever have heard of Netivot were it not for the Baba Sali, may his memory be blessed. The truth is, Rabbi Meir doesn't like Sephardim.'

Growing steadily more animated, Baruch adds: 'Rabbi Meir would have to learn for twenty straight years to know what I know in Talmud. I could write twenty learned books if I wanted. They think they're scholars. Huh! We are simply modest; our way is to conceal our learning. Our way is to go down to the people, to welcome every Jew, with love, with a smile. We never turn away a Jew . . .'

Beneath the disparagement of Baruch's prowess in Talmud learning, and of his punctiliousness in observing various mitzvot and abstaining from various sins, lies the more substantial accusation by haredi leaders that his cult is religiously undemanding – both of him and of his vast number of casual adherents. A family feast at the grave-site, a blessed bottle of water and Baruch's eyes rolling heavenward, a charm hung on a key-chain – these are becoming, in the contention of haredi critics, convenient surrogates for genuine religious practice. While Sephardic Orthodoxy throughout the Middle East and North Africa was traditionally more tolerant and less extreme than its embattled Ashkenazic counterpart, men like Rabbi Yosef believe that with Baruch, tolerance has run riot, that the religious revival of which Baba Sali's tomb is the focus is too short on religion and rather too long on commercialized superstition.

Baruch denies that he makes no religious demands on the pilgrims who come to picnic and receive water he has blessed. His office, he insists, keeps a computerized record of all visitors. There is follow-up contact. They receive religious literature in the mail; they are exhorted to step up their religious observance. 'But we never turn anyone away. That's not our way. Those who don't want to repent, to improve their religious standards, generally don't come back.'

As for his blessings, he 'never promises – unless the person promises in return to keep mitzvot. And every promise I've made, in six years here, has thank God come true. There have been literally dozens of cases of childless couples blessed with babies. A dentist from Paris, for instance, nine years married and no children. He came to me, undertook to keep mitzvot – and one year later I was the godfather at his son's circumcision. Anyone who thinks these things are mere coincidence is just a fool. There is a divine system of reward and punishment. One who truly repents is rewarded by God.'

While Baruch Abuhatseira's stewardship of his father's tomb is controversial, the cult itself is not alien to established Jewish custom. North African Jewry in particular has a strong tradition of cultivating shrines and graves as pilgrimage sites, where religion and folklore were intertwined. The tomb of Baba Sali's grandfather, Rabbi Yaacov Abuhatseira, located in Egypt west of Alexandria, was an important shrine long before Baruch built the Netivot edifice to Sali. (Baruch brings plane-loads of followers to the site each year for Rabbi Yaacov's hilula.) Every Jewish locality in Morocco had its saint's grave, or a shrine to some special miracle that a local holy man had performed. In some recorded cases, the local Muslim population would join in obeisances in the memory of a Jewish saint.

In the Ashkenazic communities, visits and prayers at rabbis' graves were – and still are – more prevalent among the hasidic sects than among the mitnagdim. In fact, some North African sages led their flocks in a manner reminiscent of hasidic rebbes, dispensing blessings and cures, offering prayers on behalf of congregants, receiving and disbursing philanthropy and generally playing the role of conduit between the community and the Almighty.

Rabbi Ovadia Yosef, his adopted mitnagdism showing through, suggests that this and the tombs cults may have been a 'foreign importation – the result of contacts between these communities and the hasidim of Europe.' At any rate, he insists, it was a strictly North African phenomenon, unknown in the major Sephardic centres of Iraq, Syria and Palestine. Baba Baruch, zealous in defence of his brand of Sephardism, maintains that if anything it was the hasidim who copied the Moroccan tradition, which was itself the authentic heir of the sixteenth-century Palestinian kabbalists. As if to drive home that claim, the decorative curtain over the Torah ark in his synagogue depicts a sort of spiritual family tree, with Baba Sali at the centre, in which the Baal Shem Tov is somehow spliced in amidst the Sephardi sages.

In the immediate aftermath of North African Jewry's geographic and cultural dislocation after 1948, the veneration of departed holy men fell into temporary abeyance. But now, with the resurgence of Sephardic ethnic pride and religious sentiment, they are coming back into their own. The cult of the late Baba Sali, nurtured by his resourceful son, is by far the biggest; but it is not the only one.

In Safed, for instance, a town in northern Israel, an otherwise modest and undistinguished family have built a quasi-mausoleum to a long-dead Moroccan sage, Rabbi David U'Moshe. They say he appeared to them in a dream and intimated that he had somehow been transferred, not corporeally but in a spiritual sense, from his tomb in Morocco to their home. Remarkably, the shrine attracts a following – as does a similar shrine, to the same tzaddik, built in similar circumstances by a family in the southern town of Ofakim.

A respected Tunisian rabbi, Chaim Choury, who emigrated to Israel in the 1950s and died soon after, has become, in death, the focus of an important and growing cult. An estimated 25,000 people come to the cemetery in Beersheba each year to attend his hilula. An Israeli academic sociologist, Alex Weingrod, in a book studying this phenomenon,* records the resentment of the Tunisian celebrants towards the hordes of unaffiliated Moroccans who, always game for a cheerful hilula, have been introducing their more boisterous – and religiously more dubious – practices at the Choury hilula. They spread out their picnics on tombstones in the graveyard; they play raucous and inappropriate music; they encourage irreverent dancing.

The biggest hilula of all in Israel, even bigger – for the moment – than Baba Sali's, is that of Rabbi Shimon Bar Yochai, a Talmudic sage whose burial place is located, according to tradition, in the Galilee village of Meron. The date is Lag Baomer, a minor festival in the springtime, commemorating both the death of Rabbi Shimon and the end of a plague that struck, according to the Talmud, at the pupils of another *tanna* (early Talmudic sage), Rabbi Akiva. This hilula is unique because of its long history – there are recorded accounts of the festivities at Meron from the sixteenth century – and because it draws both Sephardim and Ashkenazim.

Thousands of haredim from all over the country converge on Meron during the night of Lag Baomer, pray at the grave, and throw a little phial of oil on the huge bonfire that lights up the night from the top of the tomb buildings. There are klezmer bands, dancing, food and drink, and much merriment. In the daytime, the Ashkenazic custom is for three-year-old boys to have their first haircuts at the tomb, and each such shearing is accompanied by further jollity as the hitherto untrimmed tresses are snipped off, eventually leaving the toddler with a close-cropped scalp and peyot dangling to his cheeks.

But the haredi Ashkenazim are vastly outnumbered at Meron by huge throngs of Sephardim, many of whom are neither haredi nor

* *The Saint of Beersheba* (New York: SUNY Press 1990).

especially Orthodox. They come in fleets of buses and long queues of private cars; many come in extended family groups, called *hamulot* in Arabic; many bring tents and ice-boxes, and camp out around the site. A half-mile long 'mall' of stalls sprouts up overnight, selling everything from fashion shoes and designer jeans to the latest video releases from Turkey and Greece. Inspectors from the Ministry of Religion battle each year to confine the slaughtering of sheep and goats to designated areas, in the interests of hygiene as well as aesthetics.

The haredim insist on a separation of the sexes in the immediate area of the tomb. The crowd, estimated in some years at more than a quarter of a million, is good-naturedly compliant about this; most of the pilgrims pay only brief respects at the tomb and spend the rest of the time enjoying themselves. *Hilulot* are social occasions at least as much as religious ones.

'It is much simpler to take part in hilulot than to attempt to follow strict religious practices,' writes the Israeli anthropologist Shlomo Deshen, explaining the growing popularity of these events. As immigrants to Israel, the Sephardim felt their links to the traditions of the 'old country' weakening. 'The hilula is one way of freeing oneself from this feeling of loss. The participation is concentrated, dramatic and emotion-filled.'*

Professor Weingrod stresses the political significance of the hilula phenomenon. 'Identifying themselves publicly and proudly as North Africans,' he writes, 'is subsequently translated into support for political candidates who represent their ethnic group.' Moreover, there are statistically demonstrable links 'between mystical beliefs in the miraculous powers of saints on the one hand, and the emergent Israeli ideologies and movements that wed political nationalism with Jewish religious fundamentalism on the other . . . The same sensibility is there, and as a consequence, these different currents all finally flow in the same direction.'†

In the summer of 1990 one enterprising and ambitious Sephardic rabbi organized an event which he plainly hopes will turn into an

* Shlome Deshen, 'Political Ethnicity and Cultural Ethnicity in Israel in the 1960s' in A. Cohen (ed.), *Urban Ethnicity* (London: Tavistock Press 1974).
† Alex Weingrod, *The Saint of Beersheba*, p. 91.

annual hilula of major proportions. Haim Pinto, rabbi of the small southern town of Kiryat Malachi and scion of a famous family of Sephardic sages, exhumed the skeletons of four of them from their graves in Morocco and another unnamed Arab country, packed the bones into suitcases, flew back with them to Israel and reinterred them in the Kiryat Malachi cemetery. One of the four was his grandfather, also called Haim Pinto. The identities of the other three were not disclosed, apparently so as not to compromise the diplomatic discretion required for the transfer operation. The skulls, he related in a newspaper interview, were 'hot to the touch . . . The earth trembled as I removed the bones. Indeed, next morning the local newspapers reported there had been a minor earthquake in the region.'

Cabinet ministers and opposition leaders, Rabbi Ovadia Yosef and local dignitaries, were all on hand to address a throng of some 10,000 at the new tombstone dedication one evening in August, shortly after the Iraqi invasion of Kuwait. All the speakers invoked the spirits of the reinterred tzaddikim to protect Israel from the menaces of Saddam Hussein.

A stall-holder sold bottles of holy water, until he was driven off by the organizers, who said they were determined to preserve decorum and prevent commercialization. It was unclear where this holy water was purportedly from; but people bought it anyway.

Baba Baruch, coolly confident in his air-conditioned audience-chamber in Netivot, contemptuously dismisses the idea that the Pinto tomb could present competition to Baba Sali's grave-site. 'There was only one Baba Sali; everyone loved him in his life, and everyone venerates him now he is dead.' He observes, quite rightly, that Meron and Netivot are the two major national pilgrimage sites in today's Israel. No other place, not the tombs of the Patriarchs (Abraham, Isaac and Jacob) in Hebron, nor the tombs of the kabbalists in Safed, nor King David's burial site, located by tradition on Mount Zion in Jerusalem, has achieved anything approaching the mass popularity of these two venues.

As for Pinto's reinterment operation, Baruch probably reflects the views of a great many Israelis, who were shown the suitcase full of bones on television news, when he terms it 'disgusting and disrespectful'.

14

Timeless Attraction

One particular butt of Baba Baruch's vituperation is his nephew, Baba Elazar. The son of Baba Sali's first-born son Meir, who predeceased his father and who was reputedly a learned and ascetic man, Elazar has his 'court' in a nondescript suburb of Beersheba, the largest town in southern Israel. Baruch says the forty-one-year-old Elazar 'loves money', that he 'sells blessings' and that he is on bad terms with the rest of the family. 'Only God knows who is a genuine tzaddik. Anyone can cheat the public – including Elazar.' Baruch hotly denies any jealousy on his part of Elazar's growing success. 'On the contrary. I would be pleased and proud if he became the most famous tzaddik in the world. He's my flesh and blood. For years he lived in my house in Ashkelon; I brought him up.'

Whatever their shared past, there is no love lost between the two babas now. Since the brawl between their followers at Baba Sali's grave in 1985, there is hardly any contact between them. Indeed, they seem to be as different as any two persons can be, despite their close relationship and common background. 'Seem to be' is used advisedly – because Elazar cannot actually be seen by outsiders, nor indeed by his many followers. His face is covered down to below his nose by the overhanging hood of his grey cloak. Sometimes he inclines his head upwards, and lifts the edge of the cloth, like a visor, to steal a brief look at his interlocutor. But even then his own eyes and features are hardly visible.

This form of religious asceticism is called 'guarding the eyes'. It is a higher degree than merely not looking at women. He tries not to look at anything at all, other than holy books and the long and detailed kvitlach-letters in which his visitors set out their problems or requests. When he makes his way from his home – a nicely appointed but far from luxurious double flat in a modest apartment building – to his small synagogue some blocks away, he is led by an aide, so he does not have to look where he is walking.

This strange practice is in fact the lesser of the two remarkable features that distinguish this young religious leader's court. The other is that people regularly queue for up to fifteen hours for a brief audience with him. Such people, moreover, who are his hasidim in every sense of the term, as he is their Rebbe, are mainly Ashkenazim. They include many business and professional people, and as many Modern-Orthodox as strictly haredi. They arrive in Beersheba (ninety minutes from both Tel Aviv and Jerusalem) in the early afternoon. They write their names on a list outside his door. And then they wait. Sometimes they wait until dawn the next morning.

There is no registering by proxy; everyone has to write his own name, in person. Nevertheless, the audiences do not necessarily proceed according to the listed queue: sometimes the Rabbi will summon a name from low down on the list, and sometimes he will skip a name, leaving the man (no women are admitted) waiting for more long hours. Baba Elazar does not go home until he has received everyone waiting to see him, though by the small hours he is taking less time with each individual than in the afternoon.

Meanwhile, what is both remarkable and fascinating is the devotion and uncomplaining patience of the hasidim. They sit around the synagogue and study; they snooze on benches or smoke in the courtyard. The regulars can go to Elazar's home, where his wife and aides provide a running three-course buffet meal from midday to midnight. They know, each time they come down to Beersheba, that while the pilgrimage could take just an hour or two, it could equally take till the next morning, effectively spoiling two working days. And yet they keep coming. The regulars make a point of attending their leader, and hearing if not seeing him, at least once a month.

People swear by this man; by the soundness of his advice, and by his mystical prescience. He has a constant flow of non-haredi and non-Orthodox visitors, some of whom come out of curiosity, and many more out of desperation, seeking help in a medical or financial crisis. Even among his regular hasidim there are some who are non-Orthodox; and there is at least one non-Jew: an

Indian member of the Tel Aviv diamond bourse who says he never concludes a major deal without consulting Rabbi Elazar.

But the bulk of his following, which is steadily expanding, are haredim and Modern-Orthodox. Some live abroad, in the US or Europe. They phone in their questions or requests to the *rabbanit* (rabbi's wife). Some are plainly men of means: Elazar is building a large synagogue-and-residence complex on an empty plot opposite his present small facility. Once or twice each year he travels abroad to visit his followers. He is said to be a solid Talmudic scholar and, though the high-pitched voice emanating from beneath the grey cowl sounds odd at first, he is a cogent preacher.

His leadership, despite his veiled remoteness, plainly holds a powerful attraction for intelligent people who are searching to be captivated. The intense mysticism, and the disregard for the Sephardic/Ashkenazic divide, of Baba Elazar's court may well point to the shape of the haredi future.

A similar trend is discernible in the still small but significantly growing appeal of a Jerusalem-based hasidic leader, forty-one-year-old Yaacov Milikovsky, the hasidic Rebbe of Amshinov (a village near Warsaw). His hasidim, like Elazar's, also exhibit remarkably long-suffering dedication in the face of his particular form of religious zeal: complete obliviousness of time. This is not mere unpunctuality on his part, but rather a constant and deliberate disregard of the clock. In essence, it is an emulation of the early hasidic fathers, who would as a matter of dogmatic innovation deliberately not meet the halachic deadlines for the various prayers, saying *Shaharit* (the morning prayer) at mid-morning and *Mincha* (the afternoon prayer) at twilight.

Rabbi Milikovsky is considerably more exotic than that. He has been known to terminate the shabbat on Sunday evening. On Mondays and Thursdays, when a brief portion of the Torah is read during shaharit, he gets round to reading it only by tea-time, and sometimes even after nightfall (when, according to the letter of the halacha, it is no longer Monday or Thursday any more). On Hannuka, when other Jews light their menorahs each evening just after dusk, he lights his just before dawn. Scores of hasidim crowd into his apartment from 4 a.m. to watch the proceedings. After the lighting and singing, the Rebbe delivers a lengthy halachic and homiletic discourse. Then everyone files past to shake his hand. By the time the hannuka-lighting ceremony is over, the sun is streaming in and the rest of the country has begun a new day.

In every other respect he is an entirely 'normal' religious leader: a sympathetic listener, a penetrating analyst, a gripping speaker. Moreover, he insists that the congregation, and his yeshiva, do not wait for him but conduct themselves in accordance with the halacha, the calendar and the clock, while he conducts his time-consuming religious exercises alone. Still, there are occasions when being an Amshinover hasid is a strain. When the Rebbe's daughter married in the summer of 1990, the ceremony was set for mid-evening. By midnight it had not yet begun and the bride's friends had to leave on the last bus home. They returned in the morning – in time for the wedding dinner, which had become a breakfast.

The Amshinover hasidim, however, are uncomplaining. Most of them are young men who were born into other hasidic sects, but found themselves attracted by the Rebbe's intellect and self-effacing demeanour – he insists that he is not a rebbe, and he refuses to bless people – and no doubt by his strange spirituality. It is this dual appeal to mind as well as soul which is likely to characterize successful haredi leadership in the years ahead, as a religiously well educated laity, both Ashkenazic and Sephardic, confronts a broad choice of spiritual authority.

PART III

EXILED AMONG JEWS

15

Zionist Nightmare

Rabbi Shach's decision in March 1990 to support the Likud was the most momentous event in Israeli politics for years. Just when Labour seemed poised to take power, in coalition with the haredi parties, the elderly sage intervened to thwart that carefully laid plan. His decision ushered in a period of right-wing rule, after five and a half years of a Labour–Likud unity coalition. The new government stepped up settlement-building in the occupied territories, which resulted in constant tension between Israel and the United States. It participated reluctantly in the Middle East peace negotiations which began late in 1991, but took hardline positions at the talks.

For the haredim themselves, Rabbi Shach's apparent dove-to-hawk tergiversation was merely another twist in a century-long saga of ambivalence and hostility between haredism and Zionism. 'Haredi Jewry is not Zionist,' says Menahem Carmel, senior aide to Rabbi Shach and Secretary-General of the Degel Hatorah Party. 'The creation of the State of Israel was not in accordance with the wishes of the Gedolim. But the State is a fact; and with facts you don't argue.'

Given the centrality of Israel in Jewish life today, this ambivalence has become the single most offensive element of haredi identity in the eyes of other Jews. By the same token, it shapes the haredim's attitudes towards other Jews. An unreserved Zionist, whether an Israeli patriot or Diaspora supporter of the State of Israel, cannot, in the eyes of most haredim, be a haredi – no matter how Orthodox he is in his religious practice. He follows the wrong rabbis, or does not sufficiently accept the authority of the rabbis whom haredi opinion has designated as 'the Gedolim'. Worse still, his faith is flawed. Some of these Gedolim condemned Zionism as rank heresy. And even those who, over the years, reached various pragmatic accommodations with it, nevertheless retained their fundamental reservations over a political movement which was founded and led by non-Orthodox Jews, and which presumed to do what God Himself is destined to do: restore Israel to its Land.

While the Zionist founding fathers in turn-of-the-century Europe saw their movement as the effective alternative to Jewish assimilation, the haredim always saw the Zionist leaders themselves as personifying assimilationist values. Granted, the Zionists wanted to set up a Jewish State. But the State would assimilate into the family of nations. It would be just a State like all others, a far cry from the blueprint for theocracy contained in the Torah.

Immediately following the creation of Israel in 1948, there was some mitigation in the intensity of the conflict. The haredim were at their weakest. The Zionists seemed to have history on their side; they pointed to the Holocaust as the ultimate vindication of their doctrine. Leaders of both camps actively sought compromises that would enable them to live together in the new State. David Ben-Gurion, the founder of Israel and its first Prime Minister, drew up an agreement with the Orthodox parties providing that Saturday was to be the legal day of rest for the new State's Jewish citizens, that all State institutions would observe kashrut, that the laws of personal status would be administered according to halacha (shades here of the three 'major societal mitzvot' discussed in chapter 2), and also that there would be separate schools for Orthodox children.

The Ben-Gurion agreement still comprises the legal 'status quo' governing religious matters in Israel. But the conciliatory spirit of that period was short-lived. Today, even though the haredim are more numerous, much more powerful politically, and more firmly entrenched in the governing establishment, their anti-Zionist ideology has again hardened, and their rhetoric and writings are more strident and vehement than ever. If they 'don't argue', as Menahem Carmel says, with the fact of Israel's existence as a sovereign Jewish State, they certainly do not acquiesce in it ideologically or theologically. Their acceptance of it is purely pragmatic, and increasingly grudging at that. Israel's difficulties, its failure to reach peace with the Arabs and its economic and social problems – these are all seen as divine vindications of haredism's original opposition to the notion that the 'Jewish problem' could be solved by normal political means.

The Zionist dream, wrote *Yated Ne'eman*, the newspaper of Rabbi Shach's Degel Hatorah Party, on Israeli Independence Day 1990, has turned into 'a nightmare'. Headlined 'Was it all worthwhile?', the paper's editorial catalogued the country's woes – the ongoing Palestinian intifada, the housing and employment crises brought on by large-scale Soviet immigration, a widespread sense of demoralization. 'Bereaved parents of fallen soldiers wonder out loud whether it was all worthwhile,' *Yated Ne'eman* asserted.

> We do not, Heaven forbid, rejoice in the downfall of those whose dream of independence is breaking to pieces before their eyes. We are all in the same boat, and our prayer to God is that he should save us all. But we grieve the perversion of the concept of independence. In our eyes, the only true independence is spiritual independence, the independence achieved by observance of Torah and mitzvot.

Hamodia, the organ of the rival haredi party Agudat Yisrael, 'celebrates' Independence Day in much the same vein. 'There is no place on earth today other than Israel,' it noted in a recent Independence Day issue, 'where Jews are the targets of murderers. There is no place on earth where an entire community hates Jews the way [the Arabs] hate us here, in this State which was purportedly to be the haven for the Jews.'

The ideological chasm between the haredim and rest of Israeli society is not merely a matter of press polemics. On Memorial Day 1989, for instance – the day on which the nation commemorates its war dead – a group of rabbis in Bnei Brak organized an 'Assembly of Spiritual Awakening for Women' to mark 'a series of terrible accidents which have happened this past month in which a number of men and women have died in the prime of life. Women's prayers are especially efficacious in such circumstances.' The date was apparently coincidental: no mention was made of Memorial Day in the notices advertising this assembly, nor was it the theme of the sermons delivered to the women.

This was reminiscent of an incident twenty-three years earlier, also in Bnei Brak. The Israeli army had mounted a night-time reprisal operation against Palestinian guerrillas across the Jordanian border, but had run into unexpected resistance from the Jordanian army. The battle raged through the morning, with high casualties on both sides. The radio broadcast frequent bulletins, and the whole country waited anxiously. Orthodox people recited Psalms, which is the traditional recourse at times of emergency.

In a leading yeshiva, the *mashgiach* (spiritual supervisor) led the students in Psalms too, after the noontime service. His voice cracked with emotion. But he was praying for someone who was ill in hospital, someone whom he did not know personally but for whom he had been asked to recite Psalms. He made no reference to the soldiers.

'They live between two worlds: between Jewish statehood and "exile among Jews" [a phrase coined by an early twentieth-century haredi thinker, Nathan Birnbaum],' says Moshe Ishon, a Zionist-Orthodox ideologue and editor of *Hatzofe*, the newspaper of the National Religious Party, which is Modern- and Zionist-Orthodox.

The NRP consistently won between ten and twelve seats in the 120-seat Knesset during the first three decades of the State, and was an active partner in almost all the Labour-led coalitions until 1977. Over the years, it has become increasingly hardline in its policy on Greater Israel, as a younger generation of politicians inspired by the settlers in Judaea and Samaria (the West Bank, occupied since 1967) gradually elbowed out the older leadership. Despite its shift to the right – or, in the view of some observers, because of it – the party has lost votes to the Likud and its ultra-rightist satellites, and also to the Sephardic-haredi party Shas. In the Knesset election in November 1988, the NRP won only five seats. In June 1992 it managed six.

'We live,' Ishon contends, 'in an age when the Zionist-Orthodox idea has in fact triumphed. But that triumph is not reflected at the ballot-box.' In fact, he argues, the greater the success of the Zionist-Orthodox in integrating into the broader community, the less parochial its voting pattern becomes – and the weaker the

NRP. The haredim, on the other hand, seem stronger than they really are, 'because they manage to maximize their political clout'.

'A vast cadre of Zionist-Orthodox has grown up. Their symbol is the knitted *kippa* skullcap. You find them everywhere. In the army, for instance, if you saw a ranking officer with a kippa years ago, you naturally assumed he was a chaplain. Today, there are Orthodox brigadier-generals in key positions, Orthodox field commanders, officers at every level in the intelligence corps and the air force. The same goes for doctors, lawyers – every walk of life.

'At Rafael [the Weapons Research and Development Authority], you find dozens of Orthodox engineers. On television, when they screen the annual Israel Defence Prize awards and show the backs of the prize-winners' heads because they mustn't show their faces – you always see knitted *kippot*. But not everyone who wears it is necessarily a party member or party voter.'

Ishon blames his NRP leaders for failing to retain the political loyalty of this growing constituency, 'whereas the other camp, the haredim, have also grown numerically, but have remained sectarian sociologically and politically. You will rarely find a haredi voting for a non-haredi party. Hence the growth of their parties – and the decline of ours.'

The haredim for their part would not argue with Ishon; they would simply put a different construction on his facts. The stubborn sectarianism that he despises they hold up as their great success. The integration of the Zionist-Orthodox into the general society, which he sees as an historic triumph, they despise as a watering-down of pristine Orthodoxy. If Ishon's paper is in danger of folding for lack of readers, they contend, that is not because its readers have gone over to the haredi *Hamodia* or *Yated* but because they prefer *Yediot Aharonot* and *Maariv*, the racy mass-circulation papers 'full of lewd pictures and lascivious articles', in the words of rabbinical edicts banning them from haredi homes. If the haredi parties manage to maximize their potential on polling-day, that is because their rabbis are heeded when they advise their followers whom to vote for. The NRP also has its rabbis, but their pre-election calls to the faithful to vote are evidently less efficacious.

*

Rabbi Shach's speech in the basketball stadium in March 1990 was a landmark not only in party-political terms. It marked a new nadir in the worsening relationship between the haredim and the rest of Israel. Shach used the opportunity of massive media coverage at home and abroad to deliver a bitter attack on the whole of non-Orthodox Israeli society, singling out the kibbutzim, pride of the modern, secular Jewish renaissance, for special condemnation.

'I want to speak out without fear. There are kibbutz members today who do not know what Yom Kippur is, what the shabbat is, what the mikve is; they have no concept of Judaism; they rear rabbits and pigs. Do they have any link with their fathers? Can such a kibbutz survive? Did their fathers eat on Yom Kippur? . . . Can these people be called Jews? . . . If a war breaks out, how will they fight? The enemy is stronger then they.'

'We are living in terrible times,' the venerable Rabbi lamented. Israel was surrounded by enemies, 'the lamb among seventy wolves'. But the Jews had been persecuted throughout their history, and they had survived their persecutors. 'What was our secret? We are Jews! That has always made us stronger than all of them. They can kill the father, but he has raised his son, and his son will continue on the path. The father can no longer go to synagogue, but the son will go. The father can no longer study the Torah, but the son will study. The son did not cut himself adrift from the heritage of his fathers. He is tied to his fathers, all the way to Abraham, Isaac and Jacob. This is the living essence of the Jewish People. So long as the Jew continues to follow the path of his father and grandfather and doesn't seek out other wisdoms, strange new ideologies – he is alive. And those who abandoned and severed the link – they are dead!'

Rabbi Shach now dropped into Yiddish, describing the blissful scene in a poor Jewish home – presumably in pre-Holocaust Europe. The father, weary from a week of peddling in the neighbouring villages, sits at the sabbath table, 'he the king, his wife the queen, his children princes, and together they sing the sabbath songs. Is there anyone happier or more contented?'

Reverting to Hebrew again, he added: 'Some look to Labour. Some look to one [party] and some to the other. But . . . they have cut themselves adrift from the entire past and are seeking a new

Torah. We must cut ourselves off from the parties that have no link to Judaism. One is better and one is worse, but basically they're the same. They have severed themselves from their forefathers.'

Shach's attack on secular Israeli life, and especially on the kibbutzim, seemed to bring to the surface all the seething resentment in Israeli society against the haredim. The cry went up from the intelligentsia, and quickly spread through the national press: Kulturkampf! Rabbi Shach, speaking in the name of haredism, had effectively declared war on the rest of Jewry. The cartoonist in *Haaretz*, the leading morning newspaper, showed Shach on his podium in the middle of a military cemetery, surrounded by tombstones. All the graves were of kibbutz youth killed in Israel's wars. 'Are these to be called the Jewish People?' the rabbi asked his cohorts, pointing disparagingly at the graves.

The barbed message here was two-pronged: the kibbutzim have always provided a disproportionate number of officers, of volunteers for élite units – and of casualties – in the Israeli armed forces,while yeshiva students are exempted from army service for as long as they continue their studies. Most of them study so long that they never have to serve at all.

Maariv's cartoonist also depicted Shach climbing over military graves to mount his podium. The epitaphs read: 'Died in the Yom Kippur War' and Shach was shown shouting: 'In the kibbutzim they don't know what Yom Kippur is.'

With the bitterness came frustration too. Politicians and commentators, on the right as well as the left, blamed themselves, the system, the media, the public, for allowing the rabbi to hold the whole nation in the grip of his hostile rhetoric and political machinations. 'The doyen of Israeli dervishes makes one speech, and the whole country trembles,' wrote one columnist in the trade union newspaper *Davar*. 'Who are we to complain about Khomeinism in Muslim lands?' wrote Labour Party MK (Member of Knesset) Edna Solodar in an adjoining article. 'We have it at our own gates.'

The Knesset had actually had a whiff of it inside its gates. In a debate some weeks earlier, three haredi MKs had condemned Salman Rushdie's *The Satanic Verses* as an affront to religion, and demanded that it be banned in Israel. 'How would you like it if someone did that to the Bible?' one of them shouted. The Ashkenazic Chief Rabbi, Avraham Shapira, also blasted the book as 'inhuman and immoral' and supported banning it 'in Israel and everywhere else' (but not executing Rushdie).

The President of the State, Chaim Herzog, himself a former army general and later a Labour MK, asked in a radio broadcast 'if this nation knows how much it owes to the kibbutzniks, with their work-calloused hands and weather-beaten faces? When I stand at the graves of our war dead,' he added, 'who fought and sacrificed without any thought for political or religious differences, I ask myself whether we should seek their posthumous forgiveness . . .' Degel Hatorah responded by calling for the President's resignation and suggesting that he had committed the criminal offence of 'sowing dissent between one section of the populace and another'.

Degel's reaction to the furore, in fact, is instructive in the extent of the haredi community's alienation from the rest of society, but also in its resilience and confidence. In the immediate aftermath of the event, Degel, ecstatic over Shach's saturation coverage at home and abroad, engaged in a splurge of self-congratulation. 'A sanctification of God,' a *Yated Ne'eman* headline proclaimed. 'We are certain that following the massive media coverage in Israel and around the world, the main message of the convention will succeed in penetrating the hearts of all mankind: "God is the Lord. Blessed be His Name for ever and ever."'

The writer went on to thank all the reporters and cameramen for their efforts. 'This time we have no complaint that they turned their attention to us . . . On the contrary, they enabled all the citizens of Israel to participate vicariously in this spiritual gathering and to experience a taste of the fragrance of Torah-faithful Judaism . . .'

But the party's politicians and public relations men soon began to understand how inaccurate and insensitive their initial impression had been. They quickly rallied – and resumed their wonted posture of an aggrieved and misunderstood minority. But instead of merely sniping back, Degel fired off a massive broadside of its own. It reprinted the full text of Shach's speech in all the national newspapers, at a cost of tens of thousands of dollars. It also reproduced historical documents showing that Herzog's father, the late Chief Rabbi of Israel, Isaac Herzog, had similarly excoriated the kibbutzim (almost fifty years earlier) for their irreligious ways.

Yated Ne'eman published a three-page diatribe against the kibbutzim and the entire Labour movement for their 'patronizing and disparaging' treatment of the hundreds of thousands of Sephardic immigrants who came to Israel in the 1950s from countries in the Islamic world. There had been a deliberate and sustained campaign by the Labour-led government at that time, the paper charged – with, it should be said, a solid basis of truth – to divest these newcomers of their simple faith and Orthodox heritage and turn them into modern, secular (Labour-voting) Israelis bereft of any real culture or traditions. Most of Israeli Sephardic society's subsequent ills – crime, drugs, educational maladjustment and chronic unemployment – could be directly attributed to that wicked and exploitative policy, the paper maintained.

These charges were at the centre of a renewed Orthodox-secular storm a year later. Rabbi Peretz, the minister-rabbi who had linked the bus-train disaster to sabbath desecration, now serving as Minister of Immigrant Absorption, announced that the newly arrived Ethiopian immigrants would not be sent to kibbutzim 'where they would be torn from their faith'. The ensuing public uproar died down only after both sides were shocked into a transient truce by the deposit of a pig's head outside a synagogue in Bnei Brak. But Rabbi Shach, in a speech in summer 1991, hit out again at Herzog, warning that he would be 'punished' for his defence of the kibbutzim 'and their pig-eating'.

As for the media, they soon reverted in the eyes of *Yated Ne'eman* to purveyors of 'incitement against the community of the God-fearing . . . scribblers of sewer-level shallowness . . . resorting to blatantly antisemitic characterizations.'

At the same time, Degel sought to mitigate the devastation to its image by inviting kibbutz members to attend the Passover Seder in haredi homes. There were few takers, but Degel rabbis managed to persuade a handful of kibbutzim to host them for discussion evenings in which they tried to put a more tolerable slant on Rabbi

Shach's remarks. He had spoken, they assured the kibbutzniks, only out of his deep love for every Jew. One such kibbutz encounter, chronicled by a reporter, included the following exchanges:

Rabbi Moshe Frank (a Jerusalem yeshiva teacher and Degel activist): 'Whoever doesn't identify with the basic tenets of Judaism is simply not Jewish. The idea that the nation can be the supreme value is a heathen and fascist concept. Nationalism is not a Jewish concept. Jewishness is not a country or a language.'

Yariv Yaari (young kibbutz member): 'The God who is your supreme value doesn't exist for me. But you are a Jew and we are Jews; the same nation. If Rabbi Shach intended to be thought-provoking, he failed – because he spoke in slogans. As a secular person I felt no sense of guilt, but merely a sense that Shach and his people are living in the Middle Ages. He deepened the divide [between us] and no one can try to bridge it.'

Aryeh Gelber (historian and a kibbutz member): 'I reject your Judaism every bit as much as you reject mine. You have declared cultural war on us, and we will fight back.'

Rabbi Frank: 'If I had to choose between my son, God forbid, living on a kibbutz and eating unkosher food, or dying – I would rather he died. I am ready to die rather than transgress the sabbath.'

Zion Toubi (secretary of Kibbutz Maabarot): 'But where are the graveyards in which all those who proclaim "I would rather die" are buried? Our kibbutz graveyards are full of those who died in the defence of your Bnei Brak . . . [pointing at a passing helicopter]. That is a Sikorsky, like the one that ferried me to Mount Hermon when we fought for it in 1973. The haredim were sitting in their yeshiva then, and praying that we succeed.

Frank: 'And the fact is you succeeded!'

16

They Also Serve

Voting age is a moment of decision for the young Orthodox Israeli not merely in terms of his party-political preference. At eighteen, he must decide whether to become a fully fledged member of society, bearing his share of the burden, or to live, in the eyes of most Israelis, as a privileged parasite. Will he serve in the army, like everyone else? Or will he resort to the deferment scheme provided by law for yeshiva students?

Among the draftees, some fight to get into crack combat units – fewer, according to official statistics, battle doggedly to secure a comfortable desk-job for the three years of mandatory service. But everyone, except the haredi, goes in. Everyone, commando or cook, gets his basic military training, serves his stint (officers serve at least three and a half years; women serve two) – and then puts in an average of a month every year, sweating, cursing and complaining, until he is into his fifties.

It is difficult to exaggerate the importance of the army in Israeli life – and the effect, therefore, of the yeshiva deferment system in fuelling the antagonism that smoulders, never far from the surface, between the haredim and the rest of the country. It flares up in every political argument and clouds every ostensibly ideological debate. When the members of Kibbutz Mizraa, the country's largest pork producer, demonstrated in the winter of 1990 against a haredi-inspired Pig Law, their placards and chants dwelt not on the haredim's effort to dictate the nation's diet, but on their draft-dodging. That issue, unlike the ban on pigs, unites the non-haredi majority. Their resentment is always present, and impinges on every contact between the two groups.

Some 25,000 haredi men now of army age have never donned a uniform. Thousands more are now beyond army age, having deferred their service from year to year for decades. Several thousand more have spent their teens and twenties in yeshiva, emerging only after they were married with children to serve a truncated two-to-four-month stint, usually in a non-combat unit, instead of the full three years. But thereafter they do their annual reserves service along with everyone else. This latter group, if they are bearded and dress in the distinctive haredi black hat and suit, unfairly suffer the same insults and jibes on the street as the permanent deferrees. In December 1988, a number of them held a demonstration in Jerusalem, wearing their campaign ribbons and insignia, to protest at this indiscriminate discrimination.

It is probably unfair, too, to suggest that the haredi young man of eighteen has any choice to make. Most of them have been conditioned since childhood to regard deferral as the natural and automatic career option. They have no real choice, if they want to remain accepted members of the community. In haredi enclaves it is the uniformed soldier, not the black-clad yeshiva *bachur* (student), who turns heads and draws disapproving glances. At haredi weddings the question asked about the bridegroom is not 'What's he going to do?' but 'Where is he going to learn?' – at which *kollel* (yeshiva for married students) will he continue his Talmudic studies, and thus continue to defer his army call-up? Questions about career and salary are more relevant in regard to his new young wife, who will usually work as a teacher or a secretary. The kollel pays a modest stipend; the government pays child allowances and other grants; and parents are expected to help too if they can.

Yitzhak Shamir, who was prime minister from 1983 to 1984 and from 1986 to 1992, conceded in an unusually frank conversation towards the end of his term that he had 'no tolerance' for haredi draft-dodging. The Premier, whose coalitions were founded, as we have seen, on the Likud's alliance with the haredi parties, was usually careful not to give voice to his own profoundly ambivalent feelings towards haredim and haredism. A Zionist of the classical mould, Shamir brought with him to Palestine in the 1930s that spirit of rebellion against Diaspora Orthodoxy that fired much of pre-war Jewish youth in Poland.

Shamir and his wife Shulamit, who came from Bulgaria as a

young, non-Orthodox Zionist too, maintained a heartily secular lifestyle in private, but halachically impeccable practices in public. They would never be seen openly breaking the shabbat. Yet the Premier seldom went to synagogue, and clearly did not enjoy it.

But despite his caution, and worried looks from his political aide, Shamir could not contain a critical comment on the burgeoning deferral phenomenon. While he was in favour of 'tolerance' – and increased government budgets – for the haredi school system, he had 'no tolerance at all' for these schools openly educating their pupils not to serve in the army. 'But that's a special issue,' he said, sighing. 'A painful issue, a very painful issue. But I didn't innovate anything there . . .' Granted, the volume of deferrals had greatly expanded during his years as Prime Minister. 'But that's because of their growing numbers. I didn't bring in any new laws or regulations. It's expanding on the basis of the existing laws and longstanding agreements. I've done nothing to increase it.'

Shamir, in fact, even made one half-hearted stab at reducing it – and brought down on himself a hail of haredi obloquy. Visiting a *hesder* (lit. arrangement) yeshiva, where students combine Talmud study with army service over a five-year period, he let slip a remark indicating that this arrangement ought to apply, in his view, to all yeshivas. His statement won enthusiastic approval in the press, and from all parts of the political spectrum, especially the far Left and the far Right, who were both in opposition at the time to the Likud-Labour 'Government of National Unity' and could afford to anger the haredim.

It was not clear whether the Premier had actually planned to say what he said, or whether he intended to do anything about it. But if he did, he quickly withdrew in the face of the haredi fury. Rabbi Shach, speaking at his Ponevezh Yeshiva in Bnei Brak in August 1988, declared outright: 'In the event that a *gezeira* [tyrannical decree] is passed against the yeshivas, not a single yeshiva student will remain in this country; and without Torah there can be no Jewish nation . . . I am an old Jew, and I have no strength. But I say clearly: If the day comes when decrees are promulgated against the yeshiva world, I raise my hand and declare: "If I forget thee, O Jerusalem, let my right hand forget its cunning" [Psalms 137:5]. The *bnei Torah* [lit., sons of Torah – yeshiva students] will not forget the Land of Israel, but they will exile themselves from it so that the Torah will not be forgotten by the People of Israel . . .'

Yitzhak Shamir rightly insisted that he changed nothing; the rules governing yeshiva students' deferment have been in place for years. The principle was evolved during the pre-State negotiations between the founding fathers, and was applied during the War of Independence in 1948, and enshrined in law in 1949. The statutory definition was adopted from the Talmud: one 'whose Torah is his profession' was to be exempted from military service so long as that remained his situation. In the early 1950s an attempt was made to limit the deferment to four years, but this was resisted by the haredim with the then powerful support of the National Religious Party and the Chief Rabbinate. After the Likud came to power in 1977, and coopted Agudat Yisrael into its coalition, the criterion was broadened to include not only yeshiva students but teachers at yeshivas and haredi schools.

Initially, the deferment affected a few hundred men, many of them refugees from the destroyed yeshivas of Eastern Europe. David Ben-Gurion was moved by their rabbis' pleas that they must be nurtured and protected in order to preserve the last vestiges of the Talmudic heritage.

At the time, no one on the non-Orthodox side of the negotiations, and very few on the Orthodox side, foresaw the size and speed of the impending haredi renaissance, which was to centre primarily on the reconstituted yeshivas. Some of the Zionist-Socialist leaders regarded the yeshivas and indeed the whole haredi community as a quaint but doomed anachronism, or at best a living museum to a lost culture. Says Dr Zorach Warhaftig, a key NRP leader and a signatory on the 1948 Declaration of Independence: 'I don't think Ben-Gurion himself believed that Orthodoxy would fade away completely. But his wife Paula certainly did. I remember Yisrael Yeshayahu [a Labour figure of Yemenite origin who later became Speaker of the Knesset] assuring me that in twenty-five years there wouldn't be a single Yemenite in Israel who still put on tefillin.'

The veteran Agudah Knesset member Menahem Porush recalls in this connection a visit to New York in 1946 as a young journalist. Waiting outside the offices of an Orthodox Rabbis organization, Agudas Harabonim, he found himself seated alongside Rabbi Haim Meir Hager, the hasidic Rebbe of Vishnitz, then a lonely refugee. The door opened, and Porush was invited to enter. He suggested that the elderly Rabbi go in first, and the officials reluctantly agreed.

'He had come to ask their help to set up a yeshiva and housing project in Bnei Brak. When he left and I went in, they asked me: "Reb Menahem, is that guy okay in the head?" Who remembers those officials today? The Agudas Harabonim is almost defunct while the Vishnitz community in Bnei Brak is still growing and growing.' The Vishnitz Yeshiva alone accounts for hundreds of army deferrals each year.

The figure of 25,000 able-bodied deferrees is on the point of imminent, massive expansion, according to Rabbi Avraham Brun, coordinator of the hesder yeshiva network. 'The haredi baby-boom is only just beginning to reach army age in large numbers,' he says.

Brun's own organization of Zionist-Orthodox yeshivas, which started in the 1960s, is holding steady at just over 3,000 students. The students must sign up for five years, of which they spend up to two in uniform, and three in the yeshiva study-hall. All those who are medically fit to do so serve in combat units. They serve together, forming their own platoons, and thus are able to maintain some of the religious fervour and social cohesion of yeshiva life during their stints in the army.

Many hesder yeshiva graduates go on to university, and become the lawyers, doctors and engineers of whom Moshe Ishon, the editor and Zionist-Orthodox ideologue, spoke so proudly. The hesder yeshivas are also the main spiritual breeding ground of Gush Emunim, the ultra-nationalist movement that spearheads Jewish settlement-building in the occupied territories. Most of the prominent settlement rabbis and leaders are faculty members or alumni of hesder yeshivas.

Hesder soldiers have acquitted themselves well in war, and are regarded with respect in the army and by the general public. Their yeshivas are beginning, now, to turn out high-calibre Talmudic scholars on a par with the haredi yeshivas. The haredi yeshiva deans, nevertheless, consistently reject any hesder option for their own students. They have always spurned overtures from the army. They turned down even modest proposals to impart to the students the rudiments of soldiery, for use in dire national emergency. Many hesder yeshiva students, for their part, express a contempt for their haredi counterparts that is as bitter and resentful as any anti-Orthodox vituperation.

Do haredi young men go to yeshiva to dodge the draft? Or do they, as they and their rabbis maintain, defer their military service in order to enter into a no less demanding service of God, choosing a semi-cloistered existence and painfully but willingly sacrificing much of what modern life has to offer? Were the rabbis who originally negotiated the deferral scheme motivated purely by the desire to nurture their handful of refugee-students, or did their doctrinal anti-Zionism colour their insistence that their students not enlist into the army of the fledgeling Zionist State, then fighting for survival? And if the original motives were sincere, have they since been sullied by thousands of dodgers who casually aver that 'the Torah is their profession' and leave the fighting and dying to others?

The Chief Rabbi of Israel in 1948, Isaac Herzog, a passionate Zionist yet revered in haredi circles as a scholar and saintly figure, actively supported the demand that yeshiva students be exempt from army service. 'The holy yeshivas deserve a special dispensation,' Rabbi Herzog wrote to the Army Chief of Staff, 'because after the Holocaust they are the tiny remnant of the great Torah institutions . . . The very soul of the Jewish People is dependent on their existence. To require of them even partial mobilization would be to dislocate them.' At the same time, though, in a discreet dialogue with the haredi yeshiva deans, Herzog sought to persuade them that both halachically and morally the yeshiva students were duty-bound to participate in the national defence.

His pleas and arguments fell on deaf ears. Haredi rabbis contend that any dilution of the yeshiva curriculum would destroy its effectiveness. Yeshiva education, they argue, is not only an academic process. The intimate religious and social experience is an integral part of it. The yeshiva's ultimate goal is to mould bnei

Torah, men whose whole lives are dedicated to Torah study and the observance of mitzvot. Any distraction must impede the student's steady progress in acquiring 'Torah and the fear of Heaven'. They also argue that the study and prayer of the yeshiva students are as efficacious an element of the national defence as the tanks and planes of the army, and they adduce copious biblical verses and Talmudic statements to corroborate that viewpoint.

After four decades, these arguments have become part of the theology of haredism. Thus, a generation ago the question whether most yeshiva students were merely draft-dodgers would have been vividly relevant: had the draft been abolished then, the Israeli yeshivas would rapidly have emptied of a large majority of their students. Some students would have studied for a few years and then gone out into the world to earn a living. Others would not have studied at all beyond high-school age. Only a few – those with genuine academic gifts or with the ambition of becoming rabbis or dayanim – would have stayed in the yeshivas indefinitely.

Today, however, in a self-contained, self-confident haredi society, complete with deeply inculcated philosophical underpinnings to uphold and justify the deferral system on religious grounds, the distinction between draft-dodger and serious student is not so simple. The philosophy, moreover, has radiated from Israel to the Diaspora. There too young haredi men are spending long years in yeshivas and *kollelim*, far more so than a generation ago (though still far less so than in Israel).

The military deferment system has also become an integral part of the haredi community's deliberate seclusion from the general society. Yisrael Eichler, for example, editor of the Belz (a hasidic sect) weekly newspaper *Hamahane Haharedi*, assured his hasidic readers: 'Greater, even, than the obligation on a yeshiva bachur to sit and learn instead of serving in the army, is the prohibition on him to meet and talk with disgusting heretics who spread germs of abomination that poison the Jewish soul.' This was by way of reaction to a statement by the internationally acclaimed Israeli author A. B. Yehoshua, at an Orthodox-secular dialogue, that the 'basic asymmetry between haredim and others could be tolerable if the haredim would share the burden of military service.' If that obstacle were removed, a rapprochement and dialogue could follow, said Yehoshua.

'Hearing those words, from that foul mouth,' Eichler wrote, 'one's immediate reaction is: for that reason alone the present system of haredi "draft-dodging" must be maintained . . . In order to prevent any such rapprochement or dialogue with an enemy like Yehoshua, the situation must remain unchanged.'

Economics are also plainly a critical factor in the growth of the yeshivas. Before the Holocaust, young haredim could not afford to spend years in yeshivas even if they wanted to. Today, yeshivas enjoy a volume of haredi philanthropy probably unprecedented in Jewish history. The Israeli yeshivas moreover enjoy massive State support, ensured by the political power of the haredi parties. Haredi families have managed – thus far – to enable potential breadwinners to remain unproductive long into adult life.

Still, young kollel men living in poky flats with half-a-dozen children, and whose wives work long days in schools or offices while they study in the yeshiva, would do better, in material terms, to serve their truncated army stint and then go on to build a career. That they do not do so is attributable, in their own minds, solely to their religious convictions. Non-haredi critics – including the Zionist-Orthodox – cite the haredi process of conditioning, the pervasive non-identification with the Zionist State, and plain cowardice as additional factors. Since there can be no empirical determinants, the relative weight to be attributed to each of these factors is ultimately a matter of opinion. (Haredim are quick to argue that an anti-haredi opinion is attributable to anti-haredi conditioning.)

Dr Yossi Beilin MK, a rising Labour Party figure, is unequivocal. 'The whole society,' he says, 'is centred around army deferment. That is the central theme.' Nor does he accept the thesis that by now draft-dodging has been sublimated into dogma. 'They're all aware of it,' he insists. 'A lot of the so-called "yeshiva world" is artificial. If there were no draft, there would no longer be a "yeshiva world" in anything like these present proportions, a whole society in which virtually every haredi boy becomes a yeshiva bachur. Not a single one is turned away, no matter how unsuitable he might be. If he can't get into a good yeshiva, he tries for a weaker one. If he fails again, he looks for a place with even lower standards. But eventually everyone finds somewhere. It is unprecedented in Jewish history.

'But at the rate they're growing,' Beilin adds, 'there's bound to be an explosion. Israeli society won't stand for it forever.'

The issue of national service for women, on the other hand, has long ceased stirring controversy in Israeli society. In the early years of the State it provoked the most divisive and violent conflicts of all between the haredim and the rest. The leading haredi rabbis instructed girls to prefer prison, or even death, rather than succumb to army enlistment. In a Knesset debate in August 1949, the Agudat Yisrael leader, Yitzhak Meir Levin, assured the House there would be 'many parents who will obey that ruling literally, and will resist by force'.

David Ben-Gurion, who was Defence Minister as well as Prime Minister, backed off, and the law that was eventually enacted provided exemptions for women on grounds of 'conscience and religious belief'. For several years thereafter, however, pitched battles were fought, in the Knesset and in the streets, over the government's efforts to recruit Orthodox girls for some form of compulsory civilian work instead of army service. This proposal drove a wedge between the Zionist-Orthodox, who were inclined to accept it under certain conditions, and the haredim, who continued to threaten violence and civil disobedience.

The leading haredi rabbi of the day, Rabbi Avraham Yeshayahu Karelitz, known as 'the Hazon Ish' (lit., 'The Vision of a Man') after the title of his multi-volume halachic opus,* ruled that any form of national service for girls was 'totally forbidden'. Four other prominent rabbis issued a 'call to the daughters of Israel: We order you in the name of the Torah to stand and fight for your lives against those who would snatch you away to make you unclean.' In 1953 the Hazon Ish tried without success to persuade the National Religious Party ministers to resign over this issue, as

* Often, the title of a scholarly work hints at the name of its author. Thus, the word 'Ish', meaning man, is also an acrostic for Avraham Yeshayahu, so the title also means 'The Vision of Avraham Yeshayahu'.

Agudah's Levin had resigned. In the event, though, a civilian service law passed at that time remained a dead letter, and Orthodox girls have never been compulsorily recruited for any form of service.

In practice today, only 60 per cent of girls enlist in the army. Of the remainder, some make the legal declaration before a beit din that their religious convictions prevent them from serving, while others are excused for a variety of reasons. More than 3,000 girls each year from the Zionist-Orthodox community, having made the declaration, join a countrywide Orthodox volunteer network, serving for one or two years as teachers in outlying villages, paramedics in hospitals, or youth workers in disadvantaged neighbourhoods. Other Zionist-Orthodox girls enlist in the army to serve as soldier-teachers at Orthodox boarding schools or as soldier-farmers on NRP-affiliated kibbutzim.

Haredi girls spurn all of these alternatives. Haredi men revile and reject them too, which means that the age of eighteen is a decisive watershed for any Orthodox Israeli woman in terms of her future marriage prospects. By choosing the army, she effectively precludes any thought she might have had of marrying a haredi yeshiva student. Even some hesder students – especially those contemplating a career in the rabbinate or in religious education – will look askance at a girl who chose the army, and will prefer a voluntary service graduate. By the same token, though – such are the subtle but distinct gradations within Orthodoxy – a hesder alumnus will prefer a wife who has served the country rather than one who took the 'easy' (haredi) way out and did nothing.

For the young haredi woman, as for her male counterpart, arguably there is no real choice: her school and home have conditioned her to regard all the available forms of service as forms of sin. Making the declaration is an automatic act, part of growing up. It occasions no particular soul-searching among the students at haredi high schools for girls.

On the non-Orthodox side, the issue is no longer controversial because the army does not in fact need all the girls who join up, and finds it hard to provide them with useful jobs during their two-year stints. Moreover – in contrast to the War of Independence, when women fought alongside men – the army's policy for many years now has been not to expose women soldiers to danger, in combat or even in training. Hence the haredi girls' opting out does not trigger any of the resentment caused by the yeshiva students' unwillingness to share the burden and the risk of soldiering. Moreover, many of the haredi girls marry young, which automatically exempts them from army service.

There is also, in this less idealistic but more hedonistic age, a recognition among the wider Israeli public that army life is generally unsuitable for haredi young women who come from sheltered backgrounds and attended single-sex schools, and for whom the loss of virginity before marriage is both a wicked and a tragic event.

17

Holocaust Indictments

For many Jews, the Holocaust provided incontrovertible vindication – alas too late – of the Zionist thesis. It proved that antisemitism is endemic, at least in Christian European society, and that the Jews need a country of their own, at least as a refuge when all other avenues are closed to them. The starkness of that lesson helped persuade the world to support the creation of the State of Israel after the Second World War. And Israel for its part, long since grown powerful and controversial, still takes care not to let the lesson fade. Every official visit to the Jewish State begins at the Yad Vashem Holocaust Memorial in Jerusalem, where the foreign dignitary lays a wreath in memory of Hitler's six million Jewish victims.

For American Jewry, the lesson took longer to sink in. At first there was denial and suppressed guilt over what had happened in 'the old countries', and a lingering scepticism over the viability of the Zionist solution. It was the trauma and victory of the Six Day War in 1967 that sealed the bond between the Holocaust and the State of Israel in the Diaspora mind.

'In May and June of 1967,' one writer recalled, 'the Holocaust was on almost every American Jew's mind; the result was an outpouring of emotion unlike anything they had ever experienced.' Religious thinker Abraham Joshua Heschel wrote soon after the war: 'Many of us felt that our own lives were in the balance, and not only the lives of those who dwelt in the land; that indeed all of the Bible, all of Jewish history was at stake . . . The world that was silent while six million died was silent again, save for individual friends. The anxiety was gruelling, the isolation was dreadful.'

That experience released wellsprings of ethnic feeling and identity that many American Jews had kept bottled up in the post-immigration decades of determined acculturation. The era was one of awakening particularism among other groups too. But for the Jews of America, in the words of Jacob Neusner, their re-ethnicization 'could not have taken the form that it did – a powerful identification with the state of Israel as the answer to the question of the Holocaust – without a single, catalytic event . . . the 1967 war.'*

One of Jewry's leading philosophers, Emil Fackenheim, has endowed survivalism with theological dignity. 'What does the Voice of Auschwitz command?' he asks. 'Jews are forbidden to hand Hitler posthumous victories. Jews are commanded to survive as Jews, lest the Jewish People perish . . . The commanding Voice of Auschwitz singles Jews out . . . It was this Voice which was heard by the Jews of Israel in May and June 1967 when they refused to lie down and be slaughtered.'†

Some liberal critics, though, like writer Leonard Fein, have attacked this 'obsession' as 'self-defeating', a reflection of 'both confusion and shallowness'.

For the haredim, not only was the Holocaust no vindication of Zionism; it has become a vindication of their anti-Zionism. This is all the more difficult for others to comprehend since the haredim, proportionally, suffered much greater destruction in the Holocaust than non-Orthodox Jews; they comprised a substantially higher percentage of those communities that were wiped out than of those (in America, Palestine and elsewhere) that survived. Moreover, the haredim have benefited the most from what Neusner calls the 're-ethnicization' of American Jewry brought on by a belated readiness to grapple with the Holocaust. This re-focusing on Jewish particularity has helped the haredim become less self-conscious. It has enhanced their ability to retain their younger generation and to attract others to their fold. Haredism has also benefited from a parallel development in Israel: the growing capacity of second- and third-generation Israelis to deal with the Holocaust and with pre-

* Jacob Neusner, *Israel in America* (Boston: Beacon Press 1985), p. 114.
† Emil L. Fackenheim, *God's Presence in History* (New York: Harper Torchbooks 1972), p. 84.

Holocaust European Jewish life, unencumbered by the dogmatic 'rejection of the Diaspora' preached by Israel's founding fathers.

Nevertheless, the extraordinary fact is that the Holocaust and its effect on surviving Jewry changed nothing in haredism's profound opposition to the Zionist solution of 'the Jewish problem'. In the immediate aftermath of the tragedy there were, as we have seen, certain tentative signs of reassessment among some haredi survivors. But as haredi communities grew in size and assertiveness, they resumed the condemnatory attitude that had been adopted by their pre-war leaders – many of whom died in the Holocaust – to political Zionism.

One such leader who survived, the hasidic Rebbe of Satmar, Rabbi Yoel Teitelbaum (1887–1979), wrote from his post-war refuge in Williamsburg, New York, that the existence of the Zionist Movement had in fact been a primary *cause* of the Holocaust. God's wrath had been kindled against the Jews because they had sought to recover their Land and their sovereignty before His good time. After the 1967 war, he produced a second book reiterating his thesis, to disabuse anyone who might have been misled into seeing Israel's victory as a sign of God's approval.

Rabbi Teitelbaum, both before the Second World War and after, was considered an extremist even by the haredim. But this was largely due to his refusal to join with the mainstream haredi leadership in the Agudat Yisrael movement rather than to any radical ideological differences over the rights and wrongs of Zionism.

Haredi rabbis between the two world wars advised their followers not to emigrate from Europe to Israel (British-ruled Palestine as it then was), despite rising antisemitism throughout Eastern and Central Europe, and despite the looming threat of Hitler. No other country was prepared to admit large numbers of Jewish refugees. Granted, not all haredi rabbis opposed *aliyah* (lit. ascent; immigration to Israel). And those who did oppose it were not always consistent; they did not recommend their views to all of their followers at all times. The Zionist leadership, moreover, was not generously disposed towards the haredim in the disbursement of the limited number of immigration certificates made available by the British.

In the late 1930s, when the situation had become desperate, the British authorities closed the gates of Palestine almost completely, in response to Arab political pressure. Yet even in the Nazi ghettos and death camps most haredim refused to condemn or criticize their rabbis, or even admit that they had been mistaken. A bitter controversy over the rabbis' role has raged in Jewry ever since, and it accounts in large part for the poignant but often perverse complexity that characterizes the haredi attitude to the Holocaust.

'Who exactly are these heads of yeshivas and rabbis who supposedly ruled against emigrating to Eretz Yisrael [the Land of Israel]?' ask the authors of a recent major haredi work on Holocaust history and theology.* 'Agudas Yisrael was the generally recognized organization representing the anti-Zionist element of the Orthodox public prior to the Holocaust. But all the recognized leaders of Agudas Yisrael were themselves preparing before the War to emigrate to Eretz Yisrael.'

Of the three important leaders mentioned in this context, Rabbi Yisrael Meir Kagan ('the Hafetz Haim') died in 1933 at the age of ninety; Rabbi Elchanan Wasserman heroically returned from the US to Europe after war broke out, to die with his yeshiva students; and the hasidic Rebbe of Ger, Avraham Mordechai Alter, announced in Jerusalem in 1936 that he had moved permanently to Eretz Yisrael, only to succumb to his hasidim's pressures and return, several months later, to Poland.

The book, the first such comprehensive study to be published in English, argues that the fact that these leaders did not succeed in reaching Eretz Yisrael 'only underscores the almost insurmountable obstacles that stood in the way of aliyah – the same obstacles which prevented a great number of Zionists from realizing their aspirations as well.'

Scores of other revered rabbis, however, did expressly discourage aliyah, a fact that the book denies with some deft casuistry: 'A decisive majority of Torah sages did not take such a stand. The widespread misconception to the contrary is most likely due to popular confusion between the battle against Zionism with an

* Rabbi Yoel Schwartz and Yitzhak Goldstein, *Shoah – A Jewish Perspective on Tragedy in the Context of the Holocaust* (New York: ArtScroll/Mesorah 1990).

imagined battle against emigration to Israel.' But compare the Warsaw Ghetto diarist, Rabbi Shimon Huberband (1909–42): 'The Rebbe of Ger, like the majority of Polish rebbes, opposed settlement in Eretz Yisrael. If the Rebbe of Ger had ordered his hasidim, among whom were thousands of very rich industrialists, to make aliyah to Eretz Yisrael, the situation of the Jewish communities both of Eretz Yisrael and of Poland would have been different . . .'

The Rebbe of Ger, it should be noted moreover, was the most favourably disposed – or at least the most ambivalent – of all the major haredi leaders towards the Zionist settlement of Palestine. The haredi leaders in Galician Poland and Hungary were, as a rule, more extreme than the hasidic rabbis of central Poland (Ger was near Warsaw) in excoriating the entire enterprise. The sad facts are all the sadder when it is recalled that virtually all pre-Zionist aliyah to Eretz Yisrael – there was a steady trickle from Europe throughout the previous century – comprised haredim, rabbis and followers, whose piety impelled them to live and die in the holy land.

But once the non-Orthodox – and, to be fair, in many cases anti-Orthodox – Zionists took control of Jewish life in Palestine, the haredi leadership, by and large, developed reservations towards aliyah along the lines of their earlier vigorous reservations towards emigration to America. Materialistic, liberty-loving America spelt secularization to the leading haredi rabbis at the turn of the century; it is no accident that hardly any of them followed the millions of their co-religionists who were streaming across the Atlantic. Zionist Palestine spelt outright rebellion against the old religious order. Traditional religious love of Zion was superseded among the haredim by loathing for the Zionists. The historic opportunity presented by the Balfour Declaration of 1917 was not understood, and was consequently missed, by the haredi rabbis as by most of the rest of the Jews of Europe. By the late 1930s, barely half a million Jews had settled in 'the Jewish National Home in Palestine'.

Haredism blames Zionism for the Holocaust on three counts. The metaphysical charge sheet, as we have seen, was drawn up by the Satmarer Rebbe: the Zionists presumed 'to hasten the End';

1. Rabbi Eliezer Menachem Shach addressing an audience in Jerusalem.

2. Rabbi Menachem Mendel Schneerson (centre) watching a parade of his hasidim in New York.

3. Rabbi Ovadia Yosef, spiritual leader of the Sephardic or Oriental haredim.

4. The Gerer Rebbe, Rabbi Pinhas Menachem Alter.

5. A tish or festive meal at the modest 'court' of the Karliner-Pinsker Rebbe, Rabbi Aharon Rosenfeld, in the Mea Shearim quarter of Jerusalem.

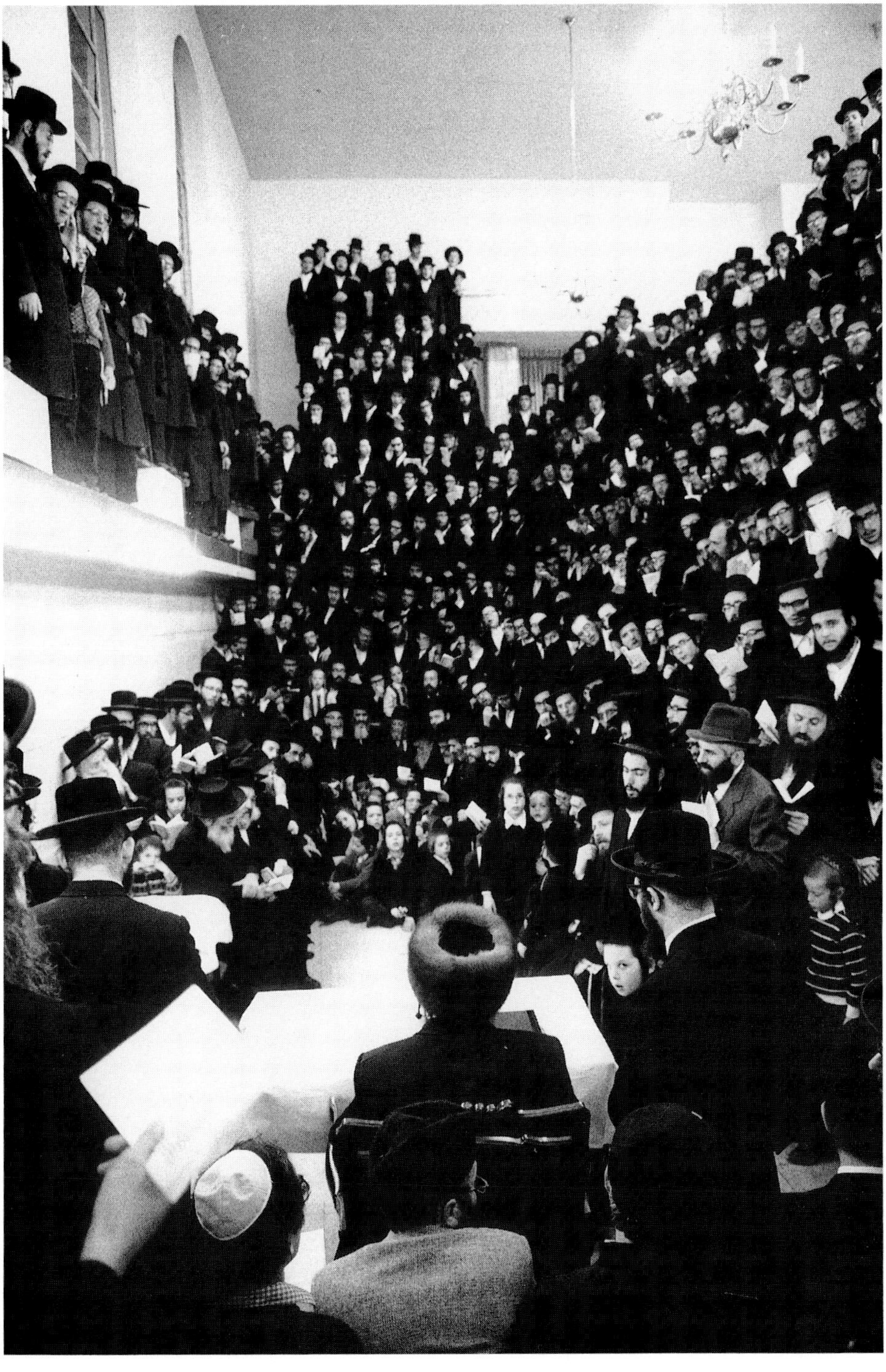

6. The Belzer Rebbe, Rabbi Yissachar Dov Rokeach, at his tish in Jerusalem.

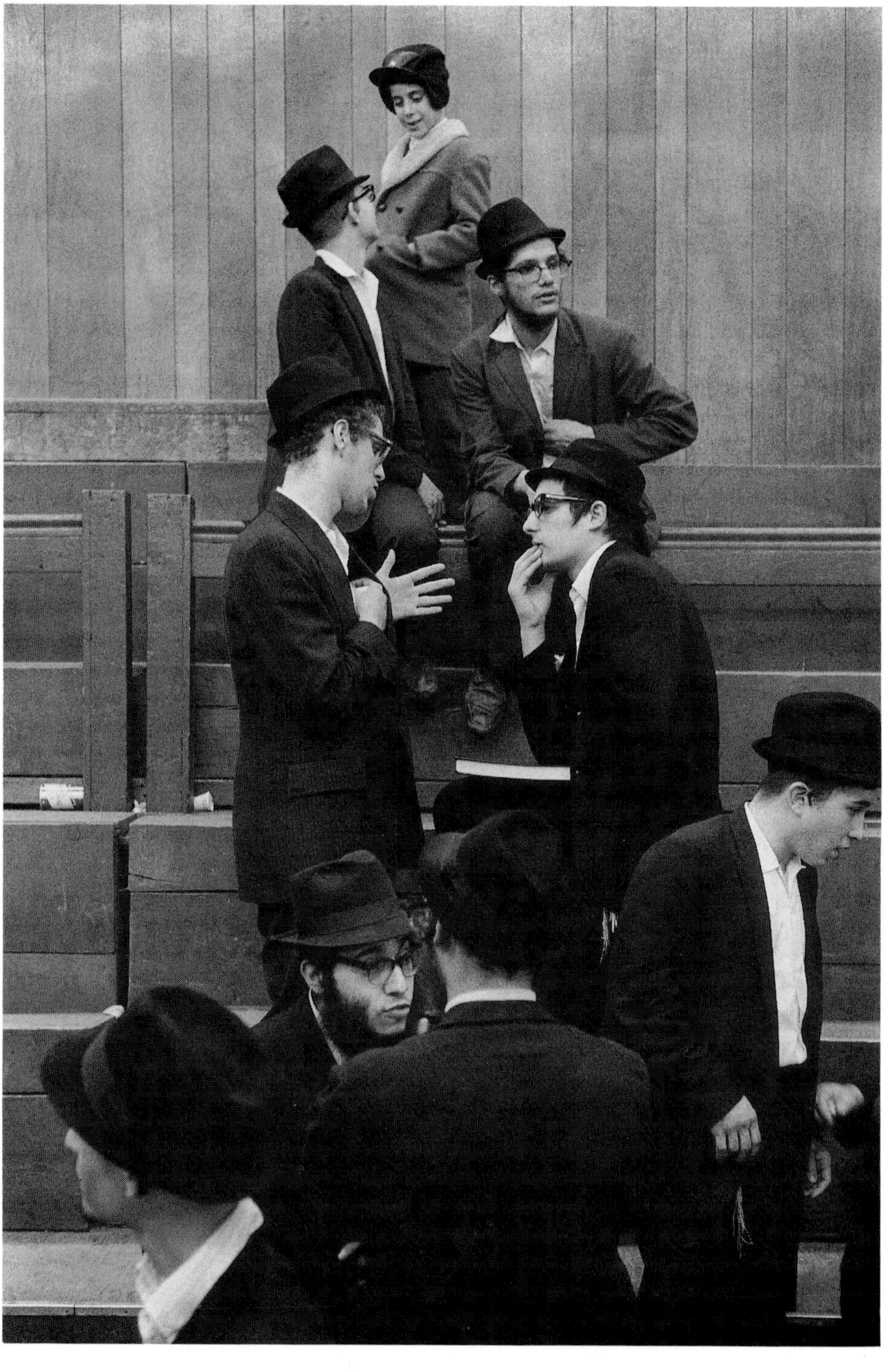

7. After the Rebbe's sermon: Lubavitcher yeshiva students at the movement's headquarters in New York.

8. First haircut, at the age of three.

9. Boys at the Belzer 'court'.

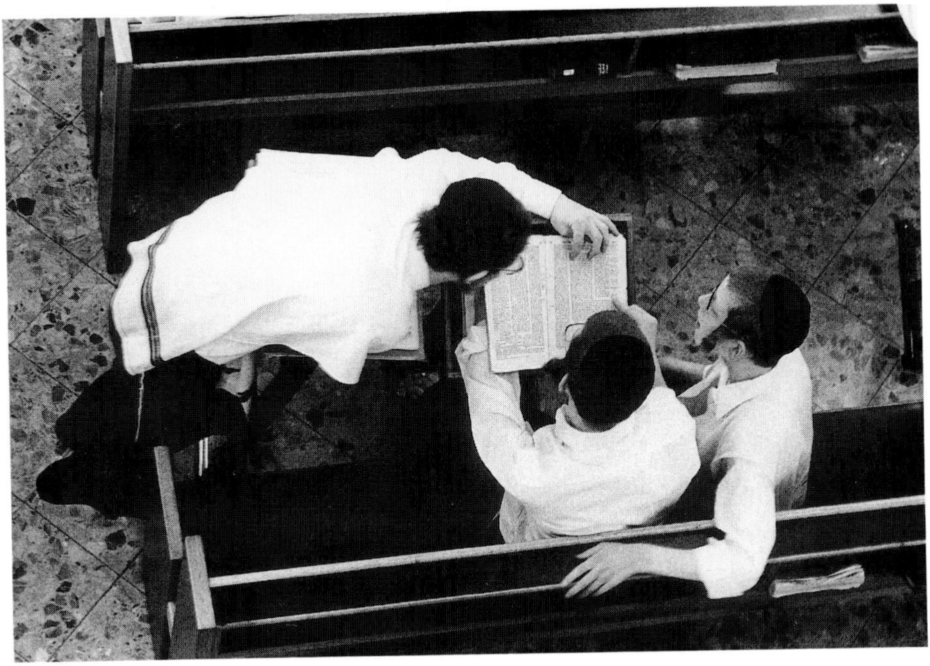

10. Yeshiva study: the core of haredi life.

11. Gerer yeshiva students in the Israeli town of Ashdod.

12. Stamford Hill, London: the telephone lines are connected to the live broadcasts of the Lubavitcher Rebbe in New York.

13. Stamford Hill.

14. Dancing at the Yeshivat Hamatmidim in Jerusalem on the festival of Lag Baomer.

15. Baking matzas for Passover. Many haredim will only eat hand-baked matzas during the week-long festival.

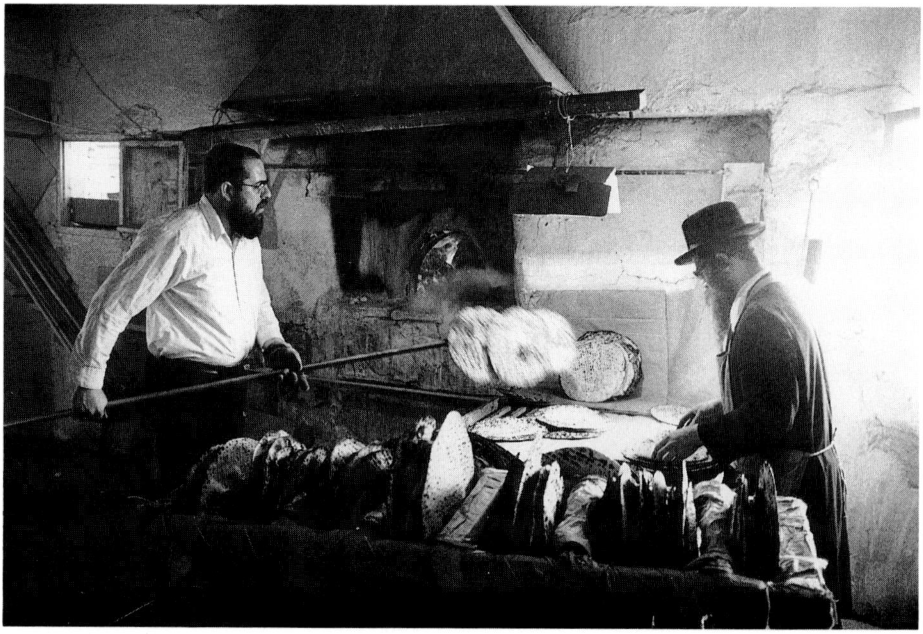

16. Cost-price supermarkets like this one in Jerusalem help haredi families to make ends meet.

17. A mikva or ritual bath in New York's Lower East Side. The child in her father's arms is converting to Judaism.

18. A hasidic bride, on her 'throne', receiving well-wishers.

19. In a Paris butcher's shop on the eve of Yom Kippur, the Day of Atonement, a hasid performing the rite of *kappara* or forgiveness. The live chicken is swung around the head in a symbolic transfer of guilt from the penitent to the bird. The chicken is then slaughtered and donated to a poor family for the pre-fast meal.

20. Priestly blessing at the Western Wall in Jerusalem during Passover. The *cohanim* or priests cover their heads with their prayer-shawls while reciting the blessing.

therefore God took terrible revenge on the whole nation. Another leading post-war American sage levelled a purportedly historical accusation against Zionism, while a third laid grave personal indictments against individual members of the Zionist wartime leadership.

The 'historical' accusation against Zionism was advanced by Rabbi Yitzhak Hutner, who was dean of the large Rabbi Chaim Berlin yeshiva in New York and greatly revered in haredi circles. 'In 1923,' he writes, 'Hitler wrote *Mein Kampf* . . . This was read by Haj Amin el-Husseini, the Grand Mufti of Jerusalem, who joined with Hitler to found one of the most significant alliances of modern times [*sic*]. There is ample documentation that not only did the Mufti visit Hitler . . . but indeed with Adolph Eichmann he visited the Auschwitz gas chamber incognito to check on its efficiency.'*

There is indeed ample evidence that el-Husseini, the leader of the Palestinian Arabs, enthusiastically supported Hitler and hoped the 'final solution' would succeed in Europe, and take care of the Jews of Palestine too. But Hutner goes on to *blame* the Zionists not only for el-Husseini's hopes, but also for the fact that Hitler realized them. 'It should be manifest,' he writes, 'that until the great public pressures for the establishment of a Jewish state, the Mufti had no interest in the Jews of Warsaw, Budapest or Vilna . . . Once the looming reality of the State of Israel was before him, the Mufti spared no effort at influencing Hitler to murder as many Jews as possible . . . This shameful episode, where the founder and early leaders of the State were clearly a factor in the destruction of many Jews, has been completely suppressed and expunged from the record.'

It was to divert attention from 'its own contribution to the final catastrophic events,' according to Rabbi Hutner, that 'those in the State in a position to influence public opinion circulated the notorious canard that Gedolei Yisrael [Great Men of Israel] were

* Rabbi Yitzhak Hutner, 'Holocaust – A Rosh Yeshiva's Response', talk originally published in *The Jewish Observer*, October 1977, and included in Rabbi Nisson Wolpin (ed.), *A Path Through the Ashes* (New York: ArtScroll 1986), pp. 39–55.

responsible for the destruction of many communities because they did not urge emigration.'

The same tendency to polemical extremism is apparent in the haredim's historical treatment of the ghetto uprisings, in Warsaw, Bialystok and other towns, which inevitably ended in failure and brutal suppression. Here the initial manifestation of tortured historiography appeared on the Zionist side. The State of Israel proclaimed the date of the Warsaw uprising as its annual Holocaust memorial day, dubbing it 'The Day of Holocaust and Heroism'. The choice of date and title implied that the handful of ghetto fighters and partisans, mostly Zionists and socialists, represented all the Jewish heroism in the Holocaust. As though the faith, humanity and dignity of so many others, even at the entrance to the gas chambers, were not heroism of a no less noble kind.

The young Zionist State was profoundly embarrassed by the 'sheep to the slaughter' image of European Jewry, by the way the victims had 'cooperated' in their own destruction, setting up 'Judenrats' (Jewish councils) to organize slave labour and eventual deportation. It took the national poet, Natan Alterman, to explain, in a controversial work originally written in 1960,* that the moral considerations of the Judenrat leaders were weighty and not necessarily despicable or dishonourable: the leaders sought to preserve as many lives as possible for as long as possible. The ghetto fighters, on the other hand, by launching their inevitably hopeless uprisings, may well have shortened whatever chances the ghetto inmates had. They, too, had to weigh up heavy moral questions, Alterman wrote. Some might have been more motivated, he suggested, by the urge to fight the fascists than by the need to save Jewish lives.

But while Alterman sought to redress the balance, the haredim in their anti-Zionist zeal distort it in the other direction. Their Holocaust literature plays down the roles of some haredi rabbis (Rabbi Menahem Zemba of Warsaw is the outstanding example) in actively supporting the Zionist-led ghetto uprisings. The Agudat Yisrael leader in wartime Palestine, Rabbi Moshe Blau, referred to

* Natan Alterman, *Al Shtei Hadrachim*, ed. Dan Laor (Tel Aviv: Hakibbutz Hameuchad Publishing House 1979).

such rabbis as 'individuals who were misled or else forced to act as they did'. Blau further accused the ghetto fighters of 'hastening their own deaths and the deaths of hundreds of thousands of others'. For him, the rebellion betrayed a 'lack of heroism, a lack of capacity to live and suffer'.

Values like honour and national pride are brushed aside as 'non-Jewish' by Blau and by post-war haredi writers. Thus, an article in the haredi newspaper *Yated Ne'eman* on Alterman's position is tendentiously headlined: 'The ghetto rebels forced suicide upon the ghetto inmates, and denied them the chance of being saved in the concentration camps.' Blau and the later haredi writers similarly ignore or downplay the reported decision by Rabbi Zemba and two other rabbis who survived in the ghetto until near the end, to reject an offer of personal asylum from local dignitaries of the Roman Catholic Church.* 'We know,' said Rabbi David Shapiro, 'that we cannot help our community in any way. But the very fact that we do not leave them, that we stay with them, may give them some encouragement. I cannot leave these people.' Rabbi Zemba delivered their reply: 'We have nothing to discuss.'

Perhaps the most telling example of haredi Holocaust historiography is the extensive (and still growing) 'miracle' literature, in which the escape stories of rabbis and yeshiva students are recounted in language of wonderment and gratitude at the divine intervention on behalf of these righteous men. Virtually every hasidic sect whose rebbe managed to flee has published an account of the episode, usually entitled 'The Miracle of the Salvation of . . .' Several mitnaged yeshivas whose students and faculty escaped from Lithuania through Siberia, China and Japan, and eventually relocated in America or Israel, have also contributed to this special genre of haredi literature.

These works, carefully compiled and edited, consistently omit any treatment of the issues that, to a non-haredi reader, cry out for consideration. They gloss over the failure of their heroes to understand the threat earlier, and to emigrate and urge their

* The incident is cited by Gideon Hausner, the Israeli State Attorney who prosecuted Eichmann, in his preface to Rabbi Shimon Huberband's diaries of the Warsaw Ghetto, *Kiddush Hashem: Jewish Religious and Cultural Life in Poland During the Holocaust* (New York: Yeshiva University Press/Ktav 1987).

followers to emigrate while there was still time. The failure is compounded because haredi rabbis – unlike Zionist leaders or any other non-Orthodox leaders – had it in their power to command their followers to emigrate, and to be obeyed. Haredism, moreover, posits as a fundamental tenet that great rabbis are endowed with prescience. In fact, haredi authors go to exegetical lengths to prove from the writings of Rabbi Meir Simcha Hacohen of Dvinsk (d. 1927), of Rabbi Wasserman and others that they knew, or at least felt, what was going to befall the Jewish People.

The 'miracle' books ignore the fact that several of the leading figures (the Rebbe of Ger, the Rebbe of Belz and the Rebbe of Satmar were among the best-known) agreed to be smuggled out of occupied Europe (usually with massive monetary and political help from the outside) while leaving other members of their families, and their followers, behind. They ignore, too, the obvious questions such conduct would seem to pose regarding these leaders' leadership. Yet the haredi literature is unanimous in praising Rabbi Wasserman for going back voluntarily to be with his yeshiva at its time of supreme agony.

Finally, and typically, the 'miracle' literature uniformly underplays the roles of non-haredim, especially Zionists, in aiding the escape of several of the haredi rabbis and yeshivas. Zorach Warhaftig, a Polish Orthodox-Zionist leader who was later to become an Israeli minister, was instrumental in the eleventh-hour flight of several rabbis and hundreds of their students from Soviet-occupied Lithuania to the Far East, before the Germans marched in. He gets scarcely a mention in the haredi books.

The haredim argue that the rabbis who saved themselves were thinking of their responsibility for the Jewish future: they fled in order to reconstitute their yeshivas and congregations. And they point out that most of the hasidim who were left behind would gladly have agreed to give their lives so that their rebbe should be saved.

There is scant evidence – though there is some – of resentment among the faithful. An Israeli researcher cites the written testimony of a Jewish gas-chamber attendant (*Sonderkommando*), who himself later perished at Auschwitz, describing a noted hasidic rebbitzin railing against the Belzer and other rebbes. They 'always calmed the people' instead of telling them to emigrate, Rebbitzin Chaya Halberstam of Stropkov noted bitterly as she walked to her death. 'Heaven concealed the truth from them. But they themselves fled to Eretz Yisrael at the last moment. They saved themselves, and left the people like sheep to be slaughtered. In my final minutes of life, I implore You, Forgive them for their great defilement of Your Holy Name.'*

But a more representative account of haredi sentiment is probably that of Hanina Shiff, now of Jerusalem, who is the *gabbai* ('chamberlain') of the Gerer hasidic court. 'God forbid,' he says, 'that we should have been resentful [that the Rebbe had escaped]. On the contrary.' Other haredi survivors recall feeling pleased and relieved to learn that their rebbe had escaped.

Shiff suffered the horrors of Treblinka and Auschwitz as a teenager. The youngsters were strengthened, he says, by older hasidim who would recount stories of rebbes. Criticism of the Rebbe of Ger for not encouraging emigration? Absolutely not, he says. 'Firstly, the Rebbe did send some people to Palestine. It was hard to make a living here. Anyway, what was was from Heaven.'

Revealingly, though, Shiff recalled that the then Rebbe's son and successor, Rabbi Yisrael Alter, who fled with his father and other relatives, but left his wife, children and grandchildren in Warsaw, 'didn't want to listen to our stories. He was like a father and mother to us [after the war. But] he couldn't bear to hear. He would turn to something else. It was too painful for him.'

Much more disturbing to historians and laymen alike than Rabbi Hutner's 'historical' accusation are the personal indictments levelled by Rabbi Michael Ber Weissmandel, a haredi leader of

* The same Sonderkommando, who may himself have been a rabbi, recorded, too, the last moments of the hasidic Rebbe of Boyan-Cracow, Rabbi Moshe Friedman. Standing naked amid his followers, he grabbed the lapel of a German officer. 'The Jewish People will never die,' he proclaimed. 'It will live for ever, and our blood will not rest until terrible vengeance has been wrought upon the bestial German nation.' Then he put on his hat and led the Jews in reciting the sacred affirmation of faith, 'Hear O Israel'. 'They were all imbued with the loftiest spiritual purity,' the diarist attested. Rebbitzin Halberstam and Rabbi Friedman are quoted in Mendel Piekarz, *Ideological Trends of Hasidism in Poland During the Interwar Period and the Holocaust* (Jerusalem: Bialik Institute 1990), pp. 412ff.

Slovakian Jewry, against Zionist emissaries in neutral Switzerland and Turkey, and against the Zionist establishment in Jerusalem and New York.

Weissmandel, a young scholar and communal leader, claimed that he, together with several other (non-haredi) Jewish leaders in Bratislava, had succeeded in stopping the deportations of Slovakian Jews to the death camps in the summer of 1942 by paying $50,000 to a senior SS officer. The Bratislava 'working group' had to beg, cajole and threaten in order to raise that sum from Western Jewish organizations. But their pleas fell on deaf ears when they subsequently urged, in innumerable cables and letters addressed to Jewish and Zionist officials, that this money-for-blood arrangement could be applied elsewhere to save Jews still alive in the Axis-occupied lands from the gas-chambers.

In a bitterly accusatory book* published after the war, Weissmandel recalled how one Zionist emissary had responded to his 'Europe Plan' by assuring the working group that the reports of Nazi atrocities in Poland were 'exaggerated in the way of *Ostjuden* [Jews from the East].' This emissary wrote to the Bratislava Jewish leaders, according to Weissmandel, that 'only with blood will we have a State.' He contended that it was 'a hutzpah for Jews to expect the Allies to grant permission to transfer money to the enemy.'

'How could we dream,' wrote Weissmandel later, 'that the nationalist Zionist would come and say: Your blood is the easier side; shed it happily, for with it we shall purchase the more important side – the Land.' In the event, the deportations in Slovakia itself resumed in 1944. Weissmandel survived by jumping off a train en route to the death camps.

Historians are divided as to whether the working group's original payment was indeed the cause of the two-year suspension in the liquidation of Slovakian Jewry. But they are united in their respect for Weissmandel as a leader, a visionary, and the victim of tragic frustration that left him a broken and bitter man. Prof.

* Rabbi Michael Dov Ber Weissmandel, *Min Hameitzar* (Jerusalem: Zeirei Agudat Yisrael 1960). See also Abraham Fuchs, *The Unheeded Cry* (New York: ArtScroll/Mesorah 1968).

Yehuda Bauer, an eminent Israeli Holocaust historian, records how Weissmandel conveyed to Jewish leaders abroad detailed maps of Auschwitz and precise timetables of the death-trains to the camp, in a desperate, futile effort to help persuade Roosevelt and Churchill to bomb the Nazi murder machine.

Some students of the period see in Weissmandel's story an example of the certain streak of callousness that permeated the Zionist establishment, in Palestine and in the US, in their rescue efforts during the war. Some discern outright antipathy towards the haredi (anti-Zionist) victims of Hitler. Certainly the Zionists' undeviating dedication to achieving their political goals *after* the war, coupled with their deep ambivalence towards the Eastern European Diaspora, sometimes generated impatience or even indifference towards the victims.

It is not at all clear, though, that the Zionist and Western Jewish organizations had as much influence as the haredim ascribe to them. Nevertheless, the haredi grievance over real and perceived instances of insensitivity or outright discrimination is deep. It is propagated with conviction, moreover, by educators and apologists throughout the haredi world. Every haredi yeshiva student knows of Weissmandel and his book (though not many have actually read it). Every one of them believes axiomatically that the Zionists turned their backs on the suffering Jews of Europe, and especially on the haredim amongst them.

In this, according to haredi thinking, the Zionists were behaving true to form, because Zionists were essentially godless Jews who had rebelled against their own faith and their people's divine destiny. Zionism was a product of Modernity, along with Reform Judaism, socialism, and assimilation. These were the scourges of our age, the causes of our suffering. The three indictments of the role of Zionism – the metaphysical, the historical and the personal – have been subsumed in haredi thought into a broader condemnation of secularism, indeed of Modernity itself, as the underlying 'reason' for the deaths of six million Jews. Lusting after Modernity was the sin, Holocaust the punishment.

The doctrine that Jewish sin causes Jewish suffering is rooted in the Torah itself. Deuteronomy 28:15 warns, for instance: 'If thou wilt not hearken unto the voice of the Lord thy God, to observe all his commandments and his statutes . . . then all these curses shall come upon thee and overtake thee.' 'Because of our sins,' says the festival prayer-book, 'we were exiled from our Land.' When private tragedy strikes, the Talmud advises the individual to 'search his deeds'. When an entire community is hit by disaster, the rabbis decree fast-days and penances.

Accordingly, the Holocaust, representing suffering on an unprecedented scale, was attributed to heinous sin. 'How terrible is the situation of our people,' wrote the Rabbi of Vilna (Vilnius), Rabbi Chaim Ozer Grodzinsky, in the summer of 1939.

> The whole Jewish People drowns in rivers of blood and seas of tears. In the Western countries, the Reform Movement has struck at the roots, and from there [i.e. Germany] the evil has gone forth now, to pursue them with wrath, to destroy them and expunge them. They [i.e. the non-Orthodox] have caused the poison of hatred against our people to spread to other lands as well.
>
> Despite all this, the people have not yet understood of why they are so persecuted; they have been struck with blindness . . .*

Rabbi Grodzinsky died before the Nazis destroyed his community. Another noted haredi thinker who fled Europe in time, wrote in England soon after the Holocaust that the monumental sin worthy of 'the awful destruction which has descended upon our generation' was the Jewish People's failure to respond religiously to the Emancipation. Rabbi Eliahu Dessler wrote:

> It is clear that the era of the Emancipation was given to us by God to serve as a time for preparation for the coming of Moshiach. To this end, the yoke of exile was eased from upon us . . . But we used the situation to mix with the Gentiles and imitate them.
>
> The process of assimilation has been progressing at an ever-quickening rate for a long time, and yet the disaster has not overtaken us until now. This is because the Holy One Blessed Be He delays his anger. He does not punish until we have

* Rabbi Chaim Ozer Grodzinsky, *Achiezer*, vol. III (Vilna 1939), Introduction.

reached the limit and there is no longer hope that kindness will lead to improvement.*

Rabbi Hutner, a multi-faceted figure who studied philosophy in Berlin as well as Talmud in the yeshivas of Lithuania, interprets the Holocaust as the culmination of Jewry's 'Era of Disappointment' in which all its misplaced hopes and expectations from the Emancipation, liberalism and Modernity were dashed. 'From trust in the Gentile world, the Jewish nation was cruelly brought to a repudiation of that trust . . . Disappointment in the non-Jewish world was deeply imprinted upon the Jewish soul.'

This in turn, Hutner argues, should lead to a national repentance, as prescribed in those Torah passages which prophesied suffering as punishment for sin. The suffering and the consequent 'disappointment in the Gentiles' are the necessary 'chronology and impetus for the teshuva [repentance] of Acharis Hayamim [the End of Days],' and Hutner takes heart from the back-to-Orthodoxy 'teshuva movement' that was then at its height in the US. Rabbi Dessler, in his Holocaust reflections, went on to exhort: 'If, after the terrible destruction, we find ourselves on the verge of a new era of Divine kindness, let us not repeat our foolishness. Let us recognize the hints from Above, and return in complete teshuva.'

It was in this context that Rabbi Shach fired off one of his controversial broadsides in December 1990. 'Another Holocaust could befall us tomorrow,' he warned, because of the secularism of Israel society. 'Remember what an old Jew is telling you. God is patient. But he keeps a tally. And one day his patience runs out, as it ran out then, when six million died.'

For many Jews, the very words 'another Holocaust' are almost sacrilegious. But haredism, in keeping with its crime-and-punishment approach to all history, including the Nazi Holocaust, refuses as a matter of dogma to invest the Holocaust with any uniqueness. It was different in degree, but not in kind, from previous punishments meted out by God to His sinful people. Indeed, Haredi theologians balk at the very term 'the Holocaust' (certainly at the definite article and capital H) and its Hebrew translation, *haShoah*.

* Rabbi Eliahu Dessler, *Michtav Me'Eliyahu*, vol. IV (Jerusalem: Vaad Lehafatsat Kitvei Hagra Dessler 1983), pp. 124–5.

They prefer the word *hurban* (destruction), which was traditionally used to denote the destruction of the Temple and major subsequent disasters. 'Is the term Shoah acceptable?' writes Rabbi Hutner. 'The answer is CLEARLY NOT.' The word 'implies an isolated catastrophe, unrelated to anything before or after it.' For Rabbi Hutner, such an approach is 'far from the Torah view of Jewish history. The Hurban of European Jewry is an integral part of our history.'*

The former British Chief Rabbi, Lord Jakobovits, who rejects the haredi Holocaust theology, nevertheless recognizes it as a key to the present strength and increasing vitality of the haredim. 'Only by recognizing in the Holocaust a replication of Jewish history's cycle of appalling catastrophes followed by survival and regeneration could they focus on the future rather than on the past. The gains derived from this outlook,' Jakobovits continues, 'have surpassed the most optimistic expectations and forecasts which could have been given credence in the shattered world of forty years ago . . . Today there is more strict observance and daily advanced Talmud study in New York, let alone in Jerusalem, than there ever was in Warsaw or Vilna.

'Single-mindedness was the one essential ingredient in the extraordinary dynamics galvanizing this colossal achievement.'†

Jakobovits's perception is trenchant. Arguably, though, it could admit of a further, vital ingredient. The haredim's single-mindedness during the Holocaust was not consciously focused on survival and regeneration, but rather on the simple – yet infinitely difficult – need to keep performing their duties as haredi Jews. 'Single-mindedness' implies a deliberate, reasoned reaffirmation of faith. Haredism, which is above all practice-oriented, enabled its stubborn, resilient adherents eventually to achieve that reaffirmation, but almost as a by-product of their ongoing practice.

The story, even if apocryphal, of the group of Jews during the Holocaust who put God on trial for abandoning His people

* Hutner, in Wolpin (ed.), op. cit.

† Rabbi Immanuel Jakabovits, *Religious Responses to the Holocaust* (London: Office of the Chief Rabbi 1988), p. 13.

exemplifies this inner strength. They found Him guilty – and then adjourned to pray the evening prayer.

On a more empirical level, Reeve Robert Brenner's study of Holocaust survivors has shown that a high proportion of the haredim amongst them remained loyal to their haredism. The more Modern-Orthodox, by contrast, suffered serious and sustained erosion of their religious commitment in the post-war years. The researcher surveyed a group of 708 Israeli Holocaust survivors, questioning them about their level of religious commitment before the war, immediately after their liberation, and twenty-five years later. He concluded:

> The more intensely observant, the more likely to remain observant; the less intensely observant, the greater the likelihood of becoming non-observant. Sixty-one percent of the ultra-observant stayed ultra, whereas only nine percent of the moderate stayed moderate. Our study conveys the case for the retentive strength of the assiduously observant, and the holding power of religious upbringing.*

Perhaps the case of the hasidic Rebbe of Klausenberg, Rabbi Yekutiel Yehuda Halberstam, later of Union City, New Jersey and Netanya, Israel, most vividly illustrates these scientific findings. He lost his wife and eleven children in the camps. On the Friday night after his liberation, the story is told (again, it may be legendary, but it is didactic, and illustrative), he set about organizing his shabbat tish, the festive meal. But he had no shtreimel, nor indeed any formal headgear. He could hardly conduct a tish without a hat. Eventually, someone produced an SS officer's cap, which Rabbi Halberstam donned with what must have been mixed feelings. The tish proceeded, as it had in Klausenberg (Kluj, Romania) before the Nazi interruption.

In the following months, Rabbi Halberstam played a major role in organizing religious and social life in the Displaced Persons camps, and many of the refugees, Orthodox and secular, remember him to this day with warmth. But his first concern had been to

* Reeve Robert Brenner, *The Faith and Doubt of Holocaust Survivors* (New York: The Free Press: 1990), p. 46.

perform his time-hallowed duties as a rebbe, holding the traditional shabbat tish.

Haredism, perhaps because of its view of history, does not torture itself with theological questions. 'For those who doubt and ask, there are no answers,' a Slovakian haredi rabbi wrote during the Holocaust. 'For those who do not doubt, there are no questions.' The Rebbe of Piastchene, a heroic figure who functioned as a spiritual leader and counsellor in the Warsaw Ghetto right up till the very end, wrote in 1942:

> Unfortunately there are some – even among those who were complete believers – whose faith has been damaged. They ask, 'Why have You abandoned us?' . . . If a Jew speaks this way as a form of prayer and entreaty, pouring out his heart to God, that is good. But if, Heaven forbid, he asks his question sceptically, if deep within his heart his faith is deficient . . . then he is torn and distanced from Him.*

Instead of asking questions about God, which could not be answered anyway and could lead to despair, haredi 'single-mindedness' in the misery of the ghettos and camps focused on specific, practical, halachic queries. A woman must immerse in the mikve on the seventh night after her menstruation ends. But the women in the ghetto of Vrbo, Slovakia, were under curfew at night, so they had to go to the mikve during the day. If her eighth day was shabbat, might a woman go on the seventh day? Rabbi Yitzhak Weiss, the local Rabbi, in his reasoned responsum, cited ancient precedents and stressed the importance of the mitzva of procreation in his decision to permit the early immersion.

In Warsaw, one of the first measures the Nazi occupiers took in 1940 was to close the mikves and forbid their use on pain of death. Orthodox women – and hasidic men, who bathe in the mikve as an act of spiritual purification – took to commuting to nearby villages. When trains and 'Aryan' trolleycars were barred to Jews, they returned to using the Warsaw mikves, slipping in through cellars and back-entrances while the main doors remained padlocked.

* Quoted in Schwartz and Goldstein, *Shoah*, p. 58.

In the words of Rabbi Huberband, the Warsaw Ghetto diarist whose writing was discovered in 1952, buried in milk-churns:

> Due to fear of detection, they heated the mikve only once a week. At night, the hole in the basement wall was sealed. 'Business' was conducted in this way for endless weeks. The official entrance to the mikve was pasted over with a notice stating that bathing in the mikve would be punished by anywhere between ten years in prison and death. Meanwhile, Jews bathed undisturbed, scoffing at the notice.*

In Treblinka concentration camp, secret prayer services took place morning and evening. The question troubling the participants, which they posed to a rabbi-inmate, was whether it was acceptable for them to pray the morning prayer before sunrise, which is its halachic time. They needed the darkness to conceal their service, and at daybreak they were marched off to their slave-labour.

Almost unbelievably, there were Jews who managed to smuggle their tefillin into the camps. According to Eliezer Berkovits, a major modern-day Jewish philosopher, in his book *With God in Hell*: 'There were Jews who hardly ever missed saying a few words of prayer with tefillin on, in Auschwitz, in Buchenwald, in Maidanek. We know of some remarkable stories of the devotion and self-sacrifice that Jews invested in their efforts to secure a pair of tefillin and put them on daily.'†

There are recorded instances of men who knew sections of the Talmud by heart 'holding classes' as they were marched to and from the slave-labour sites each day. The Jerusalem scholar Baruch-Bernard Merzel, who spent five years in Auschwitz, remembers finding odd pages of the Talmud that had been used by the Poles as wrapping paper. The inmates carefully concealed them at their workplace each night, taking them out in the morning to learn. Berkovits tells of two Dutch Jews 'who somehow managed to lay their hands on a copy of the Bible. They would squeeze into

* Huberband, *Kiddush Hashem*, p. 197.
† Eliezer Berkovits, *With God in Hell* (New York & London: Sanhedrin Press 1979), p. 5.

the middle of the ranks of the slave-labourers and study Torah together.'

Not that any form of regular religious practice was the norm in the camps, even among the haredi inmates. It was very much the exception. 'Don't exaggerate the so-called "religious life",' says Merzel. 'Even performing one mitzva was a tremendous *messirus nefesh* [self-sacrifice]. And sometimes you didn't do it for God. Putting on tefillin gave *you* strength.'

Sometimes the 'big questions' and the specific halachic queries merged. Rabbi Zevi Hirsch Meisels of Vac, Hungary, who also survived Auschwitz, recalled being asked for two halachic rulings on the same day. The first involved a congregant whose only son was about to be led away to the gas chambers. Could the father ransom his son for money, in the knowledge that another boy would be killed in his place? Then a fifteen-year-old approached the rabbi to ask whether he might offer himself in place of a noted Talmud scholar who was about to be taken to his death.

Rabbi Meisels failed to answer either of them. 'My dear friend,' he recalled saying to the first questioner. 'How can I render a clear decision for you? Even when the Temple stood, a question concerning matters of life and death would come before the Sanhedrin. But I am here in Auschwitz without any books of law, without any other rabbis, and without a clear mind because of so much suffering and grief . . . Do as you wish, as though you had not asked me at all.'*

In an incident in the Kovno Ghetto, recorded by a survivor, Rabbi Ephraim Oshry, a 'big question' and its halachic ramification were answered instinctively not by a rabbi, but by a Jewish mother. She had given birth to a baby boy after five years of childless marriage. But the Germans had forbidden Jews to have children. In Eliezer Berkovits's words: 'Just as the mohel was about to begin, the grinding of auto wheels was heard and the men of the Gestapo were getting out in front of the house. Terror struck all

* Rabbi Zvi Hirsch Meisels, *Mekadshei Hashem* (1955), vol. I, pp. 7–9; cited in Robert Kirschner, *Rabbinic Responsa of the Holocaust Era* (New York: Schocken Books 1985), pp. 111ff.

those present . . . It was the mother who showed the most courage. She turned to the mohel and ordered him: "Hurry up! Circumcise the child. Don't you see? They have come to kill us. At least let my child die as a Jew."'*

* Rabbi Ephraim Oshry, cited in Berkovits, *With God in Hell*, p. 44.

18

Success of Zeal

On the extreme edge of the haredi community are those who never wavered, not even immediately after the Holocaust, in their uncompromising rejection of Zionism. Leaders of the Netorei Karta (Aramaic: Guardians of the City) sect in Jerusalem tried to raise a white flag during the 1948 War of Independence, and surrender to the Jordanian army. The other haredim were making their accommodations with the new Zionist State, but this group had no doubts, even then, that Zionism was a mortal sin against God and Jewish destiny.

Today, they still see history unfolding their way. As the US and its allies poured troops into the Gulf region in August 1990, following Iraq's invasion of Kuwait, Netorei Karta aligned itself firmly behind the Iraqi strongman. In a letter to all UN delegates in New York (sent to the PLO delegate for distribution), Rabbi Moshe Hirsch, 'Foreign Minister' of the organization, proclaimed: 'God wants the Zionists out of the occupied territories, in order to spare the agony of His wrath on the Jewish people, but the Americans have persisted in keeping them there. So He chose another messenger, the Iraqi President Saddam Hussein, to undertake this chore, and thus benefit the Jewish nation and the world, Inshallah [Arabic: Please God]!'

Despite such exotic fulminations however, periodically published by Rabbi Hirsch in the name of the anonymous 'Seven-Man Supreme Council', Netorei Karta has fallen on hard times. It has been pushed almost beyond the fringe of Jerusalem haredi society. Its street demonstrations, once a frequent fixture in the city's calendar, are rare nowadays, and sparsely attended. Some observers blame this on Rabbi Hirsch, a controversial figure whose pamphleteering is so scurrilous that it disenchants even hard-core anti-Zionists.

Hirsch for his part attributes Netorei Karta's shrinking popularity to doctrinal backsliding among mainstream haredim. He noted with disgust that the Eda Haredit, the main ultra-haredi community centred in Jerusalem's quaint, century-old Mea Shearim quarter, put up wall-posters during the Gulf crisis calling for 'three days of prayer and Psalm-saying'. 'There was not a word of *yiddishkeit* [Jewish piety],' Hirsch snorted – meaning that the posters had not contained a ritual condemnation of the Zionist heresy, and had not specifically blamed the Israeli government for Saddam Hussein's aggression.

In fact, though, Hirsch's analysis is unduly modest, and objectively wrong. If anything, Netorei Karta is a victim of its own success. Mainstream haredism has increasingly adopted (or re-adopted after the brief post-Holocaust lapse) the hardline anti-Zionist ideology that Netorei Karta never abandoned or amended. Today's yeshiva student has no need to seek *kanoüss* (extremist zealotry) on the fringe of haredism: he has it at the heart of the movement.

But unlike the Satmarer Rebbe, Rabbi Teitelbaum, author of the 'metaphysical' brief against Zionism and mentor of Netorei Karta, and unlike his followers on both sides of the Atlantic, the mainstream haredim have managed, by Talmudic and political casuistry, to reconcile religious dogma on the one hand, and practical living on the other. Agudat Yisrael and its various offshoots have succeeded over the years in refining the theoretical zealotry so that they can justify their determined pursuit of material benefits from, and political influence in, the Zionist State.

'It's rank hypocrisy,' says Hirsch, who refuses to pay his local taxes to the city of Jerusalem and declines to take a penny in health or welfare payments from the government. He says there are 'many hundreds' of families, mainly in Mea Shearim, who likewise try to live without reference or recourse to the Zionist State. They do not pay taxes. They boycott national and local elections. And their young men do not report to the army – even to obtain the deferment automatically available to yeshiva students. 'The army usually leaves us alone,' says Hirsch. 'They don't want us; if they gave us guns, we'd shoot them. Why should they draft us? They don't draft Arabs, and we're more anti-Zionist than the Arabs . . .'

There are certainly many hundreds of families in Mea Shearim who boycott the Western Wall, vestige of the Second Temple and holiest shrine in Judaism, on the grounds that it is 'occupied by the Zionists'. (Israel took East Jerusalem, which included the Western Wall, from Jordan in the 1967 war.) Agudah-type haredim have no such qualms. They flocked to the Wall from the moment it was taken. Though the Wall has become the major national (and not just religious) shrine, and attracts Israelis and tourists of all religious stripes, it is the haredim who are its most regular devotees. Around the clock, throughout the year, haredim can be found there, praying or reciting Psalms. When Agudah's Council of Sages called for special prayers at the Wall on the eve of the Gulf War in January 1991, an estimated 80,000 haredim filled the Wall plaza – probably the largest Jewish congregation to assemble there since Temple times.

But these residents of Mea Shearim, adherents of Netorei Karta, who live barely a mile away from the Wall, never approach it. Each *Pessach* (Passover) and *Sukkot* (Tabernacles), when thousands of pilgrims visit the Wall, they hire a fleet of buses to take them southwards, *away* from the Wall to a ridge on the outskirts of the city from where they can gaze back at it and at the adjacent Temple Mount, which is now a Muslim holy site. Here they sing and pray; a klezmer band blares good cheer over loudspeakers; mothers lay out packed lunches and children romp about in holiday spirit. This is their pilgrimage.

Agudah-type haredim 'are really opposed to the State of Israel too,' the director of American Netorei Karta, Rabbi Yossef Becher, maintained in an interview with the Saudi Arabian newspaper *Riyadh Daily*. 'But they say, realistically what can we do? The State is in existence. Until the Messiah comes we have to work with the State.' For Netorei Karta, Becher explained, this was heresy. 'We believe that voting in the elections is like an act of idol-worship. They also accept money from the State for their yeshivas. Money has a way of changing one's outlook . . .'

American Netorei Karta sympathizers, mostly Satmarer hasidim but with a smattering of other denominations too, muster a sizeable showing, when the occasion calls, to demonstrate and picket against Israel outside the United Nations building in New York. And each year in May, when other Jewish organizations parade down Fifth Avenue in a 'Salute to Israel', they hold a police-protected counter-rally at Fifth and Seventy-Sixth Street which often attracts coverage in the media as a man-bites-dog type of story. 'The great adventure of the Zionists is coming to an inglorious end,' American Netorei Karta assured readers of the *New York Times* in a large display-ad before the 1985 counter-rally. 'Zionism is the opposite of Judaism, and the Zionist state is a complete falsification and caricature.'

But the death of Rabbi Teitelbaum in 1979, and the subsequent (still ongoing, sometimes violent) feuding between supporters of his nephew and successor, Rabbi Moshe Teitelbaum, and his widow, Rebbitzin Feige Teitelbaum, seem to have sapped some of the anti-Zionist zeal and diverted the Satmarer hasidim's energies to their internal troubles.

In London too, the hardening of mainstream haredi ideology leaves little separate space for the ostensibly harder-liners of Netorei Karta, and their activities are sporadic and marginal. A regular columnist in the British mainstream haredi newspaper *Jewish Tribune* wrote of himself in May 1990: 'I am not a Netorei Kartanik but I could sit at any one of their tables, share a meal and discuss any subject appertaining to Judaism, even though we might be at variance. I cannot say the same about an irreligious Jew.'

But it is in Israel that the paradox of Netorei Karta's success and eclipse is most pronounced. Rabbi Shach's stadium speech and its aftermath starkly demonstrated the depth of haredi hostility to Zionism. Moshe Hirsch nevertheless called for a demonstration against Shach – to protest against the sage's implicit decision to support the hawkish Zionist nationalism of the Likud. He could have used Shach's rhetoric against the Zionist State for his own diatribe against Shach. Perhaps because of that incongruity, barely fifty people turned up.

Israeli (or Palestinian, as they style themselves) Netorei Karta rarely hold demonstrations nowadays, and when they do they are rarely violent. Netorei Karta activists hardly ever end up in jail any more. This is a far cry indeed from the action-packed days under the sect's former leader, the colourful and charismatic Rabbi

Amram Blau (d. 1974). He marched at the head of his men against the opening of a (mixed-sex) swimming-pool in the Holy City, against motor-traffic on the sabbath through haredi districts, against a sex shop, against autopsies and against archaeological digs. (The halacha requires that bodies be buried intact, and, once buried, are never disturbed. Tampering with them before burial in the interests of medical science, or after burial – even thousands of years after – in the interests of archaeological discovery, is seen as sacrilegious invasion of posthumous privacy.) Reb Amram was undaunted by the night-sticks and water-cannon of the 'Zionist SS' (the police), and seemed to seek out confrontation.

In those days, Hirsch recalls with nostalgia, the entire Eda Haredis was *kanoï* (zealot), and Netorei Karta were its shock-troops. The Satmarer Rebbe was titular head of the Eda beit din, which would give its blessing to Reb Amram's campaigns. The Rebbe would also send money from America to cover the costs.

This simple and satisfying old order was severely shaken in the mid-1960s, however, when the middle-aged Reb Amram, who was widowed, announced his intention of marrying a beautiful young French convert to Judaism, Ruth Ben-David. This was considered improper for a man of his station and he was eventually ostracized by the Eda beit din, and 'exiled' to Bnei Brak – even though he claimed (belatedly) that he had been wounded in the testicles during the 1948 war and was therefore halachically forbidden to marry anyone but a convert. (This halacha is based on Deuteronomy 23:1: 'He that is wounded in the stones, or hath his privy member cut off, shall not enter into the congregation of the Lord.') He also reportedly claimed a mystical significance to the union and its potential issue, noting that King David is said by the Talmud to have descended from the biblical convert, Ruth the Moabite.

The Satmarer Rebbe was unable to patch up this feud, and even though Reb Amram eventually returned to Jerusalem and resumed his activities, things were never quite the same. A mild-mannered halachic scholar from Manchester, England, the late Rabbi Yitzhak Weiss, was appointed head of the beit din, and a ruling was issued: no demonstrations without a police licence, and no violence.

In any event – and this is the significant reflection of the mainstream trend – the initiative for street campaigns and demonstrations on religious issues has passed from Netorei Karta, indeed from Mea Shearim and its Eda Haredit, to the 'establishment' haredi leadership. For example, a series of mass demonstrations in the mid-1980s against an archaeological dig at the City of David, a First Temple period site which the haredim claimed had later been used as a cemetery, was spearheaded by mainstream haredi politicians of Agudat Yisrael, with Eda support and Hirsch elbowed aside. (This campaign was unsuccessful: the dig was completed. But the archaeologist, Professor Yigal Shilo, died soon after aged only forty, and a ghoulish wall-poster went up in Mea Shearim celebrating God's punishment of the sinner. Suspicion focused on Hirsch, but he denies authorship of that particular outrage.)

Hirsch, who grew up on New York's Lower East Side and came to Jerusalem as a yeshiva student in the 1950s, sees himself as Reb Amram's chosen successor. He married the daughter of another Netorei Karta leader, Rabbi Aharon Katzenellenbogen, and has adopted the flat black hat and belted coat that are the particular uniform of the 'old yishuv', the pre-State haredi community in Palestine. Slight and bespectacled, and with a straggly off-white beard, he lacks the master's physical presence and engaging ebullience (and Reb Amram's physical bravery, according to Hirsch's many detractors). But he has the imagination and resourcefulness of a Madison Avenue copywriter, and he argues with some justice that his particular brand of 'diplomacy' sometimes has a broader and more powerful impact than a mere demonstration.

Thus, for instance, in 1976 he got the PLO delegation at the UN to take up the Jerusalem Municipality's threatened closure of a Mea Shearim chicken abattoir (on sanitary grounds) at a session of the Security Council. Primed by Hirsch, Arab delegates protested against the action as an attack on religious freedom in the Holy City. And fighting a sex shop in downtown Jerusalem some years later, he appealed to PLO Chairman Yasser Arafat for support, writing to him that 'The temporary domination of Palestine by the Zionists has caused the desecration and impurity of holy places. We turn to you to help maintain the sanctity of Jerusalem.'

When US Secretary of State George Shultz visited Jerusalem in 1985, Netorei Karta invited him to 'our autonomous enclave, Mea Shearim and vicinity, the only area not ruled by the de facto Zionist government'. Hirsch added some 'practical advice' in the invitation. 'Why,' he wrote, 'should the American government invest their hard-earned dollars in a barren economy which buries its easily-earned "shnorr" [Yiddish: begging] money? The American currency bears the prestigious imprint, "In God we trust." Why can't this currency be distributed to those who place trust in God, rather than in weaponry . . . ?'

For years, bemused PLO officials and local Palestinian leaders failed to perceive the public relations potential in Hirsch's activities. Now, however, there is growing cooperation. When the 'Seven-Man Netorei Karta Supreme Council' proclaimed its 'glee and happiness at the [PLO's] long-awaited decision to form a government-in-exile' in 1988, President-designate Arafat told *Paris Match* he would recommend that a Netorei Karta representative be a minister in the government of the future State. Hirsch, in turn, announced that 'the post of Minister for Jewish Affairs will be filled by a triumvirate, comprising three members of Netorei Karta, from Jerusalem, London and New York.' At the Middle East peace conference in Madrid in 1991, an American Netorei Karta activist, Haim Yitzhak Freiman, was present as an official member of the Palestinian advisory delegation.

Hirsch, now a frequent contributor to the leading East Jerusalem newspaper *Al-Fajr*, made headlines in Israel and abroad in March 1989, and infuriated the rest of the haredim – thus achieving both of his goals – when his group distributed thousands of dollars in cash to Palestinian intifada victims lying in East Jerusalem hospitals whom he greeted as 'those afflicted by the Zionist suppressors'. Netorei Karta members also delivered aid packages to the Palestinian Red Crescent, for distribution among the families of intifada detainees, declaring, in an accompanying letter, that 'We, the anti-Zionist Palestinian Jewish Orthodox, are privileged to present to you, fellow Palestinians who find yourselves in a helpless situation, our expression of sympathy and kindness.'

19

Jewel in the Crown

There is not much sympathy and kindness left for Hirsch nowadays, even in Mea Shearim. One morning in December 1990, while walking to the synagogue, he was attacked by a hooded assailant who threw acid in his face. Thanks to his spectacles, he was not blinded, but one eye was seriously hurt. He was rushed to hospital, and later flown to London for treatment. From his sick-bed, he told reporters that although his attacker's face was concealed, he could see that 'he was not a man with a beard and peyot'.

Mea Shearim insiders suggested that a '*tzniuss* [modesty] vigilante posse' had exacted corporal punishment from the unpopular Rabbi. Such self-appointed posses exist in haredi areas of Jerusalem and in the haredi town of Bnei Brak. They are known to bruise faces and even to break the occasional rib. But an acid attack would represent an unprecedented escalation. Press speculation focused on activists of the violently anti-Arab movement, whose leader, American-Israeli Rabbi Meir Kahane, had recently been assassinated in New York. Several unsolved killings of Arabs in the occupied territories around this time were also being attributed to Kach vengeance squads.

But whatever the motive behind the attack, Mea Shearimites hardly seemed overwhelmed by grief. Hirsch sees his unpopularity as an extension of the growing hatred of Arabs in the haredi community, especially among the yeshiva students. His own group, who openly identify with the Palestinian Arab cause and the victims of the intifada, are reviled and ostracized. He blames the mainstream haredi political leadership. Rabbi Shach's alignment with the Right, he says, has exacerbated the trend.

Hirsch's analysis, though obviously subjective, contains an important insight. Mainstream haredism, while becoming more anti-Israel, is at the same time becoming more anti-Arab. Seen from the Netorei Karta perspective, this means that while the mainstream identifies with the *negative* aspect of Netorei Karta ideology – the profound theological reservations over the secular Jewish State – it firmly eschews the *positive* corollary, that is, sympathy for the Palestinians. Or put another way, during its fifteen years of political alliance with the Right, haredism embraced some of the cruder chauvinism found on the hawkish side of Zionism, while at the same time hardening in its fundamental rejection of Zionism as such.

This is a complex paradox, yet it is increasingly apparent in practice, as, for example, when an ugly wave of anti-Arab rioting broke out in Jerusalem in August 1990, following the murder by Arab terrorists of two Jewish teenagers. Arab drivers were set upon indiscriminately, dragged from their cars and beaten, and their vehicles smashed. One victim, a father of six, subsequently died. Many of the rioters were yeshiva students on their summer recess. They stalked the city in packs, stoning any passing Arab car, chanting 'Death to the Arabs.'

Haredi politics, in fact, has always had a streak of anti-Arabism in it. Arguably this is a local and contemporary form of a certain xenophobia inherent in the haredi world-view. In the period prior to the establishment of Israel, while haredi ideologues were hostile or at best ambivalent towards the very idea of Jewish statehood, hundreds of haredim joined or helped Menahem Begin's ultra-nationalist Irgun terror underground. Today, some of the haredi Knesset members match the far-right parties in their anti-Arab rhetoric. When the question of instituting the death penalty for Palestinian terrorists comes up for debate, haredi MKs are invariably in the forefront of the hanging lobby.

More recently, the creation of a haredi township, Emmanuel, in Israeli-occupied Samaria has strengthened haredi ties with the Gush Emunim settlement movement, which is ultra-nationalist and ultra-Orthodox. Observers discern a 'haredization' of the settlement movement, in terms of lifestyle and religious norms. The settlers increasingly *look* like haredim, the men with flowing beards and peyot, the women with their hair covered and long, baggy dresses. (The men do not, however, *dress* like haredim; they wear military-style anoraks and jeans, and their kippot, though as large as those of the haredim, are not black but coloured and made of crocheted cotton in the Zionist-Orthodox tradition.)

In terms of political attitudes, an influence is discernible in the other direction. Some of Gush Emunim's biblical exegesis, which equates the present-day Arab inhabitants of the Land with the Amalekites and the 'Seven Peoples' who lived there in Moses' and Joshua's day, has seeped into current haredi theology. (The Israelites were repeatedly instructed in the Bible to kill the Amalekites and the Seven Peoples, though, according to some Bible commentators, they might be spared if they agreed to live as serfs.) This is perhaps the ultimate paradox, because haredi ideology rejects any meta-historical analogy between the ancient Israelites and the modern-day Israelis, doctrinally denying the Zionist-Orthodox belief that modern Israel is the beginning of the final Redemption prophesied in the Bible.

The same dialectic is much in evidence in haredi communities abroad. Mainstream haredim in the Diaspora tend to be hawkish on Israeli issues: hardline on the territories, anti-Arab, anti-Left. Thus, for instance, the weekly newspaper *The Jewish Press*, popular in the Orthodox districts of Brooklyn, featured the late Meir Kahane as a regular columnist. The paper's editorial line is stridently nationalistic and militaristic whenever discussing Israel's policy options, and staunchly haredi on religious issues. Yet the Diaspora haredim manage all this without abandoning, at least in theory, their theological reservations over the entire Zionist enterprise. English-speaking haredim do not refer to 'Israel', which implies the State; they speak of 'Eretz Yisrael' – the Land of Israel, a biblical term devoid of political connotations.

Fortunately for the prospects of Israeli-Arab peace, the two streams of Jewish extremism, the haredi and the ultra-nationalist, though their waters have mingled, sharply separate before they reach the most sensitive issue of all, the Temple Mount in Jerusalem. Fortunately too, the haredi dogma, which forbids any access to or activity on the Mount, has prevailed, thus far at least, in this area of potential catastrophe. Zionist-Orthodox zealots who dream of destroying the Muslim shrines on the Mount, the golden Dome of the Rock and the Mosque of al-Aksa, have been pushed to the fringes of their own camp. The site continues to serve as an exclusively Muslim place of worship, administered by the Muslim Wakf, the religious authority, and guarded by the Israeli police.

Nevertheless, the danger is ever-present. It would take only a couple of home-made bombs planted by a lone fanatic to detonate a conflagration that could sweep the entire Muslim world into a jihad, a holy war, against the Jews. The Shin Bet security service is constantly on the watch for plotters. It runs under-cover agents inside various fringe groups. Six times in the past two decades, attempts have been made to attack the Muslim shrines, mostly by lone cranks, but once, in the mid-Eighties, by a well organized Jewish underground led by West Bank settlers with close ties to prominent Gush Emunim rabbis. Members of this cell were also convicted of murdering and maiming Palestinians. Some were sentenced to life imprisonment, but their sentences were commuted by President Chaim Herzog, under heavy pressure from rightist and Orthodox parties, and all were released within seven years.

In October 1990, tensions at the Mount exploded into violence. Muslims summoned by the muezzins' loudspeakers to 'defend the Mount' from a demonstration by the 'Temple Mount Faithful', an ultra-nationalist Jewish group, lobbed rocks across the Western Wall, where a large crowd of mainly haredi worshippers had been holding Sukkot services. Wild shooting by the Israeli police left seventeen Muslims dead. Israel was unanimously condemned at the United Nations Security Council. The Arabs demanded international protection for the Mount. In Israel, a wave of stabbings of Jews by young Muslim fanatics followed. In the occupied territories intifada violence increased.

Despite their leadership's ostensible dissociation from the Jewish underground and the various extremist groups, many Gush Emunim-affiliated families display in their homes an aerial photomontage of Jerusalem showing the Temple Mount with the Dome of the Rock and the Mosque of Omar removed, and the Jewish Temple standing there in their place. Yeshivas and rabbis associated with Gush Emunim engage in serious debate over the Jewish underground's theological postulate: that the Jewish People must 'force God's hand'. If the Jews try, out of sincere religious zeal and yearning, to blow up the 'abominations' – the Mosques – on the holy Mount, and that provokes an all-Muslim attack in which Israel's existence is endangered, then God will have 'no choice' but to intervene to save His people and His city.

'If the present government won't do it, a future government – the government of the kingdom of Israel – will,' said Yehuda Etzion, a leader of the Jewish underground, after his release from prison. He had been freed after agreeing to publicly recant the underground's original thesis: that a non-government, partisan group could 'do it'. 'I hope they won't have to be blown up,' he continued. 'But these buildings will have to go. That's clear. Their removal is the jewel in the crown in the process of Jewish redemption.'

While Etzion and his comrades focused mainly on 'removing the abomination', other, non-violent, enthusiasts devote themselves to planning the subsequent stages of the redemption. They envisage reconstructing the Temple and resuming the regimen of sacrifices and priestly service, interrupted 2,000 years ago. There are nationalist yeshivas in the Old City of Jerusalem that specialize in 'Temple studies'. Scholars meticulously examine the biblical and Talmudic texts and modern archaeological evidence, and draw up blueprints for future building work. They study the specifications of the Altar and the Holy Vessels and weave the priestly garments on hand-looms following the Pentateuchal instructions.

All this is anathema to the haredim. 'Forcing God's hand' was the very essence of the Zionist heresy, in haredi eyes. And even if the creation of a political, pre-Messianic State for the Jews has been grudgingly acquiesced in, post factum, on pragmatic grounds, a challenge to the existing order at the holiest spot on earth would be blatant rebellion against Heaven. After all, that existing order can hardly be an accident. In haredi thought nothing is accidental – certainly not the disposition of the Temple site, at the heart of the Israeli-Arab conflict and of world attention.

Some haredim say outright that the presence of the Mosques on the Mount, their survival intact through the 1967 war, and then-Defence Minister Moshe Dayan's decision to facilitate and protect exclusive Muslim worship on the Mount, are all Divinely Providential signposts pointing to the limitations of modern, non-

Messianic Israel in the unfolding cosmic drama (or, in a more hardline variation, tangible evidence of Divine disapproval of the Zionist State). The ultimate, apocalyptic salvation will come from God, in His own good time. 'Forcing His hand' is sinful, and also futile. A Talmudic tradition that the Third Temple will 'descend from Heaven, ready-made' expresses this faith.

The haredim, like the Orthodox nationalists, pray at least six times a day – in the three daily services and in Grace after meals – for a 'speedy return' of the Temple and the sacrifices. They, too, study all the *halachot*, the laws pertaining to the Temple service – but in a theoretical, non-practical way. Rabbi Yisrael Meir Kagan ('The Hafetz Haim'), a leader of European Orthodoxy in the early part of the century, is said to have kept himself physically fit well into his eighties, climbing up and down stairs every day for exercise, in constant anticipation of the Coming of the Messiah and the rebuilding of the Temple. As a *cohen* (priest) – and indeed a likely candidate for High Priest – he would need to be strong and agile to perform the various rituals. So he kept exercising – and waiting. But he never *did* anything to change the existing realities at the site of the Temple and would doubtless have recoiled at such an impious suggestion.

Felicitously bolstering haredism's theological passivity, the halacha actually prohibits entry to the Temple Mount. The site is considered inherently holy: no Jew may tread on it until he is cleansed from his ritual impurity. But he cannot be cleansed – and here the halacha, in its circularity, provides impregnable protection for the status quo on the Mount – until the Temple is rebuilt. Only then will everyone be restored to purity by being sprinkled with a solution of spring water and the ashes of an all-red heifer slaughtered and burned for that purpose (Numbers 19:1–22).

In practice, haredim do not set foot on the Mount, while other Jews (and Christians) visit as tourists but are forbidden by the police from holding prayer services there. The Sephardic Chief Rabbi, Mordechai Eliahu, briefly led an attempt during 1989–90 to search for, import, or clone by genetic engineering an all-red heifer. He was photographed trampling through the mud of a cattle-ranch on the Golan Heights and was reportedly in contact with a specialist bull-breeder in Sweden. He argued that the sprinkling could be done *before* the Temple was rebuilt, though this view was rejected by most rabbis.

Similarly, the former Ashkenazic Chief Rabbi, Shlomo Goren, another ultra-nationalist hardliner, has found scant rabbinical support for his halachic-geographic arguments that parts of the present Temple Mount compound are not holy, and may be trodden on by unclean persons. Goren cites copious archaeological evidence to back up his diagrams and calculations, showing that the ancient Jewish Temple did not cover the whole site. He urges that a synagogue be built on a section of the Mount where he believes it is permissible to tread.

The government, conveniently citing the haredi interpretation of the halacha, has discreetly but insistently advised both rabbis that their plans must remain in the realm of academic theory. The Mount, protected by haredi dogma and Zionist police, stays Muslim.

PART IV

LIVE AND LEARN

20

The Learning Revolution

Several years ago, the Israeli national airline, El Al, fought a bitter and eventually unsuccessful battle against demands by the haredim that it stop flying on shabbat. The airline was heavily in the red, and its executives argued that to observe the shabbat would cost a fortune in lost custom and expensive lay-overs.

El Al never really had a chance, given the political strength of the haredi party Agudat Yisrael. But the haredim did not, finally, have to resort to legislative means. Several leading rabbis threatened to pronouce a ban on the airline – and the same executives, after some hasty arithmetic, concluded that the loss of haredi custom would be more damaging than enforced weekly respites. Agudah's Knesset faction leader Rabbi Avraham Shapira, himself a major industrialist and frequent flyer, cited in the Knesset a string of Talmudic assurances to the effect that observing the shabbat never ultimately results in economic damage. God makes it up to you in other ways.

The haredim, who are the most peripatetic sector of a nation noted for its wanderlust (there are no statistics to prove this haredi trait; but any chance dalliance at JFK, Ben-Gurion, Schipol or Heathrow will provide cogent if unscientific corroboration), seem to have given El Al their preferred patronage ever since then, tacitly fulfilling their side of an unspoken bargain. And El Al for its part makes every effort to accommodate their special needs. Thus, its cabin crew are trained to turn a benevolent blind eye to prayer quorums clogging the aisles in mid-flight, oblivious of the seat-belt signs. Stewardesses even try to avoid moving across the praying men's line of vision, so as not to distract them.

In summer 1990, El Al introduced the Daf Hayomi, or daily page of Talmud, on its in-flight entertainment programme. Along with classical music, jazz, modern Israeli songs and the film soundtrack, the El Al passenger is now offered a *shiur* (lesson) in Talmud over his headphones.

Eating *glatt-kosher* (lit. smoothly kosher; super-kosher) food and praying in the aisles (or in transit lounges, while airline security men keep a watchful eye out) are not the only hallmarks of the haredi flyer. He is not just a davener; he is a learner too. And that requirement, too, is now recognized and catered for by the go-ahead company, competing for his business.

In recent years, El Al has climbed steadily into the black, and was producing a tidy annual profit for the government until the Gulf crisis, in August 1990, cast a prolonged blight on tourist travel to the region. Granted, this turnabout was achieved by creditor banks forcing the company into receivership, and by the receiver instituting a rigorous recovery programme. But for many haredim – and the point is often made by rabbis and haredi newspapers – the profits are a direct, divine consequence of El Al's obeying the halacha and thereby performing a *kiddush hashem*, or sanctification of God's name, by being the only national carrier to fly six days a week instead of seven.

This tale provides graphic illustration of the political power of the haredim. It also attests to their economic strength, to the authority of their rabbis, and to their straightforward faith in here-and-now instances of heavenly book-keeping. But more significant than all of these, in terms of understanding the inner strength of modern-day haredi society, is the fact that El Al provides the Daf Hayomi – daily study of the Talmud, a major institution among the haredim ever since its creation in the 1920s – to this sizeable and growing section of its clientele.

Learning is the internal dynamo of the haredi resurgence. Not just in schools and yeshivas and girls' seminaries, but in every haredi household the accent is increasingly on study. Ordinary people – shopkeepers, businessmen and professionals as well as scholars or yeshiva students – spend a significant part of their waking and non-working hours studying the Talmud and related religious literature. It is study for the sake of study, as well as for the sake of knowledge. Incessant revision of previously studied material is an integral part of the mitzva of study. The texts have an inherent holiness, and trying to understand them, even with limited success, is itself a necessary and sacred endeavour.

This religious relationship between the believer and the texts is unique to Jewish fundamentalism. The act of study is itself a supreme religious obligation, as incumbent on laymen as on rabbis. Neither of the other two major monotheistic faiths require of their adherents – even of their priests or judges – this constant study of the texts as a principal act of devotion. Canon Law, for instance, regulates ecclesiastical life. Every Catholic archdiocese has at least one priest who is expert in it. But he studies it in order to gain and retain expertise, so that he can dispense it. Haredi Jews study Jewish Law for no 'practical' purpose other than to discharge their religious obligation to study, and their studying in turn shapes and influences their lives, drawing them intellectually and spiritually more and more into a self-contained world of the mind. The Talmudic-halachic culture fortifies their societal separateness, providing them with a system of thought and language all their own, and a shared pool of concepts and knowledge that they regard as uniquely theirs.

Haredim traditionally spurned and scorned the Judaic and especially biblical and Talmudic studies pursued by the non-Orthodox streams of Judaism, and by academic researchers. These were considered the cutting edge of the post-Emancipation assault on Orthodox faith, scholarship and practice. In recent years there has been a flowering of Judaic studies at universities around the world, with new departments springing up, and existing ones expanding to attract more students. Interestingly, to the extent that they are aware of this development haredim have tended to respond to it without hostility, and even with a certain grudging pride that 'their' Torah and Talmud are receiving 'outside' recognition and interest. They seem no longer to fear, as in the past, that such academic institutions might tempt their own bright young scholars away from haredism. Nor do they fear that scientific, critical work on the source-material can erode their own belief-based approach to it.

Academics for their part recognize the sheer dimensions of haredi learning, which sustain a flourishing market in learning-related literature. Talmudic publishing is almost entirely in haredi hands. Haredi scholars unearth and annotate manuscripts, which are then published as new books, or as revised editions of existing books, by haredi publishing houses, and are bought mainly by the haredi public. But the gulf remains, between the academics' critical approach and the haredim's deferential treatment of the texts.

Haredim say their 'learning revolution' embraces every member of the community (women as well as men, though it is developing more slowly among the women), enveloping them all in a lifelong cycle of study. But this very inclusiveness is problematic. Not all learners possess the analytical powers, the originality or the humility required for in-depth study of the Talmud. Some lay haredim will sit at *shiurim* or study-classes night after night not understanding, but not understanding that they do not understand – or not admitting it even to themselves. Yeshiva students sit in their study-hall year after year cocooned in comfortable, cloistered unreality, without making any real progress in their studies. Scholars publish books of no great scholarly worth, which nevertheless bear the enthusiastic endorsements of well-known rabbis.

These phenomena are widespread, and they are frequently pilloried by anti-haredi polemicists. They are easily understandable, though, given the overwhelmingly ambitious pretension of the haredi 'learning revolution' – that everyone can and indeed must strive to study. And they do not overshadow the remarkable power of the 'learning revolution'. After all, intellectual honesty is often rare in the halls of academe too. In the haredi world, there is an upsurge of intellectual-cum-religious fervour unique in recent Jewish history and which, for that reason alone, deserves to be studied and understood.

Key figures at the heart of the haredi learning revolution say it has already reached unprecedented proportions. Despite the obliteration of the East European Jewish communities and their centres of scholarship less than two generations ago, there are already more students studying at more yeshivas, more laymen studying in more shiurim, and far more works of scholarship being published, than in the heyday of Polish and Russian Jewry.

This is all the more remarkable given that there are fewer haredi and Modern-Orthodox Jews today, in absolute terms, than there were before the Holocaust. And obviously there are fewer than before the Emancipation, when virtually all Jews were 'Orthodox' (although, as we have seen, that is an anachronistic use of the word).

'We're not talking about the world of the tannaim and amoraim [earlier and later Talmudic sages], the days of the Talmud itself,' says Rabbi Yosef Buxbaum of Jerusalem, editor-in-chief of Machon Yerushalayim, which is the leading publisher of scholarly works in the haredi world. 'We don't know how widespread Torah learning was then. But I have no doubt that since those times there has never been a body of Torah scholars the like of which exists today – neither in quantity nor in quality. Of course there were always outstanding individuals in each generation, great minds, far greater than exist now. But as far as "mass scholarship" is concerned, the present is unprecedented.

'In Lithuania, at its zenith just before the war, there were perhaps 13–14,000 yeshiva students. In the whole of Eastern Europe there may have been say 30–35,000. We have already passed that figure today, in Israel alone. We're close to 50,000.'

Rabbi Avraham Farbstein, veteran dean of the Hevron Yeshiva in Jerusalem, which is among the largest and most prestigious, with many overseas students, says he has 'no explanation' – meaning no rational, unmystical explanation – to account for the current dramatic growth of Torah learning among the haredim. 'There are two parallel phenomena,' he says. 'Ordinary *baalei-batim* [lit. householders; laymen] all learn; and they all send their children to yeshivas. Both phenomena are new. When I visited Golders Green for the first time, twenty-eight years ago, they just laughed at the idea of boys spending time at yeshiva. Neither the families from hasidic backgrounds nor the "Yekkes"* from Germany sent their boys to yeshiva, barring a tiny handful. Today there is virtually no one in the various Orthodox communities, both haredi and Modern-Orthodox, whose sons don't go to learn in a yeshiva. Some go for a longer time and some for a shorter, but

* Nickname of obscure origin used among Eastern European Jews to refer to Jews of German origin; nowadays has also come to denote anyone of punctual and fastidious disposition.

that's not important: the principle has been accepted that everyone goes. And it's the same in the United States.'

Farbstein, raised in Palestine, spent three years studying in Lithuanian and Polish yeshivas before the Second World War. 'In pre-war Europe in general,' he says, 'yeshiva was seen as something for individuals, not for everyone.' This was the case among hasidim, but it was true of mitnagdim too. In Lithuania, the centre of mitnagdism, yeshiva study 'may have been slightly more prevalent. A worthy layman who was himself a *ben Torah* might send his son to yeshiva; but it certainly wasn't common. 'In Poland, it was positively rare. The hasidim would learn in their shtieblach, but that was about it. Basically, the yeshiva student was a marginal factor, even in his own haredi society.'

Farbstein concedes that modern-day affluence makes it easier for families to support non-productive members and to forgo their earning power. 'But that is a contributory factor, it's not the cause of the phenomenon. Before the war, it wasn't the well-to-do who sent their sons to yeshiva. The majority of the students were absolutely destitute. They made incredible sacrifices to keep learning. I learned in Mir [a famous Polish yeshiva] and I well remember the grinding poverty.'

As for laymen's learning, says Farbstein, the revolution is no less remarkable, though here he is prepared to attach greater weight to economic circumstances. 'In Eastern Europe before the war people would only learn on shabbat,' he says. 'During the week most people were simply too tired; they were worn out at the end of the working day.' The average standard of knowledge and scholarship among the laity, therefore, he says, was considerably lower than it is today among haredi laymen. Then, many would make do with reciting Psalms or learning the 'Ein Yaakov' ('Fountain of Jacob'), a sixteenth-century anthology of the aggadic (homiletic) sections of the Talmud where the stories and homilies are much easier to follow than the halachic legalism which comprises the bulk of Talmudic literature.

The most marked change has occurred among the Sephardic Orthodox, who, says Farbstein, were until recently 'steeped in ignorance – and I'm talking about the Orthodox, the observant, obviously not about those who threw it all over. Their Judiasm – I know it's wrong to say this, but it's true – was a form of fetishism. Yes, they had some eminent Torah scholars, but very few. A mere handful. Today that's all changed. A large body of Sephardi bnei Torah has grown up, and it's growing all the time.'

Farbstein links this to 'the general Sephardic emergence from their collective inferiority complex: they wanted to get ahead, to close the gaps in all areas of life in Israel, to show that they're as good as the Ashkenazim. The haredi Sephardim want to show they're as good in Torah learning. When I was a young married yeshiva-man in Jerusalem, perhaps there were three Sephardi bnei Torah in the whole city. I say perhaps three, and I'm being generous.'

Probably there is a measure of exaggeration in these accounts – in both directions. The pre-war past was not as bleak, nor is the present as rich, as Rabbis Farbstein and Buxbaum depict them. Both rabbis (Buxbaum is younger and studied in the leading Israeli yeshivas) were products of the élitist Lithuanian rabbinic tradition, where looking down on the laity, patronizing the hasidim in particular, and despising the Sephardim, were all considered good form. Other accounts, though they perhaps err on the side of nostalgic hyperbole, depict a breadth and depth of learning among the hasidim in Poland, especially among the Gerer hasidim who were the largest sect and whose rebbes were celebrated Talmudists. But scholarship was not flaunted, they say. It was deliberately concealed, or lightly worn.

Farbstein, at any rate, recalls falling foul of the Vishnitzer Rebbe some years ago when he remarked that the hasidic world 'has drawn close to the Torah world in recent years.' 'Who does he think he is, this Litvak?' the Rebbe commented to his hasidim. 'Hasidim always learned!'

'But it's not true,' says Farbstein, 'they didn't. The Vishnitzers were known as total *amaratzim* [ignoramuses]. Even today they're not the greatest scholars. But still, they have drawn closer to Torah. The whole of *klal Yisrael* [the community of Israel] has drawn closer to Torah.'

*

Those who regard the resurgence of haredism after the Holocaust as a Divine miracle – and most haredim do so regard it – see the flowering of learning as 'a miracle within a miracle'. The fact that centrally placed haredi figures are beginning to make favourable comparisons between the present and the venerated past is a remarkable manifestation of modern-day haredi self-confidence.

Invariably, moreover, the additional assertion is made that 'this is just the beginning,' that for every yeshiva bachur there are half-a-dozen heder pupils, that the haredi baby-boom has yet to make its impact at the yeshiva and post-yeshiva stages – and that the outlook therefore is for more and ever more heders, yeshivas, kollels, learning laymen, and less learned, but enthusiastically supportive laywomen. The glorious past, they feel, has been surpassed, and the future looks even better.

21

Talmudic Mindset

Learning the Torah and keeping the mitzvot are the recipe for Jewish living, according to the haredi outlook on life. One does not learn – this is critically important – only, or even mainly, in order to know what to keep or how to keep it. Learning itself is the greatest mitzva. It 'weighs', according to a Talmudic statement incorporated into the morning prayer-service, 'as much as all the other mitzvot together.'

Nor does one learn – this is also vital for an understanding of the haredi mind, and is often misunderstood – merely in order to absorb and retain knowledge, though that is obviously an important part of what is required and expected. One learns in order to fulfil the mitzva, which is to learn, that is, to engage in the activity of learning. In other words, even if, hypothetically speaking, one were to know it all, one would nevertheless still be obliged to learn – constantly to revise and review. But the Talmud says of itself that there is no 'knowing it all', because each time one learns a section, new layers of meaning come to light. 'Learning 100 times is not the same as learning 101 times,' the rabbis of the Talmud taught. And: 'Learn [it] over and over again; for everything is in it.'

The Talmud praises dedication and diligence rather than a naturally retentive memory which, after all, is merely an accident of birth. Haredi tradition is full of stories of famous rabbis who were dunces in heder, but achieved eminence through years of dogged devotion. Torah is acquired only by one who 'kills himself over it', says the Talmud, in an aggadic play on words. These exhortations and homilies are frequently quoted in the haredi world to encourage not only dullards, but also ordinary people of average intelligence, to persevere in the lifelong enterprise of learning.

To the outsider, much of the subject-matter seems abstruse,

complicated, esoteric, of no practical relevance, or just plain boring. For the haredi, however, these considerations themselves are irrelevant. Learning is good for the soul. It is a primary purpose of life in this world, and ensures eternal reward in the World to Come. The religious dimension of learning, constantly stressed and internalized, serves to ease the anguish and frustrations of grappling with the complexities of the texts, the finely nuanced casuistry, and the vastness and diffusion of the material.

No haredi will admit that any part of 'Torah' – meaning, in this extended sense of the term, the whole corpus of Jewish law and lore – is boring. In fact, a sincerely pious haredi will not find any of it boring, or irrelevant, or too difficult. His piety necessarily precludes such attitudes, since everything in Torah is an expression of what God wants in His world. That state of awe, induced by that piety, is the goal to which every haredi must constantly aspire.

Still, it is difficult to attain, and certainly to sustain, a level of spiritual contemplation in the ordinary course of learning about, say, the classic case of the goring ox (which has gored another ox, or a human being), or the thief who steals a sheep. Most learners find themselves swept up into the intricacies of the Talmudic arguments. Many enjoy the intellectual exercise. Those who don't are probably more conscious than those who do of performing the mitzva of learning.

'You don't actually think about it [the religious aspect] at the time, when you're totally wrapped up in the subject,' says Rabbi Mordechai Becher, a yeshiva lecturer from Australia now living in Israel. 'You're trying to figure out what's in the thief's mind. What's in the thief's mind, though, has ramifications halachically, and every halachic ramification is a manifestation of the will of God, basically.'

Through learning, according to haredi belief, one can approach God and understand more about Him – since Torah is His eternal message to the Jews and to the world. 'He looked in the Torah and created the world,' is one Talmudic metaphor, expressing the universal significance of the Torah as the Creator's blueprint. 'God, the Torah and Israel are one unity,' according to another Talmudic passage that stresses the Jews' particular role in the cosmic order as the guardians of the Torah. There are two leaps of faith required here: one that Torah is Divine, or '*min Hashamayim* [from Heaven]' in the phrase which the Talmud itself uses; and secondly that studying it – all of it, even the goring ox – is the way to draw close to the Divine.

Rabbi Becher is one of the lucky ones who genuinely enjoy the legalistic cut-and-thrust of Talmud. In order, he says, to attain the desirable level of piety at least once a day, he concentrates on the words of the blessing recited before learning, the purpose of which, he explains, is to remind the learner that he is about to embark on a mitzva and not merely an enjoyable intellectual exercise. 'Blessed art Thou . . . who has chosen us from among the nations and given us His Torah . . . Blessed art Thou who teaches Torah to his people, Israel.' 'It is useful,' says Becher, 'to contemplate for a short moment, before beginning to study.'

Learners who love their learning need feel no sense of guilt. On the contrary, in the words of a famous turn-of-the-century hasidic Talmudist, Abraham Bornstein of Sochatchev, 'This is the essence of the mitzva of learning Torah – to enjoy and rejoice and delight in it, so that the words of Torah become absorbed in the very bloodstream of the learner. People are quite wrong to think,' Bornstein continues, 'that one who learns and constantly comes up with new thoughts and insights, and positively revels in his learning, is somehow not learning "for the sake of the mitzva of learning" as much as one who just studies straightforwardly and doesn't get any enjoyment out of his learning. This is a great mistake, and in fact the opposite is true . . .'*

'Learning Torah' does not refer specifically to the Pentateuch, which is one meaning of the word 'Torah' (the literal translation of Torah is teaching or law), but to the whole of the sacred literature – the 'Torah Shebiktav' (Written Law – the Bible: Pentateuch, Prophets and Hagiographa) and the 'Torah Shebaal Peh' (Oral Law). In practice, the term 'learning' means for haredim learning the Talmud and its ancillary literature.

In fact, there is no 'oral' law as such; everything is in writing. But the term is key to the evolution of the Talmud, and to the ongoing

* Rabbi Abraham Bornstein, *Iglei Tal* (Pietrkov 1905), Introduction.

significance of learning, from the haredi perspective. It is the original oral nature of Torah that creates the apparent paradox at the basis of Orthodox belief. On the one hand, the whole of Torah is Divine, immutable and eternal. Yet on the other, learning Torah is supposed to produce new insights, new interpretations, and even new laws – or new refinements of existing laws.

Published collations of Talmudic sages' teachings or commentaries are usually called *hiddushim* ('innovations'). Yet a strikingly beautiful Talmudic *aggada* asserts that every innovative insight or interpretation that any sage would ever render throughout history was communicated by God to Moses. Another Talmudic aggada, however, has Moses, in his Heavenly experience atop Mount Sinai, transported by God across 1,400 years of history into the academy of Rabbi Akiva, a famous Talmudic sage of the second century CE – where he finds, to his consternation, that he doesn't understand the halachic debate. But he is comforted when he hears a disciple asking the Rabbi: 'Whence did you derive this teaching?' and Akiva replying: 'It is a ruling handed down from Moses at Sinai.'

There, in metaphoric form, is the dialectic that construes Torah as at once ancient and new, complete yet constantly developing.

In the Orthodox construction of Jewish history, the Ten Commandments were spoken by God to the Israelites at Sinai. The rest of the Pentateuch was literally dictated by God to Moses, and is therefore also the unmediated Word of God. The remainder of the Bible is of a lesser degree of Divinity, being directly inspired by God, but not dictated word for word, to the various prophets, kings and scribes.

Just as it is heretical to believe that any of the Pentateuch was written after Moses' time, or by anyone other than Moses, so too it is heretical to believe that the Pentateuch was transmitted to Moses without an accompanying *oral* interpretation. Evolution as a theory is dogmatically rejected – both of *Homo sapiens* and of Torah. Thus, to cite a famous example, if the Pentateuch, which in Orthodox belief was written around 1,250 BCE, says 'An eye for an eye,' and the Talmud, compiled between the years 200 and 550 CE, says 'This means monetary compensation' (and not poking out the offender's eye in retribution) – that meaning was communicated to Moses by God *orally*, along with the *written* text. It was subsequently handed on by Moses to his successors. In the words of the Talmud [Mishna, Tractate Avot 1:1], 'Moses received the Torah from Sinai, and handed it down to Joshua, and Joshua to the Elders, and the Elders to the Prophets, and the Prophets to the Men of the Great Assembly . . .' and on and on until the rabbis of the Mishna.

It was at that stage, more than a century after the destruction of the Second Temple in Jerusalem in 70 CE, that the decision was made to *write* down this *oral* tradition. Until then, according to the Talmudic tradition, it had been actually forbidden 'to put into writing that which was transmitted orally', a 'ban' designed (by God Himself) to encourage 'learning' – that is constant study, review and discussion. But the rabbis of the Mishna felt that, with the loss of the nation's spiritual centre and the spread of doubts and disputes about various traditions, an 'official' text of the Oral Law should be enshrined in writing. This text, the Mishna, is veritably telegraphic in style, as though reflecting its authors' ambivalence about committing their knowledge to paper.

Over the next several generations, separately in Palestine and in Babylon, the Mishna served as the textbook of rabbinical academies, called yeshivas, in their learning, and a much larger body of interpretive and discursive material grew up around it – the Gemara. 'Gemara' means 'learning' in Aramaic, a Semitic language widely used in the ancient world. This was eventually edited and published as the Jerusalem Talmud in the fourth century and the larger Babylonian Talmud in the sixth. 'Talmud' is Hebrew for learning.

The Talmud, and subsequent Orthodox belief, depict biblical figures as halachists, engaged in the same perpetual halachic disputations with their contemporaries as the Talmudic rabbis themselves were, a millennium or more later – and with the same volume of knowledge at their disposal. King David, for instance, was not actually guilty of adultery with Bathsheba, despite the passage in the Second Book of Samuel, chapters 11–12. She was halachically no longer married to Uriah when the King seduced her, because all soldiers in the Davidic wars were required formally to divorce their wives before going into battle, in order to avoid halachic complications should they fail to return.

Uriah for his part deserved to die because he was halachically guilty of rebellion against the King. The only flaw in David's conduct was that he ought to have had him tried and sentenced by the Sanhedrin, instead of which he engineered his death on the battlefield. The Gemara, in Tractate Shabbat, contrives to squeeze linguistic hints of all this out from the biblical verses. It is a classic example of the rabbinical tradition bending over backwards to explain and exonerate apparently reprehensible actions on the part of major biblical heroes. But this kind of interpretation is more easily understandable once it is appreciated that David is seen not only as a warrior-king and lyrical poet, but as a knowledgeable and stringent halachist, a Talmudist, indeed a rabbi. As the Gemara itself observes: 'Anyone who thinks that David sinned is mistaken. For the Bible says of him elsewhere [I Sam. 18:14]: "And David behaved himself wisely in all his ways; and the Lord was with him." Is it possible that sin should have come his way if the Lord was with him?'

The Talmudic tradition even imputes halachic-Talmudic knowledge and observance to Abraham, Isaac and Jacob, though they lived and died, according to the Pentateuch, before God formally 'gave' the Torah to the Israelites through Moses. The three Forefathers of the nation are regarded as having been naturally imbued with Torah precepts because of their saintliness and close communion with God, which again underscores metaphorically the concept of Torah as beyond history and eternally valid.

This perspective is fundamentally alien to the modern, critical mind, and it lies at the heart of the deep divide between the haredi mindset and non-Orthodox scholarly and religious approach to the sources. In the eyes of a modern reader, it seems anachronistic to invest biblical figures with Talmudic knowledge, and to deny a basic element of evolution in Jewish law and theology. History, which is apparently – haredim would say fallaciously – borne out by the biblical texts themselves, describes a relatively primitive tribal culture gradually developing its legal, social and theological mores over a period of centuries. This is not to deny the radical novelty and monumental significance of the original Hebrew message of monotheism and justice. But it is to admit of further constant progress and development within the religion, both in its theology and its legal system. The *lex talionis*, in this modern interpretation, was originally conceived and applied in its literal sense: an eye for an eye. With time, however, and evolving civilization, it was transformed into a more humane and sophisticated provision for personal injury compensation, which became part of a well developed Law of Torts, clearly distinguished from a Criminal Code.

Similarly, the modern Jewish, humanistic – haredim would say Christian-influenced – reading of the Bible sees the Prophets as rebelling against the earlier cult of animal sacrifices. 'I delight not in the blood of bullocks, or of lambs or he-goats,' Isaiah thunders in the name of God. Rather, he continues, 'Learn to do good deeds, seek justice, relieve the oppressed, judge the fatherless, plead for the widow.' The Talmud's constant attempts to 'throw back' its own religious and halachic concepts to biblical times are unhistorical to the modern mind, and, by the same token, the constant efforts by post-Talmudic writers, down to the present day, to clothe – modern scholars would say disguise – any innovation or modern development in Talmud-period garb seems similarly artificial, indeed disingenuous.

But haredi Orthodoxy remains impervious to this sort of criticism. While the Modern-Orthodox find themselves in constant tension, trying to reconcile a modern outlook with Orthodoxy's fundamental (fundamentalist) ahistoricism, haredi faith is untroubled by such conflict. The traditional 'throwback' approach resolves all problems.

The problems are not new. The great medieval Jewish philosopher and halachic codifier Maimonides, in his *Guide to the Perplexed*, offers a modern-sounding psychological explanation for the biblical rites of animal sacrifice. This mode of worship was universal in the ancient world, he writes. 'It was in accordance with the wisdom and plan of God that He did not command us to give up all these rituals, for [that] would have been contrary to human nature, which generally adheres to that to which it is accustomed.'

But the tone of academic detachment is only apparent. The same Maimonides, in his monumental halachic code *Mishne Torah*, lays down detailed rules about animal sacrifice and all the other elements of ritual service in the Temple, which had ceased 1,100 years before he wrote. There are also precise instructions for (re)building the Temple and (re)making the Holy Vessels, as originally prescribed by God to Moses at Sinai and elaborated in the Talmud. The clear implication, indeed the underlying premise, is that the current prolonged lapse in the Temple service is purely temporary. Similarly, Maimonides prescribes methods of ritual purification, most of which are predicated on the existence of the Temple in Jerusalem.

As far as Maimonides is concerned in his code – and as far as the haredi learner of today is concerned – these sections of Torah are not only an integral part of the whole, but are as relevant, intellectually and religiously, as the currently valid rules pertaining to everyday life. They are not, in fact, separate 'sections'. Granted, the Mishna allocates specific sections or 'Orders' to Temple service and to the laws of ritual purity. But the diffuse nature of the Talmud precludes any notion of such separateness and defies any attempt by the modern mind to impose a categorization or rationalization upon the loosely structured and engagingly meandering course of the Gemara, which brings to life the authentic rabbinical debates in the ancient Babylonian yeshivas. The Gemara's way is to range freely throughout the corpus, mixing and matching the most disparate halachic issues.

22

The Inner Logic of Implied Infallibility

Before examining a brief sample of text, in order to illustrate the style of the Talmud and of Talmudic learning, let us look first at the six 'Orders' of the Mishna, each of which is subdivided into tractates. The tractates, in turn, are divided into chapters, and the chapters into individual paragraphs (called mishnas). In the Babylonian Talmud and the Jerusalem Talmud each of these one-paragraph mishnas is followed by the text of the Gemara, which usually begins by explaining or discussing the mishna, comparing and contrasting it with other mishnas and with other Mishnaic-type texts (Tosefta, Mechilta, Sifra, Sifri) which were collated by the tannaim in these separate and less authoritative anthologies.

This list is in no way adequate as an introduction to the substance of the Talmud; indeed some of the tractate titles seem more mystifying than enlightening. Nevertheless, within the context of this book, it may be helpful for readers, in order to appreciate the kind of subject-matter that engrosses the haredi mind.

1 *ZERAIM* ('Seeds') This Order deals with agricultural law, apart from the first tractate. There is no Babylonian Talmud on the agricultural tractates; either none was written, or none survived.

Berachot – prayers and blessings
Pe'ah – corner of the field left for the poor (Lev. 19:9) and other laws of charity
D'mai – peasants' produce which may not have been tithed
Kilayim – hybrid plants and animals (forbidden in Lev. 19:19)
Shviit – produce of the seventh (fallow) year (Lev. 25:1–7)
Terumot – tithes for the Priests (Num. 18:8–20)
Maasrot – tithes for the Levites and the poor (Num. 18:21–24)

Maaser Sheni – tithe to be eaten in Jerusalem (Deut. 12:6–18)
Halah – tithe from dough (Num. 15:17–21)
Orlah – fruit of young trees, not to be eaten (Lev. 19:23)
Bikurim – first fruits, to be taken to the Temple (Deut. 26:1–11)

2 *MOED* ('Holy days')

Shabbat – laws relating to the sabbath
Eruvin – domains, in regard to restrictions on movement on the sabbath
Pesachim – Passover laws and sacrifice
Shekalim – shekels for the Temple service (Exod. 21:11–16) and other Temple practices
Yoma – laws and Temple service of the Day of Atonement
Sukkah – laws of the Feast of Tabernacles
Betzah – miscellaneous laws relating to festivals
Rosh Hashanah – New Year laws
Taanit – fast days
Megillah – laws relating to the Feast of Purim
Moed Kattan – intermediate days of Passover and Tabernacles, and laws of mourning
Hagigah – festival pilgrimages and sacrifices

3 *NASHIM* ('Women')

Yevamot – levirate marriage; missing husbands
Ketubot – property laws in marriage
Nedarim – vows (Num. 30:27)
Nazir – vows of abstinence (from wine, etc.) (Num. 6:1–21)
Sotah – the suspected adulteress (Num. 5:11–31), and laws of war
Gittin – laws of divorce (Deut. 24:1)
Kiddushin – contracting marriage; prohibited marriages

4 *NEZIKIN* ('Damages')

Bava Kama ('First Gate') – torts (Exod. 21–2); theft
Bava Metsia ('Middle Gate') – lost property, labour law, bailee
Bava Batra ('Last Gate') – partnership, rental, purchase, loans, neighbours, inheritance
Sanhedrin – courts, evidence and procedure; capital offences; principles of faith

Makot – the punishment of lashes (Deut. 24:1–3)
Shvuot – oaths (Exod. 22:10; Lev. 5:4; Num. 30:1–3)
Avodah Zarah – idolatry (Exod. 20:2–5; Deut. 12:2–3)
Horayot – mistaken decisions by courts and priests – how they are rectified (Lev. 4:3–26)
Eduyot – miscellaneous laws
Avot – ethical sayings

5 *KODASHIM* ('Sacrifices')

Zevahim – animal sacrifices (Lev. 1–7)
Menachot – meal offerings (Lev. 2 and 6); *tsitsit* (fringed garments; Num. 15:37), *tefillin*
Hullin – kosher slaughter and dietary laws (Exod. 22:30, 23:19)
Bechorot – first-born animals
Arachin – donations to the Temple (Lev. 27)
Temurah – substituting animals earmarked for sacrifices (Lev. 5:15–16)
Kritot – sin-offerings
Me'ilah – misuse of sacred objects
Tamid – daily Temple service
Middot – the Temple structure
Kinnim – bird sacrifices (Lev. 1:14–14, 12:6–8)

6 *TOHOROT* ('Purities') There is no Babylonian Talmud on any of these tractates except Niddah, nor on the last three of the previous Order.

Kelim – how vessels can become impure (Lev. 11:24–47)
Oholot – impurity caused by a corpse (Num. 19:14–22)
Negaim – skin plagues (Lev. 13)
Parah – the red heifer, whose ashes wash away impurity (Num. 19:1–13)
Tohorot – ritual purity
Mikvaot – pools for ritual purification
Niddah – the menstruant woman (Lev. 15:19–30)
Machshirin – how objects become capable of impurity (Lev.11:34–38)
Zavin – impurity caused by venereal discharge
Tevul Yom – laws on ritual immersion
Yadayim – transmitting ritual impurity through hands
Uktsin – transmitting ritual impurity through parts of plants

המפקיד פרק שלישי בבא מציעא לז

אף בראשונה הלכה כמותו או אין הלכה כמותו אמר ליה חלוק היה ר' יוסי אף בראשונה והלכה כמותו אף בראשונה אתמר נמי אמר ר' אלעזר חלוק היה ר' יוסי אף בראשונה והלכה כמותו אף בראשונה ור' יוחנן אמר מודה היה ר' יוסי בראשונה שכבר שילם שילם אין לא שילם לא והאמר *ר' חייא בר אבא א"ר יוחנן לא שילם שילם ממש אלא כיון שאמר הריני משלם אע"פ שלא שילם אימא מודה היה ר' יוסי בראשונה שכבר אמר הריני משלם:

מתני' אמר לשנים גזלתי לאחד מכם מנה ואיני יודע איזה מכם או אביו של אחד מכם הפקיד לי מנה ואיני יודע איזה הוא נותן לזה מנה ולזה מנה שהודה מפי עצמו *שנים שהפקידו אצל אחד זה מנה וזה מאתים זה אומר שלי מאתים וזה אומר שלי מאתים נותן לזה מנה ולזה מנה והשאר יהא מונח עד שיבא אליהו *א"ר יוסי א"כ מה הפסיד הרמאי אלא הכל יהא מונח עד שיבא אליהו וכן שני כלים אחד יפה מנה ואחד יפה אלף זוז זה אומר יפה שלי וזה אומר יפה שלי נותן את הקטן לאחד מהן ומתוך הגדול נותן דמי קטן לשני והשאר יהא מונח עד שיבא אליהו א"ר יוסי א"כ מה הפסיד הרמאי אלא הכל יהא מונח עד שיבא אליהו:

גמ' אלמא מספיקא מפקינן ממונא ולא אמרינן אוקי ממונא בחזקת מריה ורמינהי שנים שהפקידו אצל אחד זה מנה וזה מאתים זה אומר שלי מאתים וזה אומר שלי מאתים נותן לזה מנה ולזה מנה והשאר יהא מונח עד שיבא אליהו א"ל פקדון אגזל קא רמית גזל דעבד איסורא קנסוהו רבנן פקדון דלא עבד איסורא לא קנסוהו רבנן ורמי פקדון אפקדון ורמי גזל אגזל פקדון אפקדון דקתני רישא או אביו של אחד מכם הפקיד אצלי מנה ואיני יודע איזה הוא נותן לזה מנה ולזה מנה ורמינהי שנים שהפקידו וכו' אמר רבא רישא נעשה כמי שהפקידו לו בשני כריכות דהוה ליה למידק סיפא נעשה כמי שהפקידו לו בכרך אחד דלא הוה ליה למידק כגון דאפקידו תרוייהו בהדי הדדי בחד זימנא דאמר להו אנא גופייכו לא קפידיתו אהדדי אנא קפידנא ורמי גזל אגזל קתני הכא אמר לשנים גזלתי לאחד מכם מנה ואיני יודע איזה מכם או אביו של אחד מכם הפקיד לי מנה ואיני יודע איזהו נותן לזה מנה ולזה מנה ורמינהי *גזל אחד מחמשה ואינו יודע איזה מהן גזל זה אומר אותי גזל וזה אומר אותי גזל מניח גזילה בינידם ומסתלק דברי ר"ט אלמא מספיקא לא מפקינן ממונא ואמרינן *אוקים ממונא בחזקת מריה וממאי דמתני' דהכא ר"ט היא *דקתני עלה דההיא מודה ר"ט באומר לשנים גזלתי לאחד מכם מנה ואיני יודע איזה מכם שנותן לזה מנה ולזה מנה התם דקא תבעי ליה הכא בבא לצאת ידי שמים דיקא נמי דקתני שהודה מפי עצמו שמע מינה אמר מר התם דקא תבעי ליה והלה מה טוען רב יהודה אמר רב הלה שותק רב מתנה אמר רב הלה

צווח

This is page 37a of Tractate Bava Metsia of the Babylonian Talmud, a typical Talmud page. The words in large letters at the top of the page read (right to left), *Hamafkid* (He who deposits), *Perek Shlishi* (Third Chapter), *Bava Metsia.*

In the centre, printed in Hebrew block-letters – comparable to 'upper case' in English – is the text of the Talmud itself. There is a mishna (from line 12 to line 26), followed by gemara (and preceded by gemara pertaining to the previous mishna). The mishna is written in Hebrew, though it is a Hebrew significantly different in both style and vocabulary from biblical Hebrew. The Mishna also contains many words borrowed from Greek and Latin, and from various Semitic languages.

This mishna begins: 'If a man said to two others, "I have robbed one of you of 100 *zuz* [a coin], but I do not know which one it was," or "The father of one of you left 100 zuz in my keeping, but I do not know whose father it was," he must give each of them 100 zuz since he himself admitted liability . . .'

The gemara is in Aramaic, heavily laced with Hebrew.

The column on the right is the commentary of 'Rashi', the early medieval French scholar Rabbi Shlomo Yitzhaki. It is written in a blend of Hebrew and Aramaic, and printed in a cursive font, midway between script and block-letters. This has traditionally been the favoured medium of Talmudic literature, ever since the earliest days of printing.

The column on the left is called *Tosafot*, which means literally 'additions'. This is also a medieval commentary, compiled by a number of French and German rabbis following Rashi's death in 1105. Whereas Rashi strives for simplicity, the Tosafists – some of whom were Rashi's grandsons – introduce deeper and more casuistic analysis. Frequently they take issue with Rashi, and delving into the myriad disputes between Rashi and Tosafot has been the stock-in-trade of Talmudists from the Middle Ages to the present day.

Every Talmud since the Soncino Edition (Venice 1520) has followed precisely this pagination, both of the text itself and of the two main commentaries. One contemporary popular edition by the Israeli scholar Adin Steinsaltz devotes two pages to every one page of the traditional format, thus still preserving the now hallowed pagination.

On the far right are cross-references to other tractates, and annotations by two post-medieval commentators. On the far left near the top are references from the Talmudic text (denoted by Hebrew letters a,b,c, etc.) to the later halachic codifications – Maimonides (12th century), the Sefer Mitzvot Gadol, and the Arabaa Turim (14th century) and Shulhan Aruch (16th century). Below them is the commentary of an early medieval North African scholar, Rabenu Hananel (11th century).

The left-to-right order is inverted on the facing or 'b' pages, so that Rashi is always on the inside of the page and Tosafot on the outside. (Hebrew is written from right to left, and Hebrew books open accordingly; 37a is a left-hand page.)

The 'back of the book' varies enormously from edition to edition. Some boast over 100 commentaries on some tractates, which explains why some Talmud tomes weigh several pounds. All editions, even the cheapest and thinnest, have the *Maharsha*, a seventeenth-century commentary on *Tosafot* by Rabbi Shmuel Edelis, a leading Polish rabbi.

Clearly the 'Orders' of the Mishna, despite their attempt at order and sequence, contain many disorderly digressions. There is no logical reason why *Nedarim* is in *Nashim* or *Hullin* in *Kodashim*. *Nezikin* trails off into a number of miscellaneous tractates that do not fit anywhere in particular.

Within individual tractates, too, there is similar laxity, with the Mishna suddenly striking out on a course quite unconnected to the central subject-matter of the tractate. The Gemara is still less disciplined and predictable. In the Babylonian Talmud, the Gemara discussion frequently wanders away from any textual or contextual connection to the specific mishna. The distinction between halacha and *aggada* (law and homiletic legends) is vague, and the Gemara slips easily from one to the other.

The Gemara's basic method of legal analysis, comparing and contrasting Mishnaic texts, is founded on a fundamental and unchallengeable postulation that the entire corpus is one integral whole, in which everything is consistent, comparable and compatible with everything else. Everything in Torah – the Oral Law and the Written – is relevant to everything else. Relevance is determined by the inner logic of the entire corpus, and by the Talmud's modes of interpreting the Pentateuch, using logical and linguistic devices to deduce, infer and imply. By the same token, everything, no matter how esoteric or impractical, is relevant to the haredi learner.

Our example is taken from Tractate Shabbat, page 76a, which was the Daf Hayomi – the daily Talmud page – on the day this passage was written. It demonstrates the seamlessness of the Talmud's method. The Mishna in the seventh chapter of Tractate Shabbat discusses the law that forbids carrying objects on the sabbath from a private domain into the public domain and vice versa. It lists a wide range of household and agricultural objects, laying down a minimal volume or size for each.

If one carries, say from one's house into the street, a smaller than minimum volume or a smaller-sized object, one has not committed the offence of carrying on the sabbath and is thus not obliged to bring a sin-offering. (The case under discussion involves carrying without malice aforethought. If the carrying is done wilfully, in deliberate disregard of the formal warning of two adult, male witnesses, the punishment is death. Carrying a smaller than minimal volume or dimension is forbidden in principle, but it does not trigger a penalty even if done wilfully. The issue in the Mishna is thus when the obligation to bring a sin-offering is incurred.)

> He who carries straw: a cow's mouthful [is the offence-creating volume]. Pea-stalks: a camel's mouthful. Ears of grain: a lamb's mouthful. Grass: a goat's mouthful. Leaves of garlic and leaves of onion: if they are fresh: a fig[-size volume]. If they are dried – a goat's mouthful. And they do not combine [i.e. are not added up together], because they each have a different minimal volume.

On this the Gemara comments: 'Rabbi Yossi son of Hanina said, they do not combine to [make up] the stricter [i.e. smaller] volume, but they do combine to [make up] the more lenient [i.e. larger] volume.'

In other words, as Rashi explains in his commentary, if one carries less than minimal volumes of two different substances, each with a different minimal offence-creating volume, the two substances will combine to trigger the offence if they add up together to the larger volume, but not if they add up only to the smaller volume. For instance, three-quarters of a cow's mouthful of straw will combine with half of a goat's mouthful of grass – if together they add up to the volume of one whole cow's mouthful.

The Gemara continues by asking against Rabbi Yossi (there is no question-mark or other punctuation in the text, but the flow of question-and-answer is discernible to the practised student):

> But do substances with different volumes ever combine [i.e. even if together they add up to the larger, more lenient volume]? Have we not learnt [elsewhere] in a mishna, 'The article of clothing – three by three; the sack – four by four; leather – five by five; a rug – six by six? And furthermore we learned [in a Tosefta on that mishna], 'The clothing and the sack, the sack and the leather, the leather and the rug combine with each other. But Rabbi Shimon said that the reason [why they combine] is that they can be joined together to become impure as the seat of a person suffering a venereal issue.' So, were it not for that reason – [they would] not [combine] . . .

The Mishna beginning 'The article of clothing', which is cited here as an analogous case, to refute Rabbi Yossi, has nothing to do with the laws of shabbat. It is from Tractate Me'ilah, in the Order of Kodashim, and deals with the ritual impurity of fabrics which are stood on or lain on by a person suffering from venereal issue. It determines that a tiny piece of cloth, three fingers by three fingers, can contract impurity; that the minimal size piece of sack for this purpose is four by four handbreadths; of leather five, and of rug six. It rules that two such fabrics can combine to make up the larger minimal measurement of the two. Rabbi Shimon provides a specific explanation for that: the various fabrics combine in another case relating to VD and ritual purity, if they are sewn together as part of a saddle-cloth; therefore they combine in this case too.

The Gemara's argument is that the Mishna recorded Rabbi Shimon's explanation in order to limit the application of the combining principle. Carrying garlic and onion on shabbat is beyond that limit – and thus the two vegetables should not combine to create the offence of carrying.

What is 'relevant' here? To the minds of most of modern mankind, including most Jews, nothing. Granted, Orthodox Jews still observe the ban on carrying on shabbat. But as we have noted, carrying any quantity is forbidden. And there have not been sin-offerings, calling into play the various volume-criteria such as a dried fig or a goat's mouth, for nigh on 2,000 years. (Nor is the death penalty for a deliberate infringement currently enforced even in the most ultra-haredi circles.)

The rules of ritual impurities have also almost all lain in abeyance since the destruction of the Temple in 70 CE – so there is no practical 'relevance' in learning about them either. Even in purely theoretical terms, it seems far-fetched to make deductions from two bits of fabric and the laws of purity and apply them to a handful of vegetables and the laws of shabbat. Nevertheless, the haredi student of Talmud finds nothing bizarre in this brief passage of Gemara, or in hundreds like it, which analogize and distinguish across the whole spectrum of the Oral Law. He, like the Gemara itself, is entirely unconcerned with any latter-day perspective of 'relevance', practical or intellectual. He, like the Gemara, is guided solely by the quest for comprehensive harmony within the Talmud's own closed system.

The inner logic of the Talmud is founded on the premise that every tanna or Mishnaic rabbi must have been consistent in all his statements and rulings throughout the corpus. Tannaim can differ with each other – though the Gemara will strive to narrow such differences and reconcile them where possible – but they cannot differ in one place with their own opinions elsewhere. Distinguishing such apparent contradictions is the classical essence of the Gemara's give-and-take debate. The same premise was extended to the amoraim, the rabbis of the Gemara, with the added proviso that an *amora* cannot differ with a tanna unless he can cite another tanna to support him.

Subsequently, the same principle was applied to the post-Talmudic scholars: the yeshiva deans of Babylon, the *geonim*, who functioned there until the early Middle Ages; then the medieval *rishonim* (lit. the early [sages]) of Spain, France and Germany; and then the *acharonim* (the later [sages]), mainly of Eastern Europe. The rule governing the study of their works was – and still is for the haredi student – that each author must always have been consistent with all his other rulings and interpretations. Moreover, he can only have disputed the opinion of an earlier sage if he cited – or can be construed to have cited – a supporting opinion from another earlier sage.

The acharonim apply these principles in trying to iron out seeming contradictions or discrepancies in the writings of a *rishon*. The special favourite is Maimonides, because his work of codification was so seminal for the development of Talmudic learning.

The same process continues to the present day in yeshivas and in learned works, with outstanding scholars still joining the ranks of the acharonim. This status is usually conferred on them posthumously by an informal but broad consensus in 'the yeshiva world'. Jerusalem sage Rabbi Yehezkel Abramsky's commentary on the Tosefta, *Hazon Yehezkel*, and New York scholar Rabbi Moshe Feinstein's (1895–1986) halachic responsa, *Igrot Moshe*, are the most recent works widely regarded as qualifying their authors as acharonim.

*

The doctrine of implied infallibility rests not only on an intellectual striving for consistency, but on a religious veneration of (earlier) sages that runs through the entire Talmudic and post-Talmudic system. 'The former generations are not like the latter generations,' says the Gemara in Tractate Berachot. 'For the former generations, studying the Torah was their constant preoccupation, and their work merely subsidiary – and they prospered at both. But for the latter generations their work is their constant preoccupation and their Torah study subsidiary – and they prosper at neither.'

The Talmud is full of accounts of the saintliness of the tannaim and amoraim, and of their ability to perform miracles or otherwise invoke divine intervention. Such attributes of holiness, albeit in watered-down versions, are attributed to subsequent generations of rabbis by still later generations. Thus, legends of extreme righteousness and mystical powers surround the figure of Rashi, the medieval commentator, while Rabbi Yosef Karo, a sixteenth-century Palestinian scholar and mystic who wrote the Shulhan Aruch, a practical halachic guide for everyday living, is believed to have been taught by the spirit of the Prophet Elijah. The Talmudic knowledge of such figures is similarly invested with a superhuman dimension: it is almost unthinkable that they would simply err, or forget something.

'Holiness', both the word and the concept, is liberally used in the course of traditional-style learning in order to accentuate this aspect of supernatural powers imputed to the 'greats' of the past. Rabbi Yehuda, editor of the Mishna, is referred to as 'Rabenu Hakadosh', Our Holy Rabbi. And many a haredi teacher will begin a shiur with the Yiddish words: '*Zogt der heiliger Tanna in der heiliger Mishna*' ('Says the holy Tanna in the holy Mishna').

In this atmosphere, heavy with posthumous deference, the haredi scholar naturally tries to 'kill himself for Torah' rather than accept an apparent contradiction that casts doubt on the Talmudic omniscience of one of the great masters. The challenge to the acute and resourceful – and pious – student is to resolve a Talmudic problem in such a way that no holy rabbi contradicts himself, and that questions are warded off by fine distinctions or by recourse to the hypothesized support of still more venerable and holy authority. The nature of such recourse is as varied and flexible – and, to the Talmudic enthusiast, as delightful – as the legalistic mind and imagination can devise. Since this delight is also an investment believed to yield eternal returns, and to provide, by intellectual infusion or by a more mystical process of spiritual osmosis, an insight into the Divine Will, what better, more fulfilling and meaningful way for a Jew to spend his time?

23

Halls of a Different Academe

The blast of noise, a cacophony of voices, incessant and deafening, is the first impression that overwhelms an outsider entering the study-hall of any large yeshiva.

The second is the constant ripple of movement. Students wave their arms about or jab the air with their fingers, adding physical vehemence to their vociferousness. Some stand, others sit, swaying rhythmically to and fro, others walk up and down the periphery of the study-hall or on the balconies or corridors outside.

All of this activity, the visitor will quickly observe, is conducted in pairs. The students, deployed in serried rows, concentrate their attention on their partners, ignoring the other pairs all around them. If the outsider is visiting in the morning, he will see that the pairs tend to pore briefly together over short pieces of text, then launch into lengthy and vigorous argument with each other. Sometimes they will go to the back of the hall to fetch more books, pore over them, then argue some more. Occasionally they will go over to one of the rabbis sitting at the front or at the side of the hall, consult with him, then return to their places, and argue again.

In the afternoon, in most yeshivas, the tempo changes. There is more poring, longer stints of reading or chanting by the pairs in unison, and less arguing. The outsider will rightly conclude that the strategy of the afternoon session is more breadth and less depth, whereas in the morning the students are expected to delve deeply into the Talmudic discussion.

At night, there is less uniformity. Some pairs – partners generally change for each session – are as agitated as in the morning; others, heads down, appear to be racing through the texts. Certain students prefer to learn alone in the evening, in silence, but others chant the text aloud, and then proceed to argue as though with themselves, even making the concomitant gesticulations. Some of the lone learners hum to themselves; some chant 'ay-ay-ay' as they rock with their *stender* (Yiddish: wooden lectern). Others sing loudly, but this does not appear to disturb anyone else.

The night *seder* (study-session) officially ends at 10.30 or 11, but there are always night owls who like to stay up to the small hours, and early birds who begin their learning before dawn. Some yeshivas pride themselves that the 'sound of Torah' is never stilled in their study-hall, twenty-four hours a day, seven days a week, except for prayers.

A visitor at dusk to many yeshivas will find the whole student body sitting and swaying and chanting 'ay-ay-ay' over small books. These are not Talmud tractates, but medieval ethical works advising how to fight the Evil Inclination, how to attain moral and spiritual excellence and how not to waste precious time on the vanities of This World.

For the outsider accustomed to any form of modern academic milieu, the obvious question has to be: how can serious study be accomplished in these conditions? What a vast difference from a university or even a high-school library, where silence and self-restraint are the norms, aspired to by the students, or imposed by the staff.

Ask the question in a yeshiva, and you will invariably be directed to the mishna in Tractate Avot which lists 'The forty-eight means by which Torah is acquired: by study, by the hearing of the ear, by the recitation of the lips . . . by consorting with fellow-students, by intense argument among students . . .' Study in pairs, which is called *chavrusa* (lit. 'friendship') in Aramaic, conducted amidst many other such pairs, is an ancient method of Talmud learning. It was naturally adopted by the first yeshivas that opened in Russia and Poland in the nineteenth century – the forerunners of the present-day haredi yeshivas. There seems no sign of it changing or being significantly amended at the end of the twentieth century.

Most yeshiva students will maintain that the noise and tumult are no distraction at all, but learning aids, without which they would find learning strange and difficult. Some will not even understand the question. That is certainly true of haredim brought up through the system of heder and *yeshiva ketana* (junior yeshiva), before reaching the *yeshiva gedola*, the fully fledged Talmudical college, which admits students in their late teens.

The traditional didactic approach in the typically run-down, dingy little heder of the East European shtetl – as in the Sephardic Middle Eastern Jewish ghetto too – was that of chanting words or phrases in unison after the 'rebbe' (meaning teacher, not to be confused with the hasidic 'rebbe', another use of the same word). He would chant the names of the Hebrew letters and the way to pronounce them, and the little children would echo them. He would sing a phrase from the Pentateuch together with its Yiddish translation, and the whole class would repeat it, time after time. Then on to Mishna, and eventually – often when the children were still only six or seven years old – to Gemara.

The chanting method, apart from successfully drilling the material into the little brains (and eventually inuring them to constant loud noise), also conveniently overcame the problem of sex-related or otherwise embarrassing or esoteric passages in the holy texts. The children understood neither the Hebrew original nor the Yiddish translation of such sections, nor did it matter as long as they could repeat them faultlessly.

The draughty heder with its bright-eyed children and ragged rebbe, portrayed with cloying, *Fiddler on the Roof* sentimentality, was the stock-in-trade of Jewish dramatists and lyricists, on both sides of the Atlantic, earlier in this century. The underlying assumption of their plays and musicals was that the world they evoked was dying. After the Holocaust, it was presumed to be dead. Today such *hadarim* (plural of *heder*) are proliferating with the haredi baby-boom. The children look happier and are certainly better fed than their pre-war shtetl or slum forebears, and the classrooms are warmer and more cheerfully decorated; but the method of instruction remains essentially unchanged.

There is of late, in fact, a revival of Yiddish, both as the language of education and of general discourse, in haredi communities. The heder, and its equivalent educational establishment for girls, is the key factor in this particular return to roots. In many families in Bnei Brak, Borough Park or Antwerp, especially among the hasidic groups, the generation now in their thirties and forties speak a lame and broken Yiddish while their children's command of the language is fluent and natural. Conversely, the children's Hebrew, English or French – the language of their native country – is less fluent than that of their parents. The parents will have had a broader early education, in a more school-like, less heder-like framework. A generation ago, with haredism weak and Modern-Orthodoxy apparently in the ascendant, haredi parents and schools were prepared to accept a modicum of compromise with secular culture. But not any more. Now, the trend in many haredi communities is to make do with as little secular study as the law of the land allows. Haredi children who are third- or fourth-generation American or British are growing up speaking with the alien lilt that their immigrant grandparents or great-grandparents tried so hard to shake off.

In yeshiva ketana, which the young haredi will attend from his bar-mitzva, secular studies taper off to nothing or almost nothing. Here he is introduced to the chavrusa format of learning in pairs in the study-hall. But long hours are still spent in the classroom, with the better teachers encouraging student participation and helping them develop textual skills and academic initiative.

In most yeshiva gedolas (though less so in the US than in Israel) the students are steadily weaned from classroom lessons (shiurim) as they advance in seniority. The top grades in many yeshivas have no class requirements at all, and students spend all their time in the study-hall. The only shiurim they attend are those of the rosh yeshiva, the dean, delivered once or twice a week in the study-hall to the entire student body. Even on these august occasions, though, the basic principle of learning through arguing is preserved. In many yeshivas, the best students, having prepared the material ahead of time, are expected to butt into the rosh yeshiva's dissertation, and argue with him. The rosh, for his part, takes huge pleasure in fencing with his brightest disciples – and nine times out of ten slashing them to ribbons.

The ceaseless babel of frenetic intellectual activity in the study-halls of the yeshivas is thus to be seen as an integral part of an ancient educational approach, an expression of the 'Oral Law' learning tradition that conditions the haredi student from his earliest childhood. It represents, for haredim, another distinct triumph over modernity: not only is the substance of Torah surviving and flourishing; even its time-hallowed teaching method is carrying the day. This triumph, moreover, has spread beyond the traditional frameworks of classical (or reconstituted) haredism. In recent years the chavrusa/study-hall format has widely established itself in Modern-Orthodox yeshiva-type high schools and colleges throughout the Jewish world.

Equally noteworthy is the fact that chavrusa learning flourishes among students at traditional yeshivas who pursue secular studies simultaneously with their yeshiva education. Thus, for instance, a seventeen- or eighteen-year-old student at the Netiv Meir yeshiva high school in Jerusalem, or in any of the twenty-odd similar institutions around Israel, will spend his mornings disputing with his Talmud partner amid the din and dissonance of the study-hall, and his afternoons in the very different discipline of the laboratory or computer-room, or of the conventional classroom. Or in suburban Baltimore, Maryland, a student will devote his whole day to chanting and arguing with chavrusas in the study-hall of the prestigious Ner Israel yeshiva gedola, and his evenings quietly taking classes or doing library work in the no less prestigious, but methodologically very different seat of learning, Johns Hopkins University.

It would not occur to either of these students, while engaged in their secular studies, to chant passages from the textbook together with a colleague, to try and find weak points in it and argue about them volubly, or to remonstrate with the teacher or professor in the middle of a lecture. But nor does it occur to them, or their rabbis, to change or challenge the old-style method of yeshiva learning.

Occasionally one comes across yeshiva students, particularly at the high-school level, who do criticize the chavrusa system as a refuge for the less academically inclined, who while away the hours comfortably enveloped in a numbing buzz of undifferentiated sound. The lazy student develops a knack of sinking into open-eyed torpor as soon as the seder has begun. As long as his chavrusa, at least, looks as if he is reading out loud or arguing, the mashgiach (his full title is *mashgiach-ruchani*: spiritual supervisor) who is the rabbi-disciplinarian of the yeshiva will not trouble the pair.

*

Despite the uniform method of chavrusa/study-hall learning which runs through the whole 'yeshiva world', that world is far from united. The traditional haredi yeshivas, as they become stronger and more numerous, are increasingly spurning any vestige of compromise with secular culture, and are distancing themselves from yeshivas where secular studies vie with Torah for the time and minds of the students. The polarization is more pronounced in Israel, though it is the prevalent trend in the Diaspora too. Top Israeli yeshivas, which used to balance their intake between haredi yeshiva ketana boys and boys from (Zionist) yeshiva high schools, now bar the latter group altogether.

Some of the outstanding haredi alumni of the Hevron Yeshiva in Jerusalem for example, men who went on to become rabbis and dayanim, are former yeshiva high-school graduates who entered the yeshiva gedola after their matriculation. Some intended originally to stay for two or three years, and stayed for ten. Others planned a rabbinical or religious career from the outset. Other high-school students followed their original plans, leaving Hevron eventually to enlist, and then pursue academic or business careers. The yeshiva would frown: any defection was considered a failure. But it would turn a blind eye, and continue admitting high-quality yeshiva high-school graduates.

Now all their kind are unwelcome, regardless of individual abilities or ambitions. 'It's not our fault,' says Rabbi Avraham Farbstein, the Hevron Dean. 'They [the yeshiva high schools] are waging all-out war against us. They're literally brainwashing their pupils. We're so strong we don't even feel it. We have to turn away hundreds of applicants each year anyway. Personally, though, this polarization pains me. I wanted to combat it, and I think we could easily combat it by sending our students to talk to the high-schoolers. But in our [haredi] circles there is no interest. People simply don't care.'

Farbstein denies that the yeshiva high-school graduates make better Talmud scholars than the boys who have come up through the heder–yeshiva ketana route. But another prominent haredi yeshiva dean, Rabbi Yissachar Meir of Yeshivat Hanegev, freely admits that he misses the intellectual input of the high-school students. 'They are more thorough in their learning,' he says. 'More analytical; less prepared to make do with superficial answers to difficult questions.'

Meir's Yeshivat Hanegev, in the southern township of Netivot, provides the most graphic example of the polarization: it has gone from a 100 per cent yeshiva high-school intake to zero. Rabbi Meir claims that the break was his deliberate doing. His policy now, he says, is 'to reject any student who has completed twelve grades in the yeshiva high-school system. Once they've gone on that far, they will rarely change.' 'That's what he tells *you*,' says Farbstein, chuckling. 'The facts are that they [the yeshiva high schools] declared war on him, he had no students, and so he had to go for yeshiva ketana students.'

Yeshiva high schools, for their part, deny any 'brainwashing'. They say their boys simply prefer, on ideological and practical grounds, to go to hesder yeshivas where they combine Talmud study with periods of military service (see p. 121), rather than to the haredi yeshivas which are based on the deferment system. The lifestyle at the hesder yeshivas is much closer to what yeshiva high-schoolers are used to. They can continue to dress casually, to wear the bright-coloured, crocheted yarmulkas that have become the badge of Zionist Orthodoxy, to read freely and to go to the theatre and cinema. The hesder yeshiva will even condone dating, although the assumption is that romances are 'serious' and will, or at least may, lead to marriage, and that there is no sex, which is halachically forbidden outside marriage.

Several of the hesder yeshivas are situated in Judaea and Samaria (the occupied West Bank). The stereotypical hesder student is a bearded, wild-eyed young man toting a Talmud in one hand and a gun in the other, always available to help set up a new settlement in the territories. This is something of a media caricature but not altogether inaccurate. At any rate, life at hesder, interspersed as it is by long stints in the army, is a far cry from the sheltered, ghettoized existence of the mainstream haredi yeshivas. In the hesder yeshivas, virtually the entire student body comes from yeshiva high schools, and most of the students go on to university or professional training at the end of their five-year learning and soldiering programme.

Plainly there is disingenuousness all round. Rabbi Farbstein *does* miss the high-schoolers, despite his protestations to the contrary. He himself is an urbane, well read and widely travelled man, like the German-born Meir. They both grew to maturity and rose to prominence in more tolerant times. Privately, neither of them is truly comfortable with the current wave of exclusivism sweeping through the haredi yeshivas. But they swim with the tide, knowing that to buck it would be to endanger their positions and court trouble with the hardliners.

And the yeshiva high schools *do* counsel their students nowadays to choose a Zionist yeshiva rather than a 'black' (that is, haredi) institution. The teachers at the yeshiva high schools, formerly drawn from the ranks of haredi yeshiva alumni, are increasingly the products of the hesder yeshivas. In turn, they influence their pupils – those who want to spend time in yeshiva – to choose the hesder option and spurn the 'black' yeshivas.

In the Diaspora, the tension between secular education and haredi exclusivity exists between yeshivas, but also within them. The issue, moreover, is not only whether students will (or may, or should) go on to university after yeshiva, but whether they can take college courses *during* their yeshiva programmes. On both counts, the exclusivist trend is gaining ground. In Gateshead Yeshiva in England, the largest in Europe, the proportion of students going on to university or to professional training after yeshiva has markedly declined in recent years. Yeshivas in America that formerly encouraged simultaneous college studies now reluctantly tolerate them. Some that once tolerated them have since banned them.

Still, the pursuit of a university education does not carry with it in American or European haredi circles the stigma of betrayal and religious backsliding that it implies for Israeli haredim. A leading haredi yeshiva like Ner Israel in Baltimore lays on buses for its students taking degree courses at Johns Hopkins and other universities in the area. A yeshiva faculty member is designated 'coordinator' with the universities, his task being to obtain as many credits as possible for each student in recognition of his Talmud studies at the yeshiva. Ner Israel also enables students to live on its campus during the summer recess in order to cram in full-day courses at the university. With application and careful planning, says Jerome Kadden, the yeshiva's associate director, students can complete a first degree in two years.

'We don't encourage university studies, but we facilitate them,' he says. 'But a student is only permitted to take college courses after he has spent at least one full year learning full-time at the yeshiva.'

'What he didn't tell you,' says Gary Rosenblatt, editor of the *Baltimore Jewish Times*, 'is that they don't permit [just] *any* courses – only those designed to lead to a professional qualification. If you want to study philosophy at university, for instance, or history or literature – forget it. They are prepared to accept university as a vocational school, but nothing more than that.'

This distinction, between study for the sake of *parnassa* (earning a living) and study for its own sake, reflects a social as well as ideological norm among American haredim. If an eligible young man took a degree in law or accounting, or even chemistry, that is acceptable, at least '*bediavad*' (post factum). The material rewards of his academic qualification are certainly acceptable. But if he studied the arts, or pure sciences, he is suspect. The burden of proof is on him, to show that he did it, for instance, in order eventually to obtain a senior teaching position in an Orthodox high school. Otherwise, the assumption is that he is ideologically rickety, and his marital eligibility will suffer accordingly.

24

Campus Life

The mashgiach, who may be a fine Talmudic scholar in his own right, is nevertheless not primarily concerned with the academic content of yeshiva life. His responsibility is the spiritual well-being of the students: their piety and the punctiliousness of their religious observance. The godly life, after all, requires both learning the Torah and keeping the mitzvot. As *mashgichim* never tire of quoting to their charges: 'The ignoramus cannot be Godfearing' (Mishna Avot 2:5), but 'The purpose of knowledge is repentance and good deeds' (Talmud Tractate Berachot 17a).

The yeshiva, like the British public school, aspires to mould its students' personalities, and not merely to inculcate knowledge or foster academic prowess. The goal is to turn out bnei Torah, 'sons of the Torah', a credential that denotes religious devotion as well as scholarship. The villains of yeshiva folklore are those turn-of-the-century students who, caught between two worlds, would lovingly learn their Gemara on shabbat while smoking a cigarette (the capital offence of kindling). Such anguished ambivalence is attributed by mashgichim, always in deprecation, to the Hebrew national poet Haim Nahman Bialik (1873–1934) and to other intellectuals and Zionist leaders who attended Volozhin or other famous Russian yeshivas before eventually throwing off the practices and beliefs of Orthodoxy.

But these figures, who became role-models for entire generations of Jewish young men in pre-Holocaust Europe, are now merely the bygone bugbears of mashgichim's harangues. The history of their defections presents no realistic enticement to the denizens of today's 'yeshiva world'. Yeshiva study is almost universal nowadays among haredi males (over 95 per cent in Israel, according to one study, almost as high in the Diaspora), and experts agree that the 'drop-out' rate among haredi yeshiva students and graduates –

that is, the complete abandonment of Orthodoxy – is negligible, some say infinitesimal.

The synthesis between learning and religious devotion in the yeshiva is immediately apparent to the outside visitor: the study-hall doubles as a synagogue. This is the case in virtually every yeshiva. At the front of the hall is the Holy Ark containing the Torah scrolls, and below it the cantor's lectern. In the centre is the *bimah*, the raised platform from which the Torah is read. Several major yeshivas have followed the example of Ponevezh, the leading Israeli yeshiva, and installed ornately carved and gilded Renaissance-period arks salvaged from disused synagogues in Italy.

Ponevezh itself, built in the late 1950s on a hilltop looking down across Bnei Brak, is a large, architecturally undistinguished edifice. But its location – and its reputation as the Oxbridge of yeshivas – give it special stature and dignity. Its broad, lofty study-hall and adjoining balconies and annexes, crowded with gnarled wooden benches and piled everywhere with books, seem to emanate an aura of learning and tradition, like an ancient Cambridge college.

When the seder is in progress in Ponevezh, a hum of hundreds of young men learning wafts out over the all-Orthodox city. But when the yeshiva is at prayer, their full-throated roar – 'Amen, May the Great Name Be Blessed Forever and Ever' – rolls like thunder down the hill.

Prayer, three times a day, is an important part of yeshiva life. It is performed much more slowly and deliberately than in a regular synagogue, where most worshippers have limited time at their disposal and must veritably speed-read through the psalms, songs, supplications, and selections from the Talmud that comprise Shaharit, the daily morning service. Mincha and Maariv, the afternoon and evening services respectively, are recited in a single time-saving session in many synagogues. In Lithuanian-style yeshivas, by contrast, a regular weekday Shaharit can take close to an hour. Mincha is said before lunch, and Maariv before dinner, and each lasts at least twenty minutes.

The central element of all three daily services – on shabbat and festivals there are four – is the *shmoneh esreh*, a series of praises and requests in the form of blessings ('Blessed art Thou O Lord . . .'), dating back to pre-Talmudic times. This prayer is said silently, while standing at attention. Anyone familiar with the text can read it, soundlessly mouthing the words, as the halacha requires, and thinking about their meaning, in three or four minutes. Many haredim will take longer, when they have the time. In yeshivas, students are expected to take much longer, to concentrate harder, to pray more fervently – not only for themselves and their families, but for the whole nation. According to the haredi belief, yeshiva students, through their learning, are the protectors of the nation and the world.

The classical mitnagdic yeshivas of Russia and Lithuania frowned on devotional movement, called *shockelling* in Yiddish, during the davening. This disapproval was in keeping with their dogmatic denigration of anything smacking of hasidic excesses. Some old-style Lithuanian rabbis still stand completely still, hands at their sides, head erect, throughout the shmoneh esreh. But the rigidity of the hasidic/mitnagdic divide has long since softened sufficiently to admit shockelling, and nowadays all yeshivas at prayer – mitnagdic, hasidic and Sephardic – present a picture of bobbing and swaying bodies.

Lay observers have long noticed a high preponderance of eyeglasses among yeshiva students and alumni, and they naturally tended to assume that this was caused by long hours of reading small and/or poor print, often under indifferent lighting. But a medical study recently published in Israel lays much of the blame on shockelling. It maintains that the incessant change of focus, as the eye approaches and recedes from the text, eventually causes myopia. The study was based on a Jerusalem yeshiva, where 90 per cent of the students were found to wear glasses – compared to 15 per cent at a nearby non-Orthodox high school.

Yeshiva students themselves, blithely unaware of the damage they may be doing to their eyes, are often more preoccupied with the effects of shockelling on their hats. For praying (but not for learning), all the students must wear their hats. The hasidim, who have closely cropped haircuts with long peyot hanging down the sides, simply ram their round black hats on hard, and *shockel* freely. But many mitnagdic yeshiva students sport careful coiffures, with a fashionable wave in the front, and they wear their hats (also black, but usually expensive snap-brimmed fedoras) jauntily angled at the back of their heads. Shockelling for them is a constant battle between the muscles of the neck and the forces of gravity.

While shockelling is pervasive among haredim in synagogues too, and is only more intensive in yeshivas, facial grimacing during davening is almost exclusively a yeshiva practice. Perhaps the students are less self-conscious than adult synagogue worshippers. Also, the yeshiva atmosphere of collective religious striving more readily encourages outward manifestations of fervour. At any rate, many students wear pained expressions during the shmoneh esreh, screw up their faces and shut their eyes, and sometimes stretch out their hands in supplicatory gestures.

In the 'Lithuanian' yeshivas the overall tone of the prayer-services is sad and sombre. The cantor, usually one of the students, intones his parts in almost dirge-like cadences, and what little singing there is is restrained and unjoyous. Hasidic yeshivas, on the other hand, follow the style or *nussach* of their particular rebbe's 'court'. Their services are generally brisk during the week, and lively with cheerful singing on shabbat and festivals. In hasidic yeshivas which physically adjoin the court, the students pray on shabbat in the rebbe's synagogue with the rest of the community. In the Gerer synagogue in Jerusalem, special galleries have been built for the students, who are not allowed to pray in the crowded main hall.

The religious life of the hasidic yeshiva student is largely rebbe-oriented, and the mashgiach's role is therefore to supervise the students' communion with the centre of spiritual inspiration, rather than to generate that inspiration himself. Between visits to the court – if the court and the yeshiva are on different continents these can be few and far between – the literature of the particular hasidic house, and other hasidic literature too, serves as day-to-day religious nourishment. The mashgiach is involved both in teaching these works and in ensuring that the boys study them themselves. (In some hasidic yeshivas, the term *mashpiah*, 'influencer', is used rather than 'mashgiach', which means 'supervisor'.)

Some hasidic yeshivas emphasize getting up before dawn as part of their religious regimen. Others encourage frequent immersions in the mikve. Whereas ritual immersion is a halachic requirement for women at the end of each menstrual cycle, there is no parallel demand on men. Nevertheless, such immersion has traditionally been considered salubrious for the soul, and physically bracing too. Legends of kabbalists and early hasidic figures often have them hacking at ice-covered rivers in their insistent enthusiasm to perform the mitzva of mikve. Nowadays, mikves are usually heated, and so the element of asceticism is mitigated. Still, rising '*fartogs*' (Yiddish: before dawn) on cold winter mornings to dip in the mikve and then study hasidic texts is fairly rigorous for young lads.

The Breslever hasidim, a sect who are disposed to mysticism, encourage their yeshiva students to spend the dawn hours in individual meditation. Their bus will drive them to a copse on the outskirts of town, and drop them off at intervals, coming back to collect them after the sun has risen.

In the 'Lithuanian' yeshivas the faculty, and especially the mashgiach, have to sustain a state of religious tension without the benefit of the rebbe and his court, or the other potent spiritual props of hasidism. It was mainly to assist them in this task that Rabbi Yisrael Salanter (1810–1883) founded the mussar (lit., moral admonishment) movement, a study programme of ethical and homiletical works for the religious betterment of yeshiva students.

Rabbi Salanter himself was a complex personality, subject to intense intellectual and psychological upheavals throughout his life. His primary purpose was to protect the 'yeshiva world' – he was instrumental in the creation of several yeshivas – and himself too, from the spiritual pitfalls of the Enlightenment and other challenges of modernity. (He spent decades commuting between the West – France and Germany – and the haredi communities in Russia). He introduced the study of mussar as part of the yeshiva curriculum. Some yeshivas, under his guidance, set aside special rooms, called 'mussar houses', where *bachurim* would meditate alone or study this literature in small groups.

Salanter's ideas were not universally popular; they even resulted in a student strike at one leading yeshiva. Different 'schools' of mussar evolved. At Slobodka, in the Lithuanian town of Kovnius (the Jews called it Kovna), they preached a form of mussar known as gadlut ha'adam, literally 'the greatness of man'. The mashgiach would constantly extol the students, stressing the important social and religious role of every ben Torah – and hence the weighty responsibility attaching to each of them. This approach was symbolized outwardly by the inordinate, almost dandyish care that the students took over their clothes and appearance, always dressing in suits and ties despite their straitened and sometimes desperate economic circumstances.

Inside the yeshiva there was another interesting expression of gadluss ha'adam: the mashgiach would always address the students, even the younger teenagers, in the deferential second-person *ihr* instead of the familiar form, *du*. Any religious correction or individual chastisement would be done in discreet privacy, and the mashgiach would emphasize the high standards expected of a 'yeshivaman' rather than dwell directly on a student's specific lapse. The *katnut ha'adam*, or 'smallness of man' school, on the other hand, tended to stress the weaknesses and inadequacies of people in general and of yeshiva bachurim in particular. Yeshivas that adhered to it, such as Novardok, fostered an atmosphere of sombre introspection. The mashgichim, in their mussar sermons or *shmuessen* (Yiddish: chats), would bemoan the sinfulness of the students.

Ulimately, though, it was – and to an important extent still is – the mashgiach's own personality and example that had the strongest religious influence on the students. Yeshiva lore is full of stories reflecting the love and concern that some of the classical mashgichim felt for every bachur in their yeshiva. Others were more distant, disciplinarian figures, but won deference and devotion from their students. Still others lacked the love, piled on the discipline – and earned only ridicule and resentment.

Today, mussar is no longer controversial, but nor is it especially influential in the yeshiva world. Some of the forms are still maintained. At the Slobodka Yeshiva in Bnei Brak the mashgiach uses 'ihr'. At the Gateshead Yeshiva in England, which follows the Novardok school, the mashgiach had no compunction about admonishing the students in summer 1990 not to hunt for television sets in town to watch the World Cup Soccer Finals. That would be *bitul zman* and *bitul Torah*, he said – wasting time that ought to be spent on Torah study.

The one mussar practice that has survived in all the non-hasidic yeshivas is the learning of ethical works – the genre has actually come to be called 'mussar' literature, even though the classics were written centuries before Rabbi Salanter founded his movement – for half an hour each evening, by the entire student body in the study-hall. This is usually done individually, not in chavrusa pairs.

The favourite works are the eleventh-century *Duties of the Heart* by the Spanish scholar Bahya ibn Pekuda, and the eighteenth-century *Path of the Just* by an Italian rabbi, poet and mystic, Moshe Hayim Luzzato. This latter book leads the reader along an ascending path of religious and moral improvement, following a course mapped out in the Talmud (Tractate Avoda Zarah 20b, also Mishna Sotah 9:16): Care, Zeal, Cleanliness (of mind), Abstinence, Purity, Piety, Humility, Fear of Sin, Holiness.

Obviously this does not appeal to every young man, and for many students the 'mussar seder' is little more than a relaxing break before Maariv and dinner. They hardly bother to focus on the dour texts. 'Too hardcore,' one New York yeshiva bachur described the *Path of the Just* in a 1982 study of American yeshivas by sociologist William B. Helmreich. 'You know, real fire-and-brimstone kind of stuff, and it depressed me too much. It was written hundreds of years ago and it's hard to relate to.' Another student noted: 'Mussar only helps people who want it to help. If a person learns mussar with the intention that he's going to change, then he will. But if he's learning just for the sake of study, then it won't affect him.' A third student interviewed by Helmreich was even more negative. 'There's a mussar seder, but it's a big joke . . . Someone will bang on the table in the *beit midrash* [study-hall/synagogue] and yell "mussar seder", and everyone will laugh.' His friend volunteered that 'Most people just stop learning and bull around for fifteen minutes.'

But there are those who take it seriously too. Usually, these are the more pious bachurim, those who daven the longest and spend the least time combing their hair and adjusting their hats. Often, but not always, these are also the students who are the 'biggest *matmidim*', that is, the most diligent and assiduous about their Talmud studies.

There are, in fact, three separate orders of merit in yeshiva life: brilliance, diligence and piety. Theoretically, the yeshiva strives to blend the three, in its quest to produce the fully rounded *talmid hacham* (religious scholar). In practice, though, yeshiva educators recognize that the three orders represent different natural endowments, and also that some students are naturally endowed with none of them in particularly generous measure. Still, diligence and piety can be 'worked on', in the mussarist sense, sometimes with remarkable results. In certain yeshivas, spending fifteen hours a day sitting in the beit midrash is the norm – from 7 in the morning to midnight, with short breaks for meals and a brief afternoon nap. The Yeshivat Hanegev, in Netivot, is famous for its exhausting standards of diligence.

In most yeshivas, though, that level of application is the exception rather than the rule. Students who reach it and maintain it are admired by their colleagues, and held up by the mashgiach as models to be emulated. The *matmid*, moreover, is a highly desirable candidate on the marriage market for the girl – and there are many such girls, the pious-minded products of mussar-equivalent influences in haredi girls' schools and seminaries – who wants a future husband guaranteed to keep learning seriously and devotedly long after he has left the yeshiva.

Piety in yeshivas can be petty, small-minded and holier-than-thou. There are sneaks and spies in some yeshivas, self-appointed or encouraged by the mashgiach to keep watch on less devout students. But yeshiva piety can also be genuinely beautiful, especially when sincerely religious students attempt to live by the biblical precept 'Love thy neighbour as thyself.' These students will make a point of befriending lonely newcomers; they will visit sick colleagues or spend time with elderly members of the wider community. They will go to inordinate lengths to fulfil the mitzva of returning lost property to its owner, pasting up notices and asking around the dining-hall over the most trifling item.

'Working on himself' to break bad habits, a pious bachur will observe 'talking-fasts', days or even whole weeks when he talks to no one except when learning. In his normal conversation he will take scrupulous care to avoid *lashon hara*, the evil tongue, which means not saying or listening to anything even vaguely uncomplimentary about anyone else. There are entire books devoted to ways of resisting this particularly tempting sin, and the pious student will study them constantly.

Here again, when the *shadchan* (marriage broker; fem. *shadchanit*) comes around, the bachur with *middot* – caring human qualities – will find himself much sought after. Many haredi girls – who must make their nuptial decision on the basis of a few brief and stilted encounters, and therefore must rely heavily on a prospective groom's yeshiva reputation – agree with the Talmudic sage Yochanan ben Zakai (Mishna Avot 2:2) that 'a good heart' incorporates most other worthy qualities and best characterizes 'the good way to which a man should cleave'.

Sometimes, years of sustained piety and spiritual asceticism in the rarefied atmosphere of a yeshiva produce a genuine tzaddik, a 'righteous man'. These are uncommon human beings, but unmistakable when encountered. Their eyes seem to shine and smile with benevolence. They never raise their voices, never get angry, always want to help. Some people look for this form of serene, radiant humanity in Eastern ashrams, or in secluded monasteries. It needs a hothouse habitat to exist, and it can be found, albeit rarely, in haredi yeshivas too.

At the other end of the scale are the students who really ought not to have been sent to a yeshiva at all, but, haredi society being what it is, end up there anyway. And once there, neither they nor the yeshiva are eager to terminate their stay peremptorily or unpleasantly. In Israel a young man not registered at a yeshiva is automatically eligible for the draft, which in haredi eyes is an additional and compelling reason not to expel any student unless there is absolutely no alternative. But even in most Diaspora yeshivas, where this consideration is absent, expulsion is still a last-resort penalty, with possibly far-reaching social repercussions (on matrimonial eligibility, for instance).

Serious halachic offence is of course the one action that will trigger automatic dismissal from almost any yeshiva. The Bialik-type heretic, the deliberate violator of shabbat, must be removed before he can influence others. (The baalei teshuva yeshivas, for newly Orthodox students, are somewhat more flexible: backsliding in observance, even if deliberate and therefore heretical, is overlooked, especially among new students.) Similarly a student caught succumbing to grave sin – sleeping with a girl, for instance, or eating non-kosher meat – must expect the ultimate punishment, even though he may have been the victim of his Evil Inclination, and not a heretical, premeditated offender. (The Evil Inclination or *yetzer hara* is each person's inborn tendency to sin – cf. Genesis 8:21. It is also linked in Jewish theology to Satan, who exploits it in order to tempt the person into sin – cf. Job 2. It is in constant strife with the *yetzer hatov* or Good Inclination.)

Even in such cases though, according to Israeli author Amnon Levy, dismissal from yeshiva is not the last word. 'At the end of the day, the [halachic rebel] gets married, and then he generally returns to the fold. Haredi society is so intense and all-encompassing that it is hard to opt out of it for ever. Only a handful make their way permanently into secular society. Most stay [within the haredi community], and adapt.'*

In any event, serious halachic offences are remarkably rare in yeshivas – as both Levy and the American sociologist Helmreich attest. 'The majority of students conform to the demands of yeshiva life,' says Helmreich, 'thereby exerting considerable influence over those who do not.'

Different yeshivas have different demands, beyond the strictly halachic. In the hasidic court of Belz, for instance, the black, round, felt hats are worn with the bow on the hat-band at the left. If a student at the Belzer yeshiva were to insist on wearing his ribbon on the right – which is the way of the Vishnitzer hasidim – that in itself could be seen as a sign that he was deliberately provoking his own institution. Relations between Belz and Vishnitz are not good, even though the Belzer Rebbe is the Vishnitzer Rebbe's son-in-law. Similarly if a student at Rabbi Shach's Ponevezh insisted on distributing the printed sermons of the Lubavitcher Rebbe in the study-hall, he would presumably be summoned to the mashgiach and urged to find another yeshiva. (In

* *The Haredim* (Jerusalem: Keter, 1989), p. 175.

both of these hypothetical cases, there might be some bodily violence from over-zealous students attendant on the expulsion.) Obviously, if a student appeared in the Belzer yeshiva, or at Ponevezh, in a colourful sports shirt and tartan slacks he would be told to look for a more appropriate institution.

The 'blackness', as it is called, of the different yeshivas is in fact a sliding scale of conformism and haredism that covers not just clothes but most aspects of a yeshiva bachur's life. In part, the scale coincides with the yeshiva's attitude to secular studies. It would be absurd, for instance, for a yeshiva to ban newspapers and serious magazines while allowing its students to attend college. At the same time, though, a student openly flaunting *Playboy* or *Penthouse* could hardly claim that he needed to be familiar with them for his university studies.

At Ner Yisrael in Baltimore, where many students go to college in the evening and during the summer recess, one student had the wall over his bed plastered with photographs of (male) basketball stars. A faculty member escorting a visitor around the modern, spacious campus, complete with football fields and basketball courts, looked mildly embarrassed at this, but indicated that it was within the bounds of the permissible. The same display would be quite unthinkable in a mainstream haredi yeshiva in Israel, but tolerable in a baal teshuva yeshiva, and acceptable at a hesder yeshiva.

Finally, there is a category of problem students who are neither heretical nor sinful nor nonconformist; they just do not study. These non-learners do not necessarily lack nautural ability; they are simply not interested in learning, and neither the mashgiach nor peer pressure can generate sufficient diligence or piety in them to draw them into the study-hall. Every yeshiva has such students. Even the top-flight yeshivas, which ostensibly admit pupils solely on the basis of entrance examinations, are susceptible to pressures from rich or rabbinic families to take their unstudious scions.

In the Diaspora, the unacademic young haredi can, in the final analysis, go out to work, and he will normally do so after spending a year or two in a yeshiva for appearance's sake. In Israel, however, he is not free to go out into the world unless he first serves in the army. So he usually stays in the yeshiva, nominally at least.

Some of these problem students gravitate to activities on the fringe of the haredi world, such as a long-established organization called Peylim ('Activists'), which campaigns against non-Jewish missionaries. Proselytizing is forbidden by law in Israel, and there are not many missionaries (on behalf of Christian sects, Jews for Jesus, Eastern cults and the like) openly operating in the country. Nevertheless, Peylim keeps going, monitoring suspicious Gentiles, harassing allegedly covert missionaries, printing leaflets, holding rallies, raising funds – providing, at any rate, a semblance of activity for bored yeshiva bachurim.

25

The Brightest and the Best

The shadchan, peeking down at an eligible student from the (empty) women's gallery during seder, need not be an old-style professional. Although the institution still exists in the haredi world, it is no longer, as it was in the shtetl – or at any rate in the literature of shtetl life – the exclusive instrument for initiating an arranged marriage. Nowadays an active and involved wife of a yeshiva dean will propose more of the matches among her husband's pupils than any professional. Relatives and friends, too, suggest and effect introductions. And sometimes, though this is strongly deplored in mainstream haredi yeshivas, and positively forbidden in the hasidic yeshivas, boys and girls actually come across each other on their own.

But whatever the eventual logistics, the matter of marriage – or *shidduchim* (matches), as it is invariably referred to in yeshiva parlance – hangs heavy over every yeshiva study-hall. Titters and knowing winks flash round the hall when a stranger arrives to chat with the dean or one of the rabbis, and stares appraisingly at a particular student. The atmosphere is such, in fact, that almost any middle-aged visitor is assumed to be a prospective father-in-law, unless there is evidence to the contrary.

The foremost hero of the study-hall, and the most eligible, is the *iluy*, the naturally brilliant student. If he fulfils his potential he might eventually be appointed to the faculty of the yeshiva, or of another yeshiva, or become a dayan or rabbi. Those career options, in that order of prestige, are the prizes that await the gifted yeshiva student who is prepared to invest long years of serious study in kollel.

The iluy is naturally the most desirable commodity on the yeshiva marriage-market, especially if he has a modicum of middot too. He for his part can do no better, career-wise, than to marry a daughter of one of the top faculty figures, or of some rich benefactor of the yeshiva.*

The Talmud itself distinguishes between two kinds of genius: *Sinai*, the phenomenally retentive memory; and *oker harim* (lit., he who 'uproots and pulverizes mountains') – the keen and powerful analytical mind. The faculty's task is to blend these two properties and ensure that the most promising students learn broadly as well as deeply, and do not spend all their time in hair-splitting *pilpul* (casuistry). Often the yeshiva rabbis will learn in chavrusa with the brightest boys.

This of course elevates the iluy still higher in the eyes of his colleagues, and the result is sometimes insufferable pride and strutting pomposity. The mashgiach and the rosh yeshiva will try to counter that, but they have to tread carefully, because the iluy, like a football star, is subject to overtures from other yeshivas. A yeshiva, ultimately, is only as good as its top students. If it cannot hold on to its own best and brightest, it will be unable to attract new star material.

The academic attainments of a top-notch oker harim-type iluy are difficult to quantify. Acuteness, clarity of thought, profundity of analysis – these are qualities that only Talmudic cognoscenti can properly assess. The age-old method by which talmidei hachamim size each other up is called in Yiddish *redn in lernen*, literally 'talking in learning'. Sometimes a prospective lay (and wealthy)

* The time-honoured tradition in yeshivas is for the best student to wind up married to the rosh yeshiva's daughter, and there is always much teasing and speculation in yeshivas surrounding such matches. But the fact is that many yeshiva deanships and community rabbinates in the haredi world are transmitted through the male line – just like hasidic *rebbistves* (positions of rebbe). Gateshead Yeshiva in northern England is a case in point: the present Dean, Rabbi Avraham Gurwicz, is the son of a previous dean, Rabbi Leib Gurwicz, and his younger brother is also a senior lecturer at the yeshiva. Both are accomplished Talmudists; but their name and blood-line hardly hurt their careers. (Avraham Gurwicz, though, is also the selected son-*in-law* of another former dean, Rabbi Leib Lopian.)

Similar filial successions have taken place in the leading American yeshiva, at Lakewood, NJ, and in many other mitnagdic yeshivas in the US and Israel. Yeshivas, indeed, can be seen as family businesses – not unlike hasidic courts (or not as unlike hasidic courts as some mitnagdim fondly pretend) – with the family reluctantly opening the boardroom to new blood only when it cannot staff all the directorships from within.

father-in-law, seeking only the finest for his daughter, will send in an outside scholar to redn in lernen with a vaunted iluy, to determine impartially whether in fact he is all he's cracked up to be in his own yeshiva.

While the oker harim needs expert appraisal, the dazzling performances of the Sinai-type student draw ready gasps of wonderment from all around. Every good yeshiva seems to have its outstanding *baki* (broadly erudite Talmudist) who, when the mood takes him, will open a tractate at random at the bottom corner of a page, and, by reading the last few lines of the Tosafot, announce what page it is and what is on it. Rabbi Pinhas Hirschsprung of Montreal, Canada, is reputedly able to do that with every tractate.

Some yeshivas place particular emphasis on *bekiut* (broad erudition). In the hasidic yeshivas of Klausenberg, for instance, in America and Israel, students receive a special award from the Rebbe himself for knowing one thousand pages of Talmud by heart (with Rashi and Tosafot). The one thousand are of course two thousand, since each 'page' is really a folio, with an 'a' and a 'b' side, and the examination is rigorous and demanding. This feat requires years of diligent study; but no amount of diligence will achieve it unless the student is also endowed with an extraordinarily agile and retentive memory.

Does a yeshiva dean or eminent haredi rabbi, or indeed a star yeshiva student, *know* more than his counterpart in the 'outside world' – the professor, judge, or postgraduate college researcher? Does he have more bytes of information, so to speak, stored in his memory?

Haredim have no doubt that he does. But if they are right, the reason for the ostensible disparity lies in the special nature of haredi Talmud learning and 'knowing'. Here, as we have seen, there is no once-and-for-all 'knowledge' but rather constant review and amplification, even of material already 'learnt' and 'known'. This ceaseless process – the fulfilment of a supreme religious precept – enables those naturally gifted with strong memories to achieve, and maintain, remarkable quantities of stored knowledge.

Thus a well-known rabbi in Bnei Brak, noted for his bekiut, was seen absent-mindedly leafing through an entire tractate of the Talmud (albeit one of the smaller tractates) during a Mincha (afternoon) service. As the cantor intoned the prayers, the rabbi's eyes ran down the columns of print, page after page. In the space of a few minutes, he had revised the entire tractate, refreshing the various themes and arguments which had been filed away in his mind.

Yeshiva folk love to swap stories about the prodigious memory feats of their rabbis. Loyalties are fierce, but there can be little doubt that the most amazingly retentive memory in the 'yeshiva world' at this time belongs to Rabbi Ovadia Yosef, the former Sephardic Chief Rabbi of Israel (1973–83) whom we have previously encountered in his role as a key figure in haredi politics. He seems able to recall and quote effortlessly from virtually every Talmudic and halachic work ever printed (he owns copies of most of them in his vast private library). On a trip to the US as Chief Rabbi in the early 1980s, he visited eight yeshivas, and, as is the custom, he delivered a Talmudic discourse in each of them. Not once, according to a companion who travelled with him, did he ask in advance what chapter of what tractate a particular yeshiva happened to be studying. As he entered the study-hall he would inquire matter-of-factly, pause briefly with his hand on his brow, and then proceed to pour forth a torrent of material, all deftly interwoven on the subject-matter of the yeshiva's current curriculum, citing verbatim from dozens of sources.

At Yeshiva University in New York, Rabbi Yosef was interrupted in mid-lecture – the accepted yeshiva practice – by a persistent questioner. He peered through his dark glasses (he has weak eyes). 'Is his excellency perchance Rabbi Herschel Schachter?' he asked, in the delightfully archaic mode of address he always uses. Schachter is a senior faculty member at YU. Yes, said the questioner, he was indeed Schachter. 'And did not his excellency make that very point [Rabbi Yosef cited the passage from memory] in his recent book . . .?' The yeshiva exploded in a gale of incredulous laughter.

Rabbi Yosef, who plainly is endowed with a photographic memory, is similarly blessed with tireless assiduity. Now into his seventies, he still never stops learning. He spends every spare moment studying, or writing his commentaries and halachic responsa. Returning to Jerusalem by helicopter after midnight from a round of revivalist rallies in Negev townships, he will study till 3 in the morning – and be at synagogue at 6.30 to lead the service. Rabbi Shach too, even at his advanced age, spends most of his waking hours bent over the Gemara, as he has done throughout his life.

But is all this cerebral energy – of Yosef and Shach and all the other scholars and learners – being sensibly expended? In the computer age, is much of their effort superfluous? At the very least, could not the laborious, time-consuming functions of memorization be performed by an electronic intelligence? Could not the analogizing and distinguishing, which are the stuff of Talmudic learning, be handled by sophisticated software? Perhaps Shach and Yosef are too old to change. But ought there not to be revolutionary change in the realm of haredi Talmud learning, in light of the computer revolution? Why do chavrusa pairs in yeshivas around the world still huddle over creaking wooden stenders, instead of over PCs or mainframe terminals? In response to such questions, haredi scholars and yeshiva deans become defensive and dismissive, as though the questions signalled a new round in the centuries-long conflict between tradition and modernity.

And in a way, they do. Modern technology and learning aids – from the fax that can immediately transmit an accurate manuscript text from a New York library, to the computer in a Tel Aviv university that contains all the centuries of halachic responsa – are indeed challenging the traditional methods. Moreover, despite their instinctive negativism in response to outside probing, scholars in the haredi community are in fact gearing up to face the challenges. The community is fearful, yet fascinated. Its leaders are innately conservative, but beneath the inertia, deep divisions are discernible as progressive innovations force themselves to the surface.

To the traditionalists, the dangers are clear: simplification and popularization. Torah must be laboured over. That, as we have seen, is the age-old essence of the Oral Law. The learner has to 'kill himself in the tent of the Torah', not have the answers dished up to him on a computer disk or in a digested summary of all the relevant source-material. 'Learning means understanding,' said an eminent yeshiva dean, explaining the conservative position. 'One must understand how the Gemara proceeded, not just how it arrived at its conclusion. The same with Rashi and Tosafot.'

Rabbi Ovadia Yosef offered the same explanation with reference to halachic decision-making. 'It's no good just totting up the sources: seven say permitted, eight say forbidden. You have to understand exactly how the key rishonim or acharonim worked out their positions. Only if you understand can you weigh up and decide. Modern aids are helpful, but they can never change the basic need to learn the texts.'

Rabbi Nota Schiller of Ohr Somayach Yeshiva made essentially the same point, using bolder imagery. 'Learning is making love to the *daf* [page of Talmud]. Relying on digested or encyclopedic material is like the difference between that and artificial insemination. The birth of an idea has to come from within, or else it hasn't been properly conceived.'

To understand, to weigh up, to love, one must learn and labour over the authentic, original texts. A labour of love; there is no other way.

In addition, haredi scholars say, computer programming does not – they say cannot – meet the needs of the learner. The entire Talmud has been put on disks by a number of different software houses, but the programs are still expensive – a sure sign that they are not selling widely. The problem, these scholars maintain, is access codes. To find a reference, every program requires the learner to punch in a key word or phrase. But often in Talmud study, the associative link is not verbal but conceptual, and for that the computer technology presently available seems unable to help.

26

Wall of Books

Computers are not inherently ideological tools, and can hardly be accused of ideological deviation. Nor, on the face of it, can a modern Hebrew commentary on the Mishna, written by the thoroughly Orthodox Rabbi Pinhas Kehati, which merely synthesizes the existing classical commentaries in a more colloquial style and readable format. Nor can an English translation of the Talmud, now being produced by ArtScroll, a highly successful English-language haredi publishing house in the United States, with enthusiastic forewords by leading American haredi rabbis. Yet neither of these seemingly innocuous – seemingly helpful – works is to be found in the study-hall of Rabbi Shach's Ponevezh yeshiva. And because they are not there, they are not in dozens of other yeshivas in Israel and the Diaspora.

Fear is a key factor; fear of Rabbi Shach. In August 1990, before his opening address to the Ponevezh *yarchei kallah* (lit. months of assembly) summer course for laymen, Rabbi Shach was rumoured to be preparing a savage attack – tantamount to a ban – on the new Art Scroll English Talmud. Telegrams and emissaries flew across the Atlantic. Panic and hysteria in New York. In the event – relief. His rambling speech ended without any mention of the new work.

A year earlier, at the same occasion, Rabbi Shach had condemned as rank heresy the vastly popular *Punctuated, Explained and Translated Talmud* produced by Jerusalem scholar Rabbi Adin Steinsaltz, along with this author's other works. 'People say that these new-style Gemaras increase the number of learners. But God doesn't need this learning,' he thundered. 'God wants the "old" learning in the "old" Gemaras. Let us therefore all cling to the old Gemaras, hold them to our breasts and kiss them. We certainly can't kiss the new-fangled type . . .'

Shach's attack was the culmination of a sudden and particularly virulent campaign he had launched against Steinsaltz earlier that summer. By the time Shach spoke in August, many other haredi rabbis in Israel and abroad – some eagerly, others succumbing to massive pressure from Bnei Brak – had joined Shach in publicly banning all Steinsaltz's works. People were commanded to remove them from their homes; in one community the rabbi had them collected up and buried.

Adin Steinsaltz (b. 1937), a brilliant and deeply spiritual scholar who began life in an irreligious family and was drawn to Orthodoxy and Talmudic study in his teens, is a major figure on the Israeli intellectual scene. In 1988 he was awarded the prestigious Israel Prize for his 'Punctuated Talmud', begun in 1964 and then in its twenty-second volume. For many secular Israelis, he is something of a guru. His lectures on history, halacha and kabbala are packed; he is an accomplished radio personality; his books are bestsellers. Each Talmud volume sells some 50,000 copies. The first volumes of the English translation made the bestseller lists in America. He is much admired among the Orthodox too (though no longer among the pro-Shach haredim), even though he is, in essence, a popularizer. He has always managed, moreover – a rare achievement for any Israeli public figure – to steer clear of party-politics. And, though closely identified with the Lubavitch movement, he has somehow avoided involvement in the hasidim-versus-mitnagdim wrangles.

So Rabbi Shach's assault came as a shock, especially since the purported heresies had appeared in books which had been published many years earlier, and frequently reprinted without any adverse comments from anyone.

'We warn the reader in advance,' wrote Rabbi Shach's party newspaper *Yated Ne'eman*, 'that the quotations cited below are full of terrible, horrible things that insult the foundations of the Torah, the Holy Forefathers, the Judges and the Prophets. No. No, it isn't easy for us to reproduce such things . . . But after the letters against Steinsaltz by our Great Men of Torah, a need has arisen to explain to the public.'

In his *The Essential Talmud* (1977), Steinsaltz had described the Gemara as 'an anthology of law, legend and philosophy . . . folk-stories and humour'. 'There is no need,' *Yated* commented between parentheses, 'to point out the seriousness of such words . . .' He had gone on to say that the Talmud was 'not particularly impressive in its structure', and had compared its 'freely associative style' to that of 'modern novels'. No comment needed on that, even in parentheses . . .

'Mister' Steinsaltz, moreover, had repeatedly used the word 'evolution' in relation to the Oral Law, which, said *Yated*, smacked of:

> the heretical theories of the haskala and of Bible Criticism. Most of our readers will probably not have heard of Hammurabi's Code, which the Bible Critics in their stupidity regarded as a source of the Torah's laws. Mister Steinsaltz, however, effectively endorses that theory. He writes: 'The existence of a written marriage contract is very ancient, and is mentioned in Hammurabi's Code, long before the Giving of the Torah. But the form and content of the contract change with time and vary according to different cultures. Our Sages were insistent that such a contract be drawn up . . .'

The newspaper then pointedly cited the Gemara in Tractate Sanhedrin to the effect that anyone denying the divine origin of the entire Torah 'has no place in the World to Come', even 'someone who says that the whole Torah is divine apart from one solitary inference or interpretation'. The paper added that this same criterion covers 'belief in the greatness and holiness of the Talmudic rabbis, who were like angels.' Steinsaltz, however, had sought to 'humanize' and 'personalize' these rabbis, describing one of them as short and dumpy, another as good-natured and a third as eccentric. 'We cannot print further disgusting quotations because they reach the level of downright obscenity.'

Steinsaltz had even presumed to attribute human dimensions to biblical figures. In a book of essays called *Characters in the Bible* (1982), he had referred to Joseph as 'a dreamer and make-believer', and to his brothers as 'ordinary'. Isaac was 'hesitant, lacking in self-confidence; Rebecca was the decisive one.' Samson was 'a young bully', and David 'an adventurer'. In a companion volume, *Women in the Bible* (1984), the Song of Deborah was characterized as 'bloodthirsty'.

Haredi pundits, looking for reasons to explain the unheralded vehemence of the onslaught, pointed to a persistent speculation in New York that the aged Lubavitcher Rebbe, who has no children, was considering naming Steinsaltz his successor. (This would be an unprecedented and remarkable move; but given Steinsaltz's personal piety, broad popularity and powerful intellect, which even his detractors concede, it is not implausible.) Others sought an explanation in the then imminent publication in the US of Steinsaltz's Talmud in English. Had would-be competitors 'gotten to' Rabbi Shach? Shach himself denied any ulterior motive. He explained that he had never been aware of Steinsaltz's works until certain baalei teshuva had drawn his attention to them some weeks earlier.

Following the initial attacks, Shach's natural enemies – the hasidic houses of Lubavitch and Ger – leaped to Steinsaltz's defence. Steinsaltz himself, in a move widely criticized as appeasement, entered into negotiations with the beit din of the Eda Haredit in Jerusalem. At one stage he claimed the two offending books *Characters in the Bible* and *Women in the Bible* had been altered in the editing, an assertion denied by the respective publishing houses. Eventually he agreed to recall and amend 'anything that requires amending, in accordance with the instructions of The Great Men of the Generation [i.e. the rabbis of the Eda beit din], may they live long lives . . . and whom I profoundly thank for their kindness to me.' Anyone sending back his copy would receive an amended one. (Hardly anyone did, of course: those who heeded the proscription obviously would not want to admit that they had bought the outlawed books in the first place . . .)

The Eda rabbis, for their part, pronounced themselves satisfied. But Shach remained unmoved. He insisted that the heresy had tainted all of Steinsaltz's output, including the monumental Talmud. 'There can be no repentance,' he asserted, 'and no recall.'

Steinsaltz clearly suffered personal anguish. But he declined to fight back, explaining in an interview that he preferred 'to keep silent and appear a fool rather than cause a great amount of *chilul hashem* [desecration of God].' He stressed that the offending books had not been written for haredi readers. 'Basically people objected to my style, my use of language. Someone once said that *Alice in Wonderland* is full of sexual symbols and advised that anyone undergoing psychoanalysis shouldn't read it. In some cases, some people who were not even meant to read my books might have been offended . . . And I say, if you are such a person, if you are so sensitive and you are offended – it wasn't meant to offend, but I still stand corrected.'

Steinsaltz's sales were hardly affected, even though haredi bookstores stopped stocking his books. His works sell to a wide market, most of which is impervious to Shach's fulminations. Many Israelis with little or no Talmud-learning experience, and now many English-speaking readers too, say the Steinsaltz Talmud opened up for them an otherwise inaccessible heritage and literature. More advanced Talmudists, including haredim, continue to refer to the Steinsaltz edition for linguistic elucidation, historical and geographical perspective and relevant economic and social information unavailable elsewhere.

The National Religious Party passed a ringing resolution of support for Steinsaltz, 'who has brought hundreds of thousands of Jews closer to the sources of our faith,' and condemned 'the haredi, anti-Zionist approach which ignores the historic process of national redemption now under way and sneeringly disregards the secular community . . .' The party asked anyone thinking of burning or burying a book to send it to them, for redistribution.

Nor has Rabbi Shach had it all his own way in his battle against other 'new-fangled' Talmudic works. The most monumental and revolutionary product of haredi scholarship, the *Anthology of Commentaries on the Talmud* (in Hebrew: *Otzar Mefarshei HaTalmud*), continues to appear, volume after volume, and each new volume is snapped up by an obviously appreciative public.

The *Otzar*, created by Rabbi Yosef Buxbaum and published by his Machon Yerushalayim, is intended as a comprehensive companion for the advanced Talmud student. As he learns the text of the Gemara, Rashi and Tosafot, he can refer to it both for elucidation of difficult points and, more especially, for a broad elaboration of the central issues. The *Otzar* cites the works of dozens of the major commentators, rishonim and acharonim. But it is much more than just a scissors-and-paste job: it digests, blends and rewrites the writings of all these commentators, in manageable paragraphs and in a modern and easily understood Hebrew style.

Buxbaum was wise enough, or lucky enough, to enlist the active and enthusiastic support of the leading American yeshiva dean, Rabbi Yitzhak Hutner, for his venture. Hutner took the title of President of Machon Yerushalayim after moving to Jerusalem in the early 1970s. But when the Machon sought to open a branch in Rehovot, near Tel Aviv, Rabbi Shach advised young haredi scholars there not to join it.

Hutner had an aide telephone Shach and inform him that he would be calling on him. Shach, always courteous, said he would call on Hutner in Jerusalem.

'I have come to live out my last days in Israel,' Hutner announced as soon as Shach had taken a seat. 'And *you* are disturbing me. If you have any critical comments to make about our *Otzar*, kindly write to me and I will do my best to reply . . .'

Shach, thunderstruck, could only mutter that 'Of course if a great man like yourself is watching over them, then of course everything is all right . . .'

Another seminal work of Talmud scholarship which is too solidly ensconced to succumb to pressures from the hardliners is the *Encyclopedia Talmudit*. Compiled by a team of haredi scholars in Jerusalem, it appears at the rate of one new volume each two years or so, and is loyally subscribed to by the Talmud-learning public worldwide. Unlike the *Otzar*, which is basically an on-the-page aid for the Gemara learner, the *Encyclopedia*'s approach is more ambitious. Each entry takes up a Talmudic or halachic theme and seeks, starting from the relevant biblical verses, to give the student a comprehensive account of all the Talmud-related scholarship on that subject.

It is a measure of the peculiar dissembling rampant in the haredi world that in many yeshivas the *Encyclopedia*, the *Otzar*, the Art Scroll English Talmud, Rabbi Kehati's Mishna and even the blacklisted Steinsaltz Talmud, while invisible in the study-hall and unavailable in the yeshiva library, are plentifully present in the dormitories. Students have constant recourse to them for their private preparatory work.

And not only students. This 'samizdat' literature is used surreptitiously by faculty members of even the most conservative yeshivas, especially the younger lecturers, in preparing their shiurim. At the very least, they have to be ready to fend off students armed with questions picked up on the sly from these works. At best, intelligent recourse to them can save the rabbi time and effort, and help him prepare a more informed and profound lecture. Some yeshiva deans openly endorse this situation as a practical compromise between the conservative and liberal approaches. They say the new works are not inherently bad or wrong, but are counterproductive for youngsters in their formative years. 'Only years of battling with the Gemara, Rashi and Tosafot will turn them into true scholars,' one veteran dean explained.

Rabbi Shach and the conservatives regard simplification and popularization as threats to the time-honoured methods of Talmud teaching. The liberals argue that Rashi himself was the greatest simplifier and popularizer: without his commentary, which doubtless seemed revolutionary in the eleventh century, the Talmud would have remained a closed book to all but a tiny circle of scholars. They argue, too, that Orthodox Talmudic scholarship over the centuries always had its encyclopedists and anthologizers, who tried to provide the scholar with fuller access to the source material. Their work was inevitably less than exhaustive, while the scholars of today have the benefit of computerized indexing and of comparative manuscript research to help them. It is especially sad and ironic, therefore, say the liberals, that these works should be cold-shouldered in hardline haredi circles, in a surge of latter-day obscurantism.

But even Buxbaum, publisher of the *Otzar*, says he was uncomfortable when the dean of a large hesder yeshiva in Jerusalem proudly showed him that almost every chavrusa pair in the study-hall was learning the *Otzar* alongside the Gemara. That, he felt, was an excessive use of the work that made learning too easy. He was happier, he says, at the Satmar hasidic yeshiva in Williamsburg, New York City, where he was shown a shelf of well-used *Otzar*s available for consultation at the back of the study-hall.

All the volumes, however, had their title pages rudely ripped out. Those pages acknowledge the support that Machon Yerushalayim receives from the Israeli government, and lists a number of official,

State-appointed rabbis associated with the project – all anathema to the virulently anti-Zionist Satmarers. 'But I don't care,' says Buxbaum philosophically. 'As long as they're using the books.'

The liberals as well as the conservatives are guilty of another form of hypocrisy: officially ignoring non-haredi scholarship while often surreptitiously plagiarizing it. The official attitude applies not only to non-Orthodox (or non-Jewish) scholars and their works, but even to academic Talmudists who are Orthodox in their personal practice, but have fallen foul of the haredi leadership on ideological or political grounds. Thus, the noted Israeli Talmudist, Professor Ephraim Uhrbach of the Hebrew University (1912–1991), whose major works on the beliefs of the Talmudic sages and on the Tosafists have become classics, is cited in works of haredi scholarship, if at all, as 'a scholar' or 'one writer'. Presumably his university professorship is in itself a black mark against him, though another Orthodox Hebrew University Talmudist, Professor Yisrael Ta-Shma, does get an occasional mention by name: Uhrbach was active politically, and was once considered as a candidate for President of the State; that too, no doubt, is held against him.

Other unmentionable scholars include the late Professor Saul Lieberman, of the (Conservative) Jewish Theological Seminary in New York, an outstanding Talmudist, and Rabbi Shlomo Goren, the long-time chief chaplain of the Israeli army and later (1973–83) Ashkenazic Chief Rabbi. A onetime iluy at Hevron Yeshiva in Jerusalem, Goren has frequently crossed swords with the haredi leadership, most stridently in a case in the 1970s when he freed a brother and sister from the dread halachic stigma of *mamzerut* (illegitimacy). Haredi vindictiveness may take extreme forms. Thus the *Encyclopedia Talmudit* (vol. 18), in a 130-page entry on electricity in halacha (kindling on shabbat), quotes from more than 100 books and articles – but not from Goren, who has written extensively on the subject.

The academics for their part, while they recognize the impressive dimensions of the haredi 'learning revolution', have little respect for much of what haredim call 'scholarship'. They regard the pilpul approach as inadequate for the modern scholar, who tackles a text and an author, however ancient and venerated, with an open and critical mind, and will turn to other contemporary sources, including Gentile sources, to help elucidate a Talmudic passage.

By the same token, the haredim consider much of the scholarly work being done in Judaic studies and Talmud at universities as irrelevant. Concerned as they are exclusively with the inner logic of the halacha, the haredim find the historical, social, economic, personal and literary backdrop to any particular text extraneous. At best it is of peripheral interest; at worst, it opens the way to an evolutionist reading of the sources of halacha, which can verge on heresy from the haredi perspective.

In effect, the two worlds of scholarship have different definitions of the word 'scholar'. Hence there is neither real dialogue, nor competition. The 'scholars' pass each other by without contact or recognition.

In the important area of manuscript research and publication, however, the two types of scholar are increasingly brushing up against each other. Almost all of the work in this field is now done by haredim. Newly discovered texts of classical and lesser-known works, mainly of the medieval period, are rolling off haredi presses in the Diaspora and Israel at a phenomenal rate, most of them copiously annotated by the researchers. Generous funding is available for this kind of work from philanthropic and State endowments in many countries, and from international Jewish foundations. The books, moreover, can count on more than just library sales: they are popular among the haredi learning public. Every haredi young man wants at least one wall of his home covered floor-to-ceiling with religious and Talmudic literature. The more recent the book, and the more esoteric, the better it attests to its owner's accomplishments as a learner.

Professor Ta-Shma, another Hevron alumnus who keeps up his links with the haredi world, welcomes all this manuscript work, although he insists that it does not qualify as original research. The Hebrew University, for example, will not award a doctorate solely on the basis of a newly edited and published manuscript. Ta-Shma, who is curator of the Hebrew University's Talmudic manuscripts, pokes gentle fun at the kollel students who 'think that to study a manuscript makes you a researcher, a man of science.' He pooh-

poohs the vast bulk of the pilpulistic annotations that adorn the haredi manuscript editions as 'needless, useless encrustation. The haredim regard this sort of thing as the apogee of Talmudic scholarship, but as far as I'm concerned it just takes up room on my shelves.' As for the biographical material on the author which haredi researchers usually include in these books, Ta-Shma dismisses it as unscholarly 'propaganda'. Since the ancient author is venerated by his haredi editor/biographer as a saint and tzaddik, regular norms of biography fall away.

27

Plugged In

'How to Turn a Traffic Jam into a Torah Class,' booms the headline on a full-page advertisement in *Jewish Action*, an American Orthodox magazine. A cartoon illustration shows irate drivers, bumper-to-bumper, looking up as one car appears to fly past them, in the air. 'While the line-up on the highway grinds to a halt,' says the blurb, 'your spirit will be soaring on a "higher-way," with Taste of Torah Tapes.'

There is a cut-out order-form to purchase tapes. 'The proceeds,' the reader is informed, 'are used to support A Taste of Torah radio which airs in New York on Mondays at 10 pm on WEVD 1050 AM.' Among the tapes on offer are: 'Abortion – an examination of this sensitive subject from the perspective of Jewish Law'; 'Vegetarianism – is it compatible with Torah thought?'; 'Women – are we really created equal?'; and 'Mikva – the metaphysical mysteries of the purifying waters.' The lecturers are all well-known rabbis.

Innovations in the method and substance of learning are only painfully and gradually penetrating the haredi world. The yeshivas, as we have seen, in their cloistered conservatism, are instinctively hesitant, even hostile, towards any new approach that appears to tamper with the content of the Talmudic corpus or its traditional modes of study. Technological innovations in transmission, however, are tolerated. The cutting edge is in lay learning – the other side of the haredi learning revolution. Tapes, telephones, videos, computers – all have been harnessed in recent years for the propagation of Torah study.

Even the old-style yeshiva deans give the often ingenious projects their blessing. The theory is that the mere mechanical (or electronic) proliferation of Torah teachings – as distinct from their substantive popularization – is acceptable. After all, not everyone can spend his whole life in a yeshiva.

In fact, another advertisement for learning tapes, in the American haredi magazine *The Jewish Observer*, invites the reader to 'relive the yeshiva experience with Rabbi Yissocher Frand, Maggid Shiur [lecturer] at Ner Israel Yeshiva in Baltimore.' This project is called 'Torah in Transit', and Rabbi Frand links each taped discourse to a weekly Torah portion. (A portion of the Pentateuch is read out in synagogue each shabbat from a parchment scroll; the whole is completed each year.) 'This dynamic young rosh yeshiva expounds on contemporary halachic issues,' the advertisement continues. 'His powerful and eloquent approach captivates both scholars and laymen alike. Free Offer: as an introduction, we'll send you "Mixed seating at weddings" FREE along with a complete catalogue listing nearly 40 tapes.'

The leading baal teshuva yeshiva, Ohr Somayach, with its main campus in Jerusalem and branches in several Diaspora communities, offers a tape library of nearly 300 lectures by its senior faculty. Topics range from 'Love and Marriage' by Rabbi Professor David Gottlieb, formerly a philosophy professor at Johns Hopkins University; through 'Usury, Selfishness and Emotion' by Rabbi Uziel Millevsky, former Chief Rabbi of Mexico; to 'Soul Stretching' by Rabbi Nota Schiller, the co-dean of Ohr Somayach.

In Paris, an enterprising young baal teshuva, Yehiel Gruner, markets a similarly wide range of tapes in French, recorded by a number of local haredi rabbis. Among them, 'Les limites de nos relations avec les Goyim', 'Le couple et la contraception dans le Judaïsme', and 'Le Roi David a-t-il fauté?'

An arresting tape-and-telephone-service advertisement in a high-holyday edition of *Jewish Action* evokes the mussar side of yeshiva learning. The headline suggests 'How to Defend Yourself on Yom Kippur' – by not talking or listening to lashon hara during the Ten Days of Penitence prior to the fast-day. 'CALL the Shmiras Haloshon Hotline for a FREE daily telephone shiur on Shmiras Haloshon [lit., guarding the tongue].' Two toll-free numbers are given, one for a shiur in English and one for Yiddish, and there is a third number to phone 'If you would like to bring this telephone shiur to your city.' If one cannot think of anything good to say about the person being discussed, the advertisement recommends 'any variation of the following: "Look, I'm probably the last person in the world who should be suggesting this, but since this conversation sounds like it could develop into lashon hara and Yom Kippur is around the corner, let's switch to something more mundane, like baseball".'

A propos of telephone services, a haredi hotline facility in the US provided by an enterprising Israeli yeshiva offers immediate prayers at the Western Wall on behalf of sick persons. Advertised as a 'high-tech prayer service', the toll-free twenty-four-hour number is 'manned by experienced data intake personnel' who give callers 'careful and unhurried attention, and when necessary a dose of compassion and a message of hope. Prayer requests, originally dispatched to Israel by telegram, are now transmitted by facsimile system for instant receipt . . .'

One useful technological device that seemed set to sweep the world of haredi learning, but has now been banned by leading rabbis as 'the instrument of Satan', is the VCR recorder. The Lubavitcher hasidim were among the first to appreciate its potential as a teaching and publicity tool. They would film every public appearance of the Rebbe, and disseminate cassettes to their libraries and to private individuals. But video-clips of Rabbi Shach are no longer available, and video-photographers are no longer welcome at haredi public events in Israel, or at weddings, where the haredim were originally introduced to this new technology. 'It is a dreadful and terrible sin,' the beit din of the Eda Haredit in Jerusalem proclaimed in July 1990. 'God forbid that anyone should have [a VCR] in his home, or in any other place.' Similar bans were announced by other haredi rabbis and rabbinical courts in Jerusalem and Bnei Brak.

'We are horrified to learn,' declared a group of rabbis of the Gerer hasidic community, 'that a terrible breach has been made in the "wall of purity" by the introduction of the weapon of destruction called VIDEO. This evil instrument has already destroyed kosher Jewish homes, and many are the corpses it leaves strewn in its wake.'

Far from being an innocent or even helpful instrument, as had been thought, the video 'turns out to be the ugliest and most loathsome instrument of debauchery. It has penetrated into our camp through its use mainly at weddings. But such is the way of the

Evil Inclination: today he tells you do this, and tomorrow do that – until the members of the family sin by watching things that are forbidden, and then degenerate even further by watching ugly VIDEO films obtainable in shops.'

The problem was apparently twofold. First, people were 'watching things that are forbidden' – that is, they were taking home their video-films after the wedding and watching that which they were physically prevented (and halachically forbidden) to watch at the wedding itself: the opposite sex dancing. Precisely because haredi weddings have such rigorous separation between men and women, each side tends to celebrate with unselfconscious abandon. The girls and young women seem as oblivious of the video-team (usually non-haredi males) as of the male waiters who pass freely between the two halves of the hall.

Second and worse, some youngsters were renting adult films. In a society where cinema-going is forbidden and television is taboo, this is indeed a serious breach. The decision, initiated in Israeli mitnagdic circles and endorsed by the hasidim too (apart from Lubavitch), was that the obvious educational and entertainment potential of the VCR would have to be forgone in order to guard the 'wall of purity'.

Computers, on the other hand, are considered unimpeachable, and many haredim have PCs for their business or professional needs, though, as we have seen, Talmudic software has yet to make a major impact on haredi learning, yeshiva or lay.

But by far the most significant, prevalent, and non-controversial use of modern technology in haredi learning life is 'Dial-a-Daf', or in its Israeli variation 'Kol Hadaf' – 'Voice of a Page'. Thousands, probably tens of thousands, of people around the world are hooked into this service for their daily page of Talmud.

The lesson, in English, Hebrew or Yiddish, takes precisely one hour. (If there are a few spare moments at the end, the telephone or tape plays a hasidic tune or a few words of mussar). The telephone service starts every hour, on the hour, around the clock (except of course on shabbat and festivals), in London, Melbourne, Antwerp and twenty-one cities across North America. In the Diaspora, where callers are deemed capable of supporting the service, there is a modest monthly subscription fee, in return for which each subscriber receives his individual dialling code. In the major cities in Israel the service is free, and the hour-long call is charged at just three local call units (instead of twenty). Cassette tapes, each comprising one telephone shiur, are available at Dial-a-Daf branch offices for a couple of dollars; they may be exchanged for a few cents.

Rabbi Mechel Silber, a Jerusalem yeshiva teacher, who is the most prolific and popular Dial-a-Daf lecturer in Hebrew and Yiddish, says he can only really relax on shabbat (when telephoning is forbidden). People constantly call him, he says, from all over the country and sometimes from abroad, to clarify points on the day's tape. Sometimes the question is about a page from a different tractate, which Silber may have recorded months or years before, but which the caller happens to be learning. So vivid and skilful are Silber's lessons, that his 'students' relate to him as though he were their personal teacher. A prominent Jerusalem rabbi pleased and embarrassed him by greeting him in public with the Talmudic salutation: 'Peace upon you, my master and teacher.'

Silber's technique, which other Dial-a-Daf lecturers try to emulate with mixed success, is to pitch his shiur simultaneously to students of different levels. He reads the text of the Gemara, translating and explaining it in line with Rashi's commentary. He weaves in several of the Tosafot on the page, compressing them and distilling their arguments. Whenever time allows, or the subject-matter requires, he broadens the discussion, drawing in other rishonim and acharonim, reading the relevant rulings of Maimonides and the Shulhan Aruch. Often he refers the more advanced students, or those with more time on their hands, to books of commentary or responsa which deal with the issue in still greater depth.

Anyone with a Talmud-learning background and reasonable powers of concentration comes away from the hour-long encounter with a solid understanding of the *blatt* or page. Those who follow up Silber's references can spend profitable hours delving into the *sugya* (the Talmudic discussion) or researching its halachic implications, as they would in a yeshiva. For the accomplished learner who has studied this tractate before, Dial-a-Daf provides a convenient method of revision – which, to stress again, is an integral part of learning.

Daf Hayomi, the universal daily page programme, was conceived in the 1920s by Rabbi Meir Shapira of Lublin, a charismatic haredi leader who represented Agudat Israel in the Polish sejm (parliament) and founded the first all-hasidic yeshiva in Poland, 'Hachmei Lublin'. The idea was supported by all the leaders of Agudah, though privately the Lithuanian 'yeshiva world' sneered at it as a hasidic cop-out for ignorant laymen. Today, 'Ivy League' yeshiva students are encouraged by faculty to adopt the Daf Hayomi schedule (and even use Dial-a-Daf tapes) for their bekiut learning.

Dial-a-Daf publishes tapes of the Jerusalem Talmud too, and there are various phone or tape services in Mishna, Halacha and Bible. But the Babylonian Talmud is the backbone of haredi learning, and the Daf Hayomi creates a unique, universal camaraderie. Any learner can walk into any Daf lecture anywhere, or call up Dial-a-Daf, and simply pick up where he left off the day before, perhaps half a world away.

Each seven-and-a-half years the cycle ends, amid much celebration in all major haredi centres. Describing a siyyum of the tenth Daf Hayomi cycle, at Madison Square Gardens on 26 April 1990, the leading New York Jewish newspaper wrote:

> The New York arena – where presidents have been nominated, rock-and-roll superstars confirmed, sports teams adored and heavyweight champions crowned – saw European-style Orthodoxy rise from what seemed to be defeat at the twin fists of the Holocaust and assimilation to reclaim its pre-eminence over the more 'modern' factions of Orthodoxy, as 17,000 black-hatted men and 3,000 modestly dressed women packed the hall . . .
>
> The arena's giant scoreboard was used to announce that the afternoon or evening services could be found on page 61 of the souvenir program. The scoreboard also announced in bright lights the 'lineup' of rabbis at the microphone . . . In the holding-areas behind the stage, austere rabbis and the side-

curled entourages stood amid the Barnum and Bailey circus wagons . . .

The Daf Hayomi is the most common curriculum at shiurim for laymen, but by no means the only one. There are shiurim at a deeper or more 'yeshivish' level, where only a few lines of Talmud text are negotiated in an hour or two, but a whole host of commentaries are brought into play, and the lecturer and students engage, in effect, in a multiple chavrusa discussion. There are shiurim in halacha, in Pentateuch and Prophets, in the writings of Maimonides, in philosophy, kabbala, hasidism, in virtually every aspect of Torah thought and literature. There are shiurim for men and for women, shiurim before dawn and late into the night, shiurim in synagogues, schools and private homes. There are lunch-hour shiurim in brokers' offices on Wall Street, in lawyers' offices in Washington DC, at the Diamond Bourse in Tel Aviv, at accountants' offices in the West End of London. There is a regular Talmud shiur in the Knesset building in Jerusalem, and one on a bus that brings haredi commuters into the city from Monsey, NY.

Modern technology has played its role here, too, though in a more prosaic way. Central heating, electricity and the internal combustion engine mean that one can drive to one's shiur in a heated car, and learn in a warm and well-lit room – unlike one's forebear in the shtetl who, if he could spare any time from the daily grind, would have to trudge through the snow or sludge to learn in a draughty shtiebel by the dim light of a smelly paraffin lamp.

It is the startling proliferation of shiurim that best reflects the strength of the lay learning revolution among the haredim. Modern Orthodoxy, too, is increasingly nurturing a shiur-attending laity – which the haredim attribute to a trickle-down effect. (Most haredim have no knowledge of or interest in the marked growth of adult education among committed Conservative and Reform laymen.)

The question of how much actual learning – in the literal sense of the English word, rather than in the more amorphous meaning of the Yiddish term '*lernen*' – is accomplished in all these various shiurim takes us back to the unique nature of lernen, at once an intellectual pursuit and a religious act. Sociologist Samuel Heilman spent years observing-cum-participating in several shiurim in America and Israel. 'From early on,' he writes:

> I realized that, for many of the Jews I was observing, this [*lernen*] was more than simply the assimilation of knowledge. For one thing, many of those I watched had been *lernen* for years, but still seemed to be unable to review the texts on their own or recall very much of the content . . . Those who had *lernt* a lot took apparent great pleasure in repeating what they had already studied. The best *lernen*, it seemed, was the sort which reiterated what everyone already knew.*

Seizing on this account, the prolific and acerbic American Talmudist, Professor Jacob Neusner, in a book on American Jewry, unleashed a withering and contemptuous denigration of virtually all 'Torah study by amateurs in synagogue and yeshiva alike'. Neusner, who is associated with the Conservative movement but some of whose work has won him a grudging regard in Orthodox circles, went on to pronounce that: 'Study of the Torah turns out to constitute a ritual of little study and virtually no torah.'

He agrees that lernen is unique in that it attempts to be 'a religious quest, a holy event'. But he insists that this cannot – and in classical settings and periods did not – detract from the literal meaning of the word: using the mind to assimilate knowledge. And that sense, he asserts, is lamentably absent in modern haredi lernen. He describes his own students, after a year of study in an Israeli yeshiva: 'When I ask them what they learned, they name the tractate. When I ask them the main point of the tractate, or of the part of it they supposedly learned, they are dumbfounded. They never learned.'

Neusner concludes that 'lernen and learning have little to do with each other.' In lernen, 'the main thing is for everyone to feel good and be happy, feel holy and be reassured. Lernen as Heilman describes it testifies to the inauthenticity of its practitioners.'†

No doubt, there is much humbug among the haredi laity, as well

* Samuel C. Heilman, *The People of the Book – Drama, Fellowship and Religion* (Chicago & London: University of Chicago Press 1987), p. 2.

† Jacob Neusner, *Israel in America – A Too-Comfortable Exile?* (Boston: Beacon Press 1985), pp. 145 ff.

as in the yeshivas. But there is much sincerity and academic competence too. Ritualized repetition does not necessarily signify quackery. Revision, rehearsal of familiar material, is part of the traditional method of lernen – and of learning. Indeed, outstanding haredi sages like Rabbi Yosef, whose academic achievements Neusner does not impugn, attained those achievements by precisely that method.

Heilman concedes that some of the lay lerners he observed 'animatedly engage in the game for years without ever assimilating much in the way of content. Such players learn to make the right moves without ever really perceiving the overarching purpose of the game.' But he insists that 'no person can consistently make the right moves without some competence . . . and intellectual contact.' And he records, with academic dispassion, his own instructive if embarrassing experience at a particularly advanced-level shiur he was observing in Jerusalem. He found the going too hard, even though he has some Talmud background and wanted to hang in, both to lern and to observe.

'They described and discussed, in what was to me a cryptic Yiddish, the order of Temple sacrifices that I could hardly decipher. While they elliptically debated the order of the priest's sprinkling of blood on the four corners of the altar, I remained ignorant of which sacrifices were being discussed or what exactly a priest was supposed to do . . .

'Nevertheless I tried. I asked questions, often inappropriate. I miscued, laughed at the wrong times, and so on.' Significantly, perhaps, this shiur was the most haredi of the half-dozen Modern-Orthodox and haredi shiurim that Heilman attended. 'Without a substantive competence, I could not keep up the pace. I found myself drifting away . . . nodding off in sleep and awakening with a sense of disorientation . . . Gradually I became more and more silent and at last found my departure from the circle inevitable.'*

* Heilman, *The People of the Book*, p. 145.

28

Late Entries

On the face of it, the accretion to haredi ranks during recent years of many thousands of formerly non-Orthodox young adults, known as baalei teshuva, penitents, might have been expected to mitigate the conflicts between haredism and secular culture. At the least, it might have been expected to produce some form of integration between the yeshiva world and the world of academic studies. Many baalei teshuva come to haredism during or immediately after their years at university.

In practice though, this assumption was never valid. Haredism's condition for accepting and welcoming the penitents has been that they wholly relinquish their former culture, and do not, as a group, seek any new synthesis between 'Torah' and secularism. Yeshivas for baalei teshuva, which mushroomed in the Seventies and Eighties, particularly in Jerusalem, are no more liberal in their attitudes to secular studies than regular haredi yeshivas. Their aim is to 'convert' their students into fully fledged haredim, not to create a separate cadre of secularly cultured haredim.

The haredim believe they are swallowing up the baalei teshuva without trace – that is, without affecting the intellectual essence of haredism. Baalei teshuva blend into the haredi milieu so as to become outwardly indistinguishable, and, apparently, inwardly metamorphosed too. Even if they continue their academic or professional careers (as they are often advised to do by rabbis), their children enter the haredi educational mainstream, emerging from yeshivas and seminaries as integral members of haredi society, as unlikely as anyone else in that society to devote intellectual energies to secular education or culture.

If the baal teshuva influx has not affected the content of haredism, it has certainly affected its form, giving impetus to an enormous outpouring of English- and French-language haredi literature. Art Scroll Publishers of New York, a flourishing partnership of enterprising rabbi-scholars and graphic artists, is the leader in an increasingly crowded field. Its hundreds of titles include all the books of the Bible, most of the classical works of Judaism including the Talmud itself, prayer-books and other ritual texts – all translated and elaborately annotated – as well as histories, biographies and children's books. They are handsomely produced, well written and tastefully illustrated.

This new form of literature is as rigidly uncritical and dogmatically adulatory as any haredi literature published in rabbinic Hebrew or Yiddish a hundred years before. Or is it? Despite its authors' and editors' determination that it be so, does the very fact that this old-new literature is written in a different language inevitably introduce differences of substance? Language, after all, is more than just words. The patterns of thought of modern American English are very different from those of Yiddish, which itself was moulded over past centuries to express the thought-patterns of the Hebrew-Aramaic Talmud.

A random example. Art Scroll's commentary to a kabbalistic sabbath hymn explains one line as follows: 'The lack of clarity in our perception of His Presence is as if we observed an event through a blurred, cloudy lens. The result is that we have a diminished appreciation of God's greatness.' That is doubtless a faithful attempt to interpret the original text. But it is written in twentieth-century English, and some of the words and phrases used have their own, twentieth-century English associations. Does it truly represent the substance of the sixteenth-century poet's intent, or is there, willy-nilly, an infiltration of modernity?

In American haredi yeshivas and lay shiurim, where the language of instruction and the native language of the students is English, teachers and students nevertheless tend to lace their speech with Yiddish words or forms, in order to express a precise and authentic Talmudic nuance. Often they will superimpose Yiddish syntax or inflection upon English words to achieve that purpose. Or they will chant their English in the special Talmud sing-song that evolved in Yiddish to accompany the question-and-answer flow of most Talmudic texts.

The same resort to a mixture of languages occurs in learning-related conversation. In Helmreich's book on American yeshivas, a New York yeshiva lecturer is quoted as follows: 'I feel that a *shiur* should cover more in terms of *gemara* and classical *meforshim* [commentators]. I think that this can be done without sacrificing basic analysis but by avoiding undue *qvetching* [pointless argumentation] and *ploidering* [discussing issues to the point of meaninglessness] which often reflects ignorance rather than profundity.'*

For some haredim, this is the way they speak English in general. Discussing the weather in London, for instance, a yeshiva graduate might say, or rather sing: '*Ma doch*, I took an umbrella in Ju-u-ne, I shouldn't take one in October?' (voice rising towards the end). He is invoking, by verbal and tonal association, the typical Talmudic process of deduction called *kal vachomer* (lit., light and serious; establishing a proposition by inference from an established case; in Latin: *a fortiori*) in order to explain why he definitely intends to protect himself against Britain's notoriously wet autumn. *Ma* means 'what' in Hebrew; *doch* means 'though' in Yiddish. Spoken together, with the appropriate intonation, they have been used for centuries by Yiddish-speaking Talmud learners to introduce a 'kal vachomer'. But for other haredi students, and certainly for the baalei teshuva, the use of traditional cadences and constructions during learning is a cultural statement. It is a deliberate use of thought-patterns and processes that are indigenous to Talmud and Talmud-study and do not entirely 'translate'.

In books, however, written in English or French or Modern Hebrew, such intonation is impossible. Art Scroll and the leading haredi rabbis who endorse its books believe the gap is bridgeable. But, as a famous sociologist has written, 'Men invent a language and then find that its logic imposes itself upon them.' The logic of modern language may yet be imposing itself, in subtle ways, upon the haredi mindset. Indeed it may well be that the recent revival of Yiddish in many haredi communities, noted above, is an unarticulated backlash to an instinctively felt linguistic, and hence cultural, threat.

* William B. Helmreich, *The World of the Yeshiva* (New York: The Free Press 1982), p. 110.

Rabbi Mendel Weinbach, co-dean of Ohr Somayach Yeshiva in Jerusalem, the largest baal teshuva institution, suggests that it is not the use of modern languages *per se* that might be subtly affecting the substance of learning, but the need to convey Talmud to beginners with cultured adult minds. That unprecedented need, brought about by the latter-day teshuva movement, he says, is creating new modes of communication within learning that may be influencing the content as well as merely the form of the material. Ohr Somayach's invariable practice is to start every student on Talmud from the very first day of his yeshiva experience (which may be his first ever experience of Orthodoxy or of any form of Judaism). Weinbach, a one-time pulpit rabbi in a Modern-Orthodox congregation in New Jersey, is convinced that this unexpected, unmediated confrontation with the source and essence of haredi culture is the best way to grip the mind and fire the spirit of the sincere seeker.

In most seminaries for *baalot* (the feminine form) *teshuva*, as in virtually all haredi girls' schools and women's seminaries, this soul-engaging confrontation is not available. Women, as a matter of religious principle, are not taught Talmud. 'He who teaches his daughter Torah, it is as though he teaches her lewdness,' the Mishna (Tractate Sotah 3:4) declares; and Jews in times past applied the ban with rigour, confining their daughters' religious education – apart from rare and exceptional cases – to a smattering of Bible stories and prayers, and a solid curriculum of cooking and sewing. The very concept of a women's seminary is a twentieth-century innovation, introduced beween the world wars by the Agudat Yisrael haredi party in an effort to stanch the flood of young women abandoning Orthodoxy in search of education. Today, all haredi groups have their girls' schools and seminaries. Some offer fairly broad *secular* curricula, with the result that many haredi women are better read and better educated than their menfolk.

In the most ultra-conservative women's institutions, such as those of the Satmar Hasidic sect in New York or the Eda Haredit in Jerusalem, the traditional ban on religious learning is still largely enforced: texts as such – even of the Pentateuch – are not studied.

Instead, material is distilled from the sources, translated into Yiddish, and taught in this digested form to the girls and young women.

In mainstream haredi seminaries – those affiliated to Agudah and the other haredi parties – the ban is interpreted as applying only to the Oral Law, that is the Talmud, but not to the Bible and its commentaries, nor to ethical and philosophical works, nor to books on practical halacha. This is also the case, for instance, in Ohr Somayach's sister-school, the 400-student Neve Yerushalayim.

'But if someone wants to study Talmud, nobody will stop her,' says Rabbi David Bowden, head of the Girls' High School at Gateshead, England. This unwonted (relative) liberalism in the bastion of European haredism may well reflect the recent appearance of an Art Scroll Talmud, with the new, rabbinically approved English-language accessibility that it brings to Talmud study. Previous translations of the Mishna and Gemara were dauntingly uncolloquial and esoteric, and the Steinsaltz translation is banned. It may also reflect a demand, not vociferous but nevertheless audible, on the part of some baalot teshuva not to be excluded from the Talmudic experience that is so central to haredi life in general, and specifically to the *chazara biteshuva* (return in penitence) process of their husbands (or likely future husbands). In Jerusalem, at least one of the more progressive yeshivas for women, Bruria College, has in effect abandoned the traditional ban altogether, and offers a curriculum that is essentially no different from that of a men's yeshiva. The women students learn in chavrusa pairs, they argue with each other and with the rabbis, they attend shiurim where the sugya is analysed in depth. They are even encouraged to spurn the Art Scroll Talmud and other modern-day study-aids, and make do with the Aramaic original, in order to better develop their independent, authentic Gemara-learning skills.

The 'baal teshuva movement', although an important phenomenon in contemporary Jewish history, has not lived up to the expectations – and fears – that it engendered in its earlier years. In its heyday in the late 1970s, it began to be seen, both among haredim and in the rest of Jewry, as a revolution of mass proportions. For haredim this was good news indeed, vindicating their subjective sense that haredism was sweeping all before it. For the others, it was profoundly disturbing, even frightening.

Families were split apart and alienated when a son or daughter suddenly changed, adopting the dress and lifestyle – and also the halachic demands and restrictions – of the ultra-Orthodox. In Israel, army generals and secular politicians cried foul when two air force combat pilots left the service after refusing to fly on shabbat and insisting on growing beards even though these interfered with their oxygen masks. The various preachers and 'converters' of the teshuva movement were barred from speaking to military audiences, and study-programmes for soldiers at baalei teshuva yeshivas were stopped by the minister of defence.

'The teshuva activists overdid their own publicity,' says Menachem Porush MK, of Agudat Yisrael, 'and it eventually boomeranged against them.' Rabbi Nota Schiller of Ohr Somayach Yeshiva blames hostile media reporting and an irrational fear of haredim in some sectors of Israeli society. 'The facts were that for every family that was unhappy about the chazara biteshuva of a child, a hundred others were overjoyed.' As for the tensions with the army: 'There are far more young Jews, mainly from abroad, serving in the Israeli army today thanks to Ohr Somayach than the number of students who have taken deferments in order to study at our yeshiva.'

Schiller agrees that the early momentum of the teshuva movement among student-age young people has peaked. He attributes this to the changes within Western student society. When the two American immigrant rabbis, Weinbach and Schiller, launched Ohr Somayach in the early Seventies, with two colleagues and five students in the borrowed backroom of a run-down Jerusalem yeshiva, Jewish hippies and backpackers of the Vietnam generation would wander in from the Western Wall, uncertain themselves what they were looking for. Some stayed and got caught up in the haredi experience; others drifted on.

Ohr Somayach mushroomed into a 500-student campus, with branches in New York, Los Angeles, Toronto, London, Johannesburg and Melbourne. Thousands of its graduates are spread throughout Jewry. But meanwhile the student body in Jerusalem has changed. Israeli enrolment, of both men and women, is slipping. And the proportion of well educated, middle-class students among the Israelis is shrinking: the majority are less well off, less well educated Sephardic youngsters. Students from overseas are no longer drifters, but achievement-minded pre-yuppies who have made a thought-out decision to give yeshiva a try. 'This type is less amenable to a sudden change in lifestyle,' says Schiller. But if they do decide to make the long-term commitment, 'it is much more cerebral, and much more serious.'

The outreach programmes conducted abroad by Ohr Somayach's branches seem to attract mainly people in their thirties and forties, veterans of the hippie generation. 'In some sense that does augur badly,' says Rabbi Pinhas Castnett, director of the 'Jewish Learning Experience', Ohr Somayach's school in Los Angeles. 'The teshuva movement has gotten older. Nowadays, college kids are much more materialistic than they used to be. Apathy and complacency are the trend on campus.' Instant 'conversions' effected by charismatic teshuva preachers are much rarer now than they were just a few years ago.

The long-term impact of the now-changing teshuva phenomenon, both in Israel and the Diaspora, is a subject of controversy and speculation. The haredim always tended to exaggerate the numbers and their import. Anti-haredim highlight the recent slowdown, and breathe sighs of relief. But the teshuva movement undoubtedly was significant beyond numbers in giving haredism a powerful *subjective* shot in the arm just as the swing from defensiveness to resurgence was getting under way. Whatever the statistics, the haredim themselves saw, and see, in the movement a dramatic, indeed Divine, affirmation of their beliefs. For them, it illustrates an historic shift: after centuries of debilitating brain-drain away from yeshivas, there was now sizeable traffic in the other direction.

The statistics are impressive. One research project, the 1981 Greater New York Population Survey directed by Paul Ritterband and Steven Cohen for the Federation of Jewish Philanthropies of New York, found that 24 per cent of New York Jews who identified as highly observant (defined as those who would not handle money on shabbat) had been brought up as less observant. The parents of 10 per cent of the highly observant Jewish New Yorkers had not even lit candles on Friday nights, a minimal and very widespread affirmation of tradition.

Academic researchers are still uncertain as to the proportion of baalei teshuva who stay Orthodox. But an American sociologist who studied the teshuva movement for years concludes that a high percentage of baalei teshuva who study at yeshivas for lengthy periods (rather than acquiring Orthodoxy in a less structured framework) stay within Orthodoxy thereafter.* Many stay within the haredi fold.

Among Sephardim, especially in Israel, the teshuva movement still retains some of its earlier vigour. Revivalist meetings still produce wholesale 'conversions', with dozens of people coming forward to publicly proclaim their resolve to live observant lives.

The most prominent among the Elmer Gantry-style popular preachers is Rabbi Reuven Elbaz, who also runs a chain of yeshivas specifically for young Sephardic baalei teshuva. Elbaz's rhetoric is dramatic and blood-curdling, with vivid images of Hell and electrifying accounts of miracles. Unrepentant sinners, he informed one audience, would be condemned to eternal entombment up to their chins in boiling excrement. A recent baal teshuva, on the other hand, who was a senior army officer, had been saved from certain death when a book of Psalms that he had begun to carry in his breast pocket deflected a stray bullet from piercing his heart.

Since Sephardic society is less rigidly categorized in its observances than Ashkenazic, the teshuva phenomenon triggers far less social and familial tension. Most Sephardic families are traditional to some degree, and so chazara biteshuva does not entail quite so sharp a break for the penitent. The rest of the family does not look upon its newly haredi member so ambivalently. There is less of the scepticism, cynicism and resentment that chazara biteshuva often stir among Ashkenazim. Sephardic families are usually proud of

* M. Herbert Danzger, *Returning to Tradition* (New Haven & London: Yale University Press 1989).

their baal teshuva relative. His status seems to change as rapidly as his outward appearance; within weeks, a quite ordinary youngster comes to be treated by his own kin as though he were a rabbi.

Sometimes, the purported capacity for instant metamorphosis is taken to bizarre extremes. In Israeli criminal courts nowadays, the number of baalei teshuva who pass through the dock seems out of all proportion to their numbers in the general public. Criminals have apparently come to believe that judges are moved by religious repentance. No sooner are they remanded in custody than they begin growing beards and peyot and chanting psalms. And sometimes it almost works. Rabbi Ovadia Yosef was persuaded to request a commutation of sentence from the President of the State for a jailed murderer, one of the most notorious underworld figures in the country, on the grounds that he had become a baal teshuva while in prison, read his Bible every day, and made large donations to haredi charities.

The Sephardic teshuva movement in Israel is closely bound up with Shas, the Sephardic-haredi political party. Shas's adult education programmes provide forums for revivalists like Elbaz. Its free nursery schools provide baalei teshuva with a practical and attractive means of imbuing their children with their own newly acquired values and lifestyle. Shas politicians make sure that the Sephardic teshuva yeshivas receive their fair share of government subsidies to the haredim. The young party (Shas was founded in 1984) has had a bumpy ride, battling accusations of political betrayal and financial impropriety. But its leaders believe the long-term prospects are bright. In the June 1992 election, despite its problems, Shas held on to its six seats and was just 36 votes away from a seventh.

Haredism's celebration and absorption of the teshuva movement is not necessarily matched by a wholehearted acceptance of the individual baal or baalat teshuva into the haredi family. The litmus test is marriage, and here baalei teshuva often find their paths blocked by an informal but strongly entrenched discrimination.

Shadchanim will generally try to set up a baal teshuva with a baalat teshuva. The whispered assumption in haredi circles is that if a haredi-born boy or girl marries a baal teshuva, there must be 'something wrong' with him or her: either they are poor, or they have a health disability, or – worst of all in some haredi eyes – they have formed an unarranged romantic attachment with the other party.

Some observers have found that the bias diminishes the longer a baal teshuva has been haredi. They attribute it, therefore, to a fear on the haredim's part of possible backsliding by relatively recent baalei teshuva. In part at least, though, the reluctance to 'intermarry' is religiously based. The baal/at teshuva, coming from a non-Orthodox home, will have been conceived by a mother who was halachically *niddah*, that is, ritually unclean because of menstruation. While conception through forbidden (because 'unclean') intercourse is not an halachic disability like illegitimacy, it nevertheless carries a certain quasi-halachic stigma.

Some newcomers, if they have indeed completely internalized the haredism to which they now subscribe, will acquiesce in this disability, and seek their marriage partners from among their own kind. Often, they prefer to do so anyway, since they are more likely to find a genuine soul-mate only in someone who underwent the same transformation, and also lives with tensions and contradictions between past and present.

But some baalei teshuva who entered into haredism with sincere commitment have found themselves gradually disenchanted in the face of subtle but sustained social rejection. A young American lawyer who chronicled his odyssey into Orthodoxy, and five years later out of it again, writes of a 'bias' against baalei teshuva. 'I'm sick of it. I'm tired of being an outsider among my own people. I'm lost to Judaism, Orthodox people believe, regardless of all I've done over the last five years . . . "Well, it's very nice [they say]. But would you want your daughter to marry one?" '*

* Michael Graubart Levin, *Journey to Tradition* (Hoboken NJ: Ktav 1986), p. 124.

PART V

BY BREAD ALONE

29

Cash or Kindness

Yechiel Michel Goodfarb, who is thirty-four years old, has been at death's door for fifteen years. He is fighting a running battle with Hodgkin's disease, a form of lymphomatic cancer. That, he says, is why his own door is open day and night to the poor of Jerusalem. 'Charity is a proven recipe for long life,' says Goodfarb, quoting Talmudic sources.

In 1990, he handed out 3 million dollars. More than half of it came from the haredi Reichmann brothers, billionaire builders from Toronto, Canada. 'Moishe [Paul Reichmann, head of the family business that was ranked eighth in the list of the world's greatest fortunes before it collapsed in 1992] said I could do what I liked with the money he gave me. I could buy a yacht and travel round the world. He trusted me blind.'

Other haredi sources confirmed that the Reichmanns had a special regard for Michel (the Yiddish version of Michael; accent on the Mi). During the 1990–91 recession in Western economies the Reichmanns cut back substantially on their vast philanthropy, which reputedly had run to hundreds of millions of dollars over the previous few years, mainly channelled to the haredi community. Michel's allocation remained untouched. He says he helped 7,000 families in 1990. 'That means about 50,000 human beings benefited from me, one way or another.' That is reason enough, he believes, for God to keep him alive.

Wayne Tanenbaum, another Toronto Jewish tycoon and philanthropist, who is not himself haredi, warned with prescience in 1991 that the growing reliance of the Israeli haredim on philanthropy was 'fearsome'. The eventual fall of the Reichmanns in 1992 accentuated the precariousness of the haredi economy. Political observers discerned a link between this and the haredi parties' eagerness to join the new coalition that emerged under

Labour after the June 1992 election in Israel. Shas joined immediately; the others teetered on the brink, deterred by Labour's alliance with the outspokenly secularist Meretz party but concerned for the material welfare of their educational and communal institutions.

Nevertheless, Wayne Tanenbaum enthusiastically assists his father, Joseph, in dispensing millions of dollars each year from the family's charitable foundation to haredi yeshivas in Israel. 'If we don't make these institutions prosper,' Wayne asserts, 'we'll lose the whole impetus of our religion.'

According to Rabbi David Refson, principal of Neve Yerushalayim, a baalot teshuva women's college in Jerusalem with 400 overseas students, the Tanenbaums are the biggest single givers to haredi education in Israel. Joseph Tanenbaum is especially interested in the teshuva yeshivas; he is regarded, with much justice, as the godfather of the teshuva movement. His own generation, Tanenbaum once wrote, received 'little inspiration' from its parents, the Jewish immigrants to North America. 'Those were tough times. Eking out a living took most of the juice out of you. And so it was no wonder that so many drifted further and further away from our sources and heritage. Now we see traffic in the other direction. Thousands of young people who received no Jewish education are today, in their adult years, searching out and reconnecting themselves with their Judaism.'

'Jewish philanthropy is just unbelievable,' says Refson. 'Jews know they have to support their fellow man. Goyim give charity either if they're hugely wealthy, or if they're feeling very, very guilty. But Jews . . . Jews are like the Talmud says they are: "Modest, merciful, and charitable." Those are the traits, and they're endemic. They're in the genes. A Jew can lose contact with everything – except his altruism.'

Refson raises most of the funds for his multi-million-dollar campus from non-Orthodox Jews. But he makes a point of involving his donors in the details of the college curriculum. 'Most Jews,' says the genial rabbi who grew up in a small town in the north of England, 'believe that other Jews should be religious. But it goes further than that. Goyim calculate carefully whom to give their money to; but Jews support causes which they *know* will give them grief!'

Wayne Tanenbaum is a case in point. 'I'm troubled,' he says, 'by the haredim's attitude to their fellow Jews. They look askance at another Jew because he doesn't come from a "black" yeshiva. I'm troubled a lot by the "Who is a Jew" thing. We came pretty close to an explosion last time, and it's bound to recur. Israeli friends of mine are honestly afraid for the future of the country because of the Orthodox-secular divide.'

He blames the haredim for this growing polarization. 'They've got blinkers on,' he sighs; but then adds quickly: 'But I don't want to talk against people I love.'

The Talmud's characterization of Jews as 'modest, merciful and charitable' is quoted incessantly throughout the haredi economy, from the shnorrers who are a fixture of haredi synagogues and shtieblach around the world, to the professional haredi lobbyists who practise essentially the same art, though on a more ambitious scale, in the corridors and committee-rooms of the Israeli Knesset. Philanthropy is not a mere facet of life for haredim. It is the breath of life; part of the essence.

'The world stands on three things,' according to the Mishna. 'On Torah, on Worship, and on Charity [*gemilut hasadim* – lit. dispensing kindnesses; *hesed* (sing.) means kindness or charity].' As far as the 'haredi world' of Israel is concerned, that has never been more true. Israel's haredim have become a 'society of learners', in the phrase of Professor Menahem Friedman, a sociologist who has devoted his academic career to studying haredism. And just as 'Torah' is not a select or élitist pursuit, but embraces the entire community, so too 'Charity' does not merely, or even mainly, follow the classical pattern of rich-to-poor assistance. Almost everyone in the Israeli haredi world is a recipient of charity, in one form or another. Yet at the same time the haredim give charity too, participating in cash or kindness in the cost of this universal Torah-learning. Israeli haredism's achievements, says Friedman, 'both in the realm of Torah learning and in the realm of mutual assistance, exceed anything previously known in the long history of the Jews.'

An entire 'society of learners' is unprecedented in Jewish history. Full-time learners were always a small minority in society, while the rest would try to make a living as best they could, and to support both the learners and fellow non-learners who couldn't make ends meet.

In recent centuries, the learners included small colonies of haredim living in the Holy Land – in the four 'holy cities': Jerusalem, Hebron, Tiberias and Safed – who were supported by their home communities in an arrangement called *halluka* (lit. handout). Whenever a particular kollel (in this sense meaning a colony founded by the Jews of a particular country or region in the Diaspora) failed to receive adequate support, it would send agents back to Europe to raise funds. The Sephardim in Palestine lived in much the same way, supported by their home communities throughout the Ottoman Empire.

Today, all of haredi Israel is a 'kollel', and all of the haredi Diaspora is its 'home community'. Today in the Diaspora, as we have seen, virtually every haredi young man and many young women devote years to yeshiva study. But eventually most of the men enter the world of commerce or the professions. The basic economic pattern of traditional haredi life is thus preserved.

In Israel, however, most haredi men seek to 'stay in learning' long after marriage, or, better still, indefinitely. In economic terms, what this means is that the productive sector of Israeli haredi society is shrinking, while an increasing proportion of Diaspora haredi philanthropy flows to Israel in a massive modern-day model of the old halluka. State funds too, wrung out of a reluctant public by the haredi parties, can be seen as a form of national philanthropy, though the haredim argue that these funds are no different from State support of universities or the arts.

Some observers, among them thoughtful haredim, believe this edifice is doomed to collapse soon under the combined weight of haredi demography and growing resentment in non-haredi Israeli society over the proportion of taxpayers' money being channelled into haredi institutions. Most haredim though, when asked to contemplate their community's economic prospects, repose in God their trust to keep the dollars flowing.

30

Who Help Themselves

A large display advertisement in the Israeli newspaper *Haaretz* announced a 'special offer for the haredi customer'. The car rental firm Avis was selling off its last year's fleet, and the 'haredi customer' was directed towards a French-made station wagon, described as 'the ideal family car, with room for seven people'. For many haredi families, even a seven-seater is not large enough. Anyway, for most Israeli haredim the cost of a relatively new car, even at Avis's knock-down prices, is far beyond their means or dreams. Cars in Israel are heavily taxed. If they have a car at all, it is usually an ancient jalopy, into which they squeeze as many of the children as fit, and hope that no policeman sees them.

But the point is well made: 'haredi' and 'large family' have become veritably synonymous, in advertising copy and in reality. Thus when the Israeli government's National Insurance Institute issued its 1990 Report on Poverty, warning that 10 per cent of the population were living below the poverty line and observing that 'poverty is more prevalent among large families than small,' the Belz hasidic newspaper *Hamahane Haharedi* headlined its story: 'They mean us!'

'The NII report does not categorize the poor according to religious background,' the paper's editor, Yisrael Eichler, wrote. 'But the implication is clear. A great many of the families living below or just slightly above the poverty line come from the haredi community . . .' Whatever the inflow of philanthropic largesse from the Diaspora, and however much can be squeezed from the government, the haredim of Israel, on average, are poor and getting poorer. The Belz newspaper continued:

> The NII report determines that a family needs 500 shekels [$250 at that time] per member per month to live above the

> poverty line. That means the average haredi family of eight children b.a.h. [Hebrew acronym: *bli ayin haraa* – 'without the evil eye' – in other words, may they continue to multiply] needs 5,000 shekels a month. How many haredi families earn anything like that, even when all its [NII] grants and salaries are taken into account? And how many of our families are blessed with ten children or more? Why aren't our leaders shouting about this?
>
> They all shout about the dire straits of the yeshivas and other institutions. And granted, that is important. We know of so many huge irreligious institutions that are bountifully endowed, and stand empty, while the housing situation of haredi schools is beyond despair. Certainly we must keep demanding funds for our institutions. But why aren't we shouting from the rooftops for all the large families, for all the young kollel students and their families, all living below the poverty line?

In fact, the haredi politicians do shout as loudly as they can on behalf of their constituents. Coalition agreements with the haredi parties have repeatedly raised the stipends that the government provides for yeshiva and kollel students. And each year at budget time, haredi lobbyists flock to the Knesset to haggle for larger grants for the institutions they represent.

At the grass-roots level, moreover, there is an impressive, concerted effort to make the community's collective resources stretch further. Haredi newspapers carry few car advertisements, but they are full of notices advertising cheap supermarkets for large families, free loan societies, low-cost wedding halls, children's clothing bazaars, all run by volunteers on a non-profit basis. In a surge of resourcefulness inspired by necessity, haredi parties and non-political groups have built up over recent years whole networks of self-help and mutual aid. These are unique to the haredi sector, and they have helped alleviate the deepening impoverishment of the rapidly expanding 'society of learners'.

Every haredi neighbourhood boasts at least one 'cheap-market' where prices are substantially lower than in regular stores and the entry ticket is an official card attesting that the family has four children or more. Some cheap-markets also want evidence of real economic need. There is no subtle lighting in these emporiums, no piped music, air-conditioning or coffee-and-pastry counters, and no elaborate display advertising. Just bare walls, and plain metal shelves piled high with foodstuffs, cleaning materials, fruit and vegetables, usually in economy-size packs, all bearing the kosher-stamps of haredi rabbis and batei din. Yet major manufacturers vie to supply these outlets, where the turnover is in inverse proportion to the luxury of the surroundings.

In some of the haredi cheap-markets – those of the Gerer hasidim for instance – there are separate shopping hours for men and women. The Gerers, moreover, do not require proof of economic need, in addition to proof of family-size. 'Our Rebbe,' says the manager of one of their seven stores around the country, 'stipulated that every large family, rich or poor, can buy here – so no one who comes in need feel embarrassed.' The Gerer shops in provincial cities are open to non-haredim, the manager adds, 'provided they come dressed modestly'.

The cheap-markets have recently branched into clothing and even furniture, growing into regular department stores – with the one key difference that they sell at cost-plus-expenses. The initial investment is usually a charitable endowment or bequest – and thereafter the store maintains itself, with no profit.

The same principle applies to haredi banqueting halls, where weddings, bar-mitzva and circumcision dinners can be booked for a fraction of the cost on the open market. Haim Yitzhak Cohen, director of the Sadagora hasidic community in Jerusalem, shows his order-book for the wedding hall he built in the basement of the Sadagora yeshiva. Hardly a night is vacant for months ahead. Given that the average haredi family is likely to celebrate several dozen weddings, bar-mitzvas and circumcisions in the course of two or three decades, the ability to hire a hall and caterer for, say, $5 a plate, instead of $15 or $20 on the open market, adds up to a major saving.

But the most important money-saver for the haredim is money itself: the availability of countless free-loan *g'machim* (singular: *g'mach*, an acrostic of *g'milut hasadim* – dispensing kindnesses) where one can borrow hundreds, and in some cases thousands of dollars without interest. There is scarcely a haredi household where the husband is 'in learning' that does not have recourse to these funds on occasion (often on the occasion of a simcha which, however cheap the hall is, is still a costly event). Many families get by on an ongoing basis by rolling loans for g'mach to g'mach, with no real prospect, or indeed intention, of ever paying them all off.

Interest, both charging it and paying it, is repeatedly forbidden in the Torah (Exodus 22, Leviticus 25, Deuteronomy 23); but Talmudic Law, in order to facilitate trade and commerce, instituted a device whereby this ban is effectively circumvented. Israeli bank branches display a framed document, called '*heter iska*' (commercial dispensation), signed by a rabbi, which halachically facilitates normal financial practices. The same device is halachically available to any creditor and borrower. But the essence of the g'mach funds is that they charge no interest. Repayment is linked to the US dollar or Swiss franc, to protect the fund against inflation; the administrators are all volunteers; there are no office expenses since there are no offices; and hence the only overheads are bad debts – of which there are remarkably few.

There are dozens of such g'machim. But, in the words of one haredi yeshiva lecturer, 'It still takes some swallowing of pride to apply and sign the forms.' This man, therefore, and thousands like him, live by borrowing privately. 'Let's take today as a typical "day in the life of",' says the lecturer. 'I needed to pay off a $1,000 loan this morning. I called up a friend last night and said, I need $1,000. He asked, How long for? I said, As long as you can. He said, One day. I took it. I paid the debt, but then I couldn't pay my friend back. So I borrowed from my brother-in-law. He said I could keep it till 9.15 this evening . . .'

The joke in Bnei Brak is that in fact there is just one sum of $1,000, perpetually circulating.

Sometimes, creative resourcefulness and the struggle to make ends meet produce bizarre ideas. For instance, advertisements have on occasion appeared in the haredi press offering to name a newborn baby after someone's departed relative in return for a sizeable lump-sum payment. Presumably these offers are intended for bereaved families in which no one is of procreative age, and hence the dead person will have no natural descendant bearing his or her name. (Ashkenazic haredim generally name new babies after departed relatives or rabbis. Sephardim name them after living persons too.)

Haredim also help each other by buying and selling within the community, in back-parlour shops, rather than in regular stores. This informal – and unregistered – retailing system is fairly common among haredim in the Diaspora, but is far more widespread in Israel, where taxes and retail mark-ups, especially on clothes, are often unwarrantedly high. (Because of the stiff tax system, even items manufactured in Israel will sell in Tel Aviv stores at twice the price they sell, say, at Britain's famous Marks and Spencer chain.)

Many haredi families travelling abroad will, as a matter of course, bring back suitcases packed with good-quality clothes to sell – garments they have bought from haredi wholesalers or back-parlour retailers abroad, or at the well-known department stores. One haredi couple from Bnei Brak say they visit their family in Europe each summer – and pay for the trip by the profit they make on selling a few coats and dresses on their return. Usually, says the wife, the specific items are ordered by customers before they set out, so there is little business risk involved.

The system works well because haredim, both men and women, require more formal and therefore more expensive clothes for their everyday wear than other people. Casual T-shirts and slacks are frowned on for men and banned outright for women. No trousers, even baggy, figure-hiding ones, are permitted for women according to the haredi interpretation of the biblical rule: 'The woman shall not wear that which pertains to a man . . . All who do so are an abomination to the Lord' (Deut. 22:5). The women wear dresses more than non-haredi women do, and even their workaday skirts and shirts imply a stiffer, and more expensive, sartorial standard then the skimpy daytime casual clothes that Israeli women favour in the long hot summers and autumns.

Unmarried girls in particular take great care, and spend much money, on their clothes. Their aim is to de-emphasize, or emphasize only subtly, physical attributes, but at the same time to project a neat and well coiffured appearance. From puberty till marriage, haredi girls are constantly on show, being appraised – openly by women, furtively by men – for potential or putative shidduchim.

*

Beyond cheap buying and free borrowing, haredi communal life provides myriad other support systems. The mainly haredi neighbourhood of Bayit Vegan in Jerusalem is a good example. Residents there are advised, in flyers printed in Hebrew and English, of the availability of the following local free-hire funds:

> Microphones [for speeches and music at family celebrations].
> Shabbat hotplates [to keep food hot through the sabbath, when cooking is forbidden].
> Ruby Stones – for healthy pregnancy and easy delivery [a folk-traditional amulet worn round the neck].
> Arbes (chickpeas) for Shalom Zachar. [This food is traditionally eaten at the family celebration held on the Friday night after a baby boy is born: the free-loan fund is designed for births on Friday afternoon when the family has not had time to cook its chickpeas before shabbat. It would be courting bad luck to cook them in advance of the birth.]
> Yad Eliezer – collection of clothing . . . please bring clean, properly mended clothes only.
> Dishes – for those adhering to strict kashrut standards only.
> Special pillow covers for Bris [circumcision: baby is placed on pillow].
> Mezuzos [small parchment scroll in metal or wooden case, placed on each doorpost].
> Sefer Torah [parchment Torah scroll, written with quill pen, for use in public worship: a new one costs upwards of $20,000].
> Tables and benches [for family occasions, joyous or sad].
> Playpens, baby-cribs (cots), and carriages (prams). [The UK-style variations are thoughtfully added in the flyer for the benefit of British and Commonwealth immigrants.]
> Artificial flower arrangements.
> Freezer space [for a simcha and the like].
> Frozen Meals – tastefully prepared (packed per person) provided in cases of: illness, after childbirth, for elderly people, etc. Volunteers are needed for packing and delivering the meals.
> Cassette tapes (Torah subjects).
> Wedding gowns.
> Maternity clothes.
> Medicines – baby needs, bottles and pacifiers, cereals and

formula, etc. Medicines are dispensed by prescription only.
Items must be returned no later than three days after receipt by purchasing the item in the pharmacy.
Breast pumps and mother's milk bank.
Bris preparations – proper organization of bris food on a voluntary basis or for a minimal fee. Volunteers for baking or preparing food needed.
Fresh flower arrangements.
Moveable partitions [used to separate men and women at family celebrations and public events].

Every listing is followed by the name, address and telephone number of the family that dispenses this particular free-loan service.

Some of the neighbourhood g'machim provide just services – hesed in the sense of kindness rather than charity:

Visiting the Sick – to cheer up long- or short-term patients.
Also to help put on tefillin. Women volunteers are needed for visiting women patients. Times and days at your convenience.
Welcoming Newcomers – both new to Israel and new to Bayit Vegan. If you have new neighbours or you want to help, please call . . .
Shabbat hospitality.
Helping Hand – for housewives in stress situations.
Help in Time of Mourning – advice and help with funeral, burial and shiva arrangements.

Nominally, the help is available to everyone, haredi and non-haredi alike. But in practice, most of the recipients and all the volunteers and contributors are haredim. 'The non-Orthodox don't seem to understand the concept of g'mach,' says Mrs Suri Frowhein, the neighbourhood coordinator.

That is not quite fair, certainly not with regard to Diaspora Jewish communities and synagogue congregations, non-Orthodox and Orthodox alike, where mutual aid and communal services are highly developed. But in Israel this aspect of social culture (and of Jewish tradition) is remarkably underdeveloped in non-haredi society, a phenomenon noted by sociologists and bemoaned by civic leaders. Perhaps the average Israeli, hard pressed by economic burdens and by army reserves duty, has little time for philanthropy or volunteering.

The Bayit Vegan flyer, written by neighbourhood rabbis, urges everyone, 'whether we are long-term residents or have recently arrived, to help by volunteering our services or donating *ma'aser* [tithe] money to help fund these programmes. If you know of someone in need, or if you know of someone who needs help, don't hesitate to contact us. We are here to help you. Our motto is: "When you can, you give; when you need, you ask." That is what mutual help is all about.'

The various kinds of free-loan funds are usually launched as private family endowments, in honour of a departed relative, often with the initial money coming from his or her estate. Most of them remain small-scale and localized, but some funds continue to raise money and enlist volunteers, growing from local to city-wide and even national enterprises.

Some years ago, for example, a young Jerusalem haredi named Uri Lupolianski conceived the idea of a free-loan fund for medical equipment – wheelchairs, crutches, blood-pressure kits and the like. He set up shop in a disused mortuary. As the fund grew, he expanded into an ancient railway carriage which he managed somehow to wheel into the courtyard of the mortuary. Today, 'Yad Sarah' – Lupolianski named the fund in memory of his mother – is a nationwide medical auxiliary organization, dispensing millions of dollars' worth of equipment, with branches inside hospitals and in all the main towns. It is partly government-funded, and serves the entire population. Lupolianski has subsequently gone into politics, and at the time of writing is a deputy mayor of Jerusalem, representing the Degel Hatorah Party.

Another haredi self-help innovation, which originated in Brooklyn, New York, is Hatsolo (Salvation), a medical emergency and ambulance service, staffed and run by volunteers. Many a New Yorker, Gentile as well as Jew, owes his life to the prompt response of Hatsolo paramedics, who man communication centres and a fleet of well equipped ambulances around the clock. Hatsolo teams usually reach the scene long before regular ambulances – which was the original rationale behind the organization.

Hundreds of haredim in New York, London, and more recently in a number of Israeli cities, take advanced first-aid courses in order to volunteer for Hatsolo. Halachic leniency regarding sabbath observance, which in the past was limited to professional doctors and nurses, has been extended by haredi rabbis to these volunteers. Shtreimel- and *sheitel*(wig)-covered heads hardly turn nowadays in Brooklyn's Borough Park or London's Stamford Hill when a hasid in his sabbath finery whips out a mobile telephone or dives out of shul and into his car to rush to an emergency.

Health is a major preoccupation among the haredim, and medicine is one aspect of the modern world that they have eagerly adopted. Granted, traditional cures and charms are still in use. One Jerusalemite haredi, for example, makes his living by raising pigeons, which are placed on the navel of jaundice-sufferers. The birds promptly die, and the patient immediately improves: there is overwhelming evidence that it works. But folk-medicine never substitutes among haredim for the best and most advanced scientific treatment that is attainable.

The haredi press is assiduous in reporting the latest medical advances, and devotes much space – much more, relatively, than other newspapers – to matters of health and sickness. Hasidic rebbes and some mitnaged rabbis too, as we have seen, devote long hours to advising people about their health problems. In a sense, the rabbi is 'dispensing hesed' in this way, by sharing with inquirers his time, experience and network of contacts with doctors and hospitals around the world.

Very often the rebbe/rabbi will dispense hard cash too to sick people, in person or through the agency of voluntary organizations. Michel Goodfarb says that more than half of the charity that he disburses goes to families facing major medical expenses. Often, a patient must go abroad for complicated surgery. The costs of the round trip plus medical fees and care can quickly reach $100,000 or more. Even for better-off families, this can spell ruin. Sometimes, Israeli hospitals are prepared to perform the required treatment, but the rabbi or rebbe advising on the case recommends treatment abroad. In such cases, the Israeli health authorities and sick funds naturally decline to cover any of the costs. But in many other cases, says Goodfarb, the local doctors themselves prescribe treatment abroad. Some procedures, such as heart-lung transplants, are not yet performed in Israel. Even then, though, a sizeable part of the cost falls on the patient and his family.

'For me,' Goodfarb says, 'a recommendation from one of the recognized rabbinical-medical authorities is the first priority. Then I will want to see the patient's complete file and a covering letter from the doctor treating the case to the doctor or hospital abroad.' Goodfarb is well connected with haredi travel agents, who will arrange bargain air tickets (their part in the hesed effort).

But even Goodfarb can rarely offer more than five or ten thousand dollars all told to any individual case. And there are not many Goodfarbs around. Frequently, therefore, haredi newspapers and synagogue bulletin-boards in Israel and abroad publicize accounts of individual medical hardship cases, signed by leading rabbis and specifying where donations should be sent. The rabbis' signatures attest to the veracity of the information.

31

The Other Half

The bulletin-boards sometimes tell the story of a haredi family, discreetly unnamed, which has fallen on hard times because of a sudden death or a business collapse. Again, well known rabbis affix their signatures as a proof of bona fides, and time and again, the community responds. This is all the more remarkable in view of the constant bombardment that the average haredi householder faces – much more so in Diaspora communities than in Israel – from an endless stream of charity collectors. It is not uncommon for the doorbell to ring a dozen times on a Sunday morning at a middle-class haredi home in New York or Los Angeles, Johannesburg or Melbourne. Each time, another bearded *meshulach* (lit. agent) stands outside, expecting to be welcomed warmly, or at least courteously, invited in, perhaps offered refreshment, and given a not inconsequential sum.

The householder will already have been accosted in synagogue that morning by a half-dozen lesser *meshulachim* and mendicants. They make do with inconsequential sums; but even these add up to sizeable amounts.

The meshulach industry has suffered the vicissitudes of the rest of the world economy, and at the time of writing it is in marked recession from the late-1980s boom years. In those days it was becoming almost standard practice in certain haredi circles in Israel for the head of a family to embark on a round-the-world begging tour each time a son or daughter reached marriageable age. This engendered much muttering and disapproval among rabbis and yeshiva heads, partly because of the inevitable frictions that arose between these unabashedly self-serving 'agents' and those sent forth by the various educational institutions. (The dividing-line is not as clear-cut as it seems, since institutional meshulachim sometimes cream off 50, 60 or even 70 per cent of their take for themselves, and this is fully understood by donors and recipients alike.)

On Sunday evening, as often as not, our householder will have been invited to – and insistently pressured to attend – an annual dinner for this or that yeshiva, school, old-age home, or other worthy cause in his own community or in Israel. He can scarcely get away with less than a three-figure contribution. If he stays home in the evening, Sunday or midweek, he may well be approached, first by telephone and then in person, by a 'major league' collector – a rosh yeshiva or noted rabbi who is also not to be fobbed off with less than a hundred dollars, and will be hoping for considerably more.

All this coming on top of school and yeshiva fees for the children and synagogue membership dues, as well as investment of time for voluntary work, can easily exceed the minimal 10 per cent tithe of one's income that the halacha requires to be allocated to charity, or even the 20 per cent that the halacha advises as the sensible ceiling. Social pressures – a rich man's standing in the haredi community is determined by his philanthropy rather than his wealth – are sometimes a contributory factor in the over-extension and eventual decline or even collapse of personal fortunes.

The ups and downs of business life are compounded among Diaspora haredim by the fact that a large number of them choose to make their money in two particularly volatile commercial fields: diamonds and real estate. These businesses are among the first to respond to shifts in the overall economic climate. When the economy is booming, the diamond and jewellery trade is quick to prosper. Similarly property prices, both commercial and residential, are the first to rise. When recession sets in, nationally or internationally, its early victims usually include the diamond trade – people simply have less to spend on precious stones, whether as gifts or investments – and the property market.

Diamonds are traditionally a Jewish business, ever since Spanish Jews settled in Amsterdam in the sixteenth century, and today, by conservative estimate, more than 70 per cent of dealers and brokers in the main world centres (London, Antwerp, New York,

Tel Aviv) are Jews. Of these, a not insignificant minority are haredim.

Jewish prominence in real estate is a more recent development in terms of Diaspora history. In Eastern Europe, Jewish landowning was rare; in some places and periods it was forbidden by the Church or the temporal authorities. Haredi prominence in this business, in North America and Europe, is of even more recent vintage, and dramatically reflects the closing of the affluence gap between the longer-established sections of Western Jewish communities, and those – most haredim amongst them – whose families arrived within the past half-century.

The Toronto-based Reichmanns, for instance, who in mid-1989, according to *The Economist*, owned the world's largest portfolio of office property (First Canadian Place, Toronto; World Financial Center, New York; and the ill-starred Canary Wharf project in London – these were some of the flagships), reached Canada only in the 1950s from Tangier, Morocco, where their parents had fled from Vienna just before the Second World War.

In the UK, the largest residential property owner in 1990, according to the *Sunday Times*, was Sighismund Berger, a publicity-shy Satmarer hasid whose father, Gershon, known as Getzel, started the business as a refugee from Nazism. The *Sunday Times* ranked Sighismund 25th in its list of the 200 richest people in Britain, just behind Paul McCartney. Another haredi property baron featured in the *Sunday Times* list was Benzion Freshwater, whose father, Osias, 'arrived as a Polish refugee in Britain three days before the outbreak of the last war. He started as a textile merchant then turned to property. By the early Seventies he was London's biggest private landlord.' The Freshwaters are relatives and hasidim of the Bobover Rebbe in New York, and an important source of philanthropic support for his court.

Property was the archetypical get-rich-quick business of the 1970s and 80s, and not all the spectacular rises to fortune were accompanied by parallel surges in ethical reputations. Interestingly, just as some Gentiles are quick to point out Jews who are convicted of economic crimes, so too some Jews are prone to making sweeping accusations about the financial probity of haredim as a group.

Certainly there are Jewish and haredi businessmen – a higher-than-average proportion of Jews, and especially of haredim, go into business – who sail close to the wind, and some who cross the line of illegality without many qualms. But there are no statistics to show that Jews do so more than others in the business world, and none to prove that haredim are better or worse than the rest. (Many of the convicted men in the headline-making 'insider trading' scandals in New York and London during 1989–90 were in fact Jews; none were haredim.)

Some students of haredi life do however claim to find a widespread disrespect for such institutions as income tax. Haredi businessmen who are scrupulous in their dealings with other individuals, Gentiles as well as Jews, seem to regard the State (Gentile or Jewish) as fair game. Thus, for example, when in July 1991 a British haredi millionaire, David Rubin, the son of the hasidic rebbe Sassov, appeared to have improperly lost vast sums of fellow haredi investors' money, only one of those investors sought legal redress, because, according to the British press, their investments had been *shvartze* (black, untaxed) money.

A source in the banking world says that while some haredim are indeed brazenly contemptuous of the law, most of them are no greedier man-for-man than the rest of mercantile mankind. But their lack of general education, he says, and their alienation from the surrounding society make the tax-evaders among them more naïve, and more blithely ignorant of the chances of being caught.

Most haredim, at any rate, profess an almost personal pride in the worldwide name for copper-bottomed honesty built up by those latter-day – but short-lived – Rothschilds, the Reichmanns. 'In an industry perhaps not noted for such qualities,' wrote *Accountancy*, the journal of the Institute of Chartered Accountants in England and Wales, the Reichmanns were said to be 'model employers as well as outstandingly upright and ethical in their business dealings.' The three Reichmann brothers, Paul, Albert and Ralph (a fourth lives in Israel and was not part of their Olympia & York Company), moreover, lived unopulently in suburban Toronto. The 'only suggestion of tycoonery,' wrote *The Economist*, 'is a corporate jet, made necessary by their trips to Canary Wharf.' There were no suggestions at the time of their company's difficulties in 1992 of wrongdoing on their part. Rather, financial circles attributed Olympia & York's collapse to a policy of over-extension which was overtaken by the worldwide recession.

Haredim were also pleased by the generally sympathetic if quizzical media coverage of the Reichmanns' Orthodoxy, especially their insistence, wherever they built, that all work must stop at their sites for shabbat (Friday afternoons in winter) and Jewish festivals. 'The builders' holidays,' wrote *The Economist* in their heyday, 'are based on the Jewish calendar. The three brothers . . . are strictly observant Jews. Their charitable donations are said, in the tradition of Jewish wealth, to be huge, though here again they avoid publicity.'

The Reichmanns' honesty, modesty and philanthropy were all spoken of in haredi communities as a 'kiddush hashem'. Rabbis and writers apostrophized them in reverent hyperbole, reminiscent of eighteenth-century Jewish religious leaders' worshipful rejoicing over Nathaniel Mayer Rothschild, the devout founder of the famous banking house.

Human nature being what it is, many Diaspora haredim, and a few Israelis too, find they cannot afford to live as unassumingly as the Reichmanns did even at their zenith, and there is much keeping up with the Cohens. Yachts, nightclubs and St Tropez are out, for religious reasons. But some well-to-do haredim live in large and lavishly furnished homes, drive expensive cars, and dress in the latest fashions (long sleeves and high necklines for the women, though).

Synagogue on shabbat and festivals is traditionally the place and the time to show what one is worth, and specifically for one's wife to show off her clothes and sheitels. No amount of rabbinical railing seems able entirely to extirpate this custom (there are written records of similar railings in Poland 300 years ago), and the women's sections of certain poky Brooklyn store-front shtieblach have been known to outdo in terms of haute couture, woman for woman, the most fashionable Manhattan temples.

The halacha itself provides plentiful opportunity for conspicuous consumption, for those who crave it. Instead of just having separate closets in the kitchen for dairy and meat utensils – the basic requirement of a kosher kitchen – some haredi rich build two entirely separate kitchens, sometimes with an additional one for Passover. The poor and the less conspicuous make do with additional sets of dishes for Passover, and with 'koshering' the regular kitchen for use on Passover by thoroughly cleaning and scouring it.

In one display of moneyed religiosity that raised embarrassed eyebrows, a British millionaire, whose real estate empire had crashed into bankruptcy some years before, chartered an airliner on his son's wedding-day, so that the bridegroom and guests could climb above the clouds and recite the monthly prayer of salutation to the moon. It is traditionally a lucky omen for a groom to perform this devotion, but the weather was overcast on that evening.

Again, as in respect of alleged financial shenanigans, many non-haredi Jews, though themselves high-livers, are apt to be accusatory and resentful of high-profile haredi affluence. They say that haredim, who purport to be more religious than others, ought to concentrate on the spiritual side of life, not on material pleasures. What they mean – and some are frank enough to spell it out – is that haredim, who are so conspicuous because of their clothes and appearance, ought not to flash their money around, for fear of causing antisemitism. Their strictures are echoed, on both counts, by the haredi rabbinate, which preaches incessantly (but not too vehemently, economic realities being what they are) against excessive materialism in the community.

Interestingly, the criticism of conspicuous consumption is often echoed too, if only transiently, by young haredi men and women who go to Israel to learn in yeshivas, and find themselves attracted by the relative absence of materialism in Israeli haredi society.

Foreign holidays are another reflection of growing haredi affluence. Israel is still by far the most frequent and popular destination for Diaspora haredim, but the Swiss ski resort of St Moritz is a particular holiday favourite among adherents of some hasidic sects and their rebbes. And several other Swiss villages and Italian coastal resorts have been 'discovered' by the haredim in recent years, and now have strictly kosher hotels, which provide a synagogue and mikve too for their guests.

Since glasnost and the crumbling of the Iron Curtain, a new form of haredi holidaymaking has evolved: grave-tours in Eastern Europe and the republics of the former USSR. A number of haredi-owned international travel agents specialize in this service, providing the pilgrims with pre-packed kosher meals as they journey by plane, train and bus from cemetery to desolate cemetery through vast tracts of Hungary and Czechoslovakia, Poland, Russia, the Ukraine and Belarus that once pulsed with Jewish life.

Some of the groups comprise hasidim of a particular sect, interested mainly in the tombs of their own rebbes. Others prefer a more eclectic itinerary, taking in centuries of rabbinical graves and praying, too, at the sites of Nazi concentration camps and in still-extant synagogues in the main cities. Sometimes a group of haredi men and women hailing from the same locality in Eastern Europe set out to search together not only for their rabbis' graves but for those of their own families too.

For vacations nearer home, many Diaspora haredim keep country cottages, but in clusters, so that they can have a minyan while on holiday. The Catskill Mountains, the mainly Jewish summer vacation area in upstate New York known jocularly as the 'borscht belt', is studded with haredi bungalow colonies. In many of them, the cottages are owned or rented by members of the same hasidic sect or yeshiva-linked group, so that their synagogue and social life during the long summer months has a comfortable home-from-home feeling. The men pray and learn together; the women and small children mix with familiar friends and neighbours.

Some families move to their bungalows for the entire summer. The men commute daily to the city, or live at home from Monday to Thursday and join the family for the weekends. Older children are generally sent to haredi camps, also located in the Catskills. There, too, they mix with their yeshiva or school classmates and continue their year-round programme of religious studies, though with long periods set aside each day for swimming, sports and hiking.

The fact that these summer retreats teem with children on

holiday is cited by residents to explain the often run-down and scruffy look of the properties and public spaces. Certain of the haredi colonies are more aesthetically maintained, set amid manicured lawns and landscaped flower-beds. These are reserved for older people who want peace and quiet. There, children and grandchildren may visit during the afternoon, but they are not expected to stay the night.

Despite the wholesale transfer of communal and religious life from the city, the atmosphere is markedly less dour in the country. People go to their bungalows to relax. The women spend the days and evenings in long, loose housecoats. (These themselves have become a fashion item: well-to-do haredi housewives will wear three of these floor-length gowns, elaborately printed or brocaded, during a single shabbat.) The men let their hair down, literally, untying their peyot to let the breeze flow through them as they stride unselfconsciously along leafy country lanes. Some hasidim take off their long coats, as a concession to country life, revealing their *talit katan* (lit. small shawl) beneath.*

The Gentile residents of Liberty, South Fallsburg, Woodbourne and the other towns and villages in the Catskills have long since ceased gawking at the haredim. A Christian child living in the area might easily assume that all Jews look and dress that way. In fact, several of the local towns are home to long-established Reform, Conservative and Modern-Orthodox Jewish communities. Moreover, by no means all the Catskill summer vacationers are haredi. (Some – though not many – are not even Jewish.) But the haredi proportion is on the rise, as other groups, less set in their ways, seek more adventurous holiday venues elsewhere. Thus, two elderly amateur fishermen, residents of a long-established bungalow colony on Lake Kiamisha, were to be heard one Sunday morning in summer 1991 bemoaning a new haredi resident's

* The observant male Jew is required to wear two *talitot* or ritual shawls, which are fringed at each corner with long white threads called *tzizit* (see Numbers 15:37–40). The *talit gadol* or large shawl, usually white or off-white with black stripes, is worn for morning prayers. The talit katan is a white, waist-length chemise that must be worn throughout the day. Some Modern-Orthodox Jews are lax about their talit katan. Those who do wear it do so under their shirts. Among the haredim, some wear it under their shirts too, but have the tzizit protruding; others wear the talit katan itself over their shirts but under their jackets.

insistence on putting up an eruv to symbolically enclose the area on shabbat. He was threatening to sue on grounds of religious discrimination if he was prevented from doing so. 'Why does he have to have the string right across the grass?' one fisherman asked. 'Can't he have it back against the trees? I tell you, they're taking over round here.'

By and large, though, a summertime spirit of relaxed tolerance seems to embrace everyone in the Catskills, Jews and Gentiles alike. On Saturday nights, after the shabbat ends, a huge haredi-run funfair is thronged with good-natured crowds of holiday-makers and locals. Hasidim in their satin bekeshes jostle with black youths in tank-tops and blondes in denim shorts. They play at adjoining pool-tables, careen and crash into each other on the race-kart track, line up together for (kosher) ice-creams and waffles.

In the city, such places of recreation are effectively out of bounds for respectable haredim. Some do not even allow their teenage children to hang out at the dozen-odd kosher pizza parlours that dot Borough Park's main thoroughfare, Thirteenth Avenue. A youngster seen there – other than to buy pizza and take it straight home – is inevitably prejudicing his or her chances of contracting a 'good shidduch' with a serious, studious, pious partner.

In the mountains, the rules are relaxed a little. Many shidduchim which are subsequently formalized by parents or marriage-brokers back in the city originate in glances, smiles and bashful introductions exchanged in the coffee-bars of Woodbourne, or at the funfair, as She furtively admires Him manfully contend against the automatic pitching machine in the baseball nets.

Of course, not all haredim meet the standards set by their rabbis and spiritual leaders. Many a Borough Park hasid and his wife – once they are married their shidduch prospects can no longer be harmed – are to be found at the pool tables and roulette wheels of Atlantic City on a Saturday night, or He with peyot slicked back and She in bikini, besporting themselves on a Florida beach. The battle against the Evil Inclination, as the rabbis would put it, is a lifelong struggle.

For the youngsters in their summer camps, sports are a central part of the programme. Campers can be seen on the baseball fields, pitching and swinging with gusto, or playing volleyball with as much dedication as any other American youth. Even the girls, in their separate camps, set aside their customary demureness for an energetic game of basketball.

There are subtle but significant differences, though, between the various haredi sects, many of which run their own camps. Non-hasidic haredi boys will wear the proper sporting attire. 'Moderate' hasidim, such as the Bobovers, will not wear shorts or T-shirts, but will play in their shirtsleeves. The more hardline Gerers will play in their long black coats, which nevertheless do not seem to detract from their zeal and enthusiasm. Only the ultra-conservative Satmarer and allied groups, who are of Hungarian origin, eschew sports altogether once the girls reach twelve and the boys thirteen, the age of bar-mitzva when, in the eyes of the halacha, adulthood begins.

In Israel, by contrast, competitive sport is frowned upon in haredi circles. Rabbi Shach, in a speech in 1989, linked sport to suicide. There had been instances, he told his audience, of sportsmen shooting themselves because they had lost the game. 'What possible enjoyment,' he asked, 'do sportsmen derive from the game itself? After all, it is only victory that gives them their satisfaction and happiness. For that gratification, they are prepared to crush and kill. And if they don't obtain their goal, they have no joy in life at all. From this we can see how far we must set ourselves apart, and stand firm on the truth of our great wisdom . . .' But such admonishments fall on deaf ears as far as American haredim are concerned. Sport is such an all-pervasive aspect of the American ethos that it has penetrated even the sheltered world of haredism.

Even in Israel, though, a breakthrough of sorts has occurred in recent years with the opening of several water-parks (sex-segregated of course) especially for haredim. These have won the approval of leading rabbis. Swimming and water sports – Israel provides segregated swimming beaches in many of its coastal resorts for the use of the haredim – are viewed more benignly by the Israeli haredi rabbis than, say, soccer, basketball or tennis. Perhaps frolicking in water is regarded as merely an extension of dipping in the mikve, which is considered a spiritually and physically healthy activity, and which many haredim, particularly hasidim, perform daily or at least weekly. Some mikves offer Turkish baths. Aficionados spend hours sweating, steaming and plunging in a relaxing and convivial clublike atmosphere, uninhibited by their collective nakedness.

Swimming, moreover, like mikve-dipping, is conducted only when the opposite sex is totally excluded. Thus it cannot lead to any of the inter-sexual levity that the rabbis are so at pains to prevent, especially between teenage yeshiva and seminary students. Girls (or boys) can wander onto a soccer field or tennis court; they cannot – because it is such a grave offence – enter a swimming-pool or bathing-beach at times reserved for the other sex. Any hint of homosexual activity at mikves or segregated swimming-pools is immediately, and on occasion violently, eliminated by modesty vigilantes or other community activists. Such episodes are rare among haredim, and are hushed up when they happen. Homosexual relations are a capital offence under the halacha.

The success, over the years, of the haredi bungalow colonies in the Catskills was a factor in persuading American haredi leaders that moving out of the crowded city permanently could be a viable option for their communities. Suburbanization need not mean a weakening of communal and cultural bonds, if a substantial group move together and transplant their religious and educational institutions to the new location.

Suburbanization can offer, moreover, a solution to worsening housing problems in the traditional haredi districts of the city. In Williamsburg, Brooklyn, an unattractive area just across the river from the Lower East Side of Manhattan, the haredi population of mainly Satmarer hasidim has long outgrown available housing space. New public housing projects are going up, but the hasidim have to vie against others for apartment allocations. The local (Yiddish-language) newspapers complain bitterly of discrimination, in that hasidic applicants are offered housing elsewhere, without reference to their need to live in close proximity to their rebbe and synagogue, while Hispanic families are enabled to move into 'Jewish Williamsburg'. In Borough Park and Flatbush, pleasant residential sections of Brooklyn with large haredi populations, property prices have become prohibitive for the average young family.

The Satmarers were among the first to take the plunge twenty-five years ago, setting up a 'colony' in the town of Monroe, about an hour's drive from the city. Other haredi groups chose Monsey, also a rustic dormitory town north of New York. The Squarer (originally Skvirer) Rebbe, head of a small but cohesive sect, formed his own officially incorporated village, New Square, on the outskirts of Monsey. Amid rolling forest- and farm-land, these groups have recreated to near perfection the ambience of the European Jewish shtetl, but set in American suburbia, with its shopping malls, gas-stations and highways all a part of the pastoral scenery. On the porches of the clapboard houses, elderly matrons sit on rocking-chairs, in the American tradition, reading their 'Tsenarena'. (*Tse'ena Ure'ena*, 'Come and See', is the title of a Yiddish anthology of Bible stories and homilies for the pious Jewish woman that was widely read in pre-Holocaust Europe.)

The rural haredi communities are expanding rapidly as more and more New York haredim choose affordable country homes and commuting over cramped and pressured city life. Local neighbours, Jews as well as Gentiles, do not always welcome the large and boisterous haredi families with open arms, and there are periodic outbreaks of muttering over the effect of their advent on property values.

32

A Woman's Place

In Israel, the housing problem in the 'society of learners' is incomparably more acute – mainly because so many haredim learn and do not work. 'The crisis is not down the road,' says Haim Yitzhak Cohen, the Sadagora hasidic executive. 'It is here now. People have nowhere to live.'

The challenge of finding somewhere to live is daunting enough for ordinary Israelis. Rental housing is scarce; people strive to buy their own homes, saddling themselves with crippling mortgages in order to pay for them. Home-building has fallen behind demand; purchase prices are sky-high, especially in comparison to the relatively low salaries and high income-tax rates prevailing in Israel. The mass influx of Soviet immigrants during 1990–91 further strained an already desperate situation. Ordinary Israelis, moreover, do not have seven or eight children to marry off, all destined to live the precarious, even penurious, existence of the 'society of learners' (and all hoping to produce at least as many children of their own).

Until Olympia & York's collapse in spring 1992, a Reichmann fund helped all haredi newlyweds in Israel – provided that the groom was registered in a kollel – with mortgages of up to $12,000 and an additional soft loan of $3,000, intended to cover basic furnishings and repayable interest-free over ten years. But that doesn't buy the apartment. According to Jerusalem journalist Micha Odenheimer, 'It is not unusual for a couple and their eight children to have to manage with two-and-a-half rooms and a porch. The real trouble starts when one of these eight children reaches marrying age. The asking price for marrying off a child in much of the haredi community today is $40,000 – the amount that each side is expected to chip in for the cost of the wedding and the apartment. Where does a father who has spent most of his life studying in yeshiva and kollel get that kind of money, once every year or two, until all his children have been married off . . .?'

The haredi newspaper *Hamodia*, writing in 1990, bemoaned 'the frightening phenomenon' of young haredi men in early middle-age being struck down, some fatally, by heart-attacks, which the paper linked to the marriage and mortgage burden. 'What's happening to us?' *Hamodia* wailed. 'Men in the prime of life dropping under the yoke of marrying off their children . . . Precious sacrifices on the altar of marriage . . . Men dying in their effort to prevent their daughters from growing grey in spinsterhood . . .'

The housing problem goes to the heart of haredi life: marriage. Crowding in with the in-laws is no solution for the long or even medium term, both because of the laws regarding intimacy between the sexes – a father-in-law and daughter-in-law, for instance, are forbidden to be in the same room alone together – and because of the more prosaic pressures of floor-space as the family's next-in-line brings home his/her new spouse.

Nor is the solution of marrying late, which similar economic exigencies have forced upon other societies, at all an option to be entertained in the haredi community. With much of haredi education designed to stifle or sublimate the sex-drive of the not yet married, the entire thrust of haredi social mores is to marry off the young as early as possible. A haredi woman of twenty-two who is still single is very definitely 'on the shelf', and people will be whispering about 'what's wrong with her'. But early marriage further exacerbates the housing shortage: it means shorter generations, with the next crop of young couples hitting the homes market much sooner than in other sectors of society.

Another aggravating factor is the haredim's insistence on living together in their own cities, suburbs or enclaves. This creates an internal price spiral. An apartment in the haredi city of Bnei Brak will cost substantially more than a similar home in any other of the satellite towns surrounding Tel Aviv. A flat in one of the all-haredi suburbs of north Jerusalem will fetch a higher price than a bigger and nicer flat in the south of the capital.

Haredi leaders in Israel have sought to grapple with this part of the problem by initiating all-haredi building projects in provincial towns and villages, and exhorting, even ordering, their followers to live in them. (One haredi township, Emmanuel, has gone up in the occupied West Bank, and a second, Betar, is being built just south of Jerusalem; but in general the haredim were reluctant to avail themselves of the heavily subsidized housing opportunities provided for settlers in the occupied territories during the years of Likud rule.)

The main pioneer both in these attempts at population distribution and in 'social legislation' designed to counter market pressures was the hasidic Rebbe of Ger, Simcha Bunim Alter (1887–1992). He forced his often reluctant young hasidim to make their homes away from Bnei Brak and Jerusalem: in Ashdod on the coast, in Hatzor in Galilee, in Arad in the barren Judaean Hills. These places had rarely seen a haredi until the black-coated Gerers moved in, first the project managers with bulldozers and cement-mixers, then the families and children, and finally the synagogues and yeshivas, to create self-contained islands of hasidic life. Belzer hasidim, Vishnitzers, Breslevers and others, and some mitnagdic groups too, have followed this pattern, building their own *krayot* (sing., *kirya*: township) of functional high-rises in 'development areas', where young families can find homes at relatively reasonable prices, with the help of generous government mortgages.

Rabbi Alter of Ger made the scheme work within his own sect by explicitly forbidding newlyweds to buy homes in Jerusalem or Bnei Brak during the first five years of their marriage. This innovative leader, who took office in 1977 at the age of eighty, applied similar consumer-pressure, with fair success, to other commodities too. One year, for instance, shortly before Sukkot, he announced that the entire community would make do with a single set of the 'four species' (citron fruit, palm branch, myrtle branch and willow branch: they are held during the festival service – Leviticus 23:40) rather than every hasid paying outrageous prices for his own set. The prices, which had topped $100, plummeted instantly.

Rabbi Alter's 'Regulations' also stipulate an upper limit on the number of guests at a wedding or bar-mitzva, and specify what food may be served. There are even rules governing what class of ceramic tiles the hasidim may install in their kitchens and bathrooms.

But all these are piecemeal panaceas; they hardly offer comprehensive protection for haredi society as the demographic and economic pressures continue to mount. Moreover, they do not address another perceived threat to the core institution of marriage caused by the exigencies of haredi economics: a sharp imbalance between the daily lifestyles of husbands and wives.

Haredi young women, who are the main breadwinners, can no longer count on a career in teaching, as they could a decade or two ago. There are simply too many girls now graduating from haredi teacher-training seminaries, and not enough teaching positions in haredi schools to go around. As a result, haredi women are looking further afield, and the seminaries offer courses in computers, graphics, professional sewing and bookkeeping. But the graduates cannot all expect to find such jobs in haredi companies or institutions, and hence many end up in a non-haredi working environment. Sociologists like Professor Menahem Friedman predict that the fact of the wife's broader general education, coupled with her daily experience in 'the outside world', could disrupt the cohesion of haredi family life. The divorce rate among haredim is rising (though it is still much lower than in non-haredi society). Micha Odenheimer suggests the rise reflects these stresses within the haredi marriage, and notes that: 'Most of the divorces in the haredi community are initiated by the women.'

Husbands face a similar employment bottleneck. How many kollel students can become yeshiva lecturers, rabbis, or even teachers in junior yeshivas? There are not enough of these posts to go around, and anyway not all kollel-men are qualified to fill them. The husbands, moreover, have no option of computer-programming or graphics: if they leave learning they must enlist in the army. (That, at least, is the strict legal position. In practice, some kollel-men work part-time 'on the side', for cash, in an informal, unregistered sub-economy that flourishes within the haredi community.) In many families, therefore, while the wife progresses in her career at the software house or advertising agency, the husband remains static as a rank-and-file kollel member, paid a pittance and with little prospect of promotion into a rabbinical or teaching position.

In addition to likely disparities between the spouses in job satisfaction and earning power, the wife's dual existence – as a professional in the non-haredi world and as a woman within the haredi community – involves a stark social dissonance within her own life. In the office she is relaxed, matter-of-fact, even bantering in her casual contact with other (non-haredi) men. She jokes and laughs, addresses them by their first names, uses the latest slang. At home, she is modest and retiring. If one of her husband's friends visits, she will greet him briefly with averted eyes, and retire to the kitchen.

This is particularly the case in hasidic homes; less so among the mitnagdim. But the 'modesty gap' is steadily closing – in the direction of the hasidic mores. A social evening in which couples meet and mingle is entirely unthinkable among hasidim, and it is becoming increasingly rare among mitnagdim. In the Diaspora, the rules in both camps are not quite as rigid as in the parallel groups in Israel. But the Israel-Diaspora gap is closing too, as the influence of hardline rabbis in Bnei Brak emanates throughout the haredi world.

The haredi kollel husband, unlike his working wife, has little cause to engage in daily contact with the non-haredi world, and he tends therefore to be gruff or gauche on occasions when such contact is unavoidable. He must avoid making small-talk with the woman teller at the bank or secretary at the doctor's office – and certainly would not wish to be heard chatting with her by his peers. The major Israeli banks, in fact, try not to place young woman tellers at their branches in all-haredi districts.

When the couple come home, he from his kollel, she from her office, how do they share their day's experiences? Does the contrast in their lives not distance her from him, and from their joint values? For the Rabbi of the Gerer hasidic community in Arad, a small town in southern Israel, the answer is Yes. He has issued an edict forbidding the women of the community from working in non-haredi institutions or companies. Since Arad is a largely non-haredi town, this means that many of the Gerer women have to travel far afield to find work, or else not work (or not live in Arad). If that edict were applied throughout the haredi community, the entire economic structure of 'the learning society' would come tumbling down.

Most haredi rabbis maintain that while it is theoretically plausible that these disparities could cause marital stress, there is, thus far at least, no compelling empirical evidence that they do. In practice, they say, the women do not grow alienated from their husbands and do not feel that there is a contradiction in their own lives. 'I've heard the theory,' says Rabbi David Refson, Dean of Neve Yerushalayim, the women baalot teshuva college, 'and I'm amazed that it isn't happening. But it isn't. If it were, I'd know about it. I think it's a tribute to the kind of education that these women have . . . that they are so unquestioning.'

Clearly, much of the credit for the society's success lies in the education system. Girls are imbued from the earliest age with the belief that learning Torah is the highest goal (for men), and that their task in life is to make it possible for their future husband and future sons to devote themselves to that end. Learning, they are taught, is its own self-contained merit-and-promotion system. If one's husband does not become a rosh yeshiva or a lecturer, that does not mean he is a failure – either in God's eyes or in the eyes of his wife.

Girls are also imbued by the system, on a more subtle, almost subconscious level, with the sense that non-haredim have a lesser status, religiously, than haredim. Chatting to the mailman or the electrician is all right, unless he has a yarmulka and beard, in which case it is forbidden. Sitting next to a non-haredi man on a bus is accepted; sitting next to a haredi man is to be avoided. Thus conversing uninhibitedly with non-haredim at work does not jar against the inhibitions by which the haredi woman lives in her social milieu.

There is an element here of the shtetl- or ghetto-Jew's attitude to the goy, carried over into haredi attitudes towards other Jews. The halacha itself, in certain aspects of sexual law, allots the Gentile less status than the Jew: a married woman, for instance, is not committing adultery, in the strict halachic sense, by sleeping with a Gentile man. The haredim apply a similar double standard to the non-haredi Jew. Non-haredi Jews may find this confusing; the haredim do not. 'I can talk to you quite freely like this,' one haredi woman explained, 'because you are not like us.'

Of course, the theory is not always borne out in practice – neither with respect to Gentiles nor to non-haredim. Isaac Bashevis Singer, in his novels of pre-Holocaust European Jewry, evokes the inner turmoil of haredi women who could not live by these rules and failed to crush their emotions into the required societal mould. In today's haredi society too, there are occasionally those who fail to keep up the double standard, and fall for a person of lesser status. Even so, knowledgeable insiders say that most instances of marital infidelity within the community – those occur too, despite all the education and sublimation, and are minutely tut-tutted over in breathless undertones – involve affairs between haredi partners rather than between haredim and non-haredim.

While no haredi insiders are prepared publicly to recognize the asymmetry within the haredi marriage as a threat to the society, the more thoughtful, or more outspoken, do speak openly of the economic pressures – and especially the housing crisis – in such bleak terms. Some predict an inevitable upheaval that will mean a new and less doctrinaire approach to army service, as more and more haredim are forced to contemplate leaving the kollel and earning their living.

'It won't happen in Rabbi Shach's lifetime,' says Rabbi Yosef Buxbaum, the head of the Machon Yerushalayim publishing house. 'But it is bound to happen. The situation just cannot carry on like this. We've reached the stage where third-generation bnei Torah are looking to marry off their children. There is no money left in the family. And with the recession in America, philanthropy is not what it used to be.'

Buxbaum factors in political considerations too. 'There are too many of us . . . the country will not allow [the draft exemption system] forever. The political demography may well shift, with the advent of more Soviet Jews. The haredi parties won't necessarily be able to impose their will indefinitely.' He predicts a form of hesder arrangement for haredi young men who want to leave the yeshiva. They would do their military service in all-haredi units, for less than the regular three-year term – and then be free to go out to work. He hints that some of the leading rabbis among the haredim see the future in similar terms, but are reluctant to speak out.

Rabbi Refson agrees that this is the outlook; but he believes the trend is already discernible. 'Five years ago,' he says, 'my friends would be sending all their sons to kollel as a matter of course. Now they're choosing *which* sons should stay in learning, while the others leave the kollel eventually to make careers elsewhere. The acceptability of working is growing. Young men are going into service occupations. *Safruss* [religious calligraphy], for instance, is becoming more popular, as the stock of *sifrei Torah* [Torah scrolls] saved from the Holocaust runs out and the prices of new scrolls rise.' He himself 'talent scouts' among Israeli kollel-men to fill teaching positions in Jewish schools abroad.

In Refson's view, this incipient trend that he claims to discern, and which he welcomes, is not the result purely of economic exigencies. People are certainly being pressed by material considerations, he says, to contemplate leaving the closed confines of 'the society of learners'. But some are also gradually realizing, he believes, 'that indiscriminate kollel admission is actually haredism's biggest problem. It is creating failures out of these people. These men are destined their whole lives to be failed talmidei hachamim. And everybody knows that they're failures – except their wives. They know it themselves, though many won't admit it. They bring back defeat into the house each night.'

Refson and Buxbaum, who might both be described as liberal haredim, offer their prognosis based on a rational analysis of the objective circumstances. Dr Yossi Beilin of Labour, as we have seen, makes the same prediction in blunter terms. 'With their natural growth,' he says, 'there has to be an explosion soon. Israeli society will not stand for their massive draft-dodge indefinitely.'

But religious movements have proved that they are not necessarily susceptible to rational, materialistic analysis. Fundamentalist groups in particular seem to have within them strength and stamina that can defy economic and political forces. It may be hazardous, therefore, to forecast that the Jewish haredi fundamentalists will break with their lifestyle merely because they seem likely to lack sufficient resources to maintain it. Resources, after all, are from God. 'He who gives life, He will give sustenance,' says the Talmud.

Feeling within the community, at any rate, is certainly not in sympathy with these two rabbis' sober predictions and Beilin's blunt warning. Haredim, both in Israel and in the Diaspora, see their divinely inspired, divinely protected 'society of learners' constantly expanding and projecting its influence ever wider. They do not anticipate having to give up any of its past achievements in order to sustain its future growth.

PART VI

SPECTRE OF SCHISM

33

Who Is a Jew?

The Jewish People is likely to split in two within the next three decades over the question, Who is a Jew? This is the common prognosis among Orthodox leaders, both haredi and Modern-Orthodox. The minority of Jews, they say, will cease to regard the majority as Jewish, and eventually the majority will cease to regard themselves as of the same religion as the minority. The historical precedent they cite is the schism between Judaism and Christianity during the century after Christ. 'In fact,' says Rabbi Dr Norman Lamm, President of Yeshiva University in New York, 'the halachic divide is deeper now than it was then.'

Some of the Modern-Orthodox, like Dr Lamm, lay part of the blame on the haredim. If Modern Orthodoxy were stronger and haredism weaker, they say, the schism would not seem so inevitable. There could be dialogue and possibly even accommodation between Orthodoxy and Reform. As it is, all attempts at compromise are foiled by haredi hardliners.

But Modern-Orthodox and haredim alike accuse the Reform movement of primary responsibility for the looming catastrophe. They say that Reform, in recent years, has broadened the battlefront in its war with Orthodoxy: from Judaism to Jewishness. The fighting is no longer over ritual or dogma, or even theology; such fighting, however bitter, has proved containable within the same religion. The struggle now is over the criteria of membership of the Jewish religion. And in the modern age of mobility among religions – more than half of American Jews marry Gentiles – the question of membership, of Who is a Jew, is seen both by the Orthodox and the non-Orthodox as crucial.

Reform (and Conservative) requirements for conversion to Judaism are condemned by the Orthodox as a parody. 'It is much more difficult,' says Rabbi Moshe Sherer, the head of Agudath

Israel of America, 'to join a country club than to become a member of the Jewish People through Reform conversion.' Recent Reform legislation on Jewish descent is condemned as heresy: 'The single most irresponsible act in contemporary Jewish history,' in the words of Dr Lamm. Reform rules on marriage and divorce are condemned as propagating halachic bastardy; and Reform (and Conservative) admission of Gentile spouses into the congregation is condemned as a wholesale abdication of Jewish particularity.

The Orthodox warnings of 'schism' and the eventual emergence of 'two peoples' appear to most other Jews as rhetorical – or fanatical – hyperbole. There is so much that unites Jews; it is hard to conceive of the Jewish People breaking apart. But the Orthodox explain that the split will not come in the form of a dramatic act or declaration. Rather, more and more Orthodox rabbis will ban marriage between Orthodox and non-Orthodox Jews, so that, in a relatively short time, two entirely separate communities will evolve, divided by marriage. Formal, dogmatic schism will be the final step.

There may still be one chance though, the Orthodox think, to avert this scenario: by bringing the State of Israel into 'their camp'. They cannot defeat Reform in a pitched battle in America; they lack the numbers. But in Israel the Reform and Conservative movements are weak, while established religion – and specifically the administration of marriage and divorce – is legally in the exclusive control of the Orthodox Rabbinate. The Orthodox believe that by defeating Reform in Israel they might be able, with time and with their own growing numbers, eventually to defeat Reform in America too in the battle over the definition of Jewishness. At the very least, they reason, if the schism becomes unavoidable, they will be able to carry the State of Israel with *them*, into their section of the divided Jewish People.

Recent battles in Israel, therefore, have been fought by both sides with the aim of affecting the religious status of Jews everywhere. In 1988–89, with the haredim in Israel politically more powerful than ever before, their demand that the State recognize only Orthodox conversion strained the ties between Israel and the Diaspora almost to breaking-point. Jewish representatives from the United States and Europe baldly threatened the Israeli leaders:

If you give in to the haredim on this – we will turn our backs on you. The 'centrality of Israel' in Jewish life, which is the bedrock of Zionism, will be destroyed.

The threats worked; Orthodoxy suffered a stinging defeat. But the conflict is bound to break out again, since neither side has shifted its basic position. The next crisis welling up is the case of a young British woman, Paula Cohen, converted by the Chief Rabbi of Israel, who is fighting haredi-led efforts to strip her and her children of their Jewishness (see chapter 35). Her fight pits Orthodoxy against Reform in a bitter contest in the British courts.

Having defined itself at its inception in 1948 as the State of the Jewish People, and having enacted a 'Law of Return' offering Israeli citizenship automatically to every Jew arriving on its soil, Israel could never escape the awkward necessity – fraught with religious, philosophical and indeed racial complexity – of deciding in its legislature who is a Jew. Was the criterion to be halachic, or would anyone who claimed to be Jewish be recognized as such by the Jewish State? Ironically, several members of the Knesset who participate in that decision each time it arises are Muslims, Christians and Druse, an irony which is invariably pointed out after each vote, by the losing side. Anti-Orthodox lobbyists, who include American Reform and Conservative representatives, always point out, too, that the Orthodox parties wield disproportionate political power as the balance-holders between Left and Right.

But it is not only party-political expediency that has determined the results of these parliamentary duels over the years. Israel's founding fathers were ambivalent in their own minds over Who is a Jew. An Orthodox leader, Dr Zorach Warhaftig, recalls David Ben-Gurion, the pre-State leader and first Prime Minister, confiding privately during one crisis that he feared for Israel's Jewish identity in the long term. While he had rebelled against Orthodoxy in his personal life, 'B-G' was less certain, says Warhaftig, about rejecting Orthodoxy's role as the guardian of the national heritage in the new Jewish State.

Menahem Begin, who led the right-wing opposition from 1948 until he finally came to power in 1977, consistently supported the

Orthodox in debates on the definition of Jewishness, even though he himself was never Orthodox. For Begin the issue was one of national pride, which he believed was embodied in the traditional, halachic approach.

Ben-Gurion first grappled with the issue in 1958, when a left-wing interior minister instructed his officials to register as Jewish (by religion and by nationality) anyone professing to be a Jew. This triggered a government crisis: the Orthodox ministers walked out of the coalition, protesting that under the halacha a Jew is only someone born of a Jewish mother or converted to Judaism – what he professes to be is irrelevant. Ben-Gurion, aware of the historic significance of the issue, decided to consult fifty Jewish sages from Israel and the Diaspora, representing all trends of Jewish thought. His specific question to them was how the State of Israel should register the children of a marriage between a Jewish father and Gentile mother, both of whose parents wanted them to be registered as Jews.

Out of forty-six replies received, thirty-eight recommended that the State apply the halachic criteria; five proposed various mixed-status solutions; and only three suggested that the parental desire alone should be the determinant, in defiance of the halacha. In the event, the controversy faded. The sages were quietly forgotten after new elections enabled Ben-Gurion to install in the interior ministry a National Religious Party minister who immediately rescinded his predecessor's regulations. The NRP was to hold on to the ministry for twenty-five years.

The next twist in the saga, in the early 1960s, involved Brother Daniel (Oswald) Rufeisen, a Polish Jew who had become a Carmelite monk and emigrated to Israel to live in the order's monastery on Mount Carmel. He petitioned the High Court to be registered as a Jew, insisting that he had never ceased regarding himself as such. There was much popular sympathy for this quixotic figure, because during the Holocaust he had saved Jews at great risk to himself. The court extolled his courage and sincerity but nevertheless held, by a majority of four to one, that someone who had converted to Christianity could not be recognized by the Jewish State as a Jew (This did not mean that Rufeisen was prevented from becoming a citizen of Israel under the regular five-year naturalization process applying to non-Jewish applicants. But he had demanded automatic citizenship under the 'Law of Return'.)

The significance of this landmark judgement was that it opened a gap between the secular law of the State and the halacha – for in the view of most halachic authority Rufeisen, once born Jewish, remained Jewish forever. No action on his part, not even becoming a Christian monk, could change his halachic status.

It was through this gap that Lt.-Col. Benjamin Shalit sought ten years later to push his two children, Oren and Galia, petitioning the High Court for the right to have them registered as Jews by nationality (and of no religion) even though their mother was not Jewish. The High Court sat in its full complement, and decided by a majority of five to four to accept the application. Once again – by now Golda Meir was Prime Minister – a crisis threatened. The Orthodox parties demanded that the gap be closed by legislation. Golda Meir and the government quickly complied. The 'Law of Return' was amended, so that it henceforth defined a Jew as '*a person born of a Jewish mother or converted to Judaism*, provided he is not a member of another religion'.

There was much debate in the Knesset over whether the word 'converted' in the amendment meant halachic (that is, Orthodox) conversion, or included Conservative and Reform conversion too. The Minister of Justice, a Labour Party man, said it did include conversions performed in the Diaspora by non-Orthodox rabbis. If an immigrant came to Israel with a conversion certificate from a Conservative or Reform community, he said, he would be registered as Jewish. But when a non-Orthodox MK proposed that the amendment spell this out, the House demurred. The Orthodox MKs for their part argued that the very concept of conversion was an halachic concept, and this therefore excluded non-Orthodox conversion. But when they proposed adding the words 'according to halacha', the House balked again.

The amendment, then, remained enshrined in its pristine ambiguity, becoming thereafter the subject of frequent and tempestuous controversy in the Knesset and the courts.

34

Who Is a Rabbi?

The shift in the focus of debate in Israel, from the broad question of Jewishness to the specific issue of conversions, created a direct link between internal Israeli politics and the religious convictions of Jews throughout the Diaspora. Millions of Reform and Conservative adherents and non-denominational Jews felt personally threatened by the prospect that the Knesset in Jerusalem might legislate 'against them'. The issue was no longer arcane or philosophical, as it must have seemed to many Diaspora Jews when the *cause célèbre* was a 'Jewish monk', or an Israeli who wanted his children to be both 'Jewish' and 'of no religion'. Brother Daniel and Lt.-Col. Shalit elicited intellectual support from Diaspora liberals; but they were hardly role-models to identify with.

Not so Susan (Shoshanna) Miller, who became the heroine of the non-Orthodox cause when the High Court of Justice in Jerusalem upheld her petition, in December 1986, to be registered in Israel as a Jew. A former part-time temple cantor from Colorado Springs, who had been converted to Judaism by a Reform rabbi years before, she had decided to try life in the Jewish State and had then been rudely rebuffed by Interior Ministry officials. (The ministry, by this time, was in the hands of the Sephardic-haredi party, Shas.)

The question, then, was not only Who is a Jew? – that is, a legitimate convert to Judaism – but Who is a rabbi? Who is legitimately qualified to convert a Gentile to Judaism? Viewed from the non-Orthodox perspective, that inevitably begs the consequent question: Who is a (Jewish) congregant? If a rabbi is not considered legitimate, then, by very brief extension, nor are his or her congregants, both the converts among them and those born Jewish. All of them, after all, choose to live and worship under his spiritual guidance. If the Jewish State does not recognize the conversions of a particular Jewish denomination – Reform or Conservative – then, by implication, it does not recognize the Jewishness of any of the adherents of that denomination.

The Hebrew word for rabbi is *rav* (literally master). In haredi books and newspapers, that word is never used to designate a Reform or Conservative cleric. Instead, the English word rabbi is transliterated into Hebrew, signalling to the readers that this is not an authentic rav. In haredi publications in English, the title rabbi, when applied to a Reform or Conservative cleric, is invariably placed in quotation marks to express the same contempt. When the rabbi is a woman, an exclamation mark is usually added too.

The Orthodox agreed that the question had indeed become Who is a rabbi? Conversion, they maintained, requires qualified rabbis, and a non-Orthodox rabbi is by (Orthodox) definition not qualified. But they insisted that there was nothing in this position to impugn the Jewishness of any Jew, whatever his denominational affiliation, provided he was born Jewish – that is, of a Jewish mother – or had been converted under the Orthodox halacha.

The Orthodox argued, too, that given the low rate of Jewish immigration from Western countries to Israel, the number of non-Orthodox immigrant-converts was tiny – and these would probably be prepared to reconvert in Israel, were it not for the exploitation of their cases by the Reform and Conservative 'lobby'. That was possibly true, but it was disingenuous. Both sides knew that there was more at stake than the status of an occasional immigrant-convert. If the legislative and judicial institutions of the Jewish State ruled against the validity of Reform and Conservative conversions, that would be a tremendous blow to the non-Orthodox movements back in America. Indeed, the leader of the Orthodox side in the Israeli battle was not an Israeli at all, but the Lubavitcher Rebbe of New York, who kept up relentless pressure on the Israeli Orthodox and haredi parties. The war, as he never tired of explaining, was over 'the integrity of the Jewish People'. And that 'integrity' was primarily threatened not in Israel, but in America.

In any given year there are probably more than 10,000 conversions to Judaism across the United States, with that figure constantly rising as intermarriage between Jews and Gentiles, the major motive for conversion, steadily increases. The vast majority of these conversions are performed by Reform or Conservative rabbis.

Under the halacha, conversion requires three conditions, administered by a beit din: immersion in a ritual bath, circumcision for males, and 'acceptance of the yoke of the commandments' – in Hebrew, *tevila, mila*, and *kabbalat ol mitzvot*. Non-Orthodox rabbis vary in what they require from conversion candidates. Some insist on immersion and circumcision; others merely recommend them, others dispense with one or both of them. All require some study-and-commitment programme, though the scope, seriousness and duration of this differs widely from rabbi to rabbi. In some cases, it is so brief and perfunctory as to be almost a formality.

As far as the Orthodox are concerned, the halachic requirements for conversion make it virtually impossible for non-Orthodox rabbis to perform it satisfactorily, even if they do insist on mila and tevila, and educate their candidates towards a sincere commitment to Judaism. Most non-Orthodox rabbis, being non-Orthodox in their personal practice, cannot constitute an acceptable beit din in the eyes of the Orthodox halachist, nor are they acceptable witnesses to the act of immersion. Substantively, moreover, the requirement of kabbalat ol mitzvot cannot be applied, in the Orthodox view, by persons (in this case rabbis) who do not themselves 'accept the yoke of the commandments'. That yoke, by Orthodox lights, means Orthodox practice. If these rabbis drive their cars on shabbat, or switch on a light, they have thrown off the yoke. In the words of Reuven P. Bulka, a Modern-Orthodox rabbi from Ottawa, Canada: 'It would be ridiculous for Reform rabbis to insist that converts be holier than they . . . By Orthodox standards, a Reform conversion is an exercise in futility, and the convert is, by Orthodox standards, as non-Jewish as before.'

That is not an overstatement or especially extremist interpretation of the Orthodox position. Indeed, Orthodox communities around the world – Modern-Orthodox as well as haredi – all conduct themselves in accordance with Rabbi Bulka's conclusion. They do not regard non-Orthodox converts as Jews, and thus will not admit them into their congregations or allow them to marry in their synagogues – unless they reconvert according to the halacha.

Conversions are the largest of three halachic problem-areas that together place an ever-growing segment of Jewry beyond the pale from the Orthodox standpoint. Rabbi Irving Greenberg of New York, who is on the liberal wing of Modern Orthodoxy, has predicted that by the year 2000 there will be some 360,000 'problematic conversions' in the United States, 'and at least 200,000 persons whose *patrilineal* connection will lead them to assume they are Jewish, but who are not Jewish according to halacha. Additionally, by the year 2000 there may well be 200,000 who are burdened with the difficulties of questionable *legitimacy*, and thus marriageability.'

As we have seen, the halacha traces genealogical Jewishness through the mother, not the father. The Reform movement, however, guided by its leader, Rabbi Alexander Schindler, long-serving President of the Union of American Hebrew Congregations, abandoned this traditional criterion in 1983 in favour of equality of the sexes. 'The child of one Jewish parent,' it declared, 'is under the presumption of Jewish descent. This presumption . . . is to be established through appropriate and timely public and formal acts of identification with the Jewish faith and people' (such as circumcision, religious study, bar-mitzva).

The decision unleashed a firestorm of Orthodox condemnation, but Schindler, looking back years later, says he has no regrets whatever. 'We have fifty thousand children of mixed marriages in our movement. In most cases, the father is the Jewish partner. Tens of thousands of them are in our schools and our summer camps. We have to make them feel that they are not discriminated against. There's an easy enough remedy from the Orthodox point of view: conversion.' But that is simply not relevant to this reality, he says. 'There are compelling sociological reasons' for patrilinealism. 'While not condoning intermarriage, we welcome the partners in mixed marriages into our communities. Once a mixed marriage is a fact, you have two choices: to bring them in, or to sit shiva [that is, to mourn as for the dead].'

For the Orthodox, 'marrying out' is indeed a disaster akin to a death. When it strikes an Orthodox family, parents and siblings of the offender will symbolically tear their clothes and sit on low stools like mourners, to receive the consolation of other relatives and friends. And even in families that are not inclined to grieve publicly in the traditional mode, the newlyweds will often be ostracized and solemnly 'cut out' of the father's or grandfather's will. Orthodox spokesmen dismiss Schindler's 'compelling sociological reasons' as 'playing a numbers game'. They accuse the Reform leader of accepting patrilineal descent in order to boost the membership figures of his dwindling congregations. 'This was one of the most evil crimes,' says Rabbi Sherer, the American haredi leader, 'almost akin to Hitler. It destroys the integrity of the Jewish People.'

Significantly, the Conservative movement too has been unimpressed by Schindler's 'compelling sociological reasons' and has flatly rejected patrilinealism. This despite the fact, documented in a 1991 survey, that 'outmarriage' among Conservative Jews is now almost as high as among Reform. Thus, while the two movements, Reform and Conservative, are united in their demand that Israel recognize their conversions, they are deeply divided over this second aspect of the Who is a Jew debate, patrilinealism.

Outmarriage in itself is not an halachic 'problem-area'; it is simply forbidden. But outmarriage is usually the reason why people undergo non-Orthodox conversions, which are then not recognized by the Orthodox, or why – when there is no conversion by the Gentile wife – their children claim patrilineal Jewishness. Sociologist Charles E. Silberman, in a widely acclaimed study, condemns Orthodoxy's rejection of mixed marriages as the deepest cause of the evolving schism. 'The Orthodox answer is clear and uncompromising,' he writes. 'Synagogue membership should be denied to the Jewish as well as the non-Jewish partner. Some would go even further: one prominent Orthodox leader has called for "the elimination from leadership roles in Jewish public life" of anyone married to a non-Jew.'*

In a similar vein, the jovial, sardonic director of the World

* Charles E. Silberman, *A Certain People* (New York: Summit Books 1985), p. 320.

Jewish Congress, Israel Singer, suggested during a conversation in New York that 'Within a few years, all the presidents of the Jewish federations around the country will be goyim!' Singer, an Orthodox rabbi by training, is one of a growing cadre of top American Jewish 'civil servants' who are Orthodox. Professional careers in the Jewish organizations, he says, mean 'visible ethnicity', and this apparently appeals to the rising generation of 'highly qualified, Jewishly educated and religiously observant public executives and social work directors'. The lay leaders of the many Jewish national and local philanthropic organizations, on the other hand, tend still to be drawn from what Singer calls a 'Waspish Jewish plutocracy' in which Orthodox membership is minimal and in which, he maintains, the proportion of non-halachic Jews – non-Orthodox converts and patrilineal descendants – is steadily rising.

The third area of halachic non-integratability (after 'problematic conversions' and patrilineal descent) seems on the face of it to pose the gravest problem of all. But, thanks to a paradoxical halachic sleight-of-hand, it has been 'solved' – after a fashion. Illegitimacy (mamzerut) in Jewish law is a much narrower, but much more devastating, designation than in canon law or Western civil codes. It is created only through a married woman's adultery or through incest. Mere out-of-wedlock sex does not produce bastardy; nor does adultery by a husband. But once a child is pronounced a bastard or *mamzer*, he may not marry any other Jew – only another mamzer, or a convert.

However, a wife's 'adultery' in Orthodox terms is often a perfectly legal and valid second marriage in the eyes of Reform rabbis and laymen. This is because Reform Jews usually do not obtain an halachic divorce when ending a marriage. They make do with a civil divorce. In Orthodox eyes civil divorce is worthless. Without a *get* – a religious bill of divorce, written by a scribe on parchment with a quill pen – the divorced woman is not divorced at all. Her subsequent marriage, therefore, is adulterous, and its offspring illegitimate.

The 'sleight-of-hand' solution was devised by the American haredi sage, Rabbi Moshe Feinstein: he simply ruled that Reform *marriages* are invalid under halacha. Thus they require no divorce, and do not give rise to adultery.

This is tidy enough in terms of pure halachic legalism. It exhibited haredi halachic thinking at its most compassionate, concerned over the plight of the individual litigant, and prepared to resort to inelegant contortions in order to help him or her. In a paradoxical way, it demonstrates the fundamental principle of non-discrimination – what British Chief Rabbi Jonathan Sacks calls 'inclusivism' – inherent in pristine haredi thought. The basic approach is to dismiss altogether the notion that Reform Judaism can affect the immutable realities of the halacha. If there was no marriage, because the (non-Orthodox) witnesses to the marriage ceremony were halachically ineligible to be witnesses, then neither the wedding itself nor all the subsequent years of cohabitation change the religio-legal situation. The two people were not man and wife in the eyes of God, and thus have been spared from the sin of adultery and its grievous consequences.

But the ruling is the most brazen insult imaginable to the Reform movement. In order to legitimize the children of a second marriage, it delegitimizes the entire religious edifice under which the second *and* the first marriage were conducted. Reuven Bulka notes that 'there are many Orthodox practitioners who are not happy with this loophole. There is a reluctance, an understandable reluctance, to delegitimize all marriages conducted by Reform rabbis.'

Bulka was the first to spell out the schism scenario, in his book *The Coming Cataclysm* (1985), which he subtitled 'The Orthodox-Reform Rift and the Future of the Jewish People'. At the time, he was dismissed even among the Orthodox as a scaremonger. Not any more. In a penetrating study of the Jewish condition as the century draws to an end, Jonathan Sacks endorses 'those who have warned that one contemporary halachic and political issue – the definition of who is a Jew – has the potential to divide the Jewish people into two in the foreseeable future.' Sacks writes:

> There were schisms in the Jewish past which led to irreparable breaches within the Jewish people: between Hellenizers and zealots, Samaritans and Pharisees, Jews and Christians,

> Rabbinites and Karaites.* Unity is undeniably a Jewish value, but not necessarily and in all circumstances a supreme and overriding one . . . One central question of modernity [is] whether the divisions between Orthodoxy and non-Orthodoxy are inherently schismatic. Is disunity an unavoidable tragedy?†

Rabbi Sherer, the American haredi leader, believes it is. 'We're on collision course,' he states baldly. 'In twenty-five years we'll end up with two Jewish Peoples.'

* The Karaite sect has its origins in the eighth century. It denies the Talmudic-rabbinic tradition (the 'Oral Law'), and regards the Bible, read literally, as the source of all religious precepts. According to Karaite sources, there are some 20,000 Karaites living in Israel today, some 10,000 in the USA, and small groups in Europe.

† Jonathan Sacks, *One People? Tradition, Modernity and Jewish Unity* (Oxford: Oxford University Press, forthcoming).

35

Why Me?

'Why do they hate me? What have I done? I'm Jewish! I'm Jewish!' Koby kept banging his head on the wall, screaming in fury.

Koby Cohen, a cheerful little boy of eight, had been growing steadily more morose and introverted for months. But this outburst early in 1990, at his home in Newcastle, in northern England, stunned his parents, Paula and Yossi. Liam, Koby's five-year-old sister, watched in silence.

'Right. We're taking them out of the school,' Paula said grimly. 'But we're not giving up the fight.'

Paula Cohen's fight, which she had taken to the House of Lords, the highest court in Britain, encapsulates the individual suffering that lies beneath the legalistic disputes and historic processes of looming schism. At the time of writing, the case appeared to be growing into another international Jewish crisis, further accelerating the slide towards schism. It showed the two sides arrayed against each other, each grimly unyielding. The Cohens were supported, morally and materially, by the American Reform movement. The Orthodox, for their part, set aside differences between them to fight, once again, for the exclusive right of Orthodox halacha to determine Who is a Jew.

Paula Cohen was born Paula Wilson in Newcastle in 1954. She says her mother's father was Jewish, and that he used to talk to her as a child about the Jews and Israel. Her first meaningful contact with the country and the people was in 1978, when she worked on a kibbutz for a month, as part of a lengthy European tour. A year later, she returned to Kibbutz Haon, on the shore of Lake Galilee. 'Something drew me,' she says. Was that 'something' kibbutznik Yossi Cohen, who ran Haon's lucrative fishing fleet on the lake? She says it was not. They hardly knew each other at that stage, she insists. The point is critical to her case.

She learned Hebrew at the kibbutz *ulpan* (adult school), and then announced that she wanted to convert. 'I wanted to be like everyone; you can't really live in Israel without being Jewish.'

Rabbi Shlomo Goren, the Ashkenazic Chief Rabbi, had set up two 'conversion *ulpanim*' at Modern-Orthodox kibbutzim, where people like Paula could live and study Judaism for a period of months in a religious but relaxed environment. If they were judged to be sincere, and serious about their studies, they were then converted by a beit din in Tel Aviv. In England, where the beit din of the United Synagogue is tough on conversion candidates as a matter of policy, the process commonly takes three or four years. The United Synagogue, which is Orthodox and presided over by the Chief Rabbi, is the main Jewish religious body in Britain.

Rabbi Goren served for many years as chief chaplain of the Israeli army, and is considered an halachic liberal. He says the London Beit Din and other conservative batei din abroad asked him to tighten up the Israeli conversion process in order to prevent Diaspora candidates from hopping over to Israel for 'quickie conversions'. It was partly for this reason, he explains, that he added to many of his conversion certificates the proviso, 'Not valid outside Israel'. The intention was not to pronounce the convert Jewish in Israel and Gentile abroad, which is an absurdity, but rather to deter him or her from reneging on the commitment to live in Israel, which lay at the basis of the conversion application. 'It was an administrative step,' Goren explains. Sometimes, he says, he would 'impound' the convert's passport for several years, to achieve the same result.

Rabbi Goren anchored this innovatory proviso in an ancient Palestinian halachic tradition, expressed in the Jerusalem Talmud, which was more welcoming to converts than the Babylonian Talmud. The Babylonian Talmud, in fact, pronounces converts to be 'as bad for Israel as sores on the skin' (Tractate Kiddushin 9a, Yevamot 47b, 109b) – this despite the biblical injunction to 'love the stranger'. Goren interpreted his Palestinian source from a strongly Zionist perspective: living in modern Israel is in itself a constant, often subconscious statement of Jewishness, whereas a convert living abroad needs consciously to reaffirm his new religious affiliation all the time. Hence a candidate for conversion intending to live in Israel can be accepted more readily, since his commitment to Judaism inspires more confidence.

The proviso, like its author, was controversial in rabbinical circles, especially haredi circles lukewarm to Zionism.

'I interviewed Paula Cohen three times,' Goren says. 'Once before she began the conversion course, then again after it ended, and finally to give her her certificate. I insisted, as I did with many candidates, that she swear an oath on the Bible that she would keep the mitzvot. She pledged not to leave Israel. I asked her if she had a boyfriend. Not that I would necessarily reject a candidate who had one. On the contrary, sometimes I would make the candidate's boyfriend do the course too, and the boyfriend would also have to undertake to keep the mitzvot.' (That approach attests to Goren's relative liberalism: other Orthodox rabbis automatically reject conversion candidates if there is a romantic motive in their application.)

Goren says he would send an aide to check out a candidate's kibbutz, to ensure that he or she would be able to eat kosher food there and not be required to work on shabbat. He knew full well that the kibbutz converts were not all likely to adopt an Orthodox lifestyle, but there had to be some serious pledge to observe the basic tenets of the faith, and no blatant flying in the face of the halacha. 'If she had said she had a boyfriend who was a *cohen*,' he says, 'I would have stopped the whole process right there.'

Here, then, is the halachic rub. Yossi Cohen is a cohen, a priest. If the Temple were standing in Jerusalem (it was destroyed in 70 CE), he would be required to serve in it for at least one month each year, offering the animal sacrifices and the incense on the altar, tending the oil-menorah, receiving the first-fruits, blessing the pilgrims. He would be forbidden to marry a divorcee, or a harlot, or a convert. And as far as Rabbi Goren or any Orthodox rabbi is concerned, he still is.

Not everyone whose family name is Cohen is a cohen, nor is every cohen called Cohen. It is a question of family tradition. Indeed many Jewish families who are thoroughly non-Orthodox nevertheless proudly cherish the knowledge that they are descended from the Priestly House of Aaron.

Nowadays, in the absence of the Temple, there are only a few rules that distinguish *cohanim* from the rest, even among the Orthodox. They are the first to be called to the Reading of the Torah (out of seven worshippers called upon on shabbat and three midweek). They are forbidden to stay under the same roof as a dead body or to walk near graves – a vestige of the laws of ritual purity. And the marriage restrictions still apply. Thus in Israel, a cohen cannot marry a divorcee. Britain's United Synagogue, which embraces most of the country's Jewish congregations, scrupulously applies these same restrictions. Like Jewishness itself, there is no opting out of being a cohen. No matter how much one disbelieves in it, or does not want it, if one was born with it, one is stuck with it.

Paula says she did not tell Rabbi Goren that Yossi Cohen was her boyfriend because he wasn't, yet. They started going out, she says, only after her conversion was completed, in June 1981. She immersed herself in a mikve in Tel Aviv, with the three rabbis of the beit din supervising from a room upstairs. When she emerged, they declared: 'Welcome to the Jewish People.' 'It was a moment I will never forget,' she says, 'and nobody will ever take it away from me.'

By September, when she went up to Jerusalem to get her certificate from Goren, she was pregnant, which she wisely omitted to divulge to the Chief Rabbi. Within days, she and Yossi were on their way to Newcastle, where they were married in the town's Reform synagogue. 'Yossi's parents wanted a Jewish wedding,' Paula says. 'And so did we. We knew no Orthodox synagogue would marry a cohen and a convert. Now I realize that going to a Reform synagogue made matters worse for me later. We didn't realize how much the Orthodox and the Reform hate each other.' Yossi adds: 'We thought, Jewish is Jewish . . .' They returned to Haon – Yossi to his fish, Paula, now called Naomi according to her conversion certificate, to the kibbutz cowsheds.

Six years later, they decided to take an open-ended break from kibbutz life and from Israel, and set out for Newcastle again.

'She duped me twice over,' Goren rails. 'She concealed her cohen boyfriend, despite her solemn oath to keep the mitzvot, and she went to live abroad despite her undertaking.'

Paula says 'went to live abroad' is tendentiously unfair. The family lived in Israel for the better part of a decade after her conversion. Anyone can want a change of scenery during the course of a lifetime. She says she knows several converts now living abroad who also have Rabbi Goren's 'Not valid outside Israel' proviso attached to their certificate. 'But they keep quiet about it.'

Paula and Yossi would have preferred to 'keep quiet' too, and quietly blend into the small Newcastle Jewish community. But by the time they arrived, the tragedy had been set in motion. Mrs Wilson, Paula's mother, had gone to the King David School, the only Jewish day-school in the town, to enrol Koby and register Liam for the nursery. A teacher at the school, from the haredi community of the neighbouring town of Gateshead, pricked up her ears. A convert, converted by the despised Goren, married to someone called Cohen . . . She rushed straight over to the Newcastle Rabbi, Moshe Baddiel.

On their first shabbat, Yossi and Paula went to the synagogue and were introduced to Baddiel, and he immediately asked to see Paula's conversion certificate. When she brought it in, he pointed to the problematic proviso. She argued that it was merely a device, designed to prevent converts from leaving Israel, but that she had been living in Israel for many years. He said he would have to send the document to the Beit Din in London. 'I'm a small fish in a big sea,' the kindly but cautious Baddiel explained. A month later, with the children settled in happily and the 'bureaucratic' glitch all but forgotten, the Beit Din's reply arrived: the conversion was invalid and the Cohens were to remove their children from the school.

They rushed to London, to remonstrate before Dayan Yitzhak Berger, the foremost halachist on the Beit Din, who is 'reckoned to have one of the finest legal brains in the country', according to the London *Daily Mail*. 'What do we tell the kids?' Yossi asked. 'Tell them the truth,' Paula recalls Berger replying. 'That they're Jewish in Israel, but not here in England.'

Normally, the Dayan explained, the Beit Din would consider reconverting Paula. But they couldn't in this case, unless she were to divorce Yossi, because he was a cohen. 'And not a fictitious divorce,' Paula quotes Berger. 'We'll have detectives watching you.'

'But you don't recognize our marriage,' Yossi argued. 'So why does it stand in the way of a reconversion?'

'You should have been a lawyer not a fish-breeder,' Berger replied.

But when the lawyers moved in – this was after the affair had been featured in the Jewish and national press – the arguments remained the same. 'You should appreciate,' wrote Messrs Beachcroft Stanleys, the solicitors of Chief Rabbi Lord Jakobovits, to Messrs Goldkorn, Davies, Mathias, the Cohens' lawyers, 'that in other cases where a similar limitation has been placed on certificates of conversion in Israel, the Beit Din has declined to recognize the conversion in this country. However, in some of those cases it has been possible to rectify the matter in this country. That is not possible in the present case, because of your client's marriage to a Cohen. Because it is not open to a convert to marry a Cohen, your client's marriage to a Cohen makes it impossible for her now to convert to Judaism.'

Paula says she warned the Dayan that she would 'make a huge stink', to which Berger replied, she says, 'Do it, by all means, and I'll help you – but do it in Israel!'

Plainly Berger's and the London Beit Din's distaste for Goren played a part in compounding the disaster. But basically neither they nor the Israeli Chief Rabbinate (Goren had retired by then), to whom the Cohens applied for help, could abrogate Goren's proviso, 'Not valid outside Israel'. As the affair developed, moreover, Rabbi Goren himself effectively abrogated the validity of Paula's conversion in Israel too. In an affidavit submitted to the British court, Goren wrote that the entire conversion was void *ab initio*, having been procured by misrepresentation.

Goren, however, says he urged a humane and caring approach towards the two children, who were needlessly victimized, he believes, by the British rabbis. He says he urged the president of the Newcastle Jewish community to let Koby and Liam stay in the school and continue studying with the other Jewish children. (Out of fifty-odd children in the King David School with Koby and

Liam, a dozen were Gentile. They did not attend Jewish Studies classes, an option offered to Koby and Liam which their parents felt added insult to injury.) Goren suggested that the two children – who, by his lights, are not Jewish because their mother is not Jewish – nevertheless be raised Jewishly, and enabled to convert formally after they reach bar- or bat-mitzva (thirteen for a boy, twelve for a girl – the halachic age of consent).

But Paula lashes out at all the Orthodox rabbis who have dealt with her. The British ones blame Goren, she says. They claim it was basically his fault that her children were thrown out of the school, just as it was his fault that she herself is rejected. By 1991, the Cohens were attending the Newcastle Reform synagogue. Koby and Liam went to a regular school, and to the Reform supplementary classes. 'These are my fellow Jews,' says Paula, 'and they are standing by me. They are the true Jews in my eyes.'

But Koby's friends are still the Orthodox children, and he still doesn't understand why he can't go to school and synagogue with them. Goren says he can reconvert after he attains the age of consent. But his mother, bitter and belligerent, says: 'I don't know what he'll be feeling when he reaches that age. His identity is so shaken.'

36

Why Now?

Why have the halachic problems of Who is a Jew become critical only now, almost two centuries after the creation of the Reform movement? Because of the 'unexpected persistence of both Orthodoxy and Reform', Jonathan Sacks explains. 'The problem arises at the boundaries: when a Reform Jew wishes to marry an Orthodox Jew.' (He might have added, when a Reform convert wishes to emigrate to Israel.) 'Neither group seriously contemplated this possibility. Orthodoxy saw Reform as destined for extinction by its rapid assimilation. Reform saw Orthodoxy as scheduled for eclipse by the inevitable tide of modernity. Each now realizes that the other has survived.'*

Sacks's predecessor, Lord Jakobovits, suggests that classical Reform deliberately avoided a confrontation over 'the oneness of our people. To give a personal example. My late sainted father was a Gemeinderabbiner, that is, Rabbi of the Grossgemeinde, of the general community of Berlin, in which there were Orthodox synagogues and Liberal or Reform synagogues, all under one synagogal roof-organization. But the Beit Din and all matters relating to it were under Orthodox control. My father was Head of the Communal Beit Din so that matters of marriage, divorce, conversion . . . were under Orthodox administration.'†

Sacks, a leading Modern-Orthodox voice and an outstanding scholar, historian and sociologist, appeals in his book for an halachic approach by the Orthodox that would avert the disaster of schism. Norman Lamm of Yeshiva University also says that he 'cannot passively acquiesce' in the schism scenario. All efforts at

* Sacks, *One People?* (forthcoming).
† Rabbi Immanuel Jakobovits, *Preserving the Oneness of the Jewish People* (London: Office of the Chief Rabbi 1988).

compromise, however, have failed, in part because of vigorous haredi opposition, which sets the tone on the Orthodox side, but in part too because of a deep-seated resistance on both sides to the realization, which Sacks claims to discern, 'that the other has survived.' In interviews with key Reform and Orthodox figures one encounters a distinct and recurrent absence of that realization.

Ironically, in more recent times some of the original doctrinal and ritual differences have narrowed. The Reform movement no longer denies a national dimension in Judaism; on the contrary, it strongly supports Zionism, which it originally rejected. There is more Hebrew in Reform services than there was half a century ago.

In other areas though, differences have deepened. When Reform rabbis voted, in summer 1990, to admit avowed gays and lesbians into the ranks of their rabbinate, declaring that 'all rabbis, regardless of sexual orientation, must be accorded the opportunity to fulfil their sacred vocation,' Rabbi Stolper of the Orthodox Union termed it 'an abomination'. A Reform rabbi from San Francisco voiced his confidence that just as women rabbis were initially shunned by Reform congregations after their formal admission into the movement, but are now widely welcomed, lesbian and gay rabbis would eventually be welcomed too. For the Orthodox, women rabbis are as unthinkable as they always were, though halachically they are a far cry from the 'abomination' of gay or lesbian rabbis.

On the most basic issue – Jewishness itself – there has clearly been no narrowing, but rather a vast widening of the gap. 'We do not have to wait for the year 2000,' the then President of the Orthodox Union, Sidney Kwestel, asserted in a message to his constituency entitled 'Overcoming the Forces of Hellenism in our Generation'. 'No longer is there an homogeneous Jewish community in which the Jewish status of individuals is basically unquestioned and each member is free to marry the other. Rather there are at present two groups living within the Jewish community, one whose Jewish status is accepted by everyone . . . and the second, consisting of those who are not Jewish according to the halacha but are accepted as Jews only by non-Torah movements. This situation is intolerable now and will only progressively worsen if the non-Torah movements continue on the course they have charted.'*

For an Orthodox leader like Kwestel, the idea, advanced by certain Jewish social scientists, that intermarriage and wholesale (non-Orthodox) conversions actually strengthen Jewish continuity in the long run is both perverse and heretical. The social scientists point to evidence suggesting that converts are often more active and committed Jewishly than other Jews in their communities. They argue, too, that conversions – entailed in about one-quarter of mixed marriages – and even intermarriage without conversion, supply fresh blood to the Jewish people which counteracts the constant haemorrhaging of assimilation. But for the Orthodox, the conviction that the non-Orthodox will fade away eventually is a tenet of faith.

Much depends, of course, on one's definition of the key criteria: Jewish continuity, identity, commitment, assimilation, and so forth. The best of the Jewish sociologists admit that they are affected by subjective considerations despite themselves. 'The controversy,' Professor Steven M. Cohen has written, 'over how to understand the past, present and future of American Jewry is not simply an argument over "facts." Even when observers agree on the evidence, they may disagree on its meaning; and even if they concur on its meaning, they may differ over its larger implications.' Cohen cautions, without taking sides, that 'the assertion that there is rampant assimilation among the non-Orthodox is a highly effective rhetorical instrument in Orthodoxy's conflict with Conservative and Reform leadership.'

Professor Cohen asserts that in the final analysis 'the big imponderable for the future concerns the Jewishness of the offspring of mixed marriages.'† The jury is still out on that, he says – which from the sociologist's perspective is doubtless impeccable. But from the Orthodox perspective the jury never needed to retire to consider its verdict. The offspring are not Jewish if the mother is not Jewish, and no sociological indicators of identification or

* Sidney Kwestel, quoted in *Jewish Action*, Winter 1988/9.

† Steven M. Cohen and Charles S. Liebman, *The Quality of American Jewish Life – Two Views* (New York: American Jewish Committee 1987), p. 27.

affiliation (nor any Reform conversion) will make any difference to the verdict of the halacha.

The 'non-Torah movements', to use Kwestel's term, plainly intend 'to continue on their course'. In a fighting sermon in 1989 to the centennial convention of the Central Conference of American Rabbis (Reform), Rabbi Schindler, who was himself born into an Orthodox family in Eastern Europe, called for vigorous resistance to Orthodox criticism of the patrilineal decision. 'Our forebears,' he declared, 'did not forge Reform Judaism to have us trade it in for a tinsel imitation of Orthodoxy.' He urged his fellow rabbis to 'stop romanticizing Orthodoxy . . . Where it alone prevails, stale repression, fossilized tradition and ethical corruption often hold sway. That is the danger in Israel today, is it not?'

37

New Battle-Lines

The danger in Israel in 1989 was that the haredim, newly powerful after the November 1988 Knesset election, were seeking to reverse by legislation the court ruling in the Susan Miller case of 1986. At that time, the interior minister, Rabbi Yitzhak Peretz of Shas, had tried to head off a judicial defeat by proposing that Ms Miller, and *all* future immigrant-converts, be registered as 'Jew (converted)'. This, he explained to the court, would satisfy the demand that they be recognized under the Law of Return, yet would 'alert' the State Rabbinate if these immigrant-converts subsequently sought to marry. The rabbis would register for marriage only persons whose conversions were satisfactory (that is, Orthodox).

The idea was widely condemned as a particularly obnoxious form of discrimination. The Torah itself repeatedly forbids any ill-treatment of converts, enjoining the Israelites to 'love the stranger, for ye were strangers in the land of Egypt' (Deut. 10:19). Peretz's device was rejected by the High Court of Justice, which ordered him to register Ms Miller as a Jew. Rather than comply, he resigned.

His party, Shas, threatened in response to support the Labour Party in a bid to bring down the government. To mollify the haredim Prime Minister Shamir undertook to push through new legislation 'within 60 days' requiring every overseas conversion to be validated by the Israeli Chief Rabbinate. This triggered an impassioned public warning from the heads of twenty-one American Jewish organizations that Shamir's pledge 'imperils the unity of the Jewish people. The result would be to deny any spiritual validity to those who identify with the Reform, Conservative and Reconstructionist movements and thus to offend millions of Jews around the world.' They predicted 'a division between the Jewish State and the Diaspora' if the proposed legislation were passed.

In the event – in no small part due to energetic lobbying by the non-Orthodox movements – the proposed amendment was defeated in the Knesset in July 1987 by a vote of 60 to 56. A handful of members of Shamir's own Likud Party refused to support their leader. Some political pundits suggested that the wily Shamir had anticipated this outcome all along. Shas railed that 'Likud's cheque has bounced', but Shamir replied that he had done his best.

The battle-lines were thus clearly drawn, and the American Jewish leaders battle-hardened, when the results of the November 1988 elections came in. The haredi parties, together with the National Religious Party, now demanded that the Law of Return be amended by adding to the Law's definition of a Jew – 'a person born of a Jewish mother or converted to Judaism' – the three words '*according to halacha*'. The Lubavitch movement spearheaded the campaign, lobbying vigorously in the Knesset corridors and mounting a major advertising effort in the media. With Likud and Labour virtually tied, the American Jewish leaders feared the worst. 'The principle behind the Law of Return must transcend partisan political gain,' the American Jewish Congress cabled Shamir and Peres in a shot across the bows two days after the election. Two weeks later, with Shamir and the Orthodox close to a deal, a delegation of top Jewish leaders flew to Jerusalem on an 'emergency mission' to prevent 'the disenfranchisement of millions of Jews' by the Jewish State. The Jewish federations of Boston, Atlanta and Pittsburgh announced officially that they would 'reevaluate' their philanthropic allocations to Israel if the amendment went through. Atlanta said baldly: 'No portion of Federation funds will be allocated overseas unless the Law of Return is satisfactorily resolved.'

This was wholly unprecedented, and would have undermined the entire structure of organized Jewish life in America. The federations in each city are the core of the communities. Each year they mount remarkably effective fund-raising campaigns, raising millions of dollars for Israel and for their own community's social and educational services.

But Israel's dependency on American Jewry is much broader and deeper than that. The US government's support for the Jewish

State – three billion dollars a year in direct military and economic aid, plus invaluable strategic cooperation and political backing – is always attributed by statesmen on both sides to shared ideals and common interests. But the role of Jewish political influence, and campaign contributions, channelled through Political Action Committees (PACs), in sustaining and enhancing this relationship can hardly be exaggerated. And the main activists, the organizers and orchestrators of that Jewish political influence, are the same communal leaders who head the Jewish federations in each city, and the national organizations, CJF (Council of Jewish Federations) and UJA (United Jewish Appeal).

The dependency, moreover, is mutual. The movers and shakers on the American Jewish scene, who so palpably enjoy their prestige and honours, draw much of their importance from the Israel nexus. Their constant involvement in the diplomatic relationship between the two States gives them access in Washington and Jerusalem, and that in turn enhances their involvement.

In Orthodox circles the accusation is often made that many of these movers and shakers are personally aggrieved by the proposal to amend the Law of Return, both because they tend to represent the longer-established, more assimilated segments of American Jewry and because their own families often contain intermarried and converted members. This latter point, indeed, may be statistically well founded. In a 1990 survey of attitudes to intermarriage among American Jewish leaders, half of the respondents said that at least one of their children was married to a person who was not born Jewish.

But the Orthodox implication that the 'Who is a Jew' controversy is artificially fanned by non-Orthodox leaders is simply wrong. Millions of ordinary American Jews, who are neither community leaders nor converts – and who harbour deep emotional, religious and psychological attachment to Israel – underwent a genuine, wrenching trauma when it appeared that Israel was about to legislate against their form of Jewish faith. In the event, the Likud-haredi negotiations fell through, and Likud and Labour joined to form a 'National Unity Coalition'. Shamir's 'solemn and irrevocable' commitment in writing to Agudat Yisrael's Council of Torah Sages that the new government would amend the Law of Return remained a dead letter. Shamir never discussed publicly the extent to which his decision to forgo a narrow coalition with the Orthodox had been influenced by pressure from America. Privately, he told certain American Jewish leaders during and after the crisis that he never really intended to amend the Law. It was all just part of the political game, he hinted. 'But we didn't believe him,' one of those leaders recalled some months later.

In the Orthodox camp, the episode provoked discord and recriminations. Orthodox leaders felt they had called their own bluff and lost. The lesson was clear: Israel could not afford to surrender to the Orthodox demand on this issue, no matter how powerful the pressures of the Orthodox parties in the Knesset. Put another way, the Orthodox in the Diaspora could not successfully harness the Israeli political process to their fight against the non-Orthodox movements, no matter how confident they (the Diaspora Orthodox) had become. Whatever Orthodox dogma might teach about the eventual demise of non-Orthodoxy, in the here-and-now, Reform and Conservative clout had prevailed.

Lubavitch found itself increasingly isolated, both in America and in Israel. 'The tactics were wrong,' said Rabbi Stolper of the Orthodox Union. 'Lubavitch wanted to shock the Jews out there who are into assimilation. They wanted to awaken them to their latent responsibility.' The President of the Modern-Orthodox Rabbinical Council of America conceded that the anti-Orthodox reaction in much of American Jewry had been 'deep and widespread, and not phoney'. Degel Hatorah, under the leadership of Rabbi Shach, was not especially enthusiastic about 'Who is a Jew' anyway: partly because of Shach's ferocious animosity towards the Lubavitcher Rebbe, and partly because Degel's strongly anti-Zionist dogma left it less exercised than the other Orthodox parties over the wording of the Law of Return.

Haredi institutions, moreover, found their charitable income from non-Orthodox contributors suffering heavily. The hardest hit was Lubavitch, which was explicitly targeted by leaders of the anti-amendment campaign. But many other haredi fundraisers found doors slammed in their faces and formerly welcoming philanthropists suddenly sour and hostile. The amendment to the Law of Return was quietly shelved.

The retreat, though, was not a rout, but rather a redeployment. 'The basic goal remains,' says Stolper. 'It is to stop crisis-level assimilation.' He attributes the intensity of the non-Orthodox movements' fight over Who is a Jew to their inner sense of approaching doom. 'They see how it's going. They see that we [the Orthodox] have made our accommodation with America, and we function as well and better than they do. And as we go on putting our act together, they'll get more and more annoyed. Look at the realities. We have kids in yeshivas who are eleven years old and have more competence with the texts than the graduates of their rabbinical seminaries . . .'

It was this unshakeable conviction – its critics call it 'triumphalism' – on the part of the Orthodox, and especially the haredim, that put paid to an important effort by Prime Minister Shamir during 1989–90 to negotiate a compromise on conversions acceptable to all three denominations. 'Yes we played a role in putting an end to that farce,' says Rabbi Sherer, the Agudah leader, 'and I'm proud we did so. If we hadn't stopped it, it would have been stopped anyway. The power of Truth would have stopped it!'

The basic plan was worked out by Elyakim Rubinstein, the Israeli Cabinet Secretary and a close Shamir aide, who negotiated secretly for months with representatives of the three rabbinical seminaries in America, Yeshiva University (Modern-Orthodox), The Jewish Theological Seminary (Conservative), and The Hebrew Union College (Reform). It envisaged a 'joint panel' that would interview candidates for conversion who were considering aliyah, and would then refer them to a special beit din. This would function in New York under the aegis of the Israeli Chief Rabbinate.

The candidates would have been prepared for conversion by their own rabbi – whether Orthodox, Conservative or Reform – in the knowledge that the conversion itself would be performed in accordance with the halacha. The joint panel would comprise representatives of the three denominations. Its referrals would have to be unanimous. The beit din would comprise Orthodox rabbis, or at any rate rabbis approved by the Israeli Chief Rabbinate.

Rubinstein, looking back on his failed effort, says the negotiating parties had actually reached agreement on three principles: that these conversions must be carried out according to the halacha; that there was no chance whatever of a joint beit din; but that there must be some tripartite dialogue mechanism somewhere in the process. Haredi rabbis whom he had canvassed privately had balked at the joint panel comprising rabbis of the three denominations; but they might have been prepared to countenance laymen. Some of the Reform negotiators had balked at the Israeli Chief Rabbinate's role; after all, their movement was opposed to the Chief Rabbinate's State monopoly over Judaism in Israel. But they might have accepted a beit din comprising American Orthodox rabbis.

As it turned out, these nuances were never reconciled. When word leaked out that Rubinstein was making progress, a group of the leading haredi rabbis and yeshiva deans in America issued a joint statement voicing their 'deep anguish and disavowal' over 'the attempts of certain Orthodox circles to join forces with the Reform and Conservative leadership in the process and procedures of Jewish conversions . . . We cannot countenance the official participation of those who have made a travesty of halacha in a process that is so vitally halachic – and so crucial to the integrity of our nation.'

A key figure in Yeshiva University itself, moreover, Rabbi Aharon Soloveitchik, published an open letter condemning Orthodox support of the joint panel as 'appeasement'. 'Through the "joint panel" approach,' he wrote, 'mamzerut will be escalated to a maximum . . . Why should the ignorant Jewish masses not make do with a so-called Jewish divorce rendered by a Reform or Conservative rabbi, when they read in the news that Orthodox leaders are in favor of a "joint panel" to screen the applicants for conversion – thus giving them legitimacy and recognition as *rabbanim* [rabbis] and spiritual leaders.'

The two Chief Rabbis of Israel, whose cooperation was critical for the success of the scheme, immediately backed off, and the deal was effectively dead. Rabbi Mordechai Eliahu, the Sephardic Chief

Rabbi, announced his 'firm opposition to any such proposal, as well as to any participation whatsoever with representatives of the Conservative and Reform movements'.

Rabbi Lamm, President of Yeshiva University, whose personal standing was shaken by the attacks on him from within the university, says the deed of which Rabbi Sherer is so proud was 'the most damaging thing he ever did in his forty-year career'. He believes that had the Rubinstein compromise succeeded it would have established a landmark precedent that he (Lamm) would then have tried to apply to the question of non-Orthodox divorce. 'I wanted to get into mamzerut,' he says. 'If Reform rabbis would only *inform* their people of the reasons why they should consider getting a halachic *get*, countless potential tragedies would be avoided.'

Ultimately, then, the scheme foundered on the Orthodox minority's refusal to extend any legitimacy, even implied, to the two larger non-Orthodox denominations. From the Orthodox standpoint there is no irony here: it is the term 'denominations' that is a misnomer. It 'imports pluralism into Judaism,' as the British Chief Rabbi, Dr Jonathan Sacks explains. 'And this itself is an accommodation to secularization. Orthodoxy does not, and cannot, make this accommodation . . . It does not see itself as a denomination among others . . . Orthodoxy sees itself as the faith, not of Orthodox Jews only, but of all Jews.' This was the theological and empirical situation before the Emancipation and the rise of Reform, Sacks continues, when there were no 'denominations' in Jewry. 'Jews were either Jews or apostates.' And this situation is immutable in Orthodox theology, modern historical and social developments nothwithstanding. 'Reform Jews are Jews, but Reform Judaism is not Judaism. This is not a contradiction but a statement of the fact that tradition is constructed in terms of a [Jewish people] united by halacha. From this vantage point it is not Orthodoxy but the existence of non-Orthodox Jewish denominations that is a contradiction in terms.'*

Sacks himself – at least before he became Chief Rabbi in

* Sacks, *One People*?

September 1991 – urged dialogue nonetheless. He argued that the halachic tradition, encompassing within it the aggadic approach and classically encouraging discussion and argument, is wide enough to embrace a good-faith debate. But most Orthodox rabbis, and all haredi ones, consider even that measure of tolerance to be theologically dangerous. They have no interest in debating with Reform Judaism or in expanding halachic definition to cover such debate. British haredim are confident of their ability, and that of the London Beit Din, to squelch Sacks's ecumenical exuberance.

As the haredi rabbis in New York were killing off the Rubinstein compromise on conversions, the haredim in Israel were marking out their new battle-line in the unending war over Who is a Jew. Their current position is shaped, in effect, by two seminal decisions handed down simultaneously in July 1989 by the High Court of Justice. One represented a crushing defeat for the Orthodox over the Law of Return. The other, however, spelled a significant victory for the Orthodox, and a signal setback for the Conservative and Reform movements, on the issue of jurisdiction over marriages.

In the first case, several non-Orthodox immigrant-converts sued the Ministry of Interior in the wake of the Susan Miller judgement. They demanded to be registered as Jews under the Law of Return. (Miller herself had meanwhile returned to the US without claiming her identity card.) The second action was brought by the World Union for Progressive Judaism (Reform) and two of its rabbis against the Minister of Religions and the Chief Rabbinate Council, demanding that the two rabbis be licensed to perform marriages.

In the first case, the President of the Court, Justice Meir Shamgar, and three of his brethren were categorical: the Law of Return said 'converted', and so if an immigrant arrived with a certificate of conversion from any Jewish congregation, that should suffice. It was not within the purview of the interior ministry to inquire into the nature of that conversion, halachic or otherwise.

The Deputy President, Justice Menahem Elon, delivered an impassioned dissenting judgement. Elon, who is Orthodox, was formerly a professor of Talmud at the Hebrew University of

Jerusalem. There is an unspoken but unbroken tradition in Israel that at least one member of the Supreme Court is an Orthodox jurist.

Elon argued that conversion is essentially an halachic concept. The Law of Return itself, he pointed out, had adopted the halachic definition of Jewishness: 'born of a Jewish mother, or converted'. The implication, he said, was that just as 'born of a Jewish mother' was an halachic determinant of Jewishness, so too the 'conversion' referred to in the Law must mean an halachically valid conversion:

> The State of Israel is the state of all the Jewish people, its individuals and its communities, its denominations and its groups, those who live in the state and those who live in the Diaspora . . . Surely it is of existential importance for us all that the act of affiliation to the Jewish people should be carried out according to a denominator that is common to all its denominations, and that in this fateful matter we should adopt a criterion which the entire nation can accept.

In the other case, it was Justice Elon who wrote the leading judgement, and his four brethren all concurred – though one of them with marked reluctance. Elon surveyed the relevant laws and regulations dating back to British Mandate days, showing that Jewish marriages were required to be performed 'according to the law of the Torah'. The Minister of Religions, moreover, was empowered to authorize certain rabbis to conduct and register Jewish marriages (and certain Muslim, Christian and Druse clerics to marry their co-religionists). The minister customarily consulted with the Chief Rabbinate Council, and could not be faulted for doing so.

The key issue was the definition of 'the law of the Torah'. The two Reform rabbinical applicants had argued that there is no single, authoritative definition. Orthodoxy's definition, they pointed out, is different from the Conservative definition, which is different again from the Reform definition. Elon hardly concealed his sarcasm. 'Let us,' he wrote, 'take as an example the applicant's statement that they regard the prohibition of marriage between a priest [cohen] and a divorcee "a ban imposed by Orthodoxy which is not accepted by Reform." And here was I thinking that it is a ban imposed by the Torah [Lev. 21:14], not by Orthodoxy which, I believe, is a movement that had not yet come into being at that time . . .'

A representative of the Chief Rabbinate Council had interviewed the two Reform rabbis, Elon continued, and had found them to be (a) Reform and (b) ignorant of the halachas relating to marriage. The Chief Rabbinate Council (which of course is Orthodox) had disqualified them on both counts, and the minister had accordingly rejected their applications to be authorized to conduct marriages. Elon found nothing illegal or improper in any of that.

Two of the Justices endorsed Elon's reasoning, especially his insistence that 'the law of the Torah' meant, in effect, the Orthodox-rabbinic corpus. Justice Shamgar, the President, concurred with Elon too, but added significantly: 'It seems to me that the problem raised by the applicants is one for the legislature.'

The fifth justice, Shlomo Levin, also agreed that the court had no legal grounds to interfere with the minister's decision. But Levin was unconvinced by Elon's other arguments. It would have been unacceptable, he wrote, had the minister vetoed the two rabbi-applicants *solely* because they were members of the Reform movement. After all, this movement had a vast following abroad, and 'not inconsiderable numbers in Israel too'. The movement in Israel, he added, was markedly more traditional in its theology and its practices than its American counterpart. In principle, moreover, it was wrong to prevent young people from being married by the rabbi they chose, Justice Levin added.

These obiter dicta from the obviously sympathetic judge offered some consolation to the two disappointed Reform rabbis, and much encouragement to the non-Orthodox movements. Next time – and there will doubtless be a next time – they will be more careful in their choice of rabbinical applicants, ensuring that they are as well versed in the small print of the halacha as any Orthodox rabbi.

The Minister of Interior, Arye Deri of Shas, announced within hours of the court verdicts that he would respect and comply with both of them. Unlike his predecessor Rabbi Peretz, in 1986, he did not bridle at the court's decision on the Law of Return, and seek to annul it by new legislation. That, following the Israel-Diaspora crisis, was not now a realistic political prospect.

Suddenly the two-decade battle over the Law of Return was over. But not the war. Deri executed a swift and elegant withdrawal from the Law of Return front, regrouping the haredi defences – reinforced by the High Court's same-day decision – around the right to perform marriages. Henceforth, he announced, all immigrant-converts would duly be registered as Jews and their identity cards would carry the word 'Jew', as the court had ruled. But *all* identity cards – of natives and immigrants, born-Jews and converts – would now bear the legend: 'According to the Law . . . the information on this card regarding "nationality" and "personal status" is not even prima facie evidence of its accuracy.' In other words, marriage registrars, who are all Orthodox rabbis, would make their own inquiries about the Jewishness of every would-be bride and groom, and not be guided by their official registration as reflected on their identity cards.

So long as Orthodoxy maintains its exclusive control over marriage, it still ultimately determines Who is a Jew as far as Israel is concerned. The rabbi-registrars, their monopoly now confirmed by the High Court, continue to prevent non-Orthodox converts, or the children of women thus converted, or persons of patrilineal Jewish descent, or halachically illegitimate persons, from marrying in Israel.

'Rabbi Deri turns court decision into victory', the haredi newspaper *Yated Ne'eman* exulted in a banner headline. 'Rabbi Deri's method of compliance left the Reform movement spluttering with rage.' In America, Rabbi Sherer praised the minister for having taken 'the right step in the right direction'. But Deri's move was widely criticized outside haredi circles. The leading Israeli newspaper *Haaretz* wrote that Deri had 'thrown down a challenge to the State of Israel. The secular public should condemn him, and bring an end to his shenanigans.'

Significantly, the sharpest attacks came from the National Religious Party. For them, as Orthodox Zionists, the defeat over the Law of Return represented a blow to the central tenet of their political-religious credo. 'Perhaps the Shas people and their ministers do not see the uniqueness of the State of Israel,' wrote the NRP daily, *Hatzofe*, 'and the holiness which it derives from the Jewish heritage. To them this is just another State, and so it hardly matters what appears in the identity cards. All that matters to them is what appears in the marriage-and-divorce registries.'

This was intended as bitter criticism. But Deri and his haredi allies were entirely impervious to it. Indeed, they agreed with it. They were fighting not for the 'holiness of the State of Israel', but for the triumph of Orthodoxy against Reform and Conservative Judaism. Israel is the instrument, not the goal. In the words of *Yated Ne'eman*: 'Rabbi Deri seems to have enraged the NRP by having made official what has been painfully obvious for over forty years: the State of the Jews is not a Jewish State.'

38

Peace in Their Time

Interior Minister Deri's decision to abandon the Law of Return battle-lines and dig in instead around the law of marriage came just in time to avert a major new conflict. Within a few months of the Shas minister's move, hundreds, and then thousands, of 'questionable' Jews began pouring into Israel – part of the vast Jewish immigration from the former Soviet Union that was to bring nearly half a million newcomers to the country by the end of 1992. A further half-million were expected by the end of the century; provided the Israeli economy could expand quickly enough to absorb them all.

After seventy years of life under communism, largely isolated from the rest of Jewry, the level of Jewish observance and identity among Soviet Jews is low, while assimilation and intermarriage are high. Many of the immigrant families reaching Israel are mixed, containing both Jews and Gentiles.

The 'questionable' immigrants fall into two categories. Some 10–12 per cent are not Jewish, do not claim to be Jewish, and are thus not registered by the Interior Ministry as Jews.* A smaller number, but also running into thousands according to informed estimates, are non-Jews who passed themselves off as Jewish at the Israeli consulates in the former USSR, and were registered on arrival as Jews.

* These Gentile family-members have the same right to immediate citizenship and to absorption assistance as the Jewish members of their families. The 1970 amendment to the Law of Return, passed in the wake of the Shalit case (see p. 295), provided that the children and grandchildren of a Jew, and their spouses, be admitted to Israel under the Law on the strength of their Jewish family connection. The Jewish grandfather or grandmother, moreover, is not required to immigrate to Israel, or even to be alive, in order for the children and/or grandchildren and/or their spouses to benefit from this provision. The amendment was intended to balance the impact of the 'Shalit amendment' itself on mixed families.

Had the Shas-run Interior Ministry been required to determine the Jewishness of each of these 'questionable' cases, Israeli politics would quickly have been engulfed by a new Who is a Jew? conflagration that would doubtless have spread once again to the Diaspora. Thanks to Deri's decision, though, the question of personal status is postponed, in effect, until the immigrant applies to marry. Thus the danger of a mass outcry posed by the mass immigration from the USSR was defused – and deferred.

But it can, of course, break out at any moment, and some well-placed observers expect it will. 'A crisis is bound to come, sooner or later,' says Rabbi Eitan Eiseman, director of the Office of the Chief Rabbis. A single test case, brought by an aggrieved immigrant denied the right to marry a Jew, could ignite a mega-crisis.

The marriage law restrictions are regularly circumvented by 'unmarriageable' Israelis – cohanim and divorcees, for instance: they fly to some convenient marriage-haven abroad and enter into matrimony there. Once officially wed under any legal jurisdiction, Israeli law too recognizes them as married. Most ex-Soviet immigrants, however, struggling to settle into their new life, are unlikely to be able to afford a trip to South America, or even to nearby Cyprus. And the number of 'unmarriageables' among them is likely to exceed by far the relatively few cases that crop up among veteran Israelis.

However, the very magnitude of the danger may, over time, inspire piecemeal, pragmatic solutions that, taken together, would amount to an historic success for Israel's exclusively Orthodox, haredi-dominated rabbinate. If, say in fifteen or twenty years' time, the wave of ex-Soviet immigration proves to have been absorbed into Israeli society *without* triggering a major Who is a Jew? crisis, then that in itself would deal a crushing defeat to Reform and Conservative efforts to disestablish Orthodoxy in Israel. It would show that Orthodoxy has the resources to cope with an halachic challenge of national proportions. It would prove Orthodoxy's contention that its war is specifically against Conservatism and Reform: that wholly estranged ex-Soviet Jews and even Gentiles can be accommodated within the fold, but Reform and Conservative converts cannot.

If such a prospect exists at all, it is due to Deri's defusing of the status issue, which enables individual rabbis to deal with individual cases as they come up, without the need for dramatic halachic pronouncements. Would-be converts among the immigrants are directed to 'conversion courses' run by rabbis in various cities. There is no formal superstructure, but the Chief Rabbinate in Jerusalem keeps a discreet eye on these different programmes, and on the different batei din that perform conversions.

The individual case-law approach, applied in the context of the mass immigration to the Jewish State, enables some Israeli rabbis to take a lenient line to the halachic requirement of kabbalat ol mitzvot, 'acceptance of the yoke of the commandments', in the conversion process (see p. 298). While all Orthodox rabbis require a sincere undertaking from the conversion candidate to observe the fundamental practices of the faith, Israeli batei din – including haredi ones – are lenient on occasion in regard to the detailed level of observance actually maintained by the convert, and there is Responsa literature supporting this approach.

In addition, there is a certain amount of flexibility built into the halacha even regarding the question of Jewishness itself, in cases where the person has become completely absorbed into Jewish society over a long period. Again, this approach is more readily applicable in Israel, a wholly Jewish society, than it would be in a Diaspora community. Again too, Israeli rabbis will have recourse to this line of precedent only on an ad hoc basis; they will not advocate its use as a general principle.*

But even a liberal halachic approach, based on individual case-law, offers no panacea for the individual immigrant – and no guarantee of success in grappling with the overall halachic problems created by the ex-Soviet immigration. In Rabbi Eiseman's words: 'We cannot make them into Jews if they don't

* The same atmosphere of rabbinical empathy encouraged some 65,000 ex-Soviet adult male immigrants to undergo circumcision between 1990 and 1992. Although no Israeli law requires circumcision, it is almost universal among Israel's Jewish citizens, and many uncircumcized ex-Soviet newcomers regard it as part of their acculturation process. But it is a painful part. Normally, the ceremony is performed eight days after birth, when it hardly hurts at all. (That, at any rate, is the popular tradition, and no one claims to remember otherwise.) At the time of writing, doctors and rabbis in the town of Beersheba were experimenting with laser surgery as a way of minimizing the (post-anaesthetic) pain in adult circumcision.

seriously want to be. The halacha gives us no way of doing that. And we are not going to kid ourselves.' Eiseman's pessimism reflects a widespread fear that the immigrant time-bomb is more likely to explode than to be successfully defused. For every Gentile immigrant who has made a serious commitment to convert, says Eiseman, there are many who prefer to ignore the entire issue. Some sign up for conversion courses, he says, on the mistaken assumption that merely signing up is sufficient. They soon realize what is required, and drop out.

Like its decision on the Law of Return, Shas's decision in 1992 to join Yitzhak Rabin's doveish government was a radical departure, with long-term significance for Israel's future and for the haredim's role in it. After fifteen years of rightist–haredi coalitions, Rabbi Ovadia Yosef led his Sephardic haredim into an 'alliance for peace' with the Left.

Unsurprisingly, it proved a troubled alliance. Shas found itself embroiled in raucous conflicts with Rabin's other partner, the left-liberal and aggressively secularist Meretz, whose leader, Ms Shulamit Aloni, Rabin had unwisely appointed as Minister of Education. The argumentative Aloni insisted on addressing the inevitably explosive subject of Creation versus Evolution as taught in non-Orthodox State schools. Attacked by Shas, she hit back with a proposal to omit the name of God from the official Prayer for the Dead. To Shas this was sacrilege; to Labour and to many in her own party, it was a gratuitous and impolitic provocation.

Despite these frictions, though, the precedent had been set: the largest haredi party had formally joined the peace camp. The Ashkenazi haredim of Agudah Yisrael were angling to join too. For Rabbi Yosef this was the practical implementation of his long-held halachic position on peace. 'To hold or conquer territories in Eretz Israel by force, in our time, against the will of the nations of the world, is a sin,' he had ruled back in 1989. 'If we can give back the territories and thereby avoid war and bloodshed, we are obliged to do so, under the Rule of Saving Life.'

Yosef delivered that ruling at a symposium in Jerusalem, where he shared the podium with the then-Defence Minister in the government of national unity, Yitzhak Rabin. The Rule of Saving

Life, Yosef noted, was a precept that took precedence over all halachic prohibitions except murder, incest and idolatry. Granted, the mitzva of living in the Land of Israel was important. One Talmudic passage even said that 'Those who live in Eretz Israel have a God; those who live abroad have no God.' Granted, too, the ancient Israelites were enjoined to drive all the heathen idolaters out of the Land, not to cede any part of it to them, nor even to sell any plots to individual heathens. But, said Rabbi Yosef, that did not apply to Muslims, who were not 'idolaters'. (He implied that it did apply to Christians, but observed that the modern-day Israelites did not have the power to extirpate such idolaters.)

Even if it were argued that the provisions about heathens did apply to modern-day Muslims – and here was the nub of Yosef's argument – they did not apply if to enforce them would be to court mortal danger. If ceding the occupied territories could prevent war, the Rule of Saving Life was paramount. 'In this sinful generation we cannot rely on miracles,' Yosef observed. 'We cannot risk war: our sins might cause us to lose . . . The territories should be returned, to prevent the danger of war . . . until He looks down upon us from on high, and brings us back to him in perfect repentance, and then he will . . . give us back all the territories with great additions, as it is written [Deut. 11:24] "Every place whereon the soles of your feet shall tread shall be yours".'

Rabbi Yosef stressed at the time that his halachic analysis was 'hypothetical'. Neither Israel nor the Arabs were prepared to enter serious negotiations. Three years later, with Rabin now heading his own government, Yosef's political support was an indispensable element in conducting such negotiations. In addition to the crucial Knesset arithmetic, it provided Rabin with the religious legitimation he needed in order to contemplate traumatic territorial concessions. Had all of Orthodox Jewry lined up against him, opposing his peace policy in the name of the Torah, Rabin would have been hard put to sustain that policy – even with a parliamentary majority.

Every Zionist leader since Herzl, and every Israeli prime minister since Ben-Gurion, has sought the support of at least part of Orthodoxy. Herzl won over the Zionist-Orthodox, while the haredim opposed him. Today, the Zionist-Orthodox are on the neo-Messianic right of the political spectrum, while the haredim of Shas, though doctrinally still opposed to secular Jewish sovereignty, in practice give their support to the moderate left. Rabbi Shach himself, though bitterly hostile to Labour, consistently favoured 'land-for-peace'. Tuvia Blubstein, a Likud government official who served during the Shamir years as the discreet go-between between Shach and the Prime Minister, concedes that the haredi sage's position remained closer to Labour than to the Likud.

In the Zionist-Orthodox camp, rabbinical opinion is almost wholly hawkish. After Yosef's landmark presentation in 1989, the National Religious Party's leading sage, Rabbi Shaul Yisraeli, wrote him an open letter, challenging both his strategic understanding and his halachic conclusions. 'What about all the settlements that have been built?' Yisraeli asked. 'Has the Eminence of his Genius [a standard mode of address in rabbinical correspondence] considered what might happen to Jewish settlers remaining under Arab sovereignty? And is the Exalted Honour of his Wisdom confident that the Arabs will not demand the rest of the Land too?'

The haredim, then, led by Shas, were on the cutting edge of Israel's move towards peace and regional conciliation. Their detractors, especially those now in the opposition, dismissed the 'peace alliance' as an incongruous quirk, a marriage of cynical convenience. The haredim, they argued, were concerned principally to get funds from the government, any government. But doveish ideologues maintain there is a genuine common denominator. 'The absence of messianism in the haredim's political approach means that their feet are firmly planted in reality,' says Meretz MK Dedi Zucker. 'They are pragmatists. They want compromise with the Palestinians. True, haredi dogma regards the State of Israel as marginal or transient. But for me, as a politician looking for political allies, that translates into pragmatism.'

Professor Avishai Margalit, a leading left-wing savant, says he feels 'very close to the haredim. I am an anarchist, like them. I see the State of Israel as a collection of disparate communities. Each should be able to build its own lifestyle with a minimum of State interference. That goes for Mea Shearim just as it goes for the Reform community. Basically the haredi concept is one of building a community for themselves, a community whose core is Torah study.'

That community, the 'society of learners', through its very growth and success, is no longer a marginal sect in Israeli life or in Diaspora Jewry. Shas's participation in the Labour-led 'alliance for peace', moreover, significantly accelerated the mainstreaming of haredism: the haredim were playing a pivotal role in national policymaking.

Internal growth, together with objective economic exigencies, as we have seen, are increasingly forcing the 'society of learners' to join the economic mainstream too. When peace does eventually come, the issue of army service – the great divide between the haredim and the rest of Israeli society – will naturally become less acute. The duration of regular army service will presumably be reduced for everyone; enlistment itself may become less than universal if the standing army is gradually allowed to grow smaller. In fact, the peace with Egypt, coupled with the steep population increase, enabled the army by the early 1990s to ease its enlistment rules. Married haredim were enabled to join up for a shorter period, and at a younger age, than before.

Influenced by the trends in Israel, and powered by their own internal growth and confidence, haredim in the Diaspora are also increasingly active in the mainstream of Jewish life there, lobbying for their own agenda, politicizing for their particular interests. As younger, American- or Israeli-born rabbis take over the leadership from the greenhorn generation, still trained in pre-Holocaust Eastern Europe, this mainstreaming seems increasingly natural, both to the haredim themselves and to the wider community.

The young leaders try to be as punctilious as their parents about minutely preserving the traditions of 'der Heim'. Nostalgia and meticulous reconstruction were the hallmarks of the successful transplantation of post-Holocaust haredism. But the opening up of Eastern Europe after the fall of communism has tempered the mystique of the pre-Holocaust 'Heim' and perhaps weakened its spell. Today, one can freely visit the shtetl of one's spiritual yearnings, and mourn there over a world destroyed. But a Western visitor to the backwaters of Poland or the Ukraine, even one steeped in haredi legend-literature, senses that shtetl life was not pure bucolic bliss. It was hard and primitive, though refined by a highly developed religious, cultural and communal civilization. This subliminal realization is spurring the development of indigenous haredi traditions in America, Israel and Western Europe, as the home-grown leadership grapples with the challenges of new places and new times.

In both political and economic terms, the outlook is for a moderation of haredi separatism within the broader Jewish society. But does that necessarily suggest a parallel moderation in the religious polarization that separates the haredim from the rest of Jewry, and ultimately threatens a schismatic crisis? Does the mainstreaming of haredism augur an opening of the haredi 'ghetto of the mind'?

Many would argue that the pressures and temptations of modern Western life make a 'dilution' of haredism inevitable. But the haredim, regarded only a few decades ago as a dying breed, have confounded forecasts of their demise. In their resurgence, they have proved that the dismissal of haredism as anachronistic may itself be an anachronism in the modern world.

Glossary

acharon (pl. *-im*): latter-day (sage): generic name given to major rabbinic authors from the 16th century to the present.
aggada (adj. *aggadic*): lit. legend; homiletic sections of Talmudic literature.
Agudat Yisrael (Agudas Yisrael, Agudath Israel, Agudah): lit. Association of Israel; haredi political movement founded in Europe in 1912, now comprises mainly hasidim.
ahavat Yisrael: love of Israel; love of fellow Jews.
AIPAC: America-Israel Public Affairs Committee.
aliyah: lit. ascent; immigration to the Land of Israel.
amora (pl. *-im*): the rabbis of the Gemara, the later Talmud sages (3rd to 6th centuries CE).
Ashkenazi (pl. *-im*; adj. *-ic*): Occidental Jew, whose medieval forebears lived in Central and Western Europe. Ashkenaz, listed in Genesis (10:3) as one of the ancient nations, came to be the Hebrew word for Germany.

baal (f. *-at*; pl. *-ei*; f.pl. *-ot*) *teshuva*: lit. master of repentance; penitent; born-again Orthodox Jew.
bachur (pl. *-im*): student; young man.
b.a.h.: acronym, *bli ayin haraa* – without the evil eye; i.e. may they continue to multiply.
baki: broadly erudite (in Talmud); *bekiut* – broad erudition.
beit (pl. *batei*) *din*: lit. house of law; rabbinical court.
bekeshe: Yiddish, long coat, silk or silk-substitute festive wear of hasidic men.
ben Torah (pl. *bnei Torah*): lit. son of the Torah; scholar.
brit (*bris*): circumcision.

chavrusa (*chavruta*): lit. companionship or friendship; learning partner or partnership.

chazara biteshuva: lit. return in penitence; repentance; adoption of Orthodox lifestyle.
cohen (pl. *cohanim*): priest; descendant of the priestly order.

daat Torah: lit. the knowledge of the Torah; opinion or ruling of recognized sage.
daf: page of Talmud.
Daf Hayomi: the daily page of Talmud, learned simultaneously around the world.
daven: Yiddish, pray; in English usage: davening, davener, davened.
Degel Hatorah: lit. Flag of the Torah; haredi party that split from Agudat Yisrael (q.v.) in 1988; comprises mainly mitnagdim. Rejoined Agudah in 1992 to form electoral alliance, 'The United Torah Front'.
Diaspora: the Dispersion (of the Jews); Jews living outside Israel.

Eretz Yisrael: the Land of Israel.
eruv: symbolic enclosure of domain in connection with halachic restrictions on movement on the sabbath.

Gaon: lit. genius; Rabbi Elijah of Vilna (1720–1797) was known as the Gaon of Vilna.
gartel: black rope-like belt worn by hasidic men for prayer.
gedolim (sing. *gadol*): great (men); great rabbis.
Gemara: lit. learning; analyses and discussions of the Mishna, conducted during the 3rd–6th centuries CE in Babylon and Palestine, edited and published as the Babylonian Talmud (6th century) and the Jerusalem Talmud (4th century).
geonim: lit. pl. of *gaon* – generic name for the leading yeshiva deans in Babylon from the 7th to the 11th centuries.
g'mach (pl. *-im*): acronym: *gemilut hasadim* – dispensing kindnesses; free loan society.

Hakadosh Boruch Hu: lit. the Holy One, Blessed Be He; God.
halacha: lit. law or rule; the corpus of Jewish law.
Hannuka: Feast of Lights, commemorating the Jews' victory over the Greeks and purification of the Temple in Jerusalem in 165 BCE.

haredi (pl. *-m*): lit. fearing or trembling; God-fearing; ultra-Orthodox Jew.
hasid (pl. *hasidim*; adj. *hasidic*; *hasidism*): lit. pious man. Hasidism was a religious revivalist movement that originated in the Ukraine in the mid-18th century. It preached joy and spontaneity in religious observance, and taught that faith and sincerity were as important as Talmudic scholarship in religious life. Its opponents were the mitnagdim (q.v.).
haskala: Enlightened intellectualism; a social and literary movement within 19th-century European Jewry, in the wake of the European Enlightenment and of Jewish political Emancipation.
hechsher (pl. *-im*): rabbinical certification that a food product is kosher, i.e. edible under the rules of the halacha.
heder (pl. *hadarim*): lit. room; elementary school.
hesder: lit. arrangement; Israeli *hesder yeshiva*: where students combine Talmud study with army service.
hesed: lit. kindness; charity.
hilula (pl. *hilulot*): lit. joyous celebration; gathering to mark the anniversary of a death (usually of a revered rabbi).

iluy: genius (usually young).

kabbala: Jewish mysticism; esoteric theological system based on occult traditions and mystical interpretations of biblical texts.
kashrut: the dietary laws.
kiddush: lit. sanctification; prayer said over wine at the start of sabbath and festival meals.
kiddush hashem: lit. sanctification of the Name (of God); acting in a way that brings credit to Judaism and/or Orthodoxy – and thus to God.
kirya (pl. *krayot*): township; residential housing project.
klezmer: traditional Jewish music, usually played on violin and clarinet.
kollel (pl. *-im*): advanced yeshiva for married men.
kvitl (pl. *kvitlach*): Yiddish, lit. small document; written request for help or advice submitted to a hasidic rebbe, bearing the name of supplicant and his mother's name and an outline of his problem. Kvitlach are also squeezed into crevices in the Wailing Wall and left at tombs of saintly rabbis.

lashon hara: lit. the evil tongue; speaking ill of others.
lechaim: lit. to life; traditional Jewish toast.

maggid: preacher.
mamzer: bastard; under halacha, the progeny of an incestuous or adulterous union.
mamzerut: bastardy.
mashgiach (pl. *mashgichim*): lit. supervisor; spiritual supervisor at yeshiva.
Mashiach (*Moshiach*): the Messiah.
mikve: ritual bath.
mincha: afternoon prayer.
minyan: prayer quorum of ten males.
Mishna: redaction of the Oral Law in concise form undertaken by rabbis in Palestine in the 1st and 2nd centures CE. A mishna is one paragraph of this work. The Talmud comprises the Mishna and the Gemara: each mishna is followed by a section of Gemara, in which it is discussed and interpreted.
mitnaged (pl. *mitnagdim*; adj. *mitnagdic*; *mitnagdism*): lit. opponent; the mitnagdim were – and are – Jews who opposed hasidism (q.v.) and regarded themselves as the repositories of the authentic Talmudic and religious tradition. They were dominant in Lithuania and Russia, and weaker in Poland and the Ukraine. Today the hasidic-mitnagdic rivalry exists only among haredim; for most other Jews it is a matter of historic interest only.
mitzva: commandment.
mussar: lit. moral admonishment; school within yeshiva life that prescribes the study of ethical and homiletical works as a means of religious improvement and character building.

Pessach: Passover.
peyot: sidelocks.
pilpul: Talmudic casuistry.

rav: lit. master; rabbi.
rebbe: hasidic rabbi and leader; elementary school teacher.
rebbitzin: rabbi's wife; saintly or scholarly woman.
rishon (pl. *-im*): early (sage); generic name given to major rabbinic authors from the 11th to the 15th centuries.

Rosh Hashana: Jewish New Year.
rosh yeshiva: lit. head of yeshiva; yeshiva dean.

seder: lit. order; study-period in yeshiva; *Seder*: festive family meal on Passover eve during which biblical story of Exodus from Egypt is recounted.
Sephardi (pl. *-im*; adj. *-ic*): Oriental Jew, whose ancestors lived in Spain and Portugal. Also applied nowadays to Jews originating from the Middle East and North Africa. *Sepharad* is found in Obadiah 1:20 and came to be the Hebrew word for Spain.
shabbat: the sabbath.
shadchan (pl. *-im*; f. *-it*): marriage broker.
shaliach (pl. *shlichim; f. shlicha*): emissary.
Shas: acrostic for Sephardic Torah Guardians; Sephardic-haredi party that split from Agudat Yisrael in 1984.
sheitel: Yiddish, wig.
shidduch (pl. *-im*): matrimonial match; arranged marriage.
shirayim: leftovers, distributed by hasidic rebbe to his followers at festive meal.
shiur: lesson (in Torah- or Talmud-related subject).
shiva: lit. seven; week-long mourning rite in which the close relatives of the deceased sit on low stools and receive consolation visits.
shlichut (*shlichuss*): mission.
shmoneh esreh: lit. eighteen (blessings); silent prayer recited while standing at attention; the high point of the thrice-daily prayer services.
shockel: Yiddish, shake or sway during prayer; in English usage: shockelling, shockelled.
shtetl: Yiddish, lit. village; wholly or largely Jewish village in pre-Holocaust Eastern Europe.
shtiebel (pl. *shtieblach*): Yiddish, lit. small room; hasidic synagogue.
shtreimel: fur hat worn by hasidim.
shul: Yiddish, synagogue.
Shulhan Aruch: Code of Jewish Law written by Rabbi Yosef Karo in the 16th century.
simcha: celebration.
siyata dishmaya: Aramaic, help from Heaven.
siyyum: lit. completion; celebration marking the completion of the

study of a tractate or a section of the Talmud, or of the study of the entire Talmud.
stender: Yiddish, wooden lectern.
sugya: text or topic of Talmudic discussion.
Sukkot: (Feast of) Tabernacles.

taharat hamishpacha: lit. purity of the family; the sexual laws.
talmid hacham (pl. *talmidei hachamim*): scholar.
Talmud: lit. learning; the Mishna and the Gemara.
tanna: early Talmudic sage cited in the Mishna.
tefillin: phylacteries; small leather boxes with thongs attached, containing parchment texts from the Torah. Tied around the head and around one arm during weekday morning prayers.
teshuva: repentance.
tish (pl. *tishen*): Yiddish, lit. table; hasidic festive meal presided over by rebbe.
torah (pl. *torot*): homily; hasidic-style discourse; *Torah*: lit. teaching; the Pentateuch; (by extension) the entire corpus of Jewish religious literature.
Tosafot: lit. additions; medieval commentary on Talmud.
Tosefta: Mishnaic-period text not incorporated into the Mishna.
tsniut (*tsniuss*): modesty.
tzaddik: lit. righteous man; hasidic rebbe.

UJA: United Jewish Appeal, national Jewish fund-raising organization in the USA for local community needs and for Israel.

yarmulka: skull-cap.
yeshiva (pl. *yeshivot, yeshivas*): Talmudical college.
yeshiva ketana: junior (lit. small) yeshiva.
yeshiva gedola: senior (lit. large) yeshiva.
Yiddish: language used by Jews from central and Eastern Europe, based mainly on German but with words from Hebrew and other languages.
Yom Kippur: Day of Atonement; a fast-day and the holiest day in the Jewish calendar. The day on which the 1973 Arab-Israeli war broke out.

zechus (*zechut*) (pl. *zechusim*): merit.

Select Bibliography

This is a list of books and monographs that I found helpful while researching and writing. From some, I have quoted directly, and for this I am grateful to their authors and publishers.

Apart from the primary (Hebrew and Aramaic) classical sources which are listed separately, all publications are listed alphabetically by author. Books published in Hebrew are indicated by an asterisk.

Eliahu Alfasi, *Baba Sali of Blessed Memory* (New York: Judaica Press 1986)

Anon., **Gedolei Torah: On the Return of Territories* (Bnei Brak 1980)

Anon., *The Lamplighters* (New York: Merkos L'Inyonei Chinuch 1989)

Anon., *Return to the Source: Selected Articles on Judaism and Teshuva* (Jerusalem & New York: Feldheim 1984)

Avraham Avi-Hai, *Ben Gurion, State-Builder* (New York, Toronto & Jerusalem: John Wiley & Sons, Israel Universities Press 1974)

Salo W. Baron, *The Russian Jew Under Tsar and Soviets* (New York & London: Macmillan 1964)

Eliezer Berkovits, *With God in Hell* (New York & London: Sanhedrin Press 1979)

Avraham R. Besdin, *Reflections of the Rav* (Jerusalem: World Zionist Organization 1979)

Abraham Bornstein. **Iglei Tal* (Pietrokov: 1909)

Reeve Robert Brenner, *The Faith and Doubt of Holocaust Survivors* (New York: The Free Press 1980)

Menahem M. Brod (ed.), **HaRebbi MiLubavitch* (Kfar Habad: Mosdot Habad 1986)

Reuven P. Bulka, *The Coming Cataclysm* (New York: Mosaic Books 1985)

—— (ed.), *Dimensions of Jewish Orthodoxy* (New York: Ktav 1983)

Steven M. Cohen, *Ties and Tensions – American Jewish Attitudes towards Israel and Israelis* (New York: American Jewish Committee 1986)
Steven M. Cohen & Charles S. Liebman, *The Quality of American Jewish Life – Two Views* (New York: American Jewish Committee 1987)
Yonah Cohen, **The National Religious Movement* (Jerusalem: Hamizrachi no date)
A 'Commentary' Symposium, *The Condition of Jewish Belief* (New York: American Jewish Committee/Aronson 1966/1989)
M. Herbert Danzger, *Returning to Tradition: The Contemporary Revival of Orthodox Judaism* (New Haven & London: Yale University Press 1989)
Shimon Dubnov, **History of Hasidism* (Tel Aviv: 1930)
Emil L. Fackenheim, *God's Presence in History* (New York: Harper Torchbooks 1972)
——, *What is Judaism?* (New York & London: Summit Books 1987)
Leonard Fein, *Where Are We?* (New York: Harper & Row 1988)
Joseph Friedenson, *A History of Agudath Israel* (New York: Agudath Israel of America 1970)
Joseph Friedenson & David Kranzler, *Heroine of Rescue* (New York: ArtScroll/Mesorah 1984)
Abraham Fuchs, *The Unheeded Cry* (New York: ArtScroll/Mesorah 1986)
Martin Gilbert, *The Holocaust* (London: Fontana/Collins 1987)
——, *The Macmillan Atlas of the Holocaust* (New York: Macmillan 1982)
Hillel Goldberg, *Between Berlin and Slobodka* (Hoboken NJ: Ktav 1989)
Heinrich Graetz, *History of the Jews* (Philadelphia: Jewish Publication Society of America 1891)
Lis Harris, *Holy Days – The World of a Hasidic Family* (New York: Summit Books 1985)
Samuel C. Heilman, *The People of the Book – Drama, Fellowship and Religion* (Chicago & London: The University of Chicago Press 1987)
William B. Helmreich, *The World of the Yeshiva* (New York: The Free Press 1982)
Arthur Hertzberg, *The French Enlightenment and the Jews* (New York & London: Columbia University Press 1968)

Samson R. Hirsch, *The Cycles of the Year* (Bnei Brak: Netzah 1986)
Moshe Horovitz, **Rabbi Shach – in Whose Hands is the Key* (Jerusalem: Keter 1989)
Shimon Huberband, *Kiddush Hashem: Jewish Religious and Cultural Life in Poland During the Holocaust* (New York: Yeshiva University Press 1987)
Louis Jacobs, *Helping with Inquiries* (London: Vallentine, Mitchell 1989)
——, *A Jewish Theology* (New York: Behrman House 1973)
Immanuel Jakobovits, *Religious Responses to the Holocaust* (London: Office of the Chief Rabbi 1988)
——, *Preserving the Oneness of the Jewish People* (London: Office of the Chief Rabbi 1988)
Jacob Katz, *Out of the Ghetto* (New York: Schocken Books 1978)
——, **Tradition and Crisis* (Jerusalem: Bialik Institute 1986)
Robert Kirschner (trans. & ed.), *Rabbinic Responsa of the Holocaust Era* (New York: Schocken Books 1985)
Zvi Kurzweil, *The Modern Impulse of Traditional Judaism* (Hoboken NJ: Ktav 1985)
Norman Lamm, *Faith and Doubt* (New York: Ktav 1986)
Yeshayahu Leibowitz, **Judaism, Jewish People and the State of Israel* (Tel Aviv: Schocken Books 1975)
Michael Graubart Levin, *Journey to Tradition – The Odyssey of a Born-Again Jew* (Hoboken NJ: Ktav 1986)
Amnon Levy, **The Haredim* (Jerusalem: Keter 1989)
Mendell Lewittes, *Principles and Development of Jewish Law* (New York: Bloch 1987)
Charles S. Liebman (ed.), **Religious and Secular – Conflict and Accommodation Between Jews in Israel* (Jerusalem: Keter 1990)
Ian S. Lustick, *For the Land and the Lord* (New York: Council on Foreign Relations 1988)
Yehuda L. Maimon, **Princes of the Century*, 5 vols (Jerusalem: Mossad Harav Kook 1953)
Egon Mayer, *From Suburb to Shtetl* (Philadelphia: Temple University Press 1979)
Ezra Mendelsohn, *The Jews of East Central Europe Between the World Wars* (Bloomington: Indiana University Press 1987)
Jacob Neusner, *Israel in America – A Too-Comfortable Exile?* (Boston: Beacon Press 1985)

Alter Pekier, *From Kletzk to Siberia* (New York: ArtScroll/Mesorah 1985)

Mendel Piekarz, **Ideological Trends of Hasidism in Poland During the Interwar Period and the Holocaust* (Jerusalem: Bialik Institute 1990)

Solomon Poll, *The Hasidic Community of Williamsburg: A Study in the Sociology of Religion* (New York: Schocken Books 1969)

Menahem M. Rabin, Bezalel Landau (ed.), **Meron Journey* (Jerusalem: Wagschal 1989)

Harry Rabinowicz, *Hasidism and the State of Israel* (London & Toronto: Associated University Presses 1982)

Dov Rabinowitz, **Dwellings of the Shepherds* (Jerusalem: published by the author 1980)

Jonathan Sacks, *Traditional Alternatives – Orthodoxy and the Future of the Jewish People* (London: Jews' College Publications)

——, *One People? Tradition, Modernity and Jewish Unity* (Oxford: Oxford University Press, forthcoming)

Letters of Rabbi Menahem M. Schneerson, **Igrot Kodesh* (Kfar Habad: Mosdot Habad no date)

Rabbi Yoel Schwartz & Yitzhak Goldstein, *Shoah, A Jewish Perspective on Tragedy in the Context of the Holocaust* (New York: ArtScroll/Mesorah 1990)

Rabbi Moshe Sherer, **Bishtei Einayim* (New York: ArtScroll/ Mesorah 1988)

S. Z. Shragai & A. Bik, **Izhbitz-Lublin* (Jerusalem: Mossad Harav Kook 1983)

Charles E. Silberman, *A Certain People – American Jews and Their Lives Today* (New York: Summit Books 1985)

Joseph B. Soloveitchik, *The Halakhic Mind* (New York: The Free Press 1986)

Shubert Spero & Yitzchak Pessin (eds), *Religious Zionism After 40 Years of Statehood* (Jerusalem: Mesilot 1989)

Avraham Steinberg, *Jewish Medical Law* (New York: Beit-Shamai 1989)

Adin Steinsaltz, *Biblical Images: Men & Women of the Book* (New York: Basic Books 1984)

——, *The Essential Talmud* (New York: Basic Books 1976)

——, **Guide to the Talmud* (Jerusalem: Keter 1988)

——, *The Strife of the Spirit* (Northvale NJ & London: Aronson 1988)

Studies in Contemporary Jewry, vols II, IV (New York & Oxford: Institute of Contemporary Jewry, The Hebrew University of Jerusalem/OUP)

Shlomo Tal, **Rabbi Naftali Zvi MiRopczyce* (Jerusalem: Mossad Harav Kook 1983)

Akiva Tatz, *Anatomy of a Search* (New York: ArtScroll/Mesorah 1979)

Hanoch Teller, *The Bostoner* (Jerusalem & New York: Feldheim 1990)

Simcha B. Unsdorfer, *The Yellow Star* (Jerusalem & New York: Feldheim 1983)

Zorach Warhaftig, **A Constitution for Israel: Religion and State* (Jerusalem: Mesilot 1988)

——, *Refugee and Survivor* (Jerusalem: Yad Vashem 1988)

Alex Weingrod, *The Saint of Beersheba* (New York: SUNY Press 1990)

Shlomo Wolbe, *Pathways* (New York: Feldheim 1983)

Nissan Wolpe (ed.), **Daat Torah: On the Situation in the Holy Land* (Kiryat Gat 1982)

Nisson Wolpin (ed.), *A Path Through the Ashes* (New York: ArtScroll/Mesorah 1986)

Gad Yacobi, **The Government* (Tel Aviv: Am Oved & Zmora, Bitan, Modan 1980)

Newspapers and Periodicals

The Israeli haredi daily newspapers: *Hamodia, Yated Ne'eman*

The Israeli daily newspapers: *Haaretz, Davar, Maariv, Yediot Aharonot, Hadashot, The Jerusalem Post, Hatzofe*

The Jewish Telegraphic Agency Daily News Bulletin, New York

The Jewish Press, New York

The Jewish Week, New York

The Jewish Chronicle, London

The Jewish Tribune, London

Shma magazine, New York

Jewish Action magazine, New York

Tikkun magazine, New York

Nekudah magazine, Jerusalem

Hamahane Haharedi weekly, Jerusalem

Classical sources

Bible:

**The Pentateuch* with major traditional commentaries edited from manuscripts (Jerusalem: Mossad Harav Kook, from 1989)

**Daat Mikra* the Old Testament with modern commentary anthologized from traditional sources (Jerusalem: Mossad Harav Kook, from 1970)

The Pentateuch & Haftorahs Hebrew text, English translations & commentary, J. H. Hertz (ed.) (London: Soncino Press 1958)

Talmud:

**The Mishna* with commentaries, 12 vols (New York: Pardes 1953)

**The Mishna* with modern commentary anthologized from traditional sources by Pinhas Kehati (Jerusalem: Hechal Shlomo Press, 9th ed. 1977)

The Mishna with introduction and brief explanatory notes by Herbert Danby (Oxford: OUP 1933)

**The Babylonian Talmud* (New York: Mesora Edition 1944)

**The Babylonian Talmud* with commentary by Adin Steinsaltz (Jerusalem: Israel Institute for Talmudic Publications, from 1965)

The Talmud with commentaries (New York: ArtScroll/Mesorah, from 1991)

The Talmud: The Steinsaltz Edition with commentaries (New York: Random House, from 1982)

**The Jerusalem Talmud* (Jerusalem: Israel Institute for Talmudic Publications, from 1989)

Marcus Jastrow, *Aramaic-English Dictionary of Talmudic Literature* (New York: Pardes 1950)

Post-Talmudic:

**Maimonides Code, Mishne Torah* (Berlin: Goldberg Edition 1866; Jerusalem: Shabtai Frenkel Edition, from 1973)

**Otzar Mefarshei Hatalmud* (Jerusalem: Machon Yerushalayim, from 1971)

**Shulhan Aruch* (Jerusalem: Hashulhan Aruch Hagadol Edition 1970)

**Tur Shulhan Aruch* (Jerusalem: Hatam Sofer Institute Edition 1965)

*Encyclopedia Talmudit (Jerusalem: Talmudic Encyclopedia Publishing Company, from 1947)
*Duties of the Heart, Bahya ibn Pekuda, with English translation by Moses Hyamson (New York: 1925; Jerusalem: Boys' Town 1962)
*Path of the Just, Moshe Hayim Luzzato, with English translation (Loeb Classical Library)

Index